STUDY GUIDE TO ACCOMPANY
WONNACOTT AND WONNACOTT:
ECONOMICS

Study Guide

TO ACCOMPANY
WONNACOTT AND WONNACOTT:
ECONOMICS
SECOND EDITION

Peter Howitt
University of Western Ontario

McGRAW-HILL BOOK COMPANY

New York   St. Louis   San Francisco   Auckland   Bogotá   Hamburg   Johannesburg
London   Madrid   Mexico   Montreal   New Delhi   Panama
Paris   São Paulo   Singapore   Sydney   Tokyo   Toronto

Study Guide
to Accompany Wonnacott and Wonnacott:
ECONOMICS

3 4 5 6 7 8 9 0 WCWC 8 9 8 7 6 5 4 3 2

ISBN 0-07-071596-3

This book was set in Caledonia and Helvetica by Better Graphics.
The editors were Bonnie E. Lieberman, Michael Elia, and Edwin Hanson;
the production supervisor was Dominick Petrellese.
New drawings were done by J & R Services, Inc.
The cover was designed by Merrill Haber;
the cover illustration was done by Bob Shein.
Webcrafters, Inc., was printer and binder.

To Pat

Contents

Preface

This study guide is intended to help the student who is taking an introductory economics course using the textbook *Economics* by Paul Wonnacott and Ronald Wonnacott. It makes no attempt to be self-contained: it can be used as a supplement to, not as a substitute for, the textbook.

Each chapter is designed for you to read and work through after reading the corresponding chapter in the textbook. Each study-guide chapter contains seven sections:

1. *Learning Objectives.* This section consists of a list of tasks that you should be able to accomplish after having studied the chapter in the textbook and in the study guide. The purpose of this section is twofold. First, it should help to give you direction and purpose while studying the rest of the chapter. Second, it should serve as a checklist to test your comprehension after reading the chapter.

2. *Chapter highlights.* This section contains a summary of the important points of the chapter. Its purpose is mainly to reinforce the textbook by going over these main points from a somewhat different perspective and adding illustrative examples. To a student learning a subject for the first time, everything is likely to appear equally important. This can be a source of great confusion. The chapter highlights should help sort out the important from the incidental by focusing more narrowly than the text upon the important points and by drawing attention to the particularly important material by such phrases as "Be sure you understand. . . ."

3. *Important terms.* Important new terms introduced in the chapter are defined in this section. The section is intended mainly to provide a source of reference for working through the chapter, but you may also benefit from going down the list to make sure you understand each term before proceeding.

4. *True-false questions;* **5.** *Multiple-choice questions;* and **6.** *Exercises.* These three sections are meant to help you learn by doing. As well as providing reinforcement through repetition, many of the questions and exercises are designed to guide you toward discovering ideas that will be explicitly introduced only later in the textbook. Each section starts with easy questions that get progressively more difficult. Particularly difficult questions are marked with an asterisk. Even students who believe they understand the chapter in the textbook well enough to proceed without using the study guide are advised to spend a few minutes going over the true-false and multiple-choice questions as a self-test. Answers to all questions in these sections are provided at the back of the book.

7. *Essay questions.* This section begins with relatively simple questions and works toward more involved ones for which clear-cut answers cannot easily be given. Again, particularly difficult questions are marked with an asterisk. The questions are meant to help you recognize and use important concepts that have been developed in the text, as well as to stimulate imagination. No answers have been provided for this section. Thus the questions may be used as material for classroom discussion.

In addition, Chapter 1 contains a lengthy appendix on some of the basic mathematical concepts and techniques used in the textbook and study guide. These concepts and techniques are not difficult, but they can be the source of a lot of unnecessary anxiety. You may find that a few hours spent early in the term going through this step-by-step account will give you the familiarity and confidence to handle them when you need to and get on with the economics.

The material from the boxes and optional sections of the text has generally been excluded from the study guide, with a few exceptions. Where such material has been included it is marked with an asterisk, as with the more difficult questions, and a footnote.

This second edition of the study guide has four new chapters, corresponding to the new chapters of the Wonnacotts' textbook. The appendix to Chapter 1 is also new. Every one of the old chapters has been reworked with a view to improving the clarity of exposition and to relating it more directly to the textbook. The sections on multiple-choice questions and exercises have been expanded, and most of the old true-false and multiple-choice questions have been replaced or reworked in an attempt to make each question as clear-cut as possible.

In preparing the study guide I have been aided by the detailed comments and suggestions of Paul and Ron Wonnacott. I also benefited from the comments of three reviewers, Ronald G. Reddall, Allan Hanock College, and Heidemarie C. Sherman and Allen R. Thompson, University of New Hampshire, and Mike Elia of McGraw-Hill. I also wish to acknowledge the assistance of Marg Gower, Yvonne Adams, and Leslie Farrant in the Economics Department of the University of Western Ontario, whose fast and efficient typing of the manuscript did more than anything else to lighten my load.

Peter Howitt

SPECIAL NOTE FOR THOSE STUDYING ONLY THE SOFT-COVER VOLUME
"AN INTRODUCTION TO MICROECONOMICS"

For students studying the microeconomics soft-cover volume, use the first six chapters of this study guide and then skip to Chapter 19, which corresponds to Chapter 7 in the soft-cover volume. The key for the balance of both books is as shown in the following chart.

Numbers referred to in this study guide	Numbering in micro-economics soft-cover volume	Key
Chapter 19, Figure 19-1, 19-2, etc.	Chapter 7, Figure 7-1, 7-2, etc.	Subtract 12 from any chapter number in this study guide. Similarly, treat any figure, appendix, box, or table number in the same way.
Parts 4 and 5.	Parts 2 and 3.	Subtract 2 from Part number in this study guide.
Pages 416–418 (ignore any references to pp. 419–421).	Pages 116–118.	
Page 422 to the end.	Page 120 to the end.	Subtract 302 from page number in this study guide.

STUDY GUIDE TO ACCOMPANY
WONNACOTT AND WONNACOTT:
ECONOMICS

PART ONE
BASIC ECONOMIC CONCEPTS

CHAPTER 1
Economic Problems and Economic Goals

Learning Objectives

After you have studied this chapter in the textbook and the study guide, you should be able to

State the difference between Adam Smith and J. M. Keynes on the issue of whether or not the government should intervene more in economic affairs

List the five major goals of economic policy

Describe the problems caused by inflation

Explain the distinction between technical efficiency and allocative efficiency

Explain some of the problems in measuring inequality

Give the arguments for and against economic growth

Give an example of two complementary economic goods, as well as an example of two conflicting economic goals

CHAPTER HIGHLIGHTS

Economics, just like physics, chemistry, biology, or psychology, is a science. Just as the other sciences do, economics helps us to understand one aspect of the world we live in. The particular aspect that economics deals with is the daily activity of making a living.

The objective of economic theory is to discover and explain the basic laws and principles that govern economic life. It helps us to understand why some prices are higher than others, why some people are richer than others, what are the underlying causes of inflation, and so forth.

Economic policy deals with such questions as: How can the government reduce the amount of unemployment? How can it reduce inflation? What are the side effects of policies aimed at reducing inflation? How does a business increase profits?

Economic theory and economic policy go hand-in-hand. Just as the physician needs to know how the human body works in order to heal his or her patients, so the applied economist needs to understand economic theory in order to prescribe economic policies that will work. Likewise, just as the pure scientist who is interested in science for science's sake has learned a great deal from applied research on such problems as how to build nuclear weapons or how to cure cancer, so the economic theorist finds it helpful to study economic policy.

However, most people become interested in economics initially because of their concern with policy issues rather than out of pure scientific curiosity. This introductory chapter discusses some of the policy issues that students find most interesting.

Probably the greatest and most hotly contested of all the issues of economic policy has been the broad question of how much the government should intervene in private economic affairs. This question motivated Adam Smith, the great eighteenth-century economist who advocated laissez faire, to conceive of the "economic system" as a self-regulating mechanism that needs little guidance by the government. Much of modern economic theory still relies upon this original conception of Smith's.

On the other hand, J. M. Keynes argued in *The General Theory* (1936) that more government intervention was necessary to prevent massive unemployment. While Keynes's position on this question is not accepted by all economists, nevertheless, his theoretical analysis lies at the core of modern macroeconomic theory (the branch of economic theory concerned mainly with explaining what determines the behavior of aggregate variables like total output, unemployment, and inflation).

Most of this chapter is devoted to a discussion of the major goals of economic policy: (1) a high level of employment, (2) price stability, (3) efficiency, (4) an equitable distribution of income, and (5) economic growth. Some economists would add other goals to this list, such as economic freedom, economic security, and the reduction of pollution.

The first two goals come under the heading of maintaining a stable equilibrium in the economy. Throughout U.S. history there has been a great deal of instability. During the 1930s, for example, the Great Depression produced a substantial drop both in the level of employment and in the average level of prices. Both of these rose dramatically during World War II. Since then, we have maintained a reasonably high level of employment, at least up until the 1970s. The problem of inflation has been particularly acute during the 1940s and 1970s.

Everyone agrees that unemployment is a serious problem. When employment falls, we have less output to enjoy, and people out of work can suffer greatly. The problems with inflation are less obvious. When inflation occurs we don't necessarily have less output; we have to give up more money to buy the things we consume, but we also receive more money when selling things we produce. However, inflation does give rise to some serious complications:

1. There is always the danger that it will turn into hyperinflation, where prices rise so quickly that the entire monetary system breaks down.

2. Inflation hurts those living on fixed incomes.

3. It can also interfere with economic decision-making because, when prices keep changing all the time, it can be difficult to keep track of how much different goods cost.

The problem of efficiency is twofold. Technical efficiency simply means getting the most output out of a given combination of inputs. On the other hand, allocative efficiency involves the problem of allocating scarce resources (such as machines, land, etc.) among different uses (such as the production of different kinds of goods) so as to avoid the kind of waste that would occur if baseball stars taught economics and were replaced on their teams by professors of economics. These two kinds of efficiency are not the same. In the example of the ball players and economists there might not be any technical inefficiency, because the baseball players might be doing as good a teaching job as they can, and the managers of the baseball teams might be getting the most out of their economist-ballplayers. Also, allocative efficiency requires not just that the right combination of factors be assigned to producing the given combination of tasks, but also that the right combination of tasks be chosen. For example, there would be allocative inefficiency if everyone were assigned to teaching economics, and nobody played baseball.

The goal of an equitable distribution of income raises several problems. Many people believe that the economic pie should be divided up more evenly than it is. But the more we try to do this the smaller the pie becomes. For example, if we were all guaranteed an equal income there would not be much incentive for anyone to work. How to measure inequality is also a problem. One common measure is the percentage share of national income earned by the poorest 20 percent of families. However, the economic well-being of these families doesn't depend only upon their incomes; it depends also upon family size, age, whether they are city or farm dwellers, and so forth. We must also remember that even when the *fraction* of the pie going to the poorest 20 percent doesn't grow, the *size* of that pie may grow, so that their standard of living improves. In other words, the degree of inequality may remain constant while the incidence of poverty has fallen.

The problem of economic growth has recently sparked a great deal of controversy. When total output is growing the additional output can be used to alleviate poverty and achieve greater equity. In this respect, growth and equity are *complementary goals*. However, faster growth requires us to sacrifice current consumption, just as each of us normally can make his or her bank account grow faster only by sacrificing current consumption. Also, growth uses up scarce natural resources, and can lead to more industrial pollution as our heavy industry expands. Thus, growth and the reduction of pollution are seen by many to be *conflicting goals*.

There is substantial agreement among economists—and among the general public at large—that all these goals are important. However, there is controversy over the best way to attain them, and whether or not any particular goal can be pursued without sacrificing one or more of the other goals. One of the main purposes of the chapters that follow is to look in more detail at these controversial issues.

IMPORTANT TERMS

Laissez faire Literally, "allow to do" in French. This is the doctrine, promoted by Adam Smith, that the best government policy is to interfere very little with the private economy.

Unemployment The situation of someone who is willing and able to work but unable to find a job. The rate of unemployment is the percentage of the total labor force that is unemployed.

Labor Force The sum of those who are actually employed plus those who are unemployed. Labor foce and unemployment statistics are tied to the traditional definition of "jobs." Thus, for example, the mother who works at home is neither "in the labor force" nor "employed."

Depression This exists when a high rate of unemployment persists over a long period of time.

Recession We say that a recession has occurred if there has been a broad decline in production, involving a rise in the rate of umemployment.

Inflation A rise in the average level of prices.

Deflation A fall in the average level of prices.

Hyperinflation An inflation so severe that the country's monetary system begins to break down. Hyperinflations usually are associated with wars.

Ratio scale Also called a *logarithmic scale*. A scale on which equal percentage changes show up as equal distances. For more details on this and other technical matters, see the appendix to this chapter.

Technical efficiency This involves getting the most output out of given inputs. Technical *inefficiency* exists whenever the same output could be produced with fewer inputs.

Allocative efficiency This involves the production of the best combination of goods using the best combination of inputs. Notice that an economy can be technically efficient without having allocative efficiency, because the wrong combination of outputs is being produced, or because some goods are being produced with inputs that would have been better allocated to producing other goods.

Equitable distribution of income A fair and not too unequal sharing of the total national income among the different individuals in society. Many people believe that equity requires a reduction of inequality, but few would argue for complete equality.

Economic growth An increase in total national output resulting from technological improvement, additional factories, machines, and other equipment, or a larger labor force. The *rate* of economic growth is usually measured as an annual percentage increase in total output.

Complementary economic goals Two economic goals are complementary if pursuit of one promotes attainment of the other. For example, anything that reduces unemployment will usually reduce poverty also.

Conflicting economic goals Two economic goals conflict if pursuit of one makes the other more difficult to attain. For example, attempts to reduce unemployment often make inflation worse.

True-False Questions

Ⓣ F   1. Output per person in the United States was higher in 1975 than it was in 1900.

T Ⓕ   2. Output per person in the United States rose every year from 1900 until 1975. *except 1930*

T Ⓕ   3. Someone who has voluntarily retired is counted as being unemployed.

T Ⓕ   4. *The General Theory* of John Maynard Keynes is famous for its advocacy of *laissez faire*. *Adam Smith*

Ⓣ F   5. A more equitable distribution of income does not necessarily involve total equality.

T Ⓕ   6. When the level of prices rises during an inflation everybody suffers from that rise. *producers/suppliers gain*

T Ⓕ   7. During the past decade the United States has experienced hyperinflation.

Ⓣ F   8. Technical efficiency can exist even without allocative efficiency.

Ⓣ F   9. The degree of inequality is commonly measured by the fraction of national income going to the poorest 20 percent of families.

T F   10. Economic growth and the reduction of pollution are generally regarded as complementary economic goals.

Multiple-Choice Questions

1. Keynes's *General Theory* argued for a larger role for the government. His principal concern in this book was with the goal of
   (a) High employment
   (b) Price stability
   (c) Efficiency
   (d) An equitable distribution of income

2. A person who believes in *laissez faire* believes that
   (a) Private schools should be abolished
   (b) The government should in most circumstances leave the economy alone
   (c) Tariffs increase the prosperity of the economy
   (d) Government regulation of wages is required to control inflation

3. In 1933 in the United States the most obvious economic problem was that of
   (a) Unemployment
   (b) Inflation
   (c) Environmental pollution
   (d) The high price of oil

4. The mother who works full time at home is officially counted as
   (a) Unemployed
   (b) Employed
   (c) Part of the labor force
   (d) None of the above

5. Someone who thinks our government's policies should mainly be directed toward preventing our standard of living from falling behind that of the countries in Western Europe is mainly concerned with the goal of
   (a) A stable price level
   (b) An equitable distribution of income
   (c) The reduction of pollution
   (d) Economic growth

6. Which of the following is *not* a common result of inflation?
   (a) People on fixed incomes suffer losses
   (b) Business mistakes become more common
   (c) The value of money increases
   (d) People who have borrowed large sums of money benefit

7. Suppose that every factory worker in the economy was in the job best suited for him or her, and that they were working as productively as possible, but that they were all employed producing cars that no one wanted to buy. This would be a situation of
   (a) Technical efficiency and allocative efficiency
   (b) Technical efficiency and allocative inefficiency
   (c) Technical inefficiency and allocative efficiency
   (d) Technical inefficiency and allocative inefficiency

8. Suppose that the average income of the poorest 20 percent of families was to rise from $4,000 per annum to $5,000, while the average income of the other 80 percent rose from $16,000 to $24,000. Then, if the cost of living didn't change, we would probably say that
   (a) The incidence of poverty rose and the degree of inequality rose
   (b) The incidence of poverty rose and degree of inequality fell
   (c) The incidence of poverty fell and the degree of inequality rose
   (d) The incidence of poverty fell and the degree of inequality fell

9. Hyperinflation is most commonly associated with
   (a) Marxist governments
   (b) Wartime
   (c) Rapid economic growth
   (d) Allocative efficiency

10. Economic growth tends to
   (a) Make it easier to reduce poverty
   (b) Increase the amount of pollution
   (c) Increase the rate of depletion of natural resources
   (d) All of the above

11. During the 1960s the government tried to reduce unemployment by policies designed to encourage people to spend more, thus creating more jobs. However, by the end of the 1960s, economists were coming to the conclusion that all this extra spending encouraged sellers to raise their prices, thus contributing to inflation. This episode provides a good example of
   (a) Conflicting economic goals
   (b) Complementary economic goals
   (c) The benefits of economic growth
   (d) Why the theories of J. M. Keynes are now widely accepted by almost all economists

12. Suppose that the incomes of all families are perfectly equal. Then the poorest 20 percent of the families will get what share of the total income?
   (a) 5 percent
   (b) 10 percent
   (c) 20 percent
   (d) 25 percent

13. Which of the following is likely to involve the most unemployment?
   (a) A recession
   (b) A depression
   (c) Environmental pollution
   (d) A moderate rate of inflation

Essay Questions

1. The textbook says that economics is a policy study. This is not true of most natural sciences, like physics. Why not? Would you call the other social sciences, such as psychology, sociology, or political science, policy studies in the same degree as economics? More?

2. Inflation is sometimes defined informally in the newspapers as "too much money chasing too few goods." What do you suppose would happen to the average level of prices if the quantity of money were to increase drastically? Why? What would happen to the average level of prices if there were

the same quantity of money but a drastic decline in the output of goods? Why? With this in mind, do you think that the two goals of economic growth and price stability should be regarded as complementary or conflicting?

3. During wartime, governments are usually hard pressed to pay the cost of their military expenditures. They often resort to printing new money in order to pay the bills. What do you suppose this has to do with the fact that most hyperinflations are associated with wars?

4. If you decide to save more, what must you sacrifice in order to do so? What do you hope to gain from this sacrifice? If the total amount of saving in the whole economy increases, what must be sacrificed? What does the economy as a whole gain? Since World War II, Japan has had the highest rate of economic growth of all developed countries, and they have also had one of the highest rates of saving. Do you think that these two facts about the Japanese economy are related? What is the connection?

5. Why do you suppose that the rate of unemployment fell so much during World War II?

*6. While economics and physics are both sciences, there are some fundamental differences between them. One can learn from controlled experiments in physics, but this is not practical in economics. Can you think of any natural sciences in which experimentation is impossible? Are there any social sciences in which controlled experiments are performed? (For example, sociology, politics, anthropology, psychology?) Economics also deals with the human factor, which is absent from physics. Do you think that this requires a fundamentally different approach than the one used in physics? Many have argued that physics deals with an unchanging physical world, whereas economic life proceeds in an environment of ever-changing institutions and political organizations. What do you think of the prospects of discovering general laws and theorems in economics when everything appears to be changing so drastically? Is there a sense in which the physical world surrounding you is also changing?

Answers

True-False Questions: **1** T **2** F **3** F **4** F **5** T **6** F **7** F **8** T **9** T **10** F

Multiple-Choice Questions: **1** a **2** b **3** a **4** d **5** d **6** c **7** b **8** c **9** b **10** d **11** a **12** c **13** b

APPENDIX 1A: SOME USEFUL TECHNIQUES

A bit of mathematics is required to study the Wonnacotts' book and to use this study guide, but not much. The bit that is required is explained in this appendix. You may find on thumbing through the appendix that most of it is familiar from high school. But, if there is anything that looks unfamiliar, you should spend some time studying it and working through the related problems at the end of the appendix until you feel comfortable with the concepts. Likewise, if in the later chapters of the textbook or study guide you are having trouble understanding a graph or equation, it might help to look back at this appendix.

Graphs

Suppose someone tells you that lawn furniture business slacks off during rainy spells, and that you can see this in the graph in Figure 1-1. If you can't see this, or if you're not sure just what the graph means, read on.

The two items marked on the graph—sales of lawn furniture and amount of rainfall—are examples of what we call variables. A variable is something that can be measured, and that can change, or

vary, from time to time or place to place. Thus, the amount of rainfall can be measured in inches per month, and can vary from April to July or Seattle to Houston.

The statement that lawn furniture business slacks off during rainy spells means that there is a

FIGURE 1-1

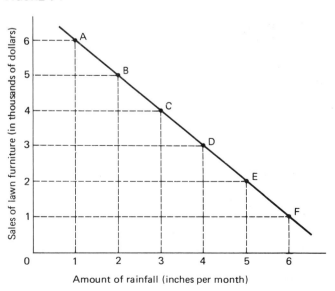

relationship between the two variables in Figure 1-1. In particular, it means that when rainfall increases, then sales decrease. We want to see how this relationship is indicated by the graph.

Notice the two *axes* with the numbers marked on them, that meet at the point labeled 0. The *vertical axis* has sales of lawn furniture on it. Every time you go up a notch this means that sales of lawn furniture have gone up by $1,000. The amount of rainfall is marked on the horizontal axis. Every time you go one notch to the right this indicates 1 more inch of rainfall per month. The point where the axes meet is the *origin*. This is the zero point on both axes—the point where there would be no rainfall and no one would sell any lawn furniture.

The relationship between the two variables is depicted by the line marked with the letters A through F. You "read" this line by using the axes. For example, consider point A. You can measure the height of this point on the vertical axis, just as you can measure a child's height on a wall. The dashed line going to the left from A is like a book held level on top of the child's head, showing that the height of A is 6. The distance that A lies to the right can be measured on the horizontal axis. The dashed line drawn down from A shows us that this distance is 1.

Here is the way to "read" point A. When there is only 1 inch of rainfall per month (when you go 1 notch to the right), then there is $6,000 worth of lawn furniture sold (6 notches up). Likewise, point B tells you that when there are 2 inches of rainfall then sales are $5,000. In this way, each time you read a point on the line you get one bit of information. These "bits" are shown in Table 1-1 below.

Table 1-1

Point	A	B	C	D	E	F
Rainfall	1	2	3	4	5	6
Sales	6	5	4	3	2	1

Thus, the rule for "reading" the graph goes as follows. Suppose you want to find out how much lawn furniture will be sold when there is some particular amount of rainfall (say 2 inches per month). Start at the origin. Now mark off that amount of rainfall to the right, along the horizontal axis (go two notches to the right). Then the height of the line directly above that point (5) is the answer to your question. Question 1 at the end of this appendix gives an exercise in reading graphs.

Slope

The statement we began with doesn't just say that rainfall and sales are related. It also says something about the *direction* of that relationship. It says

that when rainfall increases then sales don't increase, they decrease. In other words, sales are *negatively* related or *inversely* related to rainfall, because they change in the opposite direction.

You can tell the direction of this relationship by inspecting the line in Figure 1-1. Notice that it slopes downward to the right. This means that as you move to the right along the horizontal axis (as rainfall increases) then the height of the line decreases (sales decrease). For example, compare points A and B; as rainfall increases from 1 to 2, then sales decrease from 6 to 5.

A *positive* or *direct* relationship is shown in Figure 1-2. (See question 2 at the end of the appendix.) In this case, both variables change in the same direction. When snowfall increases, then sales of ski equipment increase as well. You can tell this from the way the line slopes upward to the right. As you move to the right (as snowfall increases) the line gets higher (sales increase).

You may think that a graph is a rather tedious way of showing the direction of a relationship. After all, the same idea of direction can be expressed in simple English by our original statement that lawn furniture sales slack off during rainy spells. So why bother with graphs? One reason is that a graph shows more than just the *direction* of a relationship. It also shows the *strength*. For example, when rainfall increases from 1 to 2 inches per month, Figure 1-1 doesn't just show that lawn furniture sales decrease. It also shows by *how much*—they decrease by $1,000, from $6,000 to $5,000. This goes beyond our original statement, which told us that sales would decrease, but not by how much.

The *strength* of the relationship is indicated by *how steep* the line is. For example, the steep line in Figure 1-2 shows a strong relationship between snowfall and ski equipment sales. When snowfall

FIGURE 1-2

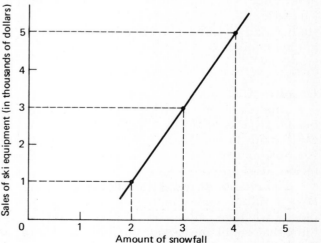

increases by 1 (going, say from 2 to 3), then sales increase by 2 (from 1 to 3). Compare this to the much weaker relationship shown by the flatter line in Figure 1-3. In this case, when snowfall increases from 2 to 3, sales increase only by ½ (from 1 to 1½).

Thus, both of these ideas—the direction and strength of a relationship—are shown by the way the line slopes. Direction is shown by whether the curve is slanted up or down. Strength is shown by how steep the line is.

There is a mathematical term that expresses both these ideas at once. This term is called the *slope.* The slope of a line is defined as *the amount by which the height of the line changes when you go one more unit to the right on the horizontal axis.* For example, the slope of the line in Figure 1-2 is 2, because when snowfall increases by 1 unit (when you go 1 unit to the right), then sales of ski equipment (given by the height of the line) change by 2 units. The slope in Figure 1-1 is −1. This is negative because when rainfall increases by 1 unit, then the change in sales (the change in the height of the line) is negative; sales decrease by 1 unit.

Thus, a positive slope indicates a line that slopes upward to right, showing a positive relationship; and a negative slope indicates a line that slopes downward to the right, showing a negative relationship.

Likewise, a larger slope indicates a steeper line, showing a stronger relationship. For example, the slope of the line in Figure 1-3 is only ½, showing that a 1-unit increase in snowfall increases sales by only $500 (½ of a unit). The slope of the steeper line in Figure 1-2 is 2, showing that the same increase in snowfall would increase sales by $2,000 (2 units). Questions 3 and 4 at the end of the appendix are designed to familiarize you with the geometric idea of slope.

Linear Equations

Sometimes the relationship between two variables is shown not by a graph, but by an equation. Suppose you are told that my expenditures each month on consumer goods (C) depend upon my monthly income (Y) according to the equation:*

$$C = \$400 + 0.5Y$$

In simple English, this equation says I will spend $400 plus half my income. As my income var-

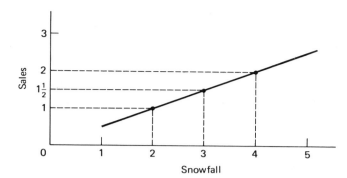

FIGURE 1-3

ies from month to month the equation tells you how my expenditures will vary. It thus describes a relationship between these two variables, Y and C. Whatever my income (Y) is, the equation tells you how much I will spend (C).

For example, choose some convenient value for my income, like $Y = 1,000$. Then substitute this into the equation to get $C = 400 + 0.5 \times 1,000 = 400 + 500 = 900$. This tells us that when my income (Y) is 1,000, my expenditures (C) will be 900. Choose any other convenient value, like $Y = 1,100$. Substituting this into the equation tells you that when my income is 1,100, then my expenditures will be $C = 400 + 0.5 \times 1,100 = 950$. Each time you choose a value of Y and make this substitution you thus get one bit of information. These two bits are shown in Table 1-2. As an exercise, fill in the rest of the table.

Figure 1-4 shows this relationship in a graph. The slope of this line is 0.5. This is because every time my income increases by $100 (go to the right one unit along the horizontal axis), I spend another $50 (the rise in the line is 0.5 of a unit). If the equation had been $C = 400 + 0.75Y$, then it would have said I spend $400 plus three-quarters of my income. In this case the slope of the line would have been 0.75, because every time my income increased by $100 I would spend another $75.

In general, any equation of the sort $C = a + bY$ represents a line with a slope equal to b. Such an equation is called a *linear* equation. For example, the linear equation pictured in Figure 1-4 has $a = 400$ and $b = 0.5$.

The number b (that is, 0.5) is known as the *coefficient* of the variable Y. It indicates the slope of the line. The number a (400) shows how high the line is where it meets the vertical axis (point A). Thus, a is

Table 1-2

Y	100	200	300	400	500	600	700	800	900	1,000	1,100
C										900	950

*Note: To represent income, economists almost always use the letter Y, not I; they reserve I to denote investment.

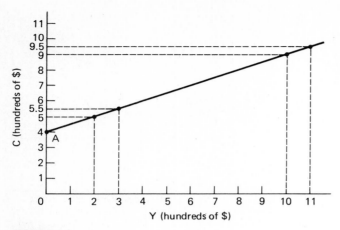

FIGURE 1-4

often called the *vertical intercept*. For example, the linear equation shown in Figure 1-4 has $a = 400$, and the line hits the vertical axis when $C = 400$.

At this point, you should try questions 5 and 6, which deal with linear equations.

Curves

So far we have drawn only straight lines. They are easy to use because they have a *constant* slope. For example, as you move down the line in Figure 1-1, from A to B, to C, and so on, every time you go 1 unit to the right the line falls by exactly 1 unit; not more or less. The slope stays constant at -1.

Not all relationships in economics can be described by straight lines. Some are described by curves, like this one in Figure 1-5. This curve shows how a student's final grade in economics depends on how many hours the student spends studying each day.

This curve does not have a constant slope. As you move to the right along the curve it gets flatter. For example, going from 0 hours to 1 hour makes the curve rise by 30—from 20 to 50. But then going

from 1 hour to 2 hours makes it rise by only 20— from 50 to 70, and going from 2 to 3 hours makes it rise by only 5. Each time you go one more unit to the right on the horizontal axis, the curve rises by less than the last time.

When dealing with a curve, we can still define the *slope* the way we did before. The slope of a curve is the amount by which the height of the curve changes when you go one more unit to the right on the horizontal axis. But we must remember that this slope changes as you move along the curve. Starting at zero hours in Figure 1-5, the slope decreases, from 30, to 20, to 5, and so on.

The decreasing slope in Figure 1-5 indicates that as you spend more and more time studying, each extra hour may raise your grade, *but not by as much as the previous hour*. The first hour raises your grade by 30 marks, the next by only 20. After 2 hours per day you are beginning to get saturated with economics and the next hour raises your grade by only 5 marks. Thus, the strength of the relationship between hours and grades is decreasing as you spend more hours. This is an example of diminishing returns; the payoff (in higher grades) diminishes as you study more and more.

Notice that, according to Figure 1-5, once you get beyond 8 hours per day, the relationship not only changes in strength, it also changes in direction, from positive to negative. After 8 hours the slope becomes negative. Studying beyond this point tires you so much it does more harm than good. Each extra hour causes your grade to decrease.

Thus, a curve with a changing slope shows a relationship whose strength or direction is changing instead of remaining constant.

Other Kinds of Graphs

Sometimes we don't bother to put numbers on the axes. For example, consider the linear relation-

FIGURE 1-5

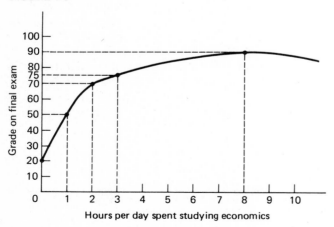

FIGURE 1-6

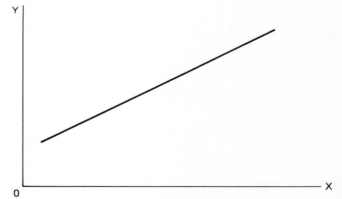

ship pictured in Figure 1-6. The variables *X* and *Y* are measured on the axes, but there are no numbers, except for the 0 at the origin. Without the numbers we can't tell exactly what the relationship is between *X* and *Y*. But the graph still tells us something. It tells us that the relationship is a positive one, because the line has a positive slope. It also tells us that the relationship is linear (with a constant direction and strength) because the line is straight (with a constant slope).

Sometimes instead of numbers we put letters, as in Figure 1-7. This still doesn't tell us the exact relationship. But the letters give us handy points of reference. For example, take point *A* on the horizontal axis. We don't know in numbers how far to the right this is. But whatever this distance is, from point *O* to point *A*, we call it the distance *OA*. Likewise, we describe the distance along the horizontal axis from point *A* to point *B* as the distance *AB*.

When describing movement from *E* to *F* along the line, it helps to look at the triangle *EFG*. The change in *X* is the difference between the distance *OB* and the distance *OA*; that is, the distance *AB*. It also equals the base of this triangle, *EG*. Likewise, the change in *Y* can be read from the vertical axis as *CD*, or from the triangle as *GF*. An exercise using this "letter code" is given in question 7.

Sometimes a graph will have numbers on it, but not starting at zero. For example, time is measured on the horizontal axis in Figure 1-8, starting at 1972. As long as each notch measures one more year, it doesn't matter that the "original" year is called 1972. We could just as easily call it year 0 provided that we understand that this refers to the year of the Watergate break-in, not of Christ's birth. In this way our choice of what number to put on the origin is purely a matter of convention. A Moslem, whose time begins with Mohammed instead of Christ,

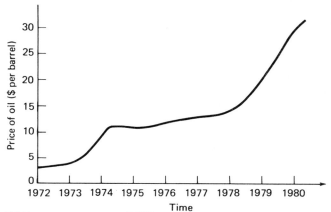

FIGURE 1-8

would put 1392 on the origin of Figure 1-8. According to the Jewish calendar we should put 5732. As long as we all know which convention is being used, the graph will mean the same to all of us.

Sometimes we start the axes at zero but "break" them, as in Figure 1-9, to focus on what's happening over a narrow range. In this case, we want to see what's happening to my expenditures as my income varies over the limited range of $100 to $110 per day. (If we didn't break the axes, and used a full graph, the range might be too small to see.)

The Ratio Scale

In Figure 1-8, every time you go one notch up the vertical axis, this represents the same change in the price of oil—$5. This is the way most graphs work—equal distances along an axis represent equal changes in the variable.

But there is an important exception to this rule. Look at Figure 1-10. In this graph, going up one notch on the vertical axis doesn't always mean the same change in the price level. The first notch takes you from 25 to 50—a change of 25. But when you move up to the second notch the price level goes from 50 to 100—a change this time of 50. The verti-

FIGURE 1-7

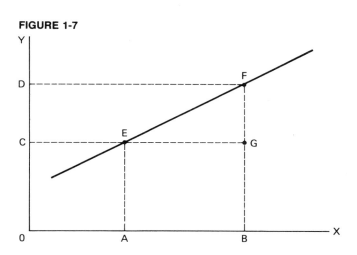

FIGURE 1-9

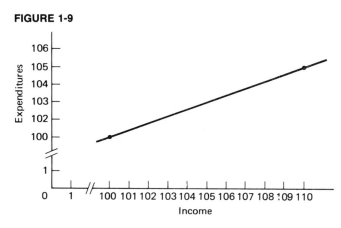

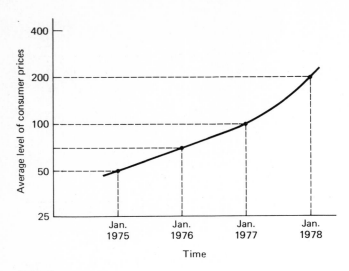

FIGURE 1-10

cal axis measures the price level not on the usual scale, but on the *ratio scale,* or *logarithmic scale.*

As you move up a ratio scale, equal distances represent equal *percentage* changes. Going up from 25 to the first notch, the price level goes up by 100 percent to 50. Going to the second notch it again goes up by 100 percent—this time to 100. In this case, every notch higher represents a price level that is 100 percent higher.

We often use a ratio scale when we're primarily interested in the annual percentage rate of growth in a variable. For instance, when we're looking at the price level we usually want to know the rate of inflation. Ten percent inflation means that the price level has been growing at that rate per year.

The percentage rate of growth from one year to the next can be measured in such a diagram by the slope of the line. For example, as we go from January 1977 to January 1978 the change in the height of the curve is one notch, or 100 percent. (This is just an illustration. In fact, the rate of inflation in the United States that year was less than 10 percent.) Thus, the slope of the curve is 100 percent. This tells us that over the calendar year 1977 there was 100 percent inflation. Starting at January 1976 the slope of the curve is half a notch, or 50 percent. Thus, there was only 50 percent inflation during 1976.

In this kind of graph, a straight line represents something that grows at a constant percentage rate. Between January 1975 and January 1977 in Figure 1-10 the curve is a straight line, showing that the rate of inflation was constant over this 2-year interval, at 50 percent. When the slope increases, as it does starting at January 1977, the rate of inflation is rising.

Geometric Series

There is one important technique that comes up frequently in economics that doesn't involve any graphs. Suppose someone gave you $1 today, then 50 cents tomorrow, then 25 cents the next day, and so on, each day giving you half as much as the day before. Let us suppose that the money is infinitely divisible so that you will continue to get 12½ cents, 6¼ cents, etc. If you stop to think how much you will be given in total, you will be faced with the problem of having to make the addition:

$$1 + \frac{1}{2} + \frac{1}{4} + \frac{1}{8} + \frac{1}{16} + \cdots$$

There is no end to the number of terms in this series. Nevertheless, there is an answer to the addition. For as each day passes the sum grows from $1 to $1.50 to $1.75 to $1.87½, to $1.93¾, and so forth. As you can see, the sum will approach an upper limit of $2. Every day, you are getting half of what it would take to get to $2. The shortfall keeps getting cut by half. You will never quite get there, because you will never get enough to bring you all the way up, just half that. But you will approach that sum asymptotically.

This is just an example of a problem that occurs often in economics. Suppose that a is some positive fraction, and you have to add the infinite sum, or series:

(1) $S = 1 + a + a^2 + a^3 + a^4 + \cdots$

This sum is called a geometric series. The previous example was obviously a special case of a geometric series, with $a = \frac{1}{2}$. There, I took a guess at the answer ($S = 2$), and showed how this would work. But it would be nice to be more systematic about it, especially when it gets to less obvious cases like $a = 0.8$. The following reasoning establishes a formula that can be used for any fraction of a.

Multiply both sides of Equation (1) by a. Then, the two sides must continue to equal one another. Thus:

(2) $aS = a(1 + a + a^2 + a^3 + a^4 + \cdots)$

If we carry out the multiplication on the right-hand side of Equation (2) term by term we get:

(3) $aS = a + a^2 + a^3 + a^4 + a^5 + \cdots$

Now, suppose we subtract this equation from equation (1):

$$\begin{aligned} S &= 1 + a + a^2 + a^3 + \cdots \\ \text{Subtract} \quad aS &= \quad\;\; a + a^2 + a^3 + \cdots \\ \hline S - aS &= 1 + 0 + 0 + 0 + \cdots \end{aligned}$$

Thus, we get the result $S(1 - a) = 1$. By dividing $(1 - a)$ into both sides of this last equation we get:

(4) $S = \dfrac{1}{1 - a}$

Equation (4) is the solution to our problem. This formula always gives the right answer. To check it out, note that when $a = \frac{1}{2}$, as in our example, then S indeed equals 2. (Now try $a = 0.8$).

Questions

1. Point A in Figure 1-11 has a height of _____, and lies a distance _____ to the right. Thus, it tells us that when there are _____ hundred police officers there will be _____ hundred crimes reported. If there are 600 officers there will be _____ hundred crimes, and with a thousand officers there will be _____ hundred crimes.

FIGURE 1-11

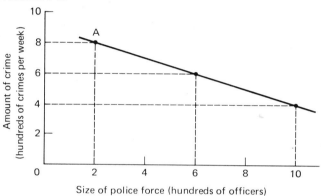

2. From Figure 1-2 fill in Table 1-3.

Table 1-3

Amount of snowfall	2	3	4
Sales of ski equipment			

3. Figure 1-12 has six different lines in it. Fill in Table 1-4 showing the slope of each line.

Table 1-4

Line	a	b	c	d	e	f
Slope						

4. Which of the lines in Figure 1-13 show a positive relationship between the variables X and Y? _____. When X increases by 1 unit, which of these lines shows the greatest increase in Y? _____. When X increases by 1 unit, which one shows the greatest decrease in Y? _____.

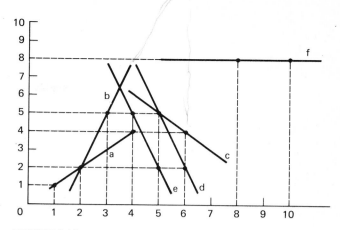

FIGURE 1-12

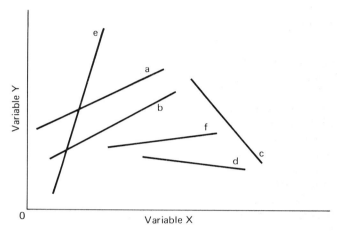

FIGURE 1-13

5. Consider any two variables, X and Y. Suppose they are related according to the linear equation:

$$Y = 8 - 2X$$

Fill in Table 1-5 according to this equation

Table 1-5

X	0	1	2	3	4
Y					

This equation represents a straight line. Draw the straight line in Figure 1-14. The slope of this line is _____. The vertical intercept is _____.

6. Consider the following linear equations, showing how one variable, Y, depends upon another variable, X.

(a) $Y = 90 + 10X$
(b) $Y = 50 + 15X$
(c) $Y = 80 - 5X$
(d) $Y = 3X$

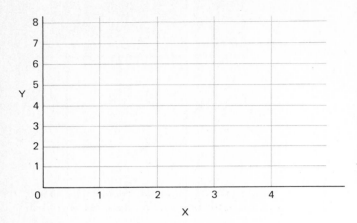

FIGURE 1-14

(e) $Y = -10 + 5X$
(f) $Y = 50$

Each of these equations describes a different line.
Line _____ has the largest vertical intercept and line _____ has the largest slope. When X increases by 1 unit, which line shows the largest increase in Y? _____. When $X = 0$, then the highest line is _____. Which show a positive relationship? _____. Which a negative relationship? _____. What is the slope of line (f)? _____. What kind of relationship do you suppose is indicated by line (f)?

_____
_____.

Which line has a vertical intercept of zero? _____. Therefore, which line passes through the origin in a graph? _____. Which line indicates that Y is always a constant multiple of X? _____. What does this suggest is always true of lines that pass through the origin? _____
_____.

What is the vertical intercept in line (e)? _____.

How would this show up in a graph? _____
_____.

7. The amount of sunshine at point A in Figure 1-15 equals the distance _____, or _____. Sales of umbrellas at point A equal _____, or _____. At B the amount of sunshine equals _____, or _____, and sales of umbrellas equal _____, or _____. Going from A to B, the amount of sunshine (increases, decreases) by _____, or _____, and sales of umbrellas (increase, decrease) by _____, or _____.

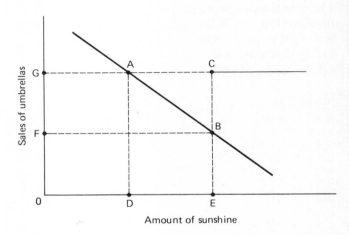

FIGURE 1-15

8. The following sum:

$$1 + 1/3 + 1/9 + 1/27 + \cdots$$

equals _____.

9. Take any positive fraction a. Then the sum $a + a^2 + a^3 + a^4 + \cdots$ equals _____. [Hint: compare this with the sum (1), and use the formula (4).]

Answers

Linear Equations:

Table 1-2 completed:

Y	100	200	300	400	500	600	700	800	900	1000	1100
C	450	500	550	600	650	700	750	800	850	900	950

Geometric Series: When $a = 0.8$, then $S = 5$.
Questions:
1. 8, 2, 2, 8, 6, 4.

2. Table 1-3 completed:

2	3	4
1	3	5

3. Table 1-4 completed:

a	b	c	d	e	f
1	3	−1	−3	−3	0

4. $(a, b, e, f), e, c.$

5. Table 1-5 completed:

X	0	1	2	3	4
Y	8	6	4	2	0

−2, 8

6. $a, b, b, a, (a, b, d, e), c, 0$; one in which Y does not vary as X changes; $d, d, d,$ they always indicate that Y is a constant multiplier of X; −10; if you extended the vertical axis down below the horizontal axis, the line would intersect the vertical axis on this lower segment.

7. OD or GA; OG or DA; OE or FB; OF or EB; increases; DE or AC; decrease; FG or BC.

8. 3/2.

9. $\dfrac{a}{1 - a}$

CHAPTER 2
Scarcity:
The Economizing Problem

Learning Objectives

After you have studied this chapter in the textbook and the study guide, you should be able to
Define the three major kinds of economic resource
Explain opportunity cost, and how it is related to the production possibilities curve (PPC)
Explain why the PPC slopes downward to the right
Explain why the PPC is bowed out from the origin
Identify the three major causes of economic growth
Explain why production occurs at a point inside the PPC in an economy with large-scale unemployment
Explain how the choice between consumption goods and capital goods affects the process of economic growth
Explain why economic theory involves simplifying assumptions

CHAPTER HIGHLIGHTS

Scarcity is one of the most fundamental concepts of economics. The purpose of this chapter is to introduce you to this concept. The basic problem of scarcity is that *material wants are unlimited but this is not true of resources* (land, labor, and capital) *available to satisfy these wants*. Hence, we cannot have everything we want, and we need to economize on our resources. Some people actually define economics as the study of scarcity.

Scarcity requires us to make choices. Since we cannot satisfy all our wants, we must choose among the limited options available to us. The most important proposition concerning choice is as follows: Whenever we choose one thing, we have to sacrifice some other thing. To use the example given in the textbook, when we choose more food, we give up some clothing.

Another fundamental concept is that of opportunity cost. The opportunity cost of producing any good is the amount of some other good (or goods) that must be given up as a result. In the example in the textbook, the opportunity cost of more food is measured by the amount of clothing that must be given up. Another way of expressing the problem of scarcity is to say that every choice has an opportunity cost.

These ideas are summarized by the production possibilities curve (the PPC). The PPC represents the range of options from which it is possible to choose. In the example in the text, the PPC depicts the various combinations of food and clothing that are possible, ranging from the extreme combination of no food and the maximum amount of clothing, to the opposite extreme of no clothing and the maximum amount of food. If there were no problem of scarcity, then we could choose any combination of food and clothing we wanted. However, with scarcity, we cannot choose a combination outside the boundary formed by the PPC (although we may, through sheer waste or unemployment of resources, end up inside that frontier).

There are two important aspects of the PPC to remember. The first is that it slopes downward to the right. This is a direct consequence of the existence of opportunity costs. If a choice is made to increase the amount of clothing produced (that is, to move to the right in the diagram), then there must be a decrease in the amount of food produced (that is, a move downward in the diagram). Indeed, the slope of the PPC is a precise measure of the opportunity cost of more clothing, because it indicates the size of the downward movement required for each movement to the right.

The second feature is that it is "bowed out" from the origin. This illustrates the important principle of *increasing* opportunity cost. The greater the production of clothing (the further to the right along the PPC), the greater is the opportunity cost of each additional unit of clothing (the greater is the slope of the PPC). This principle of increasing opportunity cost reflects the specialization of resources. For example, as the text explains, not all land is equally good for producing wheat and cotton.

There are many different kinds of choice. One of the most important ones is the choice between consumer goods and capital goods. This choice is important for the problem of economic growth. Growth can result from various fundamental causes, including technological change, and growth of the labor force. Perhaps the most important cause is the accumulation of capital goods. If we choose to produce more capital goods this year, the economy will grow faster, because next year those extra capital goods will be available to produce more output.

Consider the PPC with consumer goods on one axis and capital goods on the other (as in Figure 2-5 in the textbook). As growth occurs, this curve will shift out from the origin because our capacity to produce increases. The rate of growth is the rate at which the curve will shift out in the future. But this depends upon the point chosen on the *present* PPC. For example, suppose that society chooses to devote most of its resources to producing capital goods. Then its stock of capital goods will increase rapidly, so its capacity to produce will grow rapidly. But if society chooses to devote most of its resources to producing consumer goods, as in **Fig. 2-5a** in the text, it cannot use these resources for producing capital goods. The stock of capital goods will not accumulate as rapidly, and the capacity to produce will not grow as fast.

The final major point made by this chapter concerns the nature of economic theory. If theory is to be helpful, it must make simplifying assumptions that strip away the nonessential complications of a problem and allow you to see the important relationships. Theory should not be dismissed because it fails to account for everything; a road map can be useful even if it omits many details. But—because of this simplification—theory must be used with caution. Just as a weather map is useless for planning an auto trip, the theory that helps to explain one aspect of economic life may be inappropriate for explaining other aspects.

IMPORTANT TERMS

Economic resources Inputs that can be used to produce goods or services. These are also referred to as factors of production. They are generally classified as land, labor, and capital.

Land The nonhuman resources given by nature. This term covers more than the common notion of land, also including minerals and the environment.

Labor Human effort and ability.

Capital Any economic resource that has been produced. This definition, the one usually used by economists, includes only *real* capital such as buildings, machines, and material, and not *financial* capital, such as stocks and bonds. Such financial assets are not factors of production. (We might note that some economists speak of "human capital" which consists of the talents, skills, and knowledge built up through practice, education, or other training. However, we shall generally refer to capital as consisting simply of physical, or nonhuman capital).

Investment Accumulation of capital over time. Once again, this definition refers to *real*, not financial investment. Buying stocks or bonds isn't included in this definition, since it involves the accumulation of financial capital, not real capital.

Entrepreneur The person who (a) puts together the factors of production; (b) makes business decisions; (c) takes risks; and (d) generates innovations.

Production possibilities curve (PPC) The graphical representation of possible combinations of different goods that can be produced.

Opportunity cost The opportunity cost of a choice is the sacrifice that has to be made because, in order to make that choice, something else is *not* chosen. The opportunity cost of producing a good can be represented as the slope of the production possibilities curve drawn between it and another good.

Economic growth The outward movement of the production possibilities curve. Growth can result from (a) technological change; (b) an increase in the labor force; or (c) the accumulation of capital.

Positive economics The study of "what is" in economic life, as contrasted with *normative economics*, which is the study of "what ought to be."

True-False Questions

T F **1.** The problem of scarcity applies only to less developed countries.
T F **2.** Any factor of production is an economic resource.
T F **3.** Land is a factor of production.
T F **4.** If, for some reason, wants were limited, the production possibilities curve would slope upward to the right, not downward.
T F **5.** The production possibilities curve is bowed out from the origin because of increasing opportunity costs.
T F **6.** Just as it is possible to select a combination of goods inside the PPC, so it is possible to choose a combination that lies outside the PPC.
T F **7.** Economic growth is defined as a movement from a point inside the PPC to a point on the PPC.
T F **8.** Since economic growth shifts the PPC out from the origin, it may allow us to produce more of all goods in a given year than in the previous year.
T F **9.** Economic theory is intended to provide a detailed description of all aspects of an economy.
T F **10.** The statement that the current rate of inflation is higher than it should be is a statement of normative economics.
T F **11.** The statement that the current rate of inflation could be reduced by restricting the rate of growth of the economy's money supply is a statement of normative economics.

Multiple-Choice Questions

1. The problem of scarcity arises because
(a) Wants are limited and resources are unlimited
(b) Wants are limited and resources are limited
(c) Wants are unlimited and resources are unlimited
(d) Wants are unlimited and resources are limited

2. As economic growth occurs
(a) The production of consumer goods always grows more slowly than the population
(b) You can provide more of some goods from year to year, but only if you produce less of others
(c) The PPC shifts outward over time
(d) You cannot say what will happen to the PPC

3. An ice cream cone would be classified as
(a) Land　　　　(c) A capital good
(b) Labor　　　 (d) A consumer good

4. A government post office building would be classified as
(a) Land　　　　(c) A capital good
(b) Labor　　　 (d) A consumer good

5. A PPC between food and clothing shows
(a) How much food we ought to sacrifice in order to acquire clothing
(b) How much food and clothing will actually be produced in the economy
(c) How much potential food production would be sacrificed to produce any given amount of clothing

(d) How much of both food and clothing would have to be sacrificed in order to produce more capital goods

6. A combination of goods lying outside the PPC
(a) Can always be produced
(b) May eventually be produced if the labor force grows enough
(c) May eventually be produced even if no economic growth occurs
(d) Can presently be produced if there is some unemployment of resources

7. Which of the following is a correct definition of economic profit?
(a) Normal profits
(b) Normal profits minus opportunity costs
(c) Accounting profits plus above-normal profits
(d) Above-normal profits

8. Which of the following is *not* one of the primary roles of the entrepreneur?
(a) Taking risks
(b) Innovating
(c) Making business decisions
(d) Doing normative economics

9. The opportunity cost of a good is measured by
(a) How far the economy is operating inside the PPC
(b) The slope of a PPC

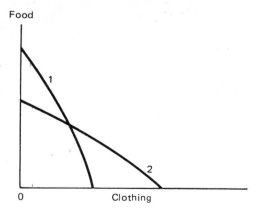

Food

Clothing

FIGURE 2-1

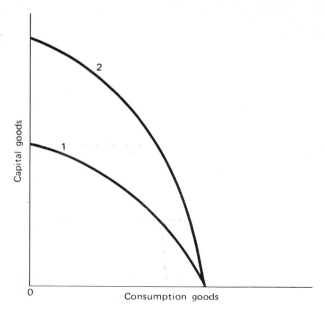

Capital goods

Consumption goods

FIGURE 2-2

(c) How far the PPC is away from the origin

(d) The speed with which the PPC is shifting out from the origin

10. In Figure 2-1, suppose that the PPC has shifted from the curve labeled 1 to the curve labeled 2. Then

— **(a)** The opportunity cost of food but not that of clothing has increased

(b) The opportunity cost of clothing but not that of food has increased

(c) The opportunity cost of both food and clothing has increased

(d) The opportunity cost of both food and clothing has decreased

11. The principle of "increasing opportunity cost" leads to the conclusion that

(a) Wants are unlimited but resources aren't

(b) Growth requires investment

(c) Points outside the PPC are not attainable

⌐ **(d)** The PPC is "bowed out" from the origin

12. Which of the following does *not* lead to increased economic growth?

(a) Faster growth in the labor force

(b) More investment

(c) More rapid technological progress

(d) More production of consumer goods

13. The "cruel dilemma" of economic development for poor countries is that

(a) More growth will cause less future consumption

– **(b)** More growth will require less present consumption

(c) More investment will cause less growth

(d) Population growth is not rapid enough

14. Technological improvements that allow us to produce more efficiently

(a) Cannot shift the PPC outward unless the labor force grows

(b) Cannot occur in a less developed country

— **(c)** Can shift the PPC outward even if there is no increase in resources

(d) Never shift the PPC

15. In Figure 2-2 suppose that the PPC shifts from the curve labeled 1 to the curve labeled 2 because of a technological improvement. This technological improvement

(a) Allows the economy to produce capital goods at less cost

(b) Allows the economy to produce consumer goods at less cost

(c) Reduces the level of unemployment

(d) Increases the total production of capital goods

Exercises

1. Consider a hypothetical economy with a labor force of 10,000 workers, each of whom can be put to work either building houses or building roads. Each worker provides 2,000 hours of labor services during each year. Thus, the economy has available a total of 20 million labor-hours during each year to produce houses and roads. Table 2-1 shows how many labor-hours it takes to build various quantities of houses. For example, in order to build 18,000 houses, 15,000,000 labor-hours are needed. Likewise, Table 2-2 indicates how many labor-hours it takes to build various quantities of

roadway. In Figure 2-3, only one point, *A*, on the PPC has been plotted out. It shows that one possi-

Table 2-1

Millions of labor-hours	Thousands of houses
20	20
15	18
10	14
5	8
0	0

Table 2-2

Millions of labor-hours	Hundreds of miles of roadway
20	10
15	9
10	7
5	4
0	0

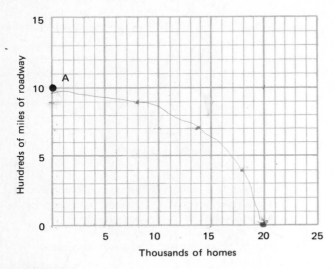

FIGURE 2-3

ble combination of houses and roadway is 1,000 miles of roadway and no houses, which is what could be produced if all 20,000,000 of the available labor-hours were used to build roads. Using the data in Tables 2-1 and 2-2, plot four other points on the PPC. Join these points with a smooth curve.

2. Figure 2-4 represents the PPC between wheat and corn. At point *A*, the output or corn equals _____ million bushels, and the output of

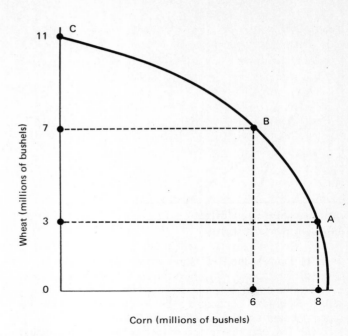

FIGURE 2-4

wheat equals _____ million bushels. At point *B*, the output of corn equals _____ million bushels, and the output of wheat equals _____ million bushels. In going from *A* to *B*, the opportunity cost of the extra 4 million bushels of wheat is _____ million bushels of corn. At point *C*, the output of corn equals _____ million bushels and the output of wheat equals _____ bushels. The opportunity cost of the extra _____ million bushels of wheat produced by going from *B* to *C* equals _____ million bushels of corn. When this opportunity cost is compared with the one in going from *A* to *B*, what general principle is illustrated? _____
_____.

Essay Questions

1. A student who spends $6,000 for books and tuition for a year at college gives up other goods that could have been bought with that $6,000. Therefore, that $6,000 should be included in the opportunity cost of going to college. Which of the following should also be included in part, or in whole, and why? (*a*) The $12,000 that the student could have earned that year in a job, (*b*) the $4,000 the student spent for room and meals at college.

2. Do you have any wants that could be satisfied entirely? If you had a million dollars, do you think you would still want more? What would you do with it? What does this imply about the fundamental principle of scarcity?

3. Some people have argued that the patent system fosters technological change. Their argument is that the system encourages people to devote their efforts to discovering better ways of doing thing by guaranteeing to inventors and innovators that the fruits of their labor cannot legally be stolen. On the other hand, some have argued that the patent system inhibits technological change because it prevents others from copying new techniques. Suppose the first argument is correct. Then, how does the patent system affect the rate of economic growth? What if the second argument is correct? In either case, what kind of government policies to you think might help to encourage economic growth?

4. The economic growth that results from accumulation of capital goods expands our capacity to produce most goods. But it does not have much effect on our capacity to produce many services, like haircuts, lawyer's services, or gardener's services, which involve relatively little capital. Show in a diagram how this kind of economic growth will "tilt" the PPC between haircuts and television sets. With this kind of economic growth, what happens to the opportunity cost of producing haircuts? How would your answer be affected if growth resulted from accumulation of human capital rather than physical capital? (See the definition of capital in the above list of important terms.)

5. John Kenneth Galbraith, a retired Harvard professor, has argued that because our economy produces so many private goods (cars, cosmetics, color television sets, etc.), it therefore produces too few public goods (parks, clean air, government-supported symphony orchestras, etc.). Is this contention an example of positive or normative economics, or are there elements of both? Explain your answer. Draw a PPC between public and private goods and show (*a*) where our economy is currently producing, and (*b*) where Professor Galbraith would like the economy to be producing. Milton Friedman, a retired University of Chicago professor, has argued that Galbraith is wrong, and that because of excessive government spending we produce too few private goods. Show in terms of this PPC how economic growth can help to reduce the conflict between those who share Galbraith's priorities and those who share Friedman's.

Answers

True-False Questions: 1 F 2 T 3 T 4 F 5 T 6 F 7 F 8 T 9 F 10 T 11 F
Multiple-Choice Questions: 1 d 2 c 3 d 4 c 5 c 6 b 7 d 8 d 9 b 10 a 11 d
12 d 13 b 14 c 15 a

Exercises: **1.** The four other points are the four columns in this table:

Hundreds of miles	9	7	4	0
Thousands of hours	8	14	18	20

2. 8, 3, 6, 7, 2, 0. 11, 4, 6, increasing opportunity cost.

CHAPTER 3
Specialization, Exchange, and Money

Learning Objectives

After you have studied this chapter in the textbook and the study guide, you should be able to

Explain why specialization requires exchange

Explain why the problem of the "coincidence of wants" makes monetary exchange preferable to barter

List four properties that the ideal money commodity should possess

Give an example of how Gresham's law works

Explain two reasons why there are gains from specialization and exchange

Explain the distinction between absolute advantage and comparative advantage

CHAPTER HIGHLIGHTS

In the last chapter, we mentioned that some people have defined economics to be the study of scarcity and choice. These problems of scarcity and choice arise even in an individual's private life. Yet, as we noted in the very first chapter, economics is a social science—one that deals with problems of interactions among different individuals. How is it that the study of scarcity, which appears to be a private affair, leads to the study of social interactions? The answer has to do with specialization. As society has progressed over the generations, people have tended to become more specialized and less self-sufficient. Rather than producing things for which we have a direct need, we each produce something quite special; we acquire the various goods and ser-

vices we need from those who, in turn, specialize in producing those items. Thus, specialization is the basis for *exchange*, the basic form of economic interaction. Economic progress has required us to become increasingly specialized, which has in turn required us to rely more and more upon exchange of goods and services. We live in a higher interdependent economy, in which each of us depends on others for so much of our material well-being, and each of us specializes in an increasingly narrow range of activities.

Although different societies have organized their exchange activities in a variety of ways, almost all economies have relied upon the use of money. We sell our specialized output for money, with which we purchase our various items of consumption. It is easy to imagine the sorts of difficulties that would arise without the use of money—that is, if we had to rely upon primitive barter for our exchange activities. The problem of finding a "coincidence of wants" (for example, the poorly clad farmer finding a hungry tailor) would make exchange very costly, thus encouraging people to produce many things for themselves rather than specializing and then having to exchange. Thus, money helps to make possible efficient specialization of economic activities. It provides people with general purchasing power, thereby relieving them of having to rely on unlikely coincidences (the poorly clad farmer still needs to find someone who is hungry, and someone who is a tailor, but they need not be the same person).

If the economy is to operate smoothly, money should be (a) of uniform value in other uses, (b) issued in stable quantities, (c) physically convenient (easily stored, carried, recognized, etc.), and (d) easily divisible into small denominations. When money is not uniform, then Gresham's law may operate so as to drive some of the money out of circulation. Nonuniformity is often the result of having some of the currency debased, as when the prisoners in the POW camp thinned out their cigarettes. When money is not issued in stable quantities, then inflation or deflation can be a problem. The resulting uncertainty concerning prices can eliminate many of the advantages of monetary exchange.

There are two reasons why there are gains from specialization and exchange: *comparative advantage* and *economies of scale*.

The notion of comparative advantage was illustrated in the text by the example of the gardener and the lawyer. The lawyer had an absolute advantage in both law and gardening. In other words, she was both a better lawyer and a better gardener than the gardener. By the same token, we say that the gardener had an absolute disadvantage at both activities. However, the gardener had a *comparative* advantage in gardening, and likewise the lawyer in the practice of law. By this we mean that while the lawyer was superior to the gardener in both activities, her superiority was greater in law than in gardening. As the example in Box 3-2 demonstrates, it was efficient for the lawyer to specialize in that activity for which she had the greater superiority, that is, in which she had a comparative advantage. Likewise, while the gardener was inferior in both activities, it paid him to specialize in the activity in which his inferiority was the least, that is, the one in which he had a comparative advantage. To be more exact, each person has a comparative advantage in the activity where his or her opportunity cost is lower than the other person's. Thus, for example, the gardener used more hours than the lawyer to produce any given amount of gardening services, but the opportunity cost, measured by the amount of legal services that could have been provided with those hours, was lower for the gardener than for the lawyer. The gardener has an *absolute* disadvantage in gardening (he uses more hours) but a *comparative* advantage (it costs him less in forgone legal services).

If there are *economies of scale,* then the cost per unit of producing an item falls as production is increased, at least up to a point. For example, the cost per car of producing 10 cars during the year would be astronomical because it would not pay to use heavy equipment and the cars would have to be handmade. However, if annual production were increased to 1 million cars, the cost per car would be significantly reduced. This clearly offers a basis for specialization and exchange. If people had to produce their own cars, few of us would be able to do so. But with large auto manufacturers doing the production, economies of scale allow most families to afford at least one car.

IMPORTANT TERMS

Specialization Specialization occurs when each of us concentrates on performing a specific task, rather than choosing to be self-sufficient. It is sometimes referred to as the *division of labor.*

Exchange The process of trading what you have for what you would rather have. Exchange is made necessary by specialization.

Barter A primitive method of exchange whereby different goods or services are exchanged directly for one another without the use of money.

Money Money is the medium of exchange (that is, the item which enters into most exchanges so as to avoid barter). It makes possible complex transactions between people by relieving them of the necessity of relying on a coincidence of wants. It also provides people with a way of storing their wealth in the form of general purchasing power. (That is, it can be used to buy *any* of the goods and services offered for sale.)

Gresham's law This is commonly expressed as the proposition that "bad money drives out good." If two different items are equally valuable as money, then the one which is the more valuable in other, nonmonetary uses will tend to disappear from circulation as money.

Absolute advantage A country (or region, or individual) has an *absolute advantage* in the production of a good if it can produce that good with fewer resources (less land, labor, and capital) than other countries.

Comparative advantage If two individuals (or regions, or nations) have different opportunity costs of producing a good or service, then the individual with the lower opportunity cost has the *comparative advantage* in producing that good.

Economies of scale These exist when a doubling of all inputs results in output which is more than doubled.

True-False Questions

T F   1. Only under a barter system can anyone possess general purchasing power.

T F   2. Economies tend to become more specialized over time because the more we specialize, the less money we need.

T (F)   3. The widespread practice of the debasing of currency is a result of Gresham's law.

(T) F   4. One reason that barter is inconvenient is because many commodities cannot readily be divided into smaller parts.

(T) F   5. One advantage of money is that it makes possible multilateral transactions that would be difficult or impossible to arrange under barter.

T F   6. A commodity can be used as money without any government intervention to certify it and regulate its supply.

T (F)   7. According to Gresham's law only the currencies with the highest nonmonetary values will continue to circulate as money.

T F   8. Specialization is efficient if everyone undertakes all those activities in which he or she has an absolute advantage.

(T) F   9. Economies of scale provide a basis for specialization even when everyone has the same abilities.

T (F)   10. The main principle which makes Adam Smith's pin factory work so much more efficiently than if each person produced pins individually is the principle of comparative advantage.

(T) F   11. Inflation is likely to result from a too-rapid increase in the quantity of money.

Multiple-Choice Questions

1. Cigarettes were used in the prisoner-of-war camp as money because
   (a) They were valuable in relation to bulk
   (b) They came in relatively small units
   (c) They were durable
   (d) All of the above

2. Not too long ago it was discovered that the price of silver had risen by so much that there was more than 10 cents' worth of silver in every dime. According to Gresham's law, you would expect that
   (a) Nickels would come to be withdrawn from circulation
   (b) Dimes would come to be withdrawn from circulation
   (c) People would start using silver itself instead of dimes
   (d) People would begin melting down nickels in order to sell the metal

3. Suppose that, in France, a person could produce one shirt in 1 hour of work while another could produce a chair in the same length of time. In Italy, on the other hand, it would take a person 1½ hours to produce a shirt and another person 2 hours to produce a chair. Then Italy has
   (a) An absolute advantage in producing shirts
   (b) An absolute advantage in producing chairs
   (c) A comparative advantage in producing shirts
   (d) A comparative advantage in producing chairs

4. Economies of scale
   (a) Are required in order for any comparative advantage to exist
   (b) Are a consequence of the principle of increasing opportunity cost

   (c) Are made easier to exploit by the widespread use of monetary exchange
   (d) Appear to be getting less important as technological progress is made toward alleviating the problem of scarcity

5. Suppose that the PPCs of Countries A and B were as they are drawn in Figure 3-1. Then we could say that
   (a) Country A has a comparative advantage in producing food
   (b) Country B has a comparative advantage in producing food
   (c) Country A has an absolute advantage in producing clothing
   (d) Nothing can be said on the basis of this diagram about comparative or absolute advantage

FIGURE 3-1

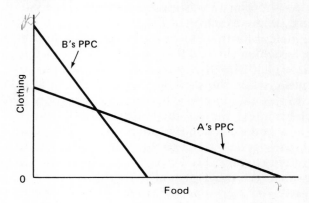

6. Which of the following is the *least* important property of money for making monetary exchange preferable to barter?

   (a) It is readily divisible into units as small as a penny

   (b) You can keep it in your pocket, even in large amounts

   (c) Everyone recognizes it

   (d) Bills of different denominations all the same size

7. Suppose that in Japan a car can be produced using $3,000 worth of capital and $2,000 worth of labor, and that a bushel of wheat can be produced using $3 worth of capital and $2 worth of labor. Then the opportunity cost to Japan of producing a car is

   (a) $3,000 worth of capital

   (b) $2,000 worth of labor

   (c) 1,000 bushels of wheat

   (d) Cannot be determined until we know the price of cars in terms of wheat

8. An unstable quantity of money results in

   (a) Money being more efficient than barter

   (b) Economies of scale

   (c) Money having general purchasing power

   (d) An unstable value of money

9. If 10 workers are put to work for a month with one machine they can produce 5 bicycles. But with 20 workers and 2 machines, 11 bicycles can be produced. This is an example of

   (a) The coincidence of wants

   (b) Economies of scale

   (c) Comparative advantage

   (d) Absolute advantage

10. Gresham's law will not be observed to operate as long as

   (a) The supply of money is stable

   (b) Money is debased

   (c) All money is completely uniform

   (d) Money is easy to store

Exercises

1. This exercise is designed to help you understand the idea of comparative advantage. Assume the following: A doctor working on home repairs can fix a leaky faucet in 10 minutes. A plumber working on the same faucet would take 15 minutes. Then the _____ has an absolute advantage in plumbing. The doctor's time, in practising medicine, is worth $50 per hour. The plumber gets paid $20 per hour.

Suppose the doctor's house has six leaky faucets. If she fixes them herself it will take _____ minutes of her own time, for a total cost of $_____. If she has the plumber do the job the plumber will take _____ minutes, which is (longer, shorter) than the doctor would take, but in this case the cost to the doctor would be $_____, which is (more, less) than if she did it herself, by $_____. Thus, the _____ has a comparative advantage in plumbing, but an _____ disadvantage.

2. Table 3-1 shows how many cars can be produced in a country with various amounts of inputs. (A unit of input is defined as a particular quantity of workers and capital.) Likewise, Table 3-2 gives the production possibilities for television sets. Suppose that the economy has 5 units of input in total with which to produce cars and television sets. Then, in Figure 3-2, plot out the PPC for the country. How is the shape of this PPC different from that of the PPCs constructed in the previous chapter? _____ _____.

In this example, are there economies of scale in the production of cars? _____ In the production of television sets? _____ Does the opportunity cost of producing cars increase or decrease as the quantity is increased? _____ Does the opportunity cost of producing television sets increase or decrease as the quantity is increased? _____ .

Table 3-1

PRODUCTION POSSIBILITIES FOR CARS	
Number of cars	Units of input
100 thousand	1
200 thousand	2
400 thousand	3
700 thousand	4
1,000 thousand	5

Table 3-2

PRODUCTION POSSIBILITIES FOR TELEVISION SETS	
Number of T.V. sets	Units of input
2 million	1
4 million	2
6 million	3
8 million	4
10 million	5

FIGURE 3-2

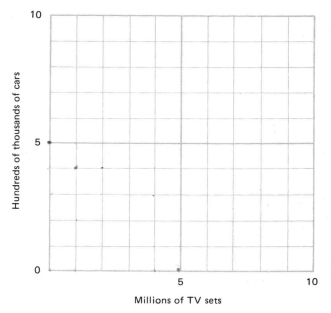

Hundreds of thousands of cars (vertical axis)

Millions of TV sets (horizontal axis)

3. This exercise is also designed to help you understand comparative advantage. Table 3-3 describes the production possibilities for clothing and food in the United States and Europe. Suppose for simplicity that there are no other countries and no other goods, and that the goods can both be produced under constant costs, with labor being the single factor of production. Then (Europe, United States) has an absolute advantage in food, and (Europe, United States) has an absolute advantage in clothing. The opportunity cost of clothing in Europe is _____ units of food, and in the United States is _____ units of food. Therefore (Europe,

Table 3-3

	Output per worker in Europe	Output per worker in the United States
Food	3	4
Clothing	1	2

United States) has a comparative advantage in clothing. The opportunity cost of food is _____ units of clothing in Europe and _____ units of clothing in the United States. Therefore (Europe, United States) has a comparative advantage in food.

Essay Questions

1. Why do you think that gold, silver, and other precious metals have commonly been used as the medium of exchange throughout history?

2. Although most transactions involve money, there are still barter transactions. For example, some people will take nonpaying boarders into their homes on the understanding that these boarders will do odd jobs around the house and take care of the garden. A less obvious but still valid example is the case of the business executive who is paid partly in the form of a salary, but also partly in the form of stock options, or a luxurious office.

Why do you suppose that people still engage in barter when they could use the system of monetary exchange? What sorts of transactions would you expect to be undertaken, nowadays, by barter rather with money?

3. There are disadvantages associated with specialization as well as advantage. One disadvantage is the feeling of alienation fostered by large organizations. What other disadvantages can you think of?

4. The textbook shows that comparative advantage is one explanation of specialization, but it does not explain why some countries, regions, or people might have a comparative advantage. How would you explain, for example, the apparent comparative advantage in corn production of the Midwestern states over the New England states? Why does Pennsylvania have a comparative advantage in steel

output by comparison with most of the other 49 states? Why do Taiwan and Hong Kong have a comparative advantage over other countries in the manufacture of textiles and light electronics components?

5. On the basis of our discussion of specialization, why do you suppose that economists are usually in favor of reducing tariffs and other barriers to international trade?

*6. Suppose that there are three people, A, B, and C, and three commodities, 1, 2, and 3. Suppose that A wants to sell one unit of 1 and buy one unit of 2, B wants to sell one unit of 2 and buy one unit of 3, and C wants to sell one unit of 3 and buy one unit of 1.

First, explain why it is impossible for A, B, and C to carry out their desired trade through the use of direct barter, in which each person is only willing to trade what he or she has for what is ultimately wanted. Show how the problems of direct barter could be overcome if indirect barter were used; that is, if each agent were willing to sell what he or she has in exchange for either of the other two commodities whether or not he or she wanted it.

What sorts of practical problems do you suppose would arise if the U.S. economy were to be conducted on the basis of indirect barter? Finally, suppose that a fourth commodity, money, were introduced. How would this help to eliminate some of the difficulties of barter?

Answers

True-False Questions: 1 F 2 F 3 F 4 T 5 T 6 T 7 F 8 F 9 T 10 F 11 T
Multiple-Choice Questions: 1 d 2 b 3 c 4 c 5 a 6 d 7 c 8 d 9 b 10 c
Exercises:
1. doctor, 60, $50, 90, longer, $30, less, $20, plumber, absolute.
2. The PPC is bowed in to the origin instead of bowed out. Yes, no, decrease, decrease.
3. United States, United States, 3, 2, United States, ⅓, ½, Europe.

CHAPTER 4
Demand and Supply:
The Market Mechanism

Learning Objectives

After you have studied this chapter in the textbook and the study guide, you should be able to

Explain what the demand curve represents and why it slopes downward to the right

Explain what the supply curve represents and why it slopes upward to the right

Explain why the equilibrium price is the only one at which the plans of buyers and sellers are mutually consistent

Explain why the actual price will move to the equilibrium price if it isn't there at first

Identify three "demand shifters" and four "supply shifters"

State the rule for determining in which directions the equilibrium price and quantity move when the demand curve shifts

State the rule for determining in which directions the equilibrium price and quantity move when the supply curve shifts

Give one example each of a pair of commodities that are (1) substitutes in demand, (2) complements in demand, (3) substitutes in supply, and (4) complements in supply, explaining in each case why they are so

Give an example illustrating why, to understand fully how the market mechanism decides what should be produced, we need to look not only at product markets but also at factor markets

Give an example illustrating why, to understand fully how the market mechanism decides "how" and "for whom," we need to look not only at factor markets but also at product markets

Explain the advantages and disadvantages of the market mechanism as a means of answering the questions posed by scarcity

CHAPTER HIGHLIGHTS

In every economy some mechanism is needed to decide *what* should be produced, *how*, and *for whom*. Different economic systems solve these three interrelated problems in different ways, but—except for Marxist countries—most countries rely heavily upon the "market mechanism." This chapter is an account of the market mechanism, how it works, and how it answers the questions of "what," "how," and "for whom."

This is a key chapter in the book and, indeed, in

27

your study of economics, because it introduces you to the central concepts of supply and demand. These concepts are essential for understanding how the market mechanism works.

The demand curve describes the amounts that demanders would willingly buy at various market prices. It has a downward slope, from left to right, because the lower the price, the more the demanders are willing to buy. Next, the supply curve presents the amounts that suppliers would be willing to sell at various prices. It slopes upward from left to right because the higher the price, the more suppliers are willing to sell.

Neither the demand curve nor the supply curve alone tells us what the market price will be or what quantity will rule in the market, we must put the two curves together, as in Figure 4-3 in the quantity will rule in the market, we must put the two curves together, as in Figure 4-3 in the textbook. The actual price and quantity that will prevail in this market is given by the point at which the supply curve intersects the demand curve. This point is the *equilibrium point*; it determines the equilibrium price and equilibrium quantity. At any higher price, sellers would be willing to sell more than demanders would be willing to buy (there would be a *surplus*); at any lower price, demanders would be willing to buy more than sellers would be willing to sell (there would be a *shortage*). Only at the equilibrium point do buyers and sellers agree; the amounts that would be willingly bought and sold are equal.

The way the market mechanism operates to establish the equilibrum price is as follows: If the price were above equilibrium, some sellers would find themselves unable to sell all they want, because sellers as a whole are trying to sell more than is being demanded. In order to attract business, sellers will compete against each other by lowering their asking prices. Thus, the price would be brought down to equilibrium. On the other hand, if the price were below its equilibrium value, some buyers would find themselves unable to buy all they want because buyers as a whole are trying to buy more than is being supplied. In order to satisfy their frustrated demands, buyers will compete against each other by offering to pay higher prices. Thus, the price will rise to the equilibrium. Once the equilibrium has been reached, buyers and sellers can all trade just the amounts they want, so no one will be encouraged to bid the price up or down.

The value of the equilibrium price depends on the location and shape of the supply and demand curves. These, in turn, depend upon various factors. Factors affecting the demand curve (demand shifters) include (1) people's incomes, (2) their tastes, and (3) prices of other goods. Factors affecting the supply curve (supply shifters) include (1) technology, (2) the weather, (3) costs of inputs, and (4) prices of related goods.

Supply and demand curves often allow us to predict what would happen to the equilibrium price and quantity when these factors change. The important rule to remember is as follows: (1) If the demand curve shifts to the right, leaving the supply curve in the same position, then both price and quantity will rise; (2) if the supply curve shifts to the right, leaving the demand curve in the same position, then quantity will rise but price will fall. (Of course, if either curve shifts to the left, then exactly the opposite consequences follow.) In short, *a change in demand tends to make price and quantity move in the same direction, whereas a change in supply tends to make price and quantity move in opposite directions.*

Supply and demand theory is usually used to analyze a single market in isolation. However, we must not forget there is often a strong interconnection between markets. When the price changes in one market, it may cause the demand or supply curve to shift in other markets. This brings us to the important distinction between *complementary* goods and *substitutable* goods. Two goods are substitutes in demand if a rise in the price of one good causes the demand curve for the other to shift to the right. For example, a rise in the price of Fords shifts the demand curve for Chevrolets to the right. At the same price of Chevrolets, more people will now buy Chevrolets instead of Fords. Two goods are complements in demand if an increase in the price of one shifts the demand for the other to the left. For example, stereo speakers and turntables are complements in demand, because people often buy them together in sets. If the price of a speaker increases, a stereo set will be more expensive; as a result, fewer sets will be demanded. Therefore, fewer turntables will also be demanded, even if their own price remains unchanged.

Likewise, two goods are substitutes in supply if a rise in the price of one shifts the supply curve of the other to the left. For example, wheat and oats can both be produced using the same land, labor, and capital. When the price of oats rises, farmers will be encouraged to produce more oats. To do so, they will divert some resources away from producing wheat. Thus, less wheat will be supplied. Finally, two goods are complements in supply if a rise in the price of one causes a rightward shift in the supply curve of the other. For example, consider wheat and straw. Suppose the price of wheat rises. Then more wheat will be supplied. But you can't produce more wheat without at the same time producing more straw. Thus, more straw will be supplied.

Figure 4-8 in the textbook illustrates how the market mechanism answers the questions "what," "how," and "for whom." "What" is determined primarily in product markets. For example, as tennis becomes more popular, the demand curve for tennis rackets shifts to the right. As a result, the price of tennis rackets rises and more tennis rackets are produced. But supply and demand theory applies also to markets for factors of production (land, labor, and capital). "How" and "for whom" are determined primarily in factor markets. For example, a sudden increase in immigration would shift the supply curve of labor to the right. As a result, the price of labor (that is, the wage rate) would fall. This would encourage producers to use more labor-intensive techniques. In other words, "how" production occurs would be affected. Likewise, this immigration would reduce the incomes of the workers who were already here, because it would reduce their wages. And it would increase the profits going to manufacturing firms, who now pay less for their labor input. Thus, more of the economy's output could now be purchased by the owners of manufacturing firms (capitalists) and less by the workers who were already here. In other words, "for whom" would be affected.

The same Figure 4-8 also illustrates the importance of links between markets. To understand how the market mechanism answers any of these questions, it is not enough to look at just one market. For example, the increased popularity of skiing may be a result of increases in people's incomes that enable them to afford such an expensive pastime. If so, we must understand why incomes have risen before we can truly understand why the production of ski equipment has increased. But, as we have seen, people's incomes are primarily determined in factor markets. Thus, we need to look also at factor markets to understand how the market mechanism decides "what." Likewise, the increase in the popularity of skiing increases the profits of equipment manufacturers, who now receive a higher price for their output, and of ski instructors, who now find they can charge more for lessons. In other words, we need to look also at product markets (in this case the market for ski equipment) to understand fully how the market mechanism decides "for whom."

Finally, the textbook briefly analyzes the strengths and weaknesses of the market mechanism as a means of answering these questions. The arguments for the market mechanism include the following: (1) It encourages producers, through high prices, to produce goods people want; (2) it encourages people, through the promise of high incomes, to acquire useful skills; (3) it encourages people, through high prices, to economize on the use of particularly scarce goods; (4) likewise, it encourages producers to economize on the use of scarce resources; (5) by leaving decisions up to private individuals it promotes economic freedom; and (6) the many prices in a market system convey information on local conditions, telling us of the relative scarcity or abundance of thousands of different goods, in a way that would be hard for any central government authority to duplicate. Criticisms of the market are that: (1) It may give no freedom to the weak and helpless except the freedom to starve; (2) it may be quite unstable, going through cycles of boom and depression; (3) when there is less than perfect competition, prices may not be the result of impersonal market forces; (4) private activities can lead to negative side effects, which the unregulated agents have no incentive to control; (5) in areas like justice, police, or national defense the market simply won't work; (6) a free market system may, like any other system, grow less flexible with age; and (7) under laissez faire some have argued that the main wants which producers satisfy are those which they themselves have instilled in consumers through manipulative advertising.

The textbook takes a look at one example of an alternative to the market mechanism—government price controls. The queues, wastage, and black markets that result (as well as the other problems in the extreme case of rent control described in Box 4-1), should serve to remind us that in weighing up the arguments for and against the market mechanism, we should bear in mind Sir Winston Churchill's assessment of democracy: "The worst system imaginable except for all the others."

IMPORTANT TERMS

Capitalist economy (free enterprise economy) One in which individuals are permitted to own large amounts of capital, and decisions are made primarily in markets, with relatively little government interference.

Mixed economy One in which the market and the government share the decisions as to what should be produced, how, and for whom.

Marxist economy One in which most of the capital is owned by the government, and political power is in the hands of a party pledging allegiance to the doctrines of Karl Marx.

Demand curve The curve showing amounts that demanders are willing to buy at various possible prices.

Supply curve The curve showing amounts that

sellers are willing to sell at various possible prices.

Excess demand Also known as shortage. The amount by which quantity demanded exceeds quantity supplied at the existing price. If this quantity is negative, it is called an *excess supply*, or surplus.

Equilibrium A situation in which quantity demanded equals quantity supplied. That is, excess demand equals zero. In this situation, the equilibrium price and the equilibrium quantity prevail.

Market The organization through which buyers and sellers interact. This is sometimes a very loose organization, as in the case of the roadside vegetable stand.

Market mechanism The interaction of demand and supply to decide *what* will be produced, *how* it will be produced, and *for whom*. An important part of the market mechanism is the tendency of competition to drive prices toward their equilibrium values, thereby eliminating shortages and surpluses.

Perfect competition The situation in which no one has any perceptible influence over the market price. Each market participant is a *price taker*. This is most likely to prevail where there are many buyers and sellers.

Oligopoly A situation where a few sellers dominate the market.

Monopoly A situation in which there is only one seller. Both this and oligopoly are examples of *imperfect competition*, because individual sellers do have some control over the market price and do not act as price takers.

Ceteris paribus Literally, "other things being equal." Supply and demand curves are constructed *ceteris paribus*. That is, they are constructed under the assumption that all factors other than the price of the good in question—factors such as income, technology, prices of other goods, etc.—are held constant.

Substitutes Two goods are substitutes in demand if an increase in the price of one causes the demand curve for the other to shift to the right. They are substitutes in supply if an increase in the price of one causes the supply curve of the other to shift to the left.

Complements The opposite of substitutes. Two goods are complements in demand if an incease in the price of one causes the demand curve for the other to shift to the left. They are complements in supply (or *joint products*) if an increase in the price of one causes the supply curve of the other to shift to the right.

Side effect The economic activity of agent *A* (by "agent" we mean, for example, a consumer or a firm) produces a side effect if the activity affects the well-being of other agents without agent *A* having to pay for it (in the case of an adverse effect on others) or receiving payment for it (in the case of a beneficial effect).

Normal good (Also called *superior* good.) A good for which the demand curve shifts to the right when there is an increase in people's incomes. The opposite of this is an inferior good, whose demand declines with a rise in incomes.

Black market One in which sales take place at a price above the legal maximum.

True-False Questions

T F **1.** In a Marxist state, the government owns most of the heavy capital equipment.

T F **2.** An oligopoly is defined as a situation where the market is dominated by a few sellers.

T F **3.** Under perfect competition, every buyer and seller takes the quantity as given and is left only with price decisions.

T F **4.** Imperfect competition can exist even when there are very many buyers.

T F **5.** The demand curve for coffee will probably shift to the right if the price of tea increases.

T F **6.** The supply curve for television sets will probably shift to the right as a result of a general rise in people's incomes.

T F **7.** A rise in incomes may actually cause a decline in demand for some goods.

T F **8.** If the price of golf clubs were to rise, the demand for golf balls would probably decrease as a result.

T F **9.** If the price of oats were to rise, the supply of barley would probably decrease as a result.

T F **10.** If the price of corn were to rise, the supply curve for corn would probably shift to the right.

T F **11.** If incomes were to rise we would expect—at least in the case of a normal good—that both price and quantity would rise.

T F **12.** If the population of the United States were to decrease suddenly as a result of an epidemic, we would expect this to produce a decrease in both the wage rate and the quantity of employment.

T F **13.** One of the advantages of the market mechanism is that it automatically results in a just distribution of incomes.

T F **14.** Most economists agree that the unregulated market mechanism is less efficient if there are major side effects than if there aren't.

T F **15.** The example of rent controls in New York City given in the textbook demonstrates not so much the perfection of the market mechanism as the unfortunate consequences that sometimes arise from well-intentioned plans for replacing it.

Multiple-Choice Questions

1. The market mechanism
- **(a)** Works only in markets for produced commodities, not in markets for factors of production
- **(b)** Operates so as to harmonize the plans of buyers and sellers
- **(c)** Works best when there are side effects
- **(d)** Does not operate in a mixed economy

2. The demand curve is drawn under the assumption that
- **(a)** There are many sellers in the market
- **(b)** There are few sellers
- **(c)** All "supply shifters" are held constant
- **(d)** All "demand shifters" are held constant

3. A high·price for a commodity provides an incentive
- **(a)** For buyers to economize in their use of that good
- **(b)** For buyers to seek alternatives to using that good
- **(c)** For producers to expand production
- **(d)** All of the above

4. A market with one buyer and only a few sellers is an example of
- **(a)** Perfect competition **(c)** Monopoly
- **(b)** Oligopoly **(d)** A black market

5. When the price of steak rises people start buying less steak, and substituting other meats such as pork and lamb for it. This is an example of
- **(a)** A movement along the demand curve for steak
- **(b)** A shift of the demand curve for steak
- **(c)** Both **(a)** and **(b)**
- **(d)** Neither **(a)** nor **(b)**

6. The demand curve for a good
- **(a)** Always shifts to the right when incomes rise
- **(b)** May shift in either direction when the price of some other good rises
- **(c)** Usually shifts when there is a technological change in producing the good
- **(d)** Shifts to the left when the price of a substitute rises

7. When the price is kept below the equilibrium price, this causes a
- **(a)** Shortage
- **(b)** Surplus
- **(c)** Shift in the demand curve
- **(d)** Shift in the supply curve

8. An excess supply in a private market would result in
- **(A)** A rise in the price
- **(b)** A fall in the price
- **(c)** No change in price
- **(d)** A rise or fall; you can't say because you aren't told whether there is a suprlus or shortage

9. A black market is most likely to develop when
- **(a)** A monopoly is unregulated
- **(b)** Side effects are present
- **(c)** The poor do not receive government assistance
- **(d)** The government imposes a price ceiling below the equilibrium price

10. A rise in the price of tea would probably be accompanied by
- **(a)** An increase in the equilibrium quantity of tea
- **(b)** A decrease in the equilibrium quantity of tea
- **(c)** An increase in the equilibrium quantity if the rise in price were caused by a shift in the demand curve with no shift in the supply curve
- **(d)** No change in the equilibrium quantity

11. If we see the price of houses rising when at the same time the production of houses is falling, then we can conclude that this may have been caused by
- **(a)** An increase in demand
- **(b)** A reduction in demand
- **(c)** An increase in supply
- **(d)** A reduction in supply

12. An increase in the cost of producing tennis rackets should cause
- **(a)** A rightward shift in the supply curve of rackets
- **(b)** A leftward shift in the supply curve of rackets
- **(c)** A rightward shift in the demand curve for rackets
- **(d)** A leftward shift in the demand curve for rackets

13. As a result of an increase in the cost of producing rackets we should expect to observe in the market for rackets
- **(a)** An increase in price and quantity
- **(b)** An increase in price but decrease in quantity
- **(c)** A decrease in price and quantity
- **(d)** A decrease in price but increase in quantity

14. Suppose that, because of a change in tastes, households become less inclined to purchase large cars and more inclined to purchase small cars. Then, assuming that small-car drivers use less gas than large-car drivers, this change in taste should result in
- **(a)** An increase in demand for gas
- **(b)** A decrease in demand for gas
- **(c)** No change in demand for gas, but a decrease in supply
- **(d)** No change in demand or supply for gas

15. This change in demand for cars will tend to cause, in the market for gas
- **(a)** An increase in price and quantity
- **(b)** An increase in price but decrease in quantity
- **(c)** A decrease in price and quantity
- **(d)** A decrease in price but increase in quantity

16. Suppose that the price of umbrellas were to rise and the quantity of umbrellas to fall. With just this amount of information, you are asked to make a guess about what happened to the weather and to the costs of production of umbrellas. Which of the following is most likely?
- **(a)** The amount of rainfall increased, and the cost of production stayed the same.
- **(b)** Rainfall decreased and cost stayed the same
- **(c)** Rainfall stayed the same and cost increased
- **(d)** Rainfall stayed the same and cost decreased

17. Beef and leather both come from the slaughter of cattle. Thus they are
- **(a)** Substitutes in production **(c)** Inferior goods
- **(b)** Unrelated goods **(d)** Joint products

18. A rise in the price of beef should cause the supply curve for
- **(a)** Beef to shift right
- **(b)** Beef to shift left
- **(c)** Leather to shift right
- **(d)** Leather to shift left

19. Suppose that an increase in people's incomes causes an increase in demand for beef but no increase in demand for leather. Then, in the leather market, we would expect
  (a) An increase in price and quantity
  (b) An increase in price but decrease in quantity
  (c) A decrease in price and quantity
  (d) A decrease in price but increase in quantity
20. An example of a side effect
  (a) The increased danger of fire to farmers whose fields lie near the right-of-way of a railroad, from which sparks fly when a train passes
  (b) The increase in your heating bill if you try to keep your house warmer in the winter
  (c) The extra satisfaction you get from painting the outside of your house

  (d) The extra incomes that farmers get when the world demand for wheat rises
21. A major problem with any alternative to the market mechanism for solving the basic problem of scarcity is that
  (a) It is difficult to think of an alternative that solves the problem of income distribution as fairly as does the market mechanism
  (b) Side effects can be dealt with most effectively by a policy of laissez faire
  (c) Any alternative is faced with the difficulty of finding a device as efficient as prices for creating incentives and disseminating information
  (d) When the government intervenes in a market the corresponding black market often disappears as a result

Exercises

1. In Figure 4-1 is plotted the supply curve, which is a straight line with the equation $Q = -30 + 4P$. The way to go about plotting a curve like this is as follows: First, choose some convenient value for P, such as 10, then put this into the equation of the supply curve to get $Q = -30 + 4 \times 10 = 10$. This tells us that when $P = 10$, $Q = 10$, so that point A is on the supply curve. Then, choose some other value of P, say, $P = 15$, and put it into the equation of the supply curve, which produces $Q = -30 + 4 \times 15 = 30$. Thus, point $P = 15$, $Q = 30$; that is, point B is on the supply curve. Once we have determined these two points, we can plot the whole supply curve by drawing the straight line that passes through A and B. **(a)** Suppose that the demand curve is also a straight line, with the equation $Q = 20 - P$. Then, if $P = 15$, the quantity demanded is _____. If $P = 5$, then the quantity demand equals _____. Plot the

demand curve in Figure 4-1. The equilibrium price is _____ and the equilibrium quantity is _____. **(b)** Suppose now that there were an increase in demand because of an increase in income, such that the quantity demanded at any price increased by 15 units; thus, the new demand curve has the equation $Q = 35 - P$. Then, with $P = 15$, the quantity demanded would be _____; with $P = 5$, the quantity demanded would be _____. Plot the new demand curve in Figure 4-1. The new equilibrium price is _____ and the new equilibrium quantity is _____. Why have both the equilibrium price and the equilibrium quantity risen? _____

(c) Now, suppose that we are back with the original demand curve, but that the supply curve is the straight line whose equation is $Q = -10 + 2P$. In this situation, when $P = 10$, the quantity supplied is _____; when $P = 15$, the quantity supplied is _____. Plot in this new supply curve. With the new supply curve but the old demand curve, the equilibrium price is _____ and the equilibrium quantity is _____. **(d)** With this new supply curve, suppose once again that the demand curve shifts because of an increase in income such that the quantity demanded rises by 15 at each price. Then the new equilibrium price is _____ and the new equilibrium quantity is _____. Why is it that, when the demand curve shifted this time, the price rose by more, and the quantity by less, than in the previous case? _____

2. The textbook discusses what happens when the government prevents the price from rising to its equilibrium value, as in the case of rent controls. In some cases, the government prevents the price from falling to its equilibrium value, as in the case of minimum wage laws. Suppose that the supply curve for labor looks like the curve labeled S in Figure 4-2

FIGURE 4-1

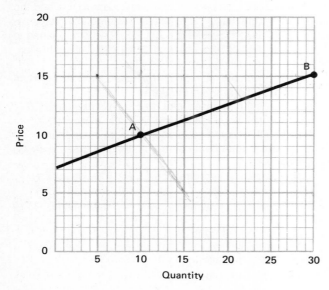

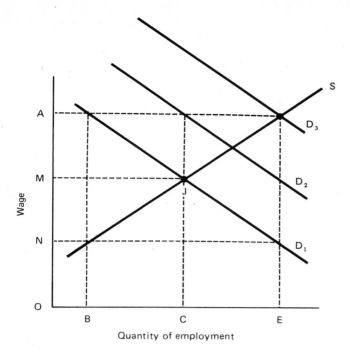

A

M

N

O

B C E

Wage

Quantity of employment

S

D₃

D₂

D₁

J

FIGURE 4-2

and that the demand curve is the one labeled D_1. (For the time being, you may ignore the curves D_2 and D_3.) In the absence of any minimum wage laws, the equilibrium would be established at point J, with a wage rate equal to OM and a quantity of employment OC. Suppose now that the government imposes a minimum wage equal to the amount OA. Then the quantity of labor demanded at that wage would be _____ and the quantity of labor supplied would be _____. Thus, there would be a surplus

equal to the amount _____. In this situation, the wage rate would normally tend to fall, but it is prevented from doing so by the minimum wage law. Thus, we may assume that it remains at the level OA. In this case, the actual amount of employment will most likely be the amount _____. One way for the government to raise the amount of employment back up to where it would have been in the absence of minimum wage laws, without giving up the minimum wage laws themselves, would be to offer a subsidy to firms for hiring workers. If, for example, the subsidy were \$1 per worker, then the "effective" wage that the firms would have to pay would be the wage received by the workers minus \$1. This would have the effect of shifting the demand-for-labor curve up by an amount exactly equal to \$1. Thus, in order for the government to restore the level of employment to its value before the minimum wage legislation, it would have to offer a subsidy equal to the amount AM, shifting the demand curve to D_2. In this situation, firms would be paying an effective wage equal to _____ and workers would be receiving a wage equal to _____. The surplus of labor would still exist, but it would now be equal to the amount _____. In order to eliminate this surplus, the government would have to increase its subsidy to the amount _____, shifting the demand curve to D_3, in which case the workers would be receiving the wage _____, the employers would be paying the effective wage _____, the amount of employment would be _____, and the total amount of subsidy paid out by the government would be _____.

Essay Questions

1. Sometimes economists distinguish between goods in different locations, even if they are the same good. Consider "milk in Washington, D.C." as one good and "milk in Baltimore, Maryland" as another. Would you expect the price of milk in these two cities to be similar? Precisely the same? Explain.

2. Suppose that, as a result of an increase in the number of children in Baltimore there were an increase in demand for milk in that city. If you were an all-powerful social planner you would probably want to persuade the people in Washington to give up some of their milk so that the children of Baltimore would not have to do without. What sort of rationing scheme might you devise to accomplish this goal? How would you know how much to allocate to each family? How large a staff do you think you would need to carry out your plan? (There are over 2 million families living in Baltimore and

Washington.) Suppose that you allowed market forces to work freely. What would happen to the price of milk in Baltimore? What would happen to the quantity of milk supplied in Baltimore? How would this price change affect the position of the supply curve for milk in Washington? What would happen to the price of milk in Washington? To the quantity of milk supplied in Washington? Draw supply and demand diagrams for these two commodities to illustrate what is happening. In what sense would your intentions as a social planner be carried out by these market forces? When the market forces are allowed to work who decides how much to allocate to each family, and how many extra people are required to carry out this allocation? Which policy—the rationing scheme or the market solution—works more efficiently? Are there any disadvantages to the more efficient scheme?

3. Try to sort out the following bit of confused

logic: "If supply *in*creases the price will fall. But if the price falls supply will *de*crease. Therefore supply cannot increase." Rewrite the passage, clearing up the ambiguities and correcting the errors.

4. The prices printed on a restaurant menu apply whether the restaurant is crowded or half-empty on any particular evening.

   (a) If you ran a restaurant, would you try to adjust prices, raising them on evenings when the restaurant was crowded (Friday and Saturday), and lowering them when demand was slack (Tuesday and Wednesday)? Explain.

   (b) Would you charge a different price for an evening meal than for an identical luncheon meal? Why or why not?

*5. People who speculate in commodity markets are often regarded as social parasites who make a living from others' misfortunes without contributing to society. Speculators buy whenever they think that the price is going to rise and sell when they think it is going to fall. Can you think of any useful social contribution that is made by speculators? To be more specific, consider the speculators in agricultural societies who used to hoard grain whenever a crop failure had just occurred. If no one had hoarded grain but had just gone on selling it at the old price, what would happen to consumption of the grain? How long would the grain have lasted? When the grain had almost run out, what would have happened to the price of grain? With this in mind, who had the better foresight, the speculators or those who would rather have seen them eliminated? Would you expect prices to fluctuate over time more if speculators were allowed to operate or if they were eliminated? Why? See if you can illustrate this with supply and demand diagrams for the two commodities: "grain now" and "grain in the future." Can you make an analogy between the milk suppliers in the previous question who had to decide whether to sell their milk in Baltimore or Washington, and the speculators in the present question who have to decide whether to sell their grain now or in the future?

Answers

True-False Questions: **1** T **2** T **3** F **4** T **5** T **6** F **7** T **8** T **9** T **10** F **11** T **12** F **13** F **14** T **15** T

Multiple-Choice Questions: **1** b **2** d **3** d **4** b **5** a **6** b **7** a **8** b **9** d **10** c **11** d **12** b **13** b **14** b **15** c **16** c **17** d **18** c **19** d **20** a **21** c

Exercises:

1. (a) 5, 15, 10, 10; (b) 20, 30, 13, 22, because the demand curve has shifted to the right; (c) 10, 20, 10, 10; (d) 15, 20, because the second supply curve is steeper.

2. *OB   OE   BE   OB   OM   OA   CE   AN   OA   ON   OE   AN × OE.*

CHAPTER 5
The Economic Role of the Government

Learning Objectives

After you have studied this chapter in the textbook and the study guide, you should be able to

Identify three levels of government

Explain the main motives for government intervention in the economy

Describe the three main forms of government intervention

Explain the difference between a progressive tax and a regressive tax and give an example of each

State four objectives of the tax system

Identify at least five different federal regulatory agencies

Explain why government regulation is sometimes justified

Describe the main problems with regulatory agencies

CHAPTER HIGHLIGHTS

The proper economic role of the government is the issue that Smith, Keynes, and other great economists have wrestled with over the generations, and which future generations of economists will undoubtedly be wrestling with also. As Figures 5-1 and 5-2 in the textbook show, the role of government in the United States has expanded greatly. The purpose of this chapter is to introduce you to the details of the expanding government sector, and to discuss some of the broad principles involved.

In the United States there are three levels of government: federal, state, and local. The textbook discusses five main motives for government activity:

1. Government's attempt to provide goods and services which the private sector would otherwise fail to provide, or would provide at a much higher cost. This is especially true of national defense, which no private person would find it in his or her interest to organize and finance because of the free-rider problem. (If I buy equipment for the army others get as much protection from it as I do. Defense cannot be left to voluntary private decisions like this because everyone would leave it up to others. That is, everyone would try to "ride free" rather than pull his or her own weight.)

2. The government also intervenes in cases where *side effects* might prevent private individuals from having the incentive to make socially desirable decisions if left on their own. For example, inoculations help to limit the spread of diseases. Thus, they generate external benefits; even people who aren't inoculated benefit from living in a more disease-free country. Because some of the benefit of my own inoculation is thus conferred on others, rather than on myself, I might decide not to bother getting it if I had to pay for it myself. This is why public health programs often pay for inoculations.

Likewise, extra taxes or penalties could be imposed on polluting firms to discourage pollution. Without this extra incentive polluting firms would not worry about the damage caused to the environment because they would not have to pay for it. It would be an *external* cost.

3. The government attempts to work toward an equitable distribution of income (see Chapter 1) mainly through its transfer payments, which are designed to boost the incomes of specific recipients such as the aged, the sick, the unemployed, and dependent children.

4. The government often assumes the paternalistic role of encouraging the consumption of "merit goods" such as education, which is heavily supported by the government, and food for children, which is provided through the food-stamp program.

5. The government may increase or decrease its expenditures in pursuit of the goal of economic stability (see Chapter 1), trying to stimulate economic activity when a recession threatens and restrain it when inflation threatens.

The economic role of the government takes three forms: spending, taxation, and regulation.

Spending

Government spending takes the form of (1) purchases of goods and services, and (2) transfer payments. As Figures 5-2 and 5-3 point out, total government purchases of goods and services have not grown over the past 20 years (as a fraction of national product), but government transfer payments have. Until 1974 national defense was the largest single item of federal government spending, but defense has now been overtaken by income security expenditures designed to augment and stabilize people's incomes.

Taxation

The biggest source of federal revenue is the personal income tax, which is a progressive tax. (That is, it takes a larger fraction of a taxpayer's income the larger is that income.) The next biggest

ship pictured in Figure 1-6. The variables *X* and *Y* are measured on the axes, but there are no numbers, local governments as a group, the biggest source is not a tax at all, but grants from the federal government. Revenue sharing by the federal government is undertaken partly to encourage particular kinds of expenditures by the states and localities (most grants are categorical, and must be spent on particular programs or areas), and partly to give state and local governments a better balance between their tax revenues and their growing expenditures. (Some have argued, however, that this last objective is misplaced. In 1978–1979 the state and local governments as a group enjoyed a budgetary *surplus* of $15 billion, whereas the federal government suffered a *deficit* of $14 billion.) Other than this, the biggest source of revenue for state governments is the sales tax, which tends to be regressive (to take a *smaller* fraction of a taypayer's income the larger is that income) because the rich tend to spend a larger fraction on nontaxable services than do the poor. The next biggest source for local governments is the property tax, which also tends to be regressive because the poor spend a larger fraction of their income on housing than do the rich. Because of these and other regressive elements in the tax structure, and because of various loopholes, the overall tax burden at all levels is much less progressive than you would gather from just looking at the personal income tax schedule. Commonly cited examples of loopholes include:

1. The investment tax credit that allows a business or individual to deduct 10 percent of the price of newly acquired business equipment from its tax bill.

2. Tax-exempt securities, like state and local government bonds, the interest on which is not subject to federal income tax.

3. The fact that only 40 percent of any capital gains on stock market investments are subject to income tax.

4. The fact that you can deduct interest on loans, like your mortgage, when calculating your taxable income.

Other than raising revenues, there are several objectives that must be considered in designing a tax system, some of which conflict with others:

1. One objective is to aim for *neutrality*. That is, to raise funds for government spending in a way that interferes as little as possible with the free market.

2. Another is to pursue various *social objectives*, in a nonneutral way, as when taxes are made especially high on cigarettes to discourage smoking, or when special tax breaks are offered to encourage business firms to spend more on new capital goods.

3. Another objective is *simplicity*. The simpler the tax code, the easier it is to pay your taxes.

4. The system should also be *fair*. But there is disagreement on just what constitutes fairness. Some argue for the benefit principle, according to which the size of your taxes should depend upon how much you benefit from programs that they finance. Others think your taxes should depend mainly upon your ability to pay.

Regulation

Government regulations run all the way from local bylaws and zoning restrictions up through the activities of the large federal regulatory bodies such as the Federal Trade Commission (FTC), the Food and Drug Administration (FDA), the Evironmental Protection Agency (EPA), and many others. The main purpose of these agencies is to oversee private affairs in areas where it is believed that the market mechanism will not attain an ideal outcome because (1) private individuals and business firms are not concerned enough about such things as product safety and environmental hazard, or (2) the unregulated market might end up as a monopoly. There are two main problems with these regulatory agencies:

1. They have a tendency to stifle productive efforts with red tape.

2. They tend to be biased toward producers, because producers in an industry find it in their own interest to put pressure on the agency that regulates the industry, whereas the consumers who buy the products of the industry usually have too many other concerns to bother organizing that sort of pressure on the other side.

IMPORTANT TERMS

Government transfers Expenditures by the government for which they acquire no good or service in return. These expenditures transfer income to the recipient from the taxpayer. Examples are social security payments and welfare payments.

Tax Credit A subtraction from the tax payable.

Deduction A subtraction from taxable income. The difference between this and a tax credit is illustrated in Exercise 1 below.

Progressive A tax is *progressive* if it takes a larger proportion of your income the larger your income is. The opposite of progressive is *regressive*. The intermediate case, in which the tax takes a constant proportion of all incomes, is called a *proportional* tax.

Average tax rate The total tax, as a fraction or percentage of income.

Marginal tax rate The additional tax, as a fraction or percentage of *additional* income.

Revenue sharing The transfer of revenue by the federal government to state and local governments. This is called *general* revenue sharing if there are no strings attached to the transfers. In 1978–1979 only 8 percent of revenue sharing was general. The remaining 92 percent consisted of *categoric grants*; that is, it could be spent only on specific programs.

Block grants These are combined categorical grants that involve fewer restrictions. President Reagan suggested in early 1981 that block grants should start replacing categoric grants. For example, instead of receiving a number of categoric grants, each for a specific educational program, a state might receive one block grant to be spent on the general area of education.

Selected government regulatory agencies
FTC: Federal Trade Commission
FDA: Food and Drug Administration
EPA: Environmental Protection Agency
SEC: Securities and Exchange Commission
FPC: Federal Power Commission
FCC: Federal Communications Commission
FAA: Federal Aviation Administration
EEOC: Equal Employment Opportunity Commission
CFTC: Commodity Futures Trading Commission
OSHA: Occupational Safety and Health Administration

Budget position The government's revenues (R) minus its expenditures (G). In symbols, $B = R - G$.

Surplus The government has a surplus if the budgetary position is positive ($R > G$).

Deficit The government has a deficit if B is negative ($R < G$).

Balanced budget This occurs when the government has neither a surplus nor a deficit ($R = G$), so that $B = 0$.

Externality A side effect (either beneficial or harmful), resulting from production or consumption, for which no payment is made.

Merit goods Goods that the government deems to be particularly desirable.

Tax neutrality The degree to which the tax system leaves unaffected the allocation of goods and services achieved by the market mechanism.

The benefit principle The principle that those who use government services are the ones who should pay for them.

Tax loophole Any provision that allows someone legally to escape paying taxes. One of the reasons why the U.S. tax system as a whole is not very progressive is the fact that the richer you are the more loopholes tend to be available.

True-False Questions

T F **1.** In the past two decades the federal government's transfer payments have risen by more than their purchases of goods and services.

T F· **2.** Unemployment compensation is a form of transfer payment.

T F **3.** The corporate income tax raises more revenue for the federal government than the personal income tax.

T F **4.** The personal income tax is designed to be progressive.

T F **5.** Most revenue sharing consists of categoric grants.

T F **6.** An external cost occurs when a firm pollutes the air.

T F **7.** Neutrality is the principal objective of taxes designed to discourage pollution.

T F **8.** The benefit principle is the principle that free riders cannot be excluded from the benefits of public goods.

T F **9.** According to recent estimates, our tax system as a whole is more progressive that you would infer from looking at the income tax schedule.

T F **10.** Capital gains are not taxed as heavily as interest income.

Multiple-Choice Questions

1. In the late 1970s defense spending was approximately what percent of national output in the United States?
- **(a)** 6 percent
- **(b)** 10 percent
- **(c)** 14 percent
- **(d)** 20 percent

2. Over the past two decades the fastest growing item of government spending has been
- **(a)** Foreign aid
- **(b)** National defense
- **(c)** Government transfers
- **(d)** Government purchases other than national defense

3. Which of the following is the *least* important role of government in the United States?
- **(a)** Spending
- **(b)** Taxation
- **(c)** Running businesses
- **(d)** Regulation of businesses

4. The personal income tax
- **(a)** Is the largest single source of federal government revenue
- **(b)** Is based on the benefit principle
- **(c)** Collects a smaller fraction of people's incomes as inflation proceeds
- **(d)** Is regressive

5. National defense is
- **(a)** The largest single item of federal government spending
- **(b)** Not left up to the free market
- **(c)** Financed mainly through revenue sharing
- **(d)** The only area where an economic justification can be provided for government spending

6. Which of the following is the largest single source of revenue for state and local governments?
- **(a)** Revenue sharing
- **(b)** Property taxes
- **(c)** Sales taxes
- **(d)** Income taxes

7. In 1972, the federal government started giving grants to state and local governments, with practically no strings attached. This is an example of
- **(a)** Categoric grants
- **(b)** Block grants
- **(c)** General tax sharing
- **(d)** Federal government expenditures net of transfers

8. Which of the following is *not* commonly cited as a loophole in our income tax system?
- **(a)** Tax-exempt securities
- **(b)** Exemptions for state and local taxes
- **(c)** Investment tax credit
- **(d)** Partial exemption from taxation of capital gains

9. If the government's revenues are $540b and its expenditures are $625b, then
- **(a)** It has a suprlus
- **(b)** It has a deficit
- **(c)** The budget is balanced
- **(d)** This is impossible; the government can't spend more than its revenue

10. When the government pays for public inoculation programs, the main justification has to do with
- **(a)** Stabilization
- **(b)** Equity
- **(c)** Merit goods
- **(d)** Externalities

11. Government food-stamp programs are justified mainly in terms of
- **(a)** Neutrality
- **(b)** Externalities
- **(c)** Merit goods
- **(d)** Stabilization

12. The provision in the personal income tax for deducting mortgage interest payments
- **(a)** Is neutral in its effects on the economy
- **(b)** Is usually justified as a means of pursuing the goal of economic stability
- **(c)** Discourages people from living in rental housing
- **(d)** Can be justified mainly by the benefit principle

13. If the taxes that finance the education of medical stu-

dents were mainly collected from families of medical students, this would be an example of
- (a) Tax neutrality
- (b) An externality
- (c) The benefit principle
- (d) The ability-to-pay principle

14. If these taxes were instead collected from everyone, in proportion to their incomes, then it would be an example of
- (a) Tax neutrality
- (b) An externality
- (c) The benefit principle
- (d) The ability-to-pay principle

15. Tax loopholes have the effect of
- (a) Making the U.S. tax system more progressive than it would otherwise be
- (b) Creating incentives and disincentives in the economy
- (c) Making the U.S. tax system neutral
- (d) Giving full scope to the benefit principle

Exercise

This exercise illustrates the difference between a tax credit and a deduction. Suppose you have calculated your 1981 taxable income to be $10,000. Your marginal tax rate is 20 percent, and you have calculated that you owe $1,100 in income taxes.

a. Now, suppose you are told that you can claim the $1,000 interest that you paid in 1981 on your mortgage as a deduction, something you had neglected to do. This will reduce your taxable income to $_____. This reduction of $_____ in your taxable income will reduce your taxes by $_____, and you will end up paying $_____ in taxes.

b. Suppose instead that you could claim the mortgage interest not as a deduction, but as a tax credit. In this case your taxable income would be $_____. But your taxes would be reduced by $_____, and you would end up paying $_____ in taxes. The (tax credit, deduction) gives you the greater tax saving.

Essay Questions

1. What would be the advantages and disadvantages of living in a country like Sweden, where the proportion of national output going to the government is larger than in the United States?

2. What do you suppose the United States would be like to live in if there were no federal government regulatory agencies? Describe what would happen if specific agencies, such as the FAA, the EPA, etc., were absent.

3. Why are local police services in most communities not provided by private security firms?

4. Explain what sort of externality is created by the following activities: someone smoking a cigarette in a movie theater, a car traveling on a highway, someone mowing the lawn, a jet plane taking off from an airport. In each case try carefully to identify all the external costs and benefits.

5. The big spurts of growth in government spending have been during wartime, and recent growth has been mainly in the form of transfer payments. Using these two facts and any others you think may be relevant can you suggest an explanation of why the government has grown so rapidly in the twentieth century? According to your explanation, will the growth of government continue for the next 50 years?

*6. When the government increases its expenditures it may increase taxes in order to finance those expenditures or it may borrow the money, thereby increasing the size of the public debt. If it borrows the money, does this mean that you do not have to pay for these government expenditures? Who must eventually pay the interest on the government debt?

Answers

True-False Questions: 1 T 2 T 3 F 4 T 5 T 6 T 7 F 8 F 9 F 10 T
Multiple-Choice Questions: 1 a 2 c 3 c 4 a 5 b 6 a 7 c 8 b 9 b 10 d 11 c 12 c 13 c 14 d 15 b
Exercise:
(a) 9,000, 1,000, 200, 900.
(b) 10,000, 1,000, 100, tax credit.

CHAPTER 6
Business Organization and Finance

Learning Objectives

After you have studied this chapter in the textbook and the study guide, you should be able to

Describe the three main types of business firm and give one example of each

List the advantages of the proprietorship or partnership as a form of enterprise

List the advantages of the corporate form of enterprise

Describe several different ways for a corporation to raise funds

Explain the advantages and disadvantages of investing your money in (a) bonds, or (b) shares

Describe the main function of financial markets

Explain the difference between a balance sheet and an income statement

State the fundamental identity of the balance sheet

CHAPTER HIGHLIGHTS

This chapter is intended to acquaint you with the various ways that business firms are organized and financed. There are three basic types of firm:

1. The *single proprietorship*, owned and operated by an individual. An example is the typical corner store.

2. The *partnership*, which is like the proprietorship except that it is owned and operated jointly by several individuals. Examples include most law firms and many small businesses.

3. The *corporation*, the form of most of the familiar giant firms, like General Motors and IBM. Corporations are owned by their shareholders. The shareholders have limited liability. That is, they are not personally responsible for the company's debts.

Small business firms often choose to be proprietorships or partnerships because (1) this form offers the greatest flexibility and freedom from legal complications, (2) it avoids the double taxation on dividend income (the profits of a corporation are taxed as corporate income and the dividends are taxed again as part of the shareholder's personal income), and (3) it may help the business to raise funds because lenders know that the owner or owners are personally responsible for repaying the company's debts.

On the other hand, the corporate form has advantages because: (1) it offers continuity of the enterprise; that is if a shareholder dies or wants to sell out, the company can continue smoothly under new ownership without having to be legally reconstituted; (2) the sale of new shares in the corporation is often an effective source of funds for expansion that the unincorporated firm can't use; (3) the limited liability of the shareholders makes their investment into the enterprise less risky than if the company's debts were considered by law as their own personal debts; and (4) the corporate form offers tax advantages that can more than offset the double taxation of dividend income.

The corporation can raise funds by (1) issuing new *common shares*, each common share representing a fraction of the ownership of the company; (2) selling *bonds*, that is, borrowing money over a long period from the bond purchasers; (3) issuing shorter-term securities like *notes* (usually between 1 and 7 years to maturity), or *bills* (less than 1 year to maturity); (4) borrowing from a bank or other financial intermediary just as you or I might do; (5) issuing *preferred shares*, which are like common shares, but whose dividends are more certain; or (6) issuing *convertible bonds*, which are like ordinary bonds except that the holder may choose to convert them, at a fixed ratio, into common or preferred shares.

All these securities can normally be bought and sold in the market. For example, if General Electric issues 20-year bonds and you buy one of them, you may decide after a year that you want to sell it. If you do sell, then General Electric owes the principal and the remaining interest to the new bondholder instead of to you.

Financial markets are mostly organized by *brokers*, who match up buyers and sellers, in return for which they charge a commission; by *investment bankers*, who arrange for the marketing of newly issued securities; and by various other *financial intermediaries*, such as banks, savings and loan associations, and insurance companies.

Because of this possibility of resale, any security has a market price that can go up or down from day to day and year to year. One source of financial return to holders of securities (indeed the main source for holders of most common shares) is the rise in market value (*capital gain*) that will occur if the company prospers. The other source consists of the *dividends* or *interest* paid by the security. The

semiannual interest payment is fixed on most bonds. Dividends are fairly certain on preferred shares, and can be highly variable on common shares. Because of the uncertainty of dividends and because the price of a share can fall, buying common shares is a *risky* venture. Buying preferred shares is less risky and buying bonds is usually less risky still (although buying "junk bonds" of corporations on the brink of bankruptcy can be risky). However, common shares probably offer the greatest prospect of gain over the very long run. That is, they give the highest *return* on average—it's just that there is a high risk that you won't get that "average." Investors also care about the *liquidity* of securities; that is, their ability to be sold for a stable or predictable price on short notice and without paying a large selling fee. Claims on financial intermediaries (for example, bank deposits) are usually the most liquid of all securities.

Just as the buyer of securities must make a complex decision regarding risk, return, and liquidity, so the issuer of the security faces a difficult choice. If a corporation raises funds by issuing new shares it will be further diluting control in the company, and it may end up selling off a part of the corporation to the new shareholders at an unreasonably low price if the stock market is temporarily depressed. On the other hand, if it borrows (either directly from a financial intermediary or by issuing new bonds), it puts itself in a risky position because the interest payments must be made. In contrast, dividends on shares can be made at the option of the corporation. But by borrowing, the firm is able to acquire *leverage*, which gives it a potential for large gains, at the expense of a greater risk of failure. Leverage is just what you or I would acquire if we were to invest borrowed money in the stock market. If the stock goes up we can make a large gain but if it goes down we can get wiped out.

The major function of financial markets is to allocate the accumulated savings of the millions of households into the millions of business investment projects that get undertaken every year. The investment bankers and others who organize these markets are basically deciding who shall have a claim upon the resources that are temporarily released when you or I decide to save part of our income rather than spend it. They do this by deciding which borrowers are credit-worthy, and which projects are economically feasible. This is one way in which we rely upon the market to cope with the problem of scarcity. In the Soviet economy, by way of contrast, the government owns these resources and decides which investment projects will be undertaken.

While there are reasons for thinking that the market solution to this allocation problem is generally good (although it does give perhaps excessive room for charlatans and swindlers to harm the ignorant and unsuspecting), there is a major economic problem associated with financial markets—the problem of instability of the economy. When the economy moves into recession many firms reduce their spending on new projects because of declining sales. This reduced spending makes the recession worse. This problem is one of the major concerns of macroeconomics, the subject of Parts 2 and 3 of the textbook.

Another major purpose of this chapter is to introduce the principles of business accounting. The two basic forms of account are the *balance sheet*, which gives a picture of the firm's stocks of assets and liabilities at a single *point* in time, and the *income statement*, which describes the flow of expenditures and receipts by the firm over an *interval* of time (usually a year). The fundamental identity of the balance sheet is that assets ≡ liabilities + net worth. (The three bars ≡ denote an identity—something that must be true simply because the terms are defined that way.) In other words, net worth is defined as the difference between the firm's assets (what it owns) and its liabilities (what it owes).

In the income statement, gross (pretax) *profit* is the firm's receipts minus its expenses. After-tax profit (net income) is partly paid to shareholders in the form of dividends; the rest is retained earnings. One component of costs is *depreciation*, the allowance for wear and obsolescence of plant and equipment. Firms generally try to make this item as large as possible (on paper!) in order to minimize their taxes. Capital that has been completely depreciated on a company's books may still be in operating condition.

IMPORTANT TERMS

Single proprietorship, partnership, corporation The three forms of business organization. These are described in the Chapter Highlights.

Bonds, convertible bonds, common shares, preferred shares, notes, bills The four most common forms of corporate securities. These too are described in the Chapter Highlights.

Commercial paper Another name for the bills issued by corporations; a form of short-term debt.

Balance sheet, income statement The two basic forms of business accounts. Once again, see the Chapter Highlights.

Asset What is owned.

Liability What is owed.

Net worth The difference between the firm's assets and its liabilities. This measures the value of ownership or *equity* in the company.

Equity The value of ownership.

Capital gain The gain to an investor as a result of selling a security or other asset for more than it was purchased. There is a *capital loss* if it is sold for less.

Dividend Income paid to shareholders by a corporation.

Interest The income paid regularly to the owner of a bond.

Book value of stock A firm's net worth, divided by the number of shares outstanding. This represents the book value of a single share in the firm.

Depreciation A cost attributable to wear and obsolescence on the firm's capital.

Financial intermediary Any institution such as a bank or a savings and loan association that borrows from savers by issuing liquid assets to them (such as deposits) and lends to ultimate borrowers. Financial intermediaries exist because they can specialize in gathering financial information and in pooling risk for savers.

Broker The representative of a buyer or seller.

Investment banker A retailer of newly issued corporate securities.

Underwrite An investment bank often underwrites the new issues of a company's securities by guaranteeing to the company that all the securities will be sold. If the investment bank fails to sell them all then it must buy the unsold securities itself.

Leverage This is usually measured by the ratio of a company's debt to its net worth. A company with high leverage is one that has borrowed a great deal in relation to its net worth.

Line of credit A commitment by a banker or other lender to lend up to a predetermined amount to a corporation or other borrower, at the borrower's option.

Liquidity This is a characteristic that investors value in a security, namely saleability at a stable and predictable price upon short notice, with little selling cost.

Risk premium The extra return, or yield, that must be paid on securities whose return is risky (such as bonds of shaky corporations).

Profit The difference between receipts and expenditures of the business firm. After-tax profits are usually referred to as *net income* or net profit. The income that is not paid out in the form of dividends is retained profit (or retained earnings).

True-False Questions

T **F**   1. Partnerships can issue preferred shares but not common shares.
T F   2. Every corporation must have issued shares at some time, although it need never issue any bonds.
T **F**   3. A shareholder has unlimited liability.
T F   4. Corporate profits that are paid out as dividends are taxed twice: once by the corporate income tax and once by the personal income tax.
T **F**   5. Preferred shares generally offer a higher yield, but are considered riskier investments, than common shares.
T F   6. One of the services that is provided by financial intermediaries is liquidity.
T **F**   7. The balance sheet indicates how a business fared during some particular interval of time, usually a year.
T **F**   8. A firm's net worth is the amount of money that shareholders initially paid for their shares when they were first issued.
T F   9. A government bond is usually a more liquid asset than a house.
T **F**   10. Business firms that try to achieve a high degree of leverage generally do so to minimize the riskiness of their operations.
T F   11. Municipal government bonds offer a lower yield than federal government bonds, mainly because of the risk premium on the federal bonds.
T **F**   12. Corporate bonds are generally regarded as a "hedge against inflation."
T F   13. The Securities Exchange Commission has the power to make publicly owned corporations disclose information concerning their operation.

Multiple-Choice Questions

1. The partnership as a form of business firm
   (a) Is used by most large law firms
   (b) Is a means of limiting the liability of any single owner
   (c) Is the most common form of business organization in the United States
   (d) Provides the simplest way for any single owner to sell his or her share of the company on the open market

2. The profits earned by a partnership
   (a) Are taxed twice under U.S. tax laws
   (b) Are often retained by the firm, in which case the owners don't count them as part of their taxable income
   (c) Are counted as capital gains for the partners
   (d) Are treated as part of the partners' taxable incomes and therefore subject to the personal income tax

3. The corporate form of business enterprise
   (a) Is typical of small businesses
   (b) Suffers from a lack of continuity when one of the owners dies
   (c) Is a social device that has been in common use ever since the industrial revolution
   (d) Can possibly make it hard for the firm to raise funds because it limits the amount that lenders can collect from the firm if it goes bankrupt

4. Normally, the riskiest type of security to buy is a
   (a) Bond   **(c)** Convertible bond
   (b) Common share   **(d)** Preferred share

5. The corporate income tax rate on profits over $100,000 is what percent?
   (a) 17   **(c)** 46
   (b) 32   **(d)** 70

6. Whenever a corporation issues bonds rather than raising funds by issuing new shares, it decreases
   (a) Its leverage
   (b) Its risk
   (c) Its liabilities
   (d) The flexibility of its financial obligations

7. Preferred shares are so called because
   (a) Shareholders prefer them to common shares
   (b) Their holders must receive preferred treatment when the corporation is deciding whether to pay dividends on some (but not all) shares
   (c) They can be converted into bonds if the holder so prefers
   (d) Dividends on preferred shares receive preferential tax treatment compared to dividends on common shares

8. The return realized by an individual owning a bond
   (a) Consists mainly of a regular interest payment
   (b) Never takes the form of a capital gain
   (c) Is paid each year only if there is enough profit to pay a dividend on the preferred shares
   (d) Is subject to the corporate income tax

9. Retained earnings
   (a) Appear only on the balance sheet of the firm
   (b) Appear only on the income statement of the firm
   (c) Are always retained in the form of cash or some other liquid asset
   (d) None of the above

10. Which of the following identities is *not* correct?
   (a) Net worth ≡ assets − liabilities
   (b) Profit ≡ receipts − expenses
   (c) Net income ≡ receipts − taxes
   (d) Retained earnings ≡ net income − dividends

11. Financial intermediaries
   (a) Offer liquidity to their creditors
   (b) Buy only common shares
   (c) Issue only long-term securities like bonds
   (d) Are prevented by the SEC from issuing shares

12. Which of the following is *not* decided primarily in financial markets?
  - **(a)** The price of commercial paper
  - **(b)** The amount of depreciation on currently existing business machinery
  - **(c)** Which among the many potential borrowers will succeed in getting the funds they seek
  - **(d)** Which among the many risky projects that businesses would like to undertake actually get financed

13. When New York City faced bankruptcy in 1975 their bonds sold for much less than comparable bonds of other municipal governments. The New York bonds
  - **(a)** Offered investors a risk premium
  - **(b)** Offered investors more liquidity than other cities' bonds
  - **(c)** Offered investors a relatively sure way of getting a large rate of return
  - **(d)** Yielded interest payments that were subject to income tax

14. Which of the following does *not* act as a financial intermediary?

  - **(a)** An underwriter
  - **(b)** An investment banker
  - **(c)** A broker
  - **(d)** The Securities Exchange Commission

15. A commitment by a bank to lend any amount up to some predetermined limit, at the borrower's option, is a
  - **(a)** Warrant
  - **(b)** Stock option
  - **(c)** Line of credit
  - **(d)** Commercial paper

16. The major purpose of the Securities and Exchange Commission (SEC) is to require corporations to
  - **(a)** Issue common stock periodically so as to reduce leverage
  - **(b)** Issue preferred stock periodically in order to meet the demands of the stock-buying public
  - **(c)** Issue bonds periodically so as to provide lenders a stable source of income
  - **(d)** Make information public about the corporation's position

Exercises

1. From the following data, prepare a balance sheet as of December 31, 1982, for the ABC Corporation in Table 1. All figures refer to December 31, 1982 (in thousands of dollars). You may assume that there are no assets or liabilities other than those explicitly listed. If in doubt refer to the example of Table 6-1 in the textbook.

Accounts payable	$800
Accounts receivable	900
Long-term bonds issued	1,800
Plant and equipment	3,000
Inventory on hand	1,000
Cash on hand	400
Accrued liabilities	600
Common stock	1,200
Holdings of marketable securities	50
Preferred stock	700

2. The balance sheet for Chremastics Incorporated (CI) on December 31, 1980, included the following information (in thousands of dollars):

Cash	$ 65
Long-term debt	700
Plant and equipment	500
Accounts receivable	135
Retained earnings	100
Accounts payable	15
All other assets	250
Short-term debt	55
All other liabilities	30

Table 1

BALANCE SHEET OF ABC

Assets	Liabilities and net worth

Therefore, at this date CI's total assets were $_____, its total liabilities were $_____, and its net worth was $_____. If the firm had 3,000 shares outstanding at this date, the book value of its stock was $_____ per share.

For the calendar year 1981 CI's income statement showed that its sales were $480,000 and its costs (including depreciation) were $380,000. Therefore, its before-tax profits were $_____. If it paid an average tax rate of 20 percent, its net income was $_____. It paid $22,000 in the form of dividends, so its retained earnings for the year were $_____.

CI's capital equipment in 1981 consisted of one minicomputer, bought (new) for $140,000 3 years ago; an office building bought for $200,000, 6 years old, and other office equipment, bought for $160,000 all over 5 years old. Suppose that CI has been using a straight-line method of depreciation on its capital equipment, assuming a lifetime of 40 years on its building and 5 years on everything else. Then its total depreciation cost for 1981 was $_____. In its balance sheet of December 31, 1981, CI would report retained earnings of $_____.

Essay Questions

1. Why is it that very large companies tend to be corporations rather than partnerships or single proprietorships? Why has the twentieth century seen such a large growth in the corporate form of business enterprise? Do you think that the rise of the corporation has helped or hindered the development of the American economy in the twentieth century? Explain your answers.

2. Would it be possible for a firm's net worth to be negative? If so, what would this mean? Would it ever pay you to buy shares in a firm with negative net worth? Explain why or why not.

3. Suppose that all firms were charged by the government for the external costs resulting from their operations, and were paid by the government for the external benefits that they rendered to others. How do you suppose this would affect the income statement and balance sheet of the typical firm engaged in strip-mining? Of the typical firm that sells lawn-care services?

4. Suppose that for purposes of calculating depreciation a firm estimates the lifetime of a machine as 3 years rather than as 5 years. What difference will this make to the total amount of depreciation cost that the firm will claim over a 5-year period following the purchase of the machine? What difference will it make to the timing of these depreciation costs (that is, to how the depreciation costs are spread out over the 5-year period)? Explain carefully why it would be generally in the best interest of the firm to estimate the lifetime as 3 years rather than 5 years. Hint: Remember that a dollar this year is worth more to the firm than a dollar 4 years from now, because a dollar this year can be put into the bank where it will gather interest.

5. Explain carefully what is meant by Gilbert and Sullivan's lines, "If you succeed, your profits are stupendous and if you fail, pop goes your eighteen pence" which are quoted in Box 6-1 in the textbook. What basic concept explained in the textbook do these lines illustrate? How do they illustrate it?

6. Why do you suppose that corporations publish their income statements and their balance sheets? Who is interested in reading these? Would corporations publish this information if they were not forced to by government regulations? Suppose that they did publish this information but that there were no laws regulating the way these numbers could be calculated. What difference do you suppose this would make to the accounts published by the firms?

7. Suppose that you are in charge of finance for a large corporation. How would you go about raising funds for (a) the construction of a large plant, expected to remain in operation for at least 25 years; (b) the acquisition of larger inventories of raw materials; and (c) a temporary cash deficit resulting from the decision of a lot of your customers not to pay their bills until next month?

*8. In 1975 there was a threat that New York City might go bankrupt (indeed it did default on some of its debt). Many felt that if it did go bankrupt there would be serious consequences for economic stability in the United States. Explain the chain of events that such a bankruptcy might have created.

Answers

True-False Questions: **1** F **2** T **3** F **4** T **5** F **6** T **7** F **8** F **9** T **10** F **11** F **12** F **13** T
Multiple-Choice Questions: **1** a **2** d **3** d **4** b **5** c **6** d **7** b **8** a **9** d **10** c **11** a **12** b **13** a
14 d **15** c **16** d

Exercises:

1. Table 6-1

BALANCE SHEET OF ABC CORPORATION					
Assets			Liabilities and net worth		
Cash	$ 400		Accounts payable	$800	
Marketable securities	50		Accrued liabilities	600	1,400
Receivables	900		Long-term debt		1,800	3,200
Inventories	1,000	2,350			
Land, plant, and equipment		3,000	Net worth			2,150
Total assets		$5,350	Capital stock		1,900
			Retained earnings		250

2. 950, 800, 150, 50, 100, 80, 58, 33, 158

PART TWO

HIGH EMPLOYMENT AND A STABLE PRICE LEVEL

CHAPTER 7
Measuring National Product and National Income

Learning Objectives

After you have studied this chapter in the textbook and the study guide, you should be able to

Explain what national product measures

Explain the main reason why an increase in the dollar value of national product does not necessarily mean that more output is being produced

State the difference between the GNP price deflator and the consumer price index

State why the concept of "value added" is important for national income accounting

Explain the relationships between net investment, gross investment, depreciation, and changes in the country's capital stock

State and explain the equation $GNP = C + I_g + G + X - M$

State the difference between GNP and NNP, between NNP and NI, between NI and DI, and between DI and PI

Explain what the measure of economic welfare (MEW) attempts to measure, and how it differs from GNP

Explain why the "underground economy" poses a problem for national income accountants

Explain why the "underground economy" may be growing

CHAPTER HIGHLIGHTS

The purpose of this chapter is to explain how national product is measured, and some of the limitations of GNP as a measure of economic welfare.

When we calculate national product we must somehow add apples and oranges, tons of steel and bushels of wheat. The only practical way to do this is the one actually used, namely to add up the monetary value of all these goods and services, at their going market prices. There are many reasons why this method is less than ideal, but the most important one is that the value of money is not the same from one year to the next. If national product rises from one year to the next it might be because prices rose, not because of an increase in the quantity of goods and services produced. To deal with this problem, *current dollar*, or *nominal* national product is adjusted to remove the effects of inflation and find *constant dollar*, or *real* national product. Specifically, current dollar GNP is divided by an index of prices (then multiplied by 100). The price index so used "deflates" the nominal measure of GNP. So it is called the GNP price deflator. Study Box 7-1 and Table 7-2 in the textbook to understand how price indices are constructed and used.

Every price index is a *weighted average* of individual prices where different prices are given different weights. In the price index used in Table 7-2—that is, the GNP price deflator—the weights reflect the relative importance of the different goods in our gross national product (GNP). Make sure you understand the difference between this index and the consumer price index (CPI), in which the weights reflect the relative importance of goods in the budget of a typical urban family.

In measuring national product, care must be taken to avoid double counting. In other words we want to count the golf clubs that were produced but we don't also want to count the production of the steel, leather, wood, aluminum, glue, and so forth that went into the clubs. The golf clubs we call *final products* and the ingredients we call *intermediate products*. We only want to count the total final product. As shown in Box 7-2 in the text, this is the same as computing all the *value added* at each stage of production.

The most common measure of national product is *gross national product* (GNP). This measures the total production of goods and services in the economy over a particular year. It equals the sum of personal consumption expenditures (C), gross private domestic investment (I_g), government purchases of goods and services (G), and exports of goods and services (X) minus imports of goods and services (M). In symbols: $GNP = C + I_g + G + X - M$. This important equation states that all output of the country is bought in the country for use as a consumption good, for use as a private investment good, or for the government, or else it is sold abroad. Imports are subtracted because some of the items included in C, I_g, and G are goods and services produced in other countries, whereas we want to measure only U.S. production.

Gross private domestic investment (or gross investment, for short) includes all current production of plant and equipment for private use, as well as the net increase in business inventories. Even if a good (like steel) is intended to be used eventually

as an intermediate good, some of it will be counted as a final investment good this year if it is added to inventories. Government purchases do not include all government expenditures. *Transfer payments* (such as unemployment insurance benefits) are not included because nothing is produced in exchange for the payments.

During the year the capital stock *depreciates*; that is, it wears out or becomes obsolescent. Gross investment (I_g) represents the new plant and equipment acquired, plus the net additions to inventories. By subtracting depreciation we find the net addition to the country's capital stock; that is, *net* investment (I_n); $I_n = I_g -$ depreciation. Net national product (NNP) is the same as GNP except that it counts net investment rather than gross investment; in symbols, $NNP = C + I_n + G + X - M$. Thus, $NNP = GNP -$ depreciation.

National product and national income (NI) mean almost the same thing. The reason can best be understood by referring to the circular flow of spending, which is represented in the textbook by Figure 7-3. The basic idea is simple—one person's expenditure is another person's receipt. If I buy a dollar's worth of output, this creates a dollar's worth of income for the seller of that product. There is one complication. Some of that dollar might go directly to the government in the form of sales tax, so it doesn't count as anyone's income. Thus, $NI = NNP -$ sales taxes (this is not exactly correct, as it ignores several other minor adjustments). National income measures the total income (wages and salaries, rent and interest, proprietors' income, and corporate profits) in the economy resulting from current productive activity. It does not include such items as transfer payments that are not a reward for productive activity. Thus, it is not the same as *personal income* (PI), which measures the income received by households. This in turn is not the same as disposable personal income (DI), which measures the income actually available to the individual or family for personal use. The relationship between these measures of national product and income is given by Figure 7-5 in the textbook. Make sure you can reproduce all of this figure on your own, and that you can state the definitions of these measures given in the following list of important terms.

This chapter also explains the ambitious attempt by two Yale economists (William Nordhaus and James Tobin) to calculate a better measure of economic well-being, MEW (measure of economic welfare). This measure includes an estimate of the value of our leisure as well as of the goods and services we produce, and it makes adjustments for the quality of life that take into account environmental pollution and urban congestion. Finally, the chapter describes the attempts by Professor Edgar Feige and others to measure the national output produced in the "underground economy"—output that does not get included in the official statistics because people do not report the corresponding income for tax purposes. The important aspect of the underground economy is its potential size and growth. Although it is difficult to get reliable estimates, Feige has calculated that the underground economy was 19.1 percent of GNP in 1976 and 26.2 percent in 1978.

IMPORTANT TERMS

National product The dollar value of all final goods and services produced in the country during the year.

Nominal national product National product measured at the prices existing when production took place. Also called *current-dollar* national product.

Real national product National product measured at the prices existing in one specific *base* year. Also called *constant-dollar* national product.

Price index A weighted average of prices, expressed as a percentage of prices in the base year. To compute real national product, divide nominal national product by the price index for that year, then multiply by 100.

GNP price deflator The price index used in computing real GNP from nominal GNP. The weights used in this index depend upon the relative importance of various goods in national product.

Consumer price index (CPI) An index of consumer prices paid by the typical urban family. In this index goods and services are weighted according to their importance in the budget of a typical urban family.

Final product A good or service that was produced during the year and not used up as an input into the production of some other good or service.

Intermediate product A good used as an input in producing some other good or service. These are not counted separately when national product is calculated. To avoid double counting we include only final products.

Value added The value of a firm's output minus the value of intermediate products acquired by the firm. National income can be computed as the sum of all value added in the economy.

Personal consumption expenditures (C) Expenditures by residents of the country on consumer goods.

Government purchases of goods and services (G) All government expenditures for the purpose of acquiring goods (like paper or guns) or services (like those of soldiers or social workers).

Gross private domestic investment expenditures (I_g) The total amount spent in the country on capital goods that were produced during the year. It includes expenditures on plant and equipment and net additions to inventories. (It also includes, under the heading "residential construction," expenditures on building or renovating houses and apartments).

Depreciation A dollar estimate of the deterioration of the country's capital stock.

Net private domestic investment expenditures (I_n) The net addition to the country's capital stock. It is defined as: $I_n = I_g -$ depreciation.

Exports of goods and services (X) The total value of all goods and services produced by residents of the country but sold to residents of other countries.

Imports of goods and services (M) The total expenditures by residents of the country on foreign-produced goods and services.

Gross national product (GNP) Defined as $GNP = C + I_g + G + X - M$.

Net national product (NNP) Defined as $NNP = C + I_n + G + X - M$, or equivalently, as $NNP = GNP -$ depreciation.

National income (NI) The total value of all income received during the year by residents of the country in return for current productive activity. It includes the sum of wages and salaries, rent, interest, and profits. It equals NI minus sales taxes and other minor items.

Personal income Equals NI + transfer payments − corporate profit taxes − undistributed corporate profits − social security taxes paid by employers.

Personal disposable income Equals personal income minus personal taxes.

Personal saving Equals personal disposable income − consumption − interest paid by consumers.

Measure of economic welfare (MEW) A measure computed by two Yale economists, which is like NNP except that it includes the value of leisure and adjusts for environmental pollution and urban congestion.

True-False Questions

T F **1.** Nominal GNP is the same thing as current-dollar GNP.
T F **2.** Nominal GNP is computed by dividing real GNP by a price index.
T F **3.** If nominal GNP has gone up then real GNP also must have gone up.
T F **4.** A price index is an average of all prices, in which all prices are given the same weight.
T F **5.** National income is defined in such a way that it must always be equal to net national product.
T F **6.** In measuring GNP we try to avoid counting the production of any intermediate products except those that are added to inventories.
T F **7.** Government purchases of goods and services do not include all government expenditures.
T F **8.** National income can be greater than gross national product.
T F **9.** GNP ≡ C + I_n + G + X − M.
T F **10.** Gross investment is greater than the net annual addition to the country's stock of capital.
T F **11.** Personal income includes some profit income.

Multiple-Choice Questions

1. This year's real GNP measures the value of
  (a) Current output at current prices
  (b) Current output at base-year prices
  (c) Base-year output at current prices
  (d) Base-year output at base-year prices

2. Suppose that national product consisted simply of guns and butter. You are given the following data (1972 is the base year):

	Production of guns	Price of guns	Production of butter	Price of butter
1972	80	$10 each	1,100 lbs.	$1 per lb.
1980	100	$15 each	1,500 lbs.	$2 per lb.

Then nominal national product for 1980 is
  (a) $1,900   **(c)** $3,800
  (b) $2,500   **(d)** $4,500

3. Using the same data as in the previous question (and remembering the answer to question 1), we may conclude that real national product for 1980 is
  (a) $1,900   **(c)** $3,800
  (b) $2,500   **(d)** $4,500

4. From the answers to the previous two questions we may conclude that in 1980 the GNP price deflator is
  (a) 132   **(c)** 200
  (b) 180   **(d)** 237

5. If the price index goes up and real GNP goes down, then
  (a) Nominal GNP must rise
  (b) Nominal GNP must fall
  (c) Nominal GNP will rise if the percentage fall in real GNP is greater than the percentage rise in the price index
  (d) Nominal GNP will rise if the percentage rise in the price index is greater than the percentage fall in real GNP

6. The consumer price index
  (a) Is the index used in deriving real GNP from nominal GNP
  (b) Uses weights for different goods and services according to their relative importance in the budget of the typical urban family
  (c) Is the only price index which equals 100 in the base year
  (d) Rises less rapidly than the GNP price deflator

7. GNP minus national income equals
  (a) Sales taxes
  (b) Transfer payments plus depreciation
  (c) Transfer payments
  (d) Sales taxes plus depreciation

8. The sum of wages and salaries plus rents, interest, and profits equals
  (a) Net national product
  (b) National income
  (c) Personal income
  (d) Personal disposable income

9. Suppose a firm incurs economic costs of $100 in wages and salaries, $50 in rent and interest, and $160 for inputs purchased from other firms. If it produces an output worth $400, then its value added is
  (a) $240   **(c)** $300
  (b) $250   **(d)** $350

10. Suppose that the firm described in the previous question has $40 of depreciation, then its profit is

(a) $50   (c) $140
(b) $100   (d) $150

11. If during the year I paid $1,000 in social security taxes and collected $800 in unemployment insurance benefits, then the combined effect of these two items was to
(a) Reduce national income by $200
(b) Reduce personal income by $1,000
(c) Increase national income by $800
(d) Reduce disposable personal income by $200

12. If I buy $20,000 worth of common stock in the Xerox Corporation, then this will contribute $20,000 to
(a) Gross investment   (c) National income
(b) Consumption   (d) None of the above
    expenditure

13. If during a year gross investment equaled 150 and net investment equaled 30, then the country's capital stock rose by

$$I_g - D = I_N$$
$$150 - D = I_n 30$$

(a) Negative 120   (c) 120
(b) 30   (d) 150

14. If during the year gross investment equaled 150 and net investment equaled 30, then depreciation was
(a) Negative 120   (c) 120
(b) 30   (d) 150

15. Which of the following is *not* true of measure of economic welfare?
(a) It includes the output of the underground economy
(b) It takes into account the value of our leisure time
(c) It makes adjustment for the quality of life
(d) It takes environmental pollution into account

16. Feige estimated that in 1978 the underground economy was what percent of GNP?
(a) 1.9   (c) 26.2
(b) 11.3   (d) 43.8

Exercises

1. You are given the following (incomplete) data for country A during a particular year:

C	$900
I_n	400
Wages and salaries	800
Interest and rent	100
Corporate profits (after taxes)	250
Personal taxes	350
Depreciation	50
G	450
Corporate income taxes	150

Contributions to social security	0
Sales taxes	200
Transfer payments	200
Undistributed corporate profits	150
Proprietors income	400

Compute the following:
NI _____
NNP _____
GNP _____
$X - M$ _____
Personal income _____
Personal disposable income _____
I_n _____

2. Suppose that country Y produces two goods, a consumption good and an investment good. The first two rows of Table 7-1 give the current-dollar value of the total production of the two goods. Fill in the next row indicating nominal GNP each year in country Y. The next two rows indicate the market prices of the two goods each year. Fill in the next two rows giving the number of units of each good produced each year. Then fill in the next two rows giving the value of production of each good in constant dollars (i.e., at 1972 prices). Fill in the next row giving real GNP, and the next row giving the value of the price index, using 1972 as the base year.

Table 7-1

	1972	1977	1982
Current-dollar value of C production	200	450	600
Current-dollar value of I production	100	150	200
Nominal GNP			
Price of C	5	9	10
Price of I	20	25	40
Quantity of C production			
Quantity of I production			
Constant-dollar value of C production			
Constant-dollar value of I production			
Real GNP			
Index of prices			

Essay Questions

1. In what sense does the gross national product tend to overstate the level of economic well-being in a country in a particular year? In what sense does it tend to understate it?

2. Explain step by step how you would go about computing the net national product of a country by measuring the flows in the upper loop of the circular flow (see Figure 7-3 in the textbook). How would you do it by measuring the flows in the lower loop? Explain why you should arrive at the same answer using either approach.

3. Why do you suppose that the statistics on depreciation are unreliable? How is this connected to the tax system?

4. Consider a man who has been spending his time as a homemaker, without being paid by anyone. Suppose he were to take a job in a factory, and that the factory worker whom he replaced went to work for him as a domestic servant, doing all the things he used to do as a homemaker. Suppose that the former homemaker is just as good a factory worker as the former factory worker and that the former factory worker is just as good a homemaker as the former homemaker. What has been the effect on economic well-being? When the government statistician computes GNP, how will this role-switching affect the value that is obtained? Will the resulting change in GNP overstate or understate the change in economic welfare?

5. Suppose that the house which you bought at the beginning of the year increases in value by $15,000 by the end of the year. Would you consider this as part of your income? As part of your disposable income? Should the national income accountant count is as part of national income? As part of disposable personal income?

6. Why do the GNP price deflator and the CPI use different weights? What would be the problem if you tried to use the GNP price deflator to measure the cost of living? If you used the CPI to compute real GNP from nominal GNP?

7. Why is the concept of "value added" important for national income accounting? Is it used in the upper-loop or the lower-loop approach of Figure 7-3 in the textbook?

8. Why doesn't production in the "underground economy" normally get included in GNP?

*9. What do you suppose is the purpose of distinguishing government expenditures from transfer payments? If you wanted to measure the total size of the government sector, which do you think would be a better measure, the total level of spending by the government or the amount of purchases of goods and services by the government?

Answers

True-False Questions: 1 T 2 F 3 F 4 F 5 F 6 T 7 T 8 F 9 F 10 T 11 T

Multiple-Choice Questions: 1 b 2 d 3 b 4 b 5 d 6 b 7 d 8 b 9 a 10 a 11 d 12 d 13 b 14 c 15 a 16 c

Exercises:

1.

NI	1,700
NNP	1,900
GNP	1,950
$X - M$	200
Personal income	1,600
Personal disposable income	1,250
I_n^*	350

2. Table 7-1

	1972	1977	1982
Nominal GNP	300	600	800
Quantity of C production	40	50	60
Quantity of I production	5	6	5
Constant-dollar value of C production	200	250	300
Constant-dollar value of I production	100	120	100
Real GNP	300	370	400
Index of prices	100	162	200

CHAPTER 8
Equilibrium with Unemployment:
An Introduction to Keynesian Economics

Learning Objectives

After you have studied this chapter in the textbook and the study guide, you should be able to

Show how national output and the price level react to increases in aggregate demand (a) when the aggregate supply schedule is horizontal, and (b) when it is vertical

State the difference between the aggregate supply curves assumed by classical economics and Keynesian economics

List the four components of aggregate demand

Explain what the MPC means and how the size of the MPC is indicated by the diagram of a consumption function

Derive the saving function from the consumption function

Explain the relationship between the MPC and the MPS

Explain why the level of national product at which the aggregate demand schedule intersects the 45-degree line is an equilibrium

State and derive the formula for the multiplier in a simple economy without taxes

Explain the distinction between leakages and injections

Express the equilibrium condition for national product in three different ways

$AD = AS$

$AD = c + I_g + g + x - m$

$AD = c + I_g + g + x - m$

CHAPTER HIGHLIGHTS

The purpose of this chapter is to introduce the basic theory of Keynesian macroeconomics. Keynes revolutionized macroeconomics in 1936 with his *General Theory*. In this book he attacked "classical" theory on the grounds that it was unable to explain large-scale unemployment or to suggest policies to

deal with it. This chapter discusses Keynes and his attack on "the classics" in order to put modern macroeconomic theory into historical perspective. But the main objective of the chapter is to understand the theory; the history is just a means to this end.

The first element of this theory is *aggregate supply*. As illustrated in Figure 8-2 in the textbook, when the economy is at less than full employment firms can supply more output at existing prices. However, once full employment is reached more demand will cause higher prices. The theory of this chapter assumes that the economy is on the horizontal range of the aggregate supply function, where an increase in demand can cause output to increase with no rise in prices. This simplifying assumption may be justified when there is large-scale unemployment, but this is not always the case. The "classical" economics that Keynes attacked dealt with the vertical segment of the aggregate supply function. This too is a simplifying assumption, which might be reasonably close to the truth when there is not much unemployment.

The next element of the the theory is *aggregate demand*. This consists of (1) consumption demand, (2) investment demand, (3) government expenditures on goods and services, and (4) net export demand (exports minus imports). As you can see by drawing your own diagram, if the supply curve is horizontal then the price of output will be determined by the position of the supply curve, but the quantity of output will be determined by aggregate demand. Since we are interested in the quantity of aggregate output (national product), aggregate demand is the key concept for Keynesian economics.

The determination of aggregate demand can be quite complex. In order to illustrate the basic principles this chapter considers what would happen in a very simplified economy with no government sector, no foreign trade, no depreciation, and no undistributed corporate profits. In such an economy, GNP = NNP = NI = personal disposable income. (Make sure you know why, using the definitions in the last chapter.) The only components of aggregate demand are consumption and investment. To make things even simpler we suppose that the demand for investment, I^*, is fixed at some constant value, and we focus upon consumption.

Consumption expenditures (C) depend upon personal disposable income (DI). The relationship between C and DI is called *the consumption function*. This is one of the most important concepts of macroeconomic theory. The consumption function has three main characteristics:

1. As DI increases, this causes C to increase.

2. When this happens, the change in C (ΔC) is less than the change in DI (ΔDI); the fraction $\Delta C/\Delta$DI is called the marginal propensity to consume (MPC).

3. Below some level of DI (called the "break-even" point) C will actually be larger than DI; this is possible because people can spend more than their disposable incomes by running down their assets or going into debt.

These characteristics are all illustrated by Figure 8-4 in the textbook. As an exercise, try drawing consumption functions that do *not* have each of these three characteristics.

Saving (S) equals DI minus C. (This is a simplification of the definition given in Chapter 7. Here we are assuming that no interest is being paid by consumers.) Thus, a saving function can be derived directly from the consumption function, and it has three main characteristics:

1. If DI increases then so will S.

2. The change in S (ΔS) is less than the change in DI (ΔDI); the fraction $\Delta S/\Delta$DI is the marginal propensity to save (MPS). Also, what is not consumed is saved. Therefore, $\Delta C + \Delta S = \Delta$DI. Dividing both sides by ΔDI we find that MPS + MPC = 1.

3. Below some level (the break-even point again) people will dissave (that is, S is negative).

Figure 8-5 in the textbook illustrates these characteristics of the saving function.

Figure 8-7 in the textbook shows how the equilibrium quantity of output is determined. The aggregate demand schedule is constructed by adding the given level of investment demand on top of the consumption function. The "45-degree line" allows us to measure national product on the vertical axis. Point E represents an equilibrium quantity of output because at that output firms are producing a quantity that is just equal to what is being demanded. At larger quantities of NP, aggregate demand is less than NP; and at lower quantities of NP, aggregate demand is greater than NP. Business firms will want to meet the demand for their product, but they will not want to produce more than they can sell. Thus, they will be led to produce the equilibrium level of NP.

A key concept is *the multiplier*. If investment demand increases, the resulting rise in output will be greater than the increase in investment demand; that is, it will be some *multiple* of the increase in investment demand, which we call the multiplier. The increase in output caused by the initial increase in investment demand will create extra income. Households with higher income will increase their consumption expenditures. This generates more output, more income, and so forth as the effects of the initial increase in demand ripple through the economy.

The exact size of the multiplier is $1/(1 - \text{MPC})$. To derive this formula, let's look in detail at what happens when aggregate demand shifts up by $1 ($\Delta I^* = 1$). If firms increase output to meet this extra demand, NP increases by $1. But now households with one more dollar of income will increase their consumption demand by an amount equal to $1 \times$

MPC. If firms again meet this increase in demand, NP will increase again, this time by the amount MPC. But this gives households another increase in their income, this time an increase equal to MPC. The resulting increase in consumption this time is just this change in income times the MPC; that is, $(MPC)^2$. Next time the increase in consumption will be $(MPC)^3$, and so on. As you can see, this process can go on forever, with the changes in income getting smaller and smaller. If NP keeps increasing to meet the increased demand, the total change in NP will be the sum of all those changes: $\Delta NP = 1 + MPC + (MPC)^2 + (MPC)^3 + \cdots$. But remember our discussion of geometric series from the appendix to Chapter 1. (Or see footnote 6 in Chapter 8 of the textbook.) There we saw that an infinite sum like this can be added up, and the total is $\Delta NP = 1/(1 - MPC)$. This gives the total effect on NP of each dollar's increase in I^*. Therefore, the multiplier equals $1/(1 - MPC)$.

The equilibrium quantity of NP is described by three different conditions, all of which amount to the same thing: (1) NP equals aggregate demand. This is the condition that we have been using so far.

(2) Actual investment (I) equals the demand for investment (I^*). When NP exceeds aggregate demand, the unsold goods that pile up in firm's inventories are actually part of investment, but this investment was *not* demanded. When aggregate demand exceeds NP the inventories of business firms will be running down faster than firms wanted. Only when aggregate demand equals NP is actual I just equal to the desired I^*, because only then is there no unintended investment (or disinvestment) in inventories. (3) Desired investment, I^*, equals saving. One way to see this is as follows. By the definition of DI:

$$(a) \qquad DI = C + S$$

But, as we have already mentioned, in this simplified economy, DI and NP are the same. So we can rewrite (a) as:

$$(b) \qquad NP = C + S$$

The level of aggregate demand is:

$$(c) \qquad AD = C + I^*$$

Now subtract (c) from (b):

$$(d) \qquad NP - AD = S - I^*$$

Equation (d) states that if NP = AD (the first equilibrium condition), then $S = I^*$ (the third equilibrium condition)

IMPORTANT TERMS

Aggregate supply The relationship between the average level of prices and the amount of output that firms are willing to produce. Aggregate supply shows how the average level of prices and output respond to changes in aggregate demand.

Aggregate demand Total spending on goods and services. That is, aggregate demand = consumption demand + investment demand + government purchases of goods and services + net exports.

Consumption function The relationship between personal disposable income and personal consumption expenditures.

Break-even point The amount of disposable income where $C = DI$; that is, where $S = 0$.

Marginal propensity to consume (MPC) $\Delta C/\Delta DI$. That is, the slope of the consumption function.

45-degree line The line through the origin with slope equal to one. Since this line is equidistant from each axis, it serves as a visual aid to translate what is on the horizontal axis to the vertical axis.

Saving function The relationship between personal disposable income and personal saving.

Marginal propensity to save (MPS) $\Delta S/\Delta DI$.

That is, the slope of the saving function. (Remember that MPS + MPC = 1.)

Undesired inventory investment The investment in inventories that occurs not because firms wanted the investment but because they incorrectly estimated demand when making their production decisions. It can be positive or negative.

Actual investment (I) The amount of new plant and equipment acquired during the year, plus the increase in inventories. All inventory accumulation is included, whether the inventories were desired or not.

Investment demand (I*) The amount of investment demand that firms would like to undertake. Also called *desired investment*, or *planned investment*. It includes new plant and equipment, plus additions to inventories that businesses want to acquire. It excludes undesired inventory accumulation.

Equilibrium national product The quantity of national product at which aggregate demand equals national product. It is also the quantity at which undesired inventory investment is zero, and also the quantity at which desired investment and saving are equal.

Full-employment national product The quantity of national product that the economy is capable of producing with its existing quantities of land, labor, and capital.

The multiplier The ratio of the change in national product to an initial change in aggregate demand. In the simple model studied in this chapter, it equals $1/(1 - \text{MPC})$, or $1/\text{MPS}$.

Leakage Any withdrawal from the circular flow of spending. In the simple model of this chapter, the only leakage is saving.

Injection Any addition to the circular flow of spending. In the simple model of this chapter, the only injection is investment.

True-False Questions

T F **1.** According to Keynesian theory, the assumption of a horizontal aggregate supply curve is likely to be reasonably close to the truth when there is large-scale unemployment.

T F **2.** If the aggregate supply curve is horizontal, then the level of prices does not depend upon aggregate demand.

T F **3.** The multiplier measures the change in investment that would be caused by a shift in the consumption function.

T F **4.** The slope of the consumption function is equal to the MPC.

T F **5.** One minus the slope of the saving function is the MPS.

T F **6.** At the "break-even" point saving is zero.

T F **7.** The vertical difference between the consumption function and the 45-degree line equals saving.

T F **8.** If the MPC is positive then the MPS must be negative.

T F **9.** If national product exceeds its equilibrium value, then saving is more than desired investment.

T F **10.** If output equals aggregate demand then actual inventory investment must be zero.

T F **11.** The equilibrium national product is always the full-employment national product.

T F **12.** The size of the multiplier is always greater than unity as long as the MPC is a positive fraction.

T F **13.** The multiplier equals the ratio of additional consumption to additional investment.

T F **14.** Saving is an injection into the circular flow of spending.

T F **15.** When desired investment increases, then to restore equilibrium, national product must continue to rise until the resulting increase in saving equals the increase in desired investment.

Multiple-Choice Questions

1. In Keynesian economics the aggregate supply curve is
- **(a)** Assumed to be horizontal for levels of output below full employment
- **(b)** Assumed to be horizontal for levels of output above full employment
- **(c)** The same as in "classical" economies
- **(d)** Vertical throughout its length

2. If the aggregate supply curve is horizontal, then
- **(a)** No more output will be produced unless the price level increases
- **(b)** The price level is determined by aggregate demand
- **(c)** Real NP is determined by aggregate demand
- **(d)** Further increases in aggregate demand will just cause inflation

3. Which of the following is *not* one of the four major components of aggregate demand?
- **(a)** Net exports
- **(b)** Saving
- **(c)** Government purchases of goods and services
- **(d)** Planned investment

4. The MPC is the ratio of
- **(a)** Additional *C* to additional disposable income
- **(b)** Additional *C* to total disposable income
- **(c)** Total *C* to additional disposable income
- **(d)** Total *C* to total disposable income

5. Which of the following is generally true?
- **(a)** The consumption function is the same thing as the 45-degree line
- **(b)** The slope of the consumption function is greater than one
- **(c)** The greater the slope of the consumption function, the larger will be the multiplier
- **(d)** The slope of the saving function equals the slope of the consumption function.

6. At levels of disposable income above the break-even point
- **(a)** Saving is negative
- **(b)** Intended investment is negative
- **(c)** Output exceeds aggregate demand
- **(d)** None of the above

7. If the MPS equals 1/3, then the multiplier equals
- **(a)** 1/3
- **(b)** 1-1/2
- **(c)** 3
- **(d)** The multiplier depends upon the MPC, not upon the MPS

8. In the simple economy studied in this chapter, even when NP is not at its equilibrium, actual investment equals
- **(a)** Saving
- **(b)** Undesired inventory investment

(c) The demand for investment

(d) Consumption

9. Undesired inventory investment is negative if

(a) National product exceeds aggregate demand

(b) C is less than disposable income

‑ (c) Desired investment exceeds saving

(d) (a) and (b)

10. In Figure 8-1, the equilibrium level of national product equals the distance

(a) 0A   ‑(c) 0D

(b) 0B   (d) 0E

11. In the same figure, the MPC equals the ratio

(a) 0E/0A   (c) BD/FH

(b) 0H/0D   ＼(d) FG/0B

12. In the same figure, the multiplier equals the ratio

(a) 0E/0A

(b) 0H/0D

＼(c) BD/FH

(d) FG/0B

13. If national product is less than its full-employment quantity, then

(a) Aggregate demand exceeds national product

‑(b) National product will increase if aggregate demand increases

(c) The aggregate supply curve must be vertical

(d) There must be some undesired inventory investment taking place

14. According to Keynesian theory, which of the following would *not* produce an increase in the equilibrium national product?

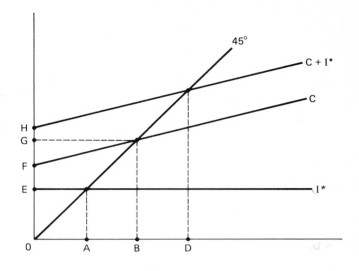

FIGURE 8-1

(a) An increase in intended investment

(b) An upward shift in the consumption function

‑ (c) An upward shift in the saving function

(d) An increase in injections into the circular flow

15. National product is at its equilibrium level if

(a) National product equals aggregate demand

(b) Actual investment equals investment demand

(c) Investment demand equals saving

(d) All of the above

Exercises

1. Table 8-1 below represents the same sort of simple economy as the one studied in this chapter. Suppose that the MPC = 0.8. Fill in the second column, giving the level of consumption demand at each level of DI. Suppose that the demand for investment is 40. Then fill in the third column, giving the level of aggregate demand at each level of NP. Now fill in the fourth and fifth columns, giving (respectively) the amount of saving and the amount of undesired inventory investment that would occur at

each level of NP. Then fill in the sixth column, giving S minus investment demand. The equilibrium level of NP equals _____. The break-even level of DI equals _____.

2. Suppose that the equation of the consumption function is C = 25 + (0.75) DI. In other words, if DI equals, say, 100, then C = 25 + (0.75 × 100) = 100. Plot out the consumption function in Figure 8-2. Plot the saving function in Figure 8-3. Suppose that the demand for investment equals 25.

Table 8-1

(1) DI (= NP)	(2) C	(3) 40 C+I Aggregate demand	(4) DI-C Saving	(5) Undesired inventory investment	(6) -20 S minus investment demand
0	20	60	-20	_____	-60
100	100	140	0	_____	_____
200	_____	_____	_____	_____	_____
300	_____	_____	_____	_____	_____
400	_____	_____	_____	_____	_____
500	_____	_____	_____	_____	_____

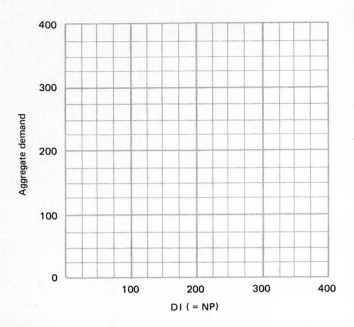

FIGURE 8-2

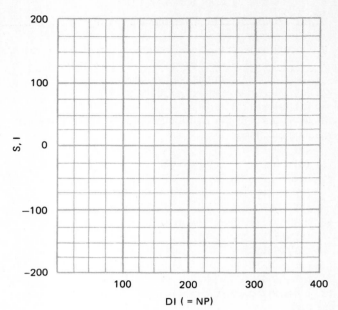

FIGURE 8-3

Plot the demand for investment in Figure 8-3. Plot the aggregate demand schedule and the 45-degree line in Figure 8-2. The MPC equals _____, the MPS equals _____, the multiplier equals _____, and the equilibrium level of NP equals _____. Now, suppose that the demand for investment increases by 25; it now equals 50. Plot the new aggregate demand schedule in Figure 8-2 and the new investment demand schedule in Figure 8-3. The new equilibrium NP equals _____. At the value of NP that used to be the equilibrium, aggregate demand is now (more,less) than NP by the amount _____, saving is now (more,less) than the demand for investment by the amount _____, and the level of undesired inventory investment equals _____.

3. In Figure 8-4, the equilibrium quantity of NP equals __O F__. At that quantity of NP, C equals __F F__, S equals __I M__, investment demand equals __I M__, actual investment equals __I M__, and undesired inventory investment equals __O__. When NP equals *OB*, then *C* equals __B J__, *S* equals _____, investment demand equals _____, actual investment equals _____, undesired inventory investment equals _____, *S* minus investment demand equals _____, and actual investment minus desired investment equals _____. When NP equals *OX*, then undesired inventory investment equals _____, *S* minus investment demand equals _____, and actual investment minus planned investment equals _____.

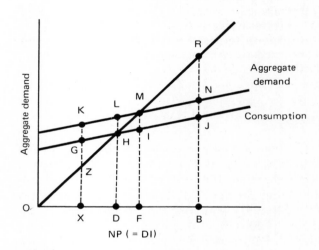

FIGURE 8-4

4. Suppose that the MPC equals 0.5 and that investment demand rises by 400. In the first column of Table 8-2 below fill in the increase in demand at each round of spending, as in Table 8-3 in the textbook. In the second column fill in the total increase in demand (investment plus consumption) that has occurred up to and including that round. The total increase in demand in *all* the rounds (if the series is continued indefinitely) will be _____.

Table 8-2

		(1) Change in aggregate demand	(2) Cumulative total
First round	Investment of		
Second round	Consumption of		
Third round	Consumption of		
Fourth round	Consumption of		
Fifth round	Consumption of		
Sixth round	Consumption of		
Seventh round	Consumption of		

Essay Questions

1. "Keynesian theory works best when there is large-scale unemployment." Do you agree? Explain.

2. In the textbook, personal disposable income was stated as the main determinant of consumption expenditures. What variables other than personal disposable income do you think would be important in determining consumption expenditures? Explain how you think they will affect consumption expenditures.

3. In the textbook, the level of investment demand was assumed to be constant. What variables do you think would be important in determining investment demand? How do you think they would affect it?

4. In the simple model of this chapter, the only component of aggregate demand that depended upon national income in any way was consumption. What other components would you think would depend upon national income in a more realistic model? Why?

5. Draw a diagram illustrating the situation that would exist if the MPC were greater than unity. In such a situation is there an equilibrium level of national product? If so, what would happen if the actual level of national product was greater than the equilibrium level? In this case, what would the size of the multiplier be?

6. "If the demand for investment goods rises that will just divert some of our resources from producing consumption goods and put them to work in producing investment goods. The economy can't produce both more investment goods and more consumption goods unless the production possibilities frontier shifts out." Do you agree with this statement? Do you think a Keynesian economist would agree with it? Explain why or why not.

*7. Explain why saving is a leakage. Try to identify two other leakages, and explain why they are leakages.

*8. One of the conditions characterizing the equilibrium level of national product is that desired investment and saving are equal. Show that it is always true that actual investment and saving are equal, whether national product is at its equilibrium level or not. How would this result have to be altered if saving was not the only leakage?

Answers

True-False Questions: **1** T **2** T **3** F **4** T **5** F **6** T **7** T **8** F **9** T **10** F **11** F **12** T **13** F **14** F **15** T

Multiple-Choice Questions: **1** a **2** c **3** b **4** a **5** c **6** d **7** c **8** a **9** c **10** c **11** d **12** c **13** b **14** c **15** d

Exercises:

1. 300,100

Table 8-1

DI(NP)	C	Aggregate demand	Saving	Undesired inventory investment	S minus investment demand
0	20	60	−20	−60	−60
100	100	140	0	−40	−40
200	180	220	20	−20	−20
300	260	300	40	0	0
400	340	380	60	20	20
500	420	460	80	40	40

2. 0.75, 0.25, 4, 200, 300, more, 25, less, 25, −25
3. OF, FI, IM, IM, IM, O, BJ, JR, JN, JR, NR, NR, NR, $-ZK$, $-ZK$, $-ZK$
4. 800

Table 8-2

	1	2
First	400	400
Second	200	600
Third	100	700
Fourth	50	750
Fifth	25	775
Sixth	12½	787½
Seventh	6¼	793¾

CHAPTER 9
Fiscal Policy

Learning Objectives

After you have studied this chapter in the textbook and the study guide, you should be able to

Explain why government expenditures are injections, and taxes are leakages

Show how the introduction of a government changes equilibrium output

Show how aggregate demand is affected by a lump-sum tax

Show how aggregate demand is affected by a proportional income-tax

Explain why an increase in government spending has a greater effect upon aggregate demand than does a decrease in taxes of the same amount

Explain how automatic stabilizers work and give an example

Describe how the full-employment budget is measured

Explain why the full-employment budget is a better indicator of the effects of fiscal policy than is the actual budget

State the connection between fiscal drag and automatic stabilizers

Explain why balancing the actual budget every year can be a policy trap

State under what circumstances deficit spending is likely to help the economy, and under what circumstances it is likely to create problems (explaining why)

Explain why a large national debt can cause economic problems

CHAPTER HIGHLIGHTS

The government can influence aggregate demand through monetary and fiscal policies. This chapter deals with fiscal policy; that is, the government's policy regarding expenditures and taxes.

When aggregate demand is too low to provide full employment, a recessionary gap exists. An increase in government spending or a decrease in taxes may close this gap by raising aggregate demand and bringing national product up to its full-employment level. When aggregate demand is higher than needed to provide full employment, an inflationary gap exists, which may be closed by a decrease in government spending or an increase in taxes.

Government spending, like investment, is an injection into the circular flow of spending; and taxes, like saving, are a leakage. As in the last chapter, planned injections and leakages must be equal for national product to be at its equilibrium level. In other words, G plus planned I must equal T plus S.

Government spending, like investment spending, contributes directly to aggregate demand. Changes in government spending have the same multiplied effects on national income as do changes in investment spending. Changes in taxes also affect national income, but not to the same extent, because they only affect aggregate demand indirectly. Any increase in taxes immediately produces a dollar-for-dollar decrease in disposable income. This in turn causes households to reduce consumption spending, which is one component of aggregate demand. Because the marginal propensity to consume is less than one, a $1 increase in taxes causes the consumption function to shift down by less than $1. This means that if government spending and taxes are increased by equal amounts, the effects do not cancel out. Rather, national product will rise.

Not all changes in the amount of taxes and government spending are a result of changes in fiscal policy. For example, when national product rises, more income tax must be paid; this produces an *automatic* rise in the amount of taxes collected without any change in tax rates.

Any tax whose collections rise automatically when national income rises is an *automatic stabilizer*. Likewise, any item of government spending that falls whenever national income rises is an automatic stabilizer. Automatic stabilizers are like shock-absorbers that prevent national income from "bouncing around" too much. For example, an increase in investment demand will cause national product to increase. But the increase in taxes that automatically accompanies that increase will prevent disposable income from rising by as much as it otherwise would. This in turn prevents consumption expenditures from rising as much as they otherwise would, thus damping the increase in aggregate demand.

Automatic stabilizers are not always beneficial. When there is less than full employment, we may want national income to increase. But any increase will be dampened by automatic stabilizers. This effect is called *fiscal drag*.

Automatic stabilizers tend to produce government deficits when the economy is in recession by making taxes low and government spending high.

Likewise, they tend to produce surpluses during prosperity. Most economists regard this as a small price to pay for the benefits of stabilization.

However, many would argue for the principle of balancing the budget, as a restraint on government spending and tax policy. This principle could be implemented by any one of a number of different guidelines. For example, balancing the *full-employment* budget every year would allow automatic stabilizers to work but would not permit spending programs or budget cuts to restrain a recession. A bolder strategy is to aim for a full-employment deficit during recession and full-employment surplus during prosperity. This may mean that the actual budget is in deficit on average; thus, some economists argue that the government should aim for a "cyclically balanced" budget. Not much support can be found for balancing the *actual* budget every year. This would require higher tax rates and budget cuts during a recession to make up for falling tax revenues; such policies would aggravate the recession by causing aggregate demand to fall even further.

Restraint on government spending can also be accomplished by placing direct limits upon the size of government spending, or upon the amount of taxes that the government is allowed to collect. Such limits have been imposed upon various state governments in recent referenda, such as the 1978 Proposition 13 in California.

The full-employment budget is often used as an indicator of whether the government's fiscal policy is working to increase aggregate demand or to reduce it. It is a better indicator than the actual budget, which includes effects of automatic stabilizers as well as those of deliberate policy. For example, an actual budget deficit does not necessarily indicate an expansionary fiscal policy. The deficit may simply be the result of a fall in national income.

One long-run problem of government deficits is that they add to the national debt. Some regard this debt as a burden upon future generations of taxpayers. However, for the most part, repayment of the debt is just a transfer from one group of citizens (the general taxpayers) to another (the holders of government bonds).

Nevertheless, the national debt may be a burden if (1) the transfer to bondholders creates an "undesirable" distribution of income; (2) the taxes required to pay the interest generate an "excess burden;" or (3) to avoid raising taxes the government creates new money to pay the interest, thus fueling inflation.

IMPORTANT TERMS

Fiscal policy The use of changes in government spending programs or tax rates to affect aggregate demand.

Recessionary gap The amount by which the aggregate demand function would have to shift upward to produce full employment. Sometimes called *deflationary gap*.

Output gap The amount by which national product falls short of the full-employment quantity. In a diagram like Figure 9-2 in the textbook, it is measured along the *horizontal* axis, whereas the recessionary gap is measured along the vertical axis. The output gap is larger than the recessionary gap (it equals the recessionary gap × the multiplier).

Inflationary gap The amount by which the aggregate demand schedule lies above the 45-degree line, when measured at the full-employment national product.

Lump-sum tax A tax whose amount does not depend upon the level of national product.

Marginal tax rate When more taxes are paid because of an increase in national income, the marginal tax rate is the change in tax collections as a fraction of the change in income. (That is, $\Delta T/\Delta NI$.)

Government budget surplus Government receipts minus transfer payments minus government purchases of goods and services. A *negative* surplus is called a budget *deficit*.

Full-employment surplus The budget surplus that would exist if the economy were at full employment, with the existing tax rates and government spending programs.

Automatic stabilizer Any tax or government spending program that makes the government surplus increase automatically (without any change in government policy) when national product rises, and fall automatically when national product falls.

Fiscal drag The retarding effect on aggregate demand produced by automatic stabilizers when an increase in aggregate demand is desired.

Fiscal dividend The increase in the budget surplus caused when national product rises and tax collections automatically increase.

Cyclically balanced budget A government budget designed so that the surpluses received during the expansion phase of the business cycle are equal to the deficits incurred during recessions. In other words, a budget that is balanced "on average" over the business cycle.

Excess burden The decrease in efficiency in the economy which results when people change their behavior to reduce their taxes. (The primary burden of taxes is measured by the amount of taxes collected.)

True-False Questions

T F **1.** The effect of a discretionary increase in government spending is to increase the equilibrium national product.

T F **2.** If an inflationary gap exists, then the equilibrium quantity of national product is below the full-employment quantity.

T F **3.** Lump-sum taxes constitute an automatic stabilizer.

T F **4.** With a proportional income tax, if the marginal tax rate rises, then the aggregate demand schedule becomes flatter.

T F **5.** If the schedule of unemployment insurance benefits were increased, the aggregate demand schedule would become steeper.

T F **6.** Fiscal drag can arise only if automatic stabilizers are not strong enough.

T F **7.** If the full-employment budget is balanced and national income is below its full-employment level, then the actual budget will be in surplus.

T F **8.** In the absence of discretionary fiscal policy, the full-employment surplus would tend to rise when national income rose.

T F **9.** Automatic stabilizers do not tend to stabilize the actual budget deficit.

T F **10.** The national debt is more burdensome if the spending which it financed occurred when national income was above its full-employment level than if that spending occurred during a recession.

Multiple-Choice Questions

1. Suppose that the MPC equals 2/3, and that all taxes are lump-sum taxes. Then, if taxes increase by 75, the aggregate demand schedule will shift

(a) Up by 75
(b) Down by 75
(c) Up by 50
(d) Down by 50

2. An increase in lump-sum taxes will
   (a) Make the aggregate demand schedule flatter
   (b) Make the aggregate demand schedule steeper
   (c) Leave the slope of the aggregate demand schedule unchanged
   (d) Increase or decrease the slope depending upon the size of the MPC

3. Suppose that the MPC equals 0.75 and that all taxes are lump-sum taxes. If the equilibrium value of national product is $140 billion and the full employment value is $200 billion, then the size of the recessionary gap is
   (a) $15 billion   (c) $60 billion
   (b) $45 billion   (d) $160 billion

4. In this example the size of the output gap is
   (a) $15 billion   (c) $60 billion
   (b) $45 billion   (d) $160 billion

5. Pick the best example of an automatic stabilizer
   (a) Local property taxes
   (b) The corporate income tax
   (c) Temporary tax increases legislated by Congress to reduce inflationary pressures
   (d) Inheritance taxes

6. A proportional income tax
   (a) Makes the consumption function steeper than it would be with only lump-sum taxes
   (b) Makes the multiplier larger than it would be with only lump-sum taxes
   (c) Acts as an automatic stablizer
   (d) None of the above

7. Which of the following could result from the automatic increase in taxes caused by a rise in national product?
   (a) Fiscal drag
   (b) A fiscal dividend
   (c) A rise in the actual surplus
   (d) All of the above

8. The full-employment budget will be in
   (a) Surplus if the economy is below full employment and the actual budget is balanced
   (b) Deficit if the economy is below full employment and the actual budget is balanced
   (c) Surplus if there is an inflationary gap and the actual budget is in surplus
   (d) Deficit if there is an inflationary gap and the actual budget is in surplus

9. In the absence of discretionary fiscal policy
   (a) The full-employment surplus would rise when national product rose
   (b) The actual surplus would rise when national product rose
   (c) The full-employment surplus would fall when national product rose
   (d) The actual surplus would fall when national product rose

10. The policy of achieving a balanced budget on the average over each business cycle
   (a) Requires a full-employment surplus on average if there is less than full employment (on average) over the business cycle
   (b) Requires the actual budget surplus to fall when national income rises
   (c) Cannot be achieved if the actual budget is always in balance
   (d) None of the above

11. The excess burden of the debt exists only if
   (a) The federal government prints money to pay off the debt
   (b) Holders of government bonds are wealthier on average than the typical taxpayer
   (c) People change their economic behavior to reduce their taxes
   (d) There is a full-employment deficit

12. The federal government cannot go broke because
   (a) With the power to tax, they can always raise the revenue to pay their debt
   (b) They can print more bonds if they are in financial difficulties
   (c) They can print more money to pay their debts
   (d) The constitution prohibits it from going that far into debt

13. The size of the recessionary gap is equal to
   (a) The multiplier times (actual income minus full-employment income)
   (b) The multiplier times (full-employment income minus actual income)
   (c) (Actual income minus full-employment income) divided by the multiplier
   (d) (Full-employment income minus actual income) divided by the multiplier

Exercises

1. The equation of the consumption function in Figure 9-1 is $C = 200 + 0.5Y$, where C denotes consumption and Y national income. The variable on the horizontal axis is national income, and the consumption function is plotted under the assumption that no taxes are collected ($T = 0$). The MPC = _____. Suppose now that a lump-sum tax of 200 is collected. When $Y = 400$, disposable income will be _____, and consumption will be _____. When $Y = 600$, disposable income will be _____, and consumption will be _____. Plot this consumption function in the same diagram. As a result of the lump-sum tax, the consumption function has shifted down by _____. Suppose now that instead of a lump-sum tax, a proportional income tax is collected, where $T = (1/3)Y$. The marginal tax rate is _____. When $Y = 300$, $T = $ _____, disposable income = _____, and $C = $ _____. When $Y = 600$, $T = $ _____, disposable income = _____, $C = $ _____. Plot this new consumption function on the same diagram.

2. In Figure 9-2 the full-employment national

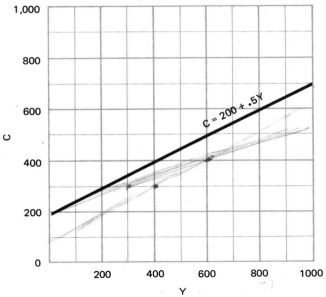

FIGURE 9-1

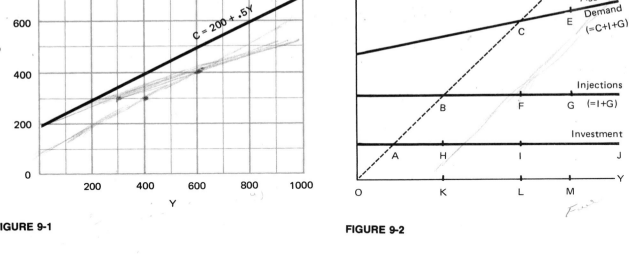

FIGURE 9-2

product is equal to the distance *OM*. The size of the recessionary gap is ___. The equilibrium national product is ___. If a line were drawn indicating the total amount of leakages (saving plus taxes), then that line would pass through the injec-

tions line at point _____. At the full-employment national product, would the leakages line lie above or below the injections line? _____ The vertical distance between these two lines at full employment would be equal to ___.

Essay Questions

1. If the government increases transfer payments, how does this affect aggregate demand? Will it have the same dollar-for-dollar effect as an increase in government purchases of goods and services? Explain.

2. Critically evaluate the following statement: "Any system of unemployment insurance is inherently self-defeating as a measure to combat cyclical unemployment, because even though the payment of benefits to the unemployed will help to raise aggregate demand, the contributions (taxes) from employed workers will lower aggregate demand."

3. Suppose that there are no undistributed corporate profits, no depreciation, and no interest payments by households. Define *TR* as the size of government transfer payments, and *T* as the total amount of taxes collected by the government. Prove that the following relationship holds: $GNP = C + S + T - TR$. Next, prove that $I_g + G + TR + X = S + T + M$. Do these equations hold at all levels of national product, or just at the equilibrium levels? Explain.

4. The government can finance its expenditures through taxes, debt financing, or printing money. Contrast and compare the advantages and disadvantages of each of these three forms of finance.

***5.** Several economists have argued that the income tax should be indexed to the cost of living. That is, the basic exemptions and all tax brackets should go up, say, by 10 percent whenever the cost of living rises by 10 percent. How would indexation affect the role of the income tax as an automatic stabilizer? (Hint: Whenever national income rises, the cost of living usually rises too. That is, the aggregate supply curve is not perfectly horizontal.)

***6.** According to the theory of fiscal policy outlined in this chapter, when taxes rise, national income falls. On the other hand, when automatic stabilizers were discussed in the text, it was pointed out that when national income falls, taxes fall. Putting these two together we are led to the nonsensical result that when taxes rise, taxes fall. What's wrong with this logic?

Answers

True-False Questions: **1** T **2** F **3** F **4** T **5** F **6** F **7** F **8** F **9** T **10** T
Multiple-Choice Questions: **1** d **2** c **3** a **4** c **5** b **6** c **7** d **8** a **9** b **10** a **11** c **12** c **13** d
Exercises:

1. 0.5, 200, 300, 400, 400, 100, 1/3, 100, 200, 300, 200, 400, 400

2. *DE*, *OL*, *F*, above, *DE*.

CHAPTER 10
Money and the Banking System

Learning Objectives

After you have studied this chapter in the textbook and the study guide, you should be able to

Describe the three basic functions of money

Explain the difference between checking deposits and time and savings deposits

Define M1-A, M1-B, M-2, and M-3

Explain the difference between a commercial bank and a central bank

Describe five functions of the Federal Reserve

Explain how the process of deposit expansion works

State the formula for the deposit multiplier

Give two reasons why this formula sets only an upper limit on the expansion of bank deposits

CHAPTER HIGHLIGHTS

The purpose of this chapter is to introduce some of the basic concepts of money and banking as a preliminary to studying the workings of monetary policy.

Money performs three basic functions:

1. It is a *medium of exchange*; that is, it is the item that you give up when you buy something and acquire when you sell something.

2. It is a *standard of value*; that is, we keep accounts, quote prices, and sign contracts in units of money.

3. It is a *store of value*; that is, by holding money you can defer purchases until later.

Banks evolved from medieval goldsmiths, who issued warehouse receipts as "claim checks" on gold that was deposited with them for safekeeping. These warehouse receipts were the forerunners of modern bank deposits. The goldsmiths found that they could lend out some of the gold that had been deposited. Thus, they held in the warehouse only a fraction of these deposits. This worked as long as not too many depositors came in at once to withdraw their gold, as long as the loans were repaid, and as long as the goldsmith kept enough gold in reserve (not lent out). This practice was the beginning of the modern fractional-reserve banking system.

There are several definitions of the money supply. M1-A is the sum of currency in the hands of the public plus demand deposits. (These are deposits with commercial banks payable on demand, against which checks may be written.) M1-B includes everything in M1-A plus all other checkable deposits like NOW and ATS accounts, both of which are described in the list of important terms below. M-2 includes everything in M1-B plus any savings deposits not already included, as well as all time deposits of less than $100,000. (A time deposit, unlike a savings deposit, cannot be withdrawn before a certain time without penalty.) M-3 includes everything in M-2 as well as all time deposits of $100,000 or more. (These large deposits are mainly certificates of deposit held by businesses.) Even broader definitions of money include other liquid assets.

The banks at which most people keep their checking deposits are "commercial banks." There are about 15,000 of these in the United States. Like the early goldsmiths, their major roles are to accept money on deposit for saving and for writing checks, and to lend money to businesses, individuals, and governments.

The Federal Reserve is the *central bank* of the United States. The roles of the "Fed" are to (1) control the quantity of money, (2) issue paper currency, (3) act as the banker of the commercial banks—lending to them and accepting deposits from them, (4) supervise and inspect the commercial banks, and (5) act as the federal government's bank.

Less than half the commercial banks in the United States are members of the Federal Reserve System, but these member banks account for about 70 percent of all bank deposits. All national banks must be members, and about 10 percent of state banks choose to belong. All deposit-taking institutions are required by law to hold reserves equal to specified percentages of their deposits. The precise percentages are set by the Fed, within limits set by law. Banks can hold reserves in the form of currency or deposits with the Fed.

The purpose of the required reserve ratio is to limit the amount of money that can be created by the banking system. As the example in the textbook illustrates, the volume of checking deposits, D, can potentially expand up to the level $D = A/R$, where R is the required reserve ratio, and A is the amount of reserves that the banks have acquired. This expansion of deposits takes place following a deposit of currency by the public. As one bank lends out its excess reserves to a customer, the proceeds of the loan may be deposited in a checking account in another bank. This second institution can lend out its excess reserves, and so on until deposits have expanded to the point where no more excess reserves remain. However, the maximum expansion A/R is unlikely to be reached because banks hold excess reserves and, more importantly, people hold some of their new money in the form of currency rather than deposits.

IMPORTANT TERMS

Currency Federal reserve notes (paper currency) and coins.

Demand deposits Deposits with commercial banks, payable on demand. Until recently, these were the only checking deposits in the United States.

Savings and time deposits Deposits that yield interest. Some savings accounts are checkable. Every time deposit has a specific date before which it cannot be cashed without a penalty.

NOW Negotiable order of withdrawal. This is a check written against a special kind of savings account, called a NOW account.

ATS Automatic transfer from savings. An ATS account is a savings account against which you can write checks indirectly. If your regular checking account is insufficient to cover a check, it gets replenished automatically by an ATS.

Certificate of deposit (CD) A large time deposit (over $100,000) held mainly by businesses. It has the advantage of being negotiable. Unlike smaller time deposits, CDs can be sold on the market before they reach maturity.

Liquid asset Otherwise known as *near-money*. An asset that is readily convertible into cash at low cost and a predictable dollar value. An example is a short-term government bill.

Federal Reserve The central bank of the United States.

Commercial banks The banks you are familiar with, that deal directly with the public.

Bank reserves Commercial banks' holdings of currency and deposits with the Federal Reserve.

Required reserve ratio The fraction of its deposit liabilities that a commercial bank or other deposit-taking institution is required to hold in the form of reserves.

Required reserves Reserves that deposit-taking institutions must hold as a consequence of the required reserve ratio.

Excess reserves Any reserves held over and above required reserves. The sum of required reserves plus excess reserves equals total reserves.

Secondary reserves A financial institution's holdings of liquid assets.

Federal funds market The market in which banks with excess reserves lend to banks with inadequate reserves.

Checking deposit multiplier The maximum amount by which checking deposits may expand as a result of someone originally depositing $1. This multiplier is the reciprocal of the required reserve ratio.

True-False Questions

T F 1. Money is a store of value.
T F 2. Money is the only store of value.
T F 3. Fractional reserve banking started with the creation of the Federal Reserve System.
T F 4. Bank panics would not occur if banks held reserves equal to 100 percent of their deposit liabilities.
T F 5. The only function of the Federal Reserve is to set the reserve requirements for banks.
T F 6. All national banks are members of the Federal Reserve System.
T F 7. Only national banks are members of the Federal Reserve System.
T F 8. Demand deposits are now the only checkable deposits.
T F 9. M-2 is greater than M1-B.
T F 10. A noncheckable savings deposit is a liquid asset.
T F 11. Banks are more likely to hold excess reserves in a depression than during prosperity.
T F 12. The required reserve ratio applies only to secondary reserves.

Multiple-Choice Questions

1. Which of the following is *not* a role of money?
   (a) Store of value
   (b) Instrument of barter
   (c) Medium of exchange
   (d) Standard of value
2. Which of the following is largest?
   (a) Currency in the hands of the public
   (b) M1-B
   (c) M-3
   (d) Time and savings deposits
3. Checks can be written
   (a) Only against demand deposits
   (b) Against CDs
   (c) Against some savings deposits
   (d) Against all deposits
4. Which of the following are *not* included in M-2?
   (a) Currency in the hands of the public
   (b) NOW accounts
   (c) ATS accounts
   (d) CDs
5. One difference between commercial banks and central banks is that
   (a) Central banks are not in the business of lending money to private individuals
   (b) Commercial banks do not create money
   (c) A central bank does not take deposits
   (d) Commercial banks all have branches
6. The number of commercial banks in the United States is about
   (a) 15,000   (c) 70,000
   (b) 30,000   (d) 150,000

7. Deposits with member banks constitute what percent of total deposits?
   (a) 10   (c) 70
   (b) 47   (d) 92
8. Which of the following is *not* one of the roles of the Federal Reserve?
   (a) To regulate commercial banks
   (b) To act as a bankers' bank
   (c) To act as the federal government's bank
   (d) To conduct fiscal policy
9. Short-term government bills held by a commercial bank
   (a) Are liquid assets
   (b) Cannot be counted to satisfy reserve requirements
   (c) Are secondary reserves
   (d) All of the above
10. If a bank holds $30 million in actual reserves and has $25 million required reserves, then without acquiring any more reserves it can legally lend out another
   (a) $5 million
   (b) $25 million
   (c) $30 million
   (d) It must contract its loans to meet its requirements
11. If the required reserve ratio is 0.125, then the deposit multiplier equals
   (a) 1.25   (c) 8.0
   (b) 8/7   (d) 12.5
12. If I deposit $20,000 in a commercial bank and the required reserve ratio is 10 percent, then the potential expansion of checking deposits resulting from this act is
   (a) 2,000   (c) 22,000
   (b) 20,000   (d) 200,000

13. A decision by many people to hold a larger fraction of their money in the form of currency would

  (a) Reduce the total amount of money that would eventually result from an original deposit of $100 in a checking account
  (b) Increase the size of the checking deposit multiplier
  (c) Reduce the required reserve ratio
  (d) Increase the quantity of excess reserves held by banks, at least initially

14. An increase in the required reserve ratio on checking accounts would most likely cause

  (a) An increase in the money supply
  (b) An increase in demand deposits
  (c) An increase in the checking deposit multiplier
  (d) A decrease in M-1B

Exercises

1a. If I deposit $100,000 in currency into a checking deposit with Bank A and the required reserve ratio is 20 percent, then the immediate increase in Bank A's total reserves is $_____, and the immediate increase in Bank A's required reserves is _____. Thus, the immediate increase in Bank A's excess reserves is _____. As a result of this transaction, the total amount of currency in the hands of the public has gone (up, down) by the amount _____, the total amount of checking deposits has gone (up, down) by the amount _____, the total amount of M-1B has (increased, decreased, not changed) and the total amount of M-2 has (increased, decreased, not changed).

1b. If Bank A now lends its new excess reserves and the proceeds of the loan are deposited into a checking deposit in Bank B, then the immediate effect is to make Bank A's total reserves go (up, down) by _____, to make Bank A's required reserves (increase, decrease, stay unchanged), to make Bank A's excess reserves go (up, down) by _____, to make Bank B's total reserves go (up, down) by _____, to make Bank B's required reserves go (up, down) by _____, to make Bank B's excess reserves go (up, down) by _____. As a result of this loan and subsequent deposit, the total amount of currency in the hands of the public has (increased, decreased, stayed the same), the total amount of checking deposits has (increased by _____, decreased by _____, stayed the same), the total amount of M-1B has gone (up, down) by _____, and the total amount of M-2 has (increased by _____, decreased by _____, stayed the same).

1c. If the process continues like this until all excess reserves have been eliminated, then the result of the whole process, starting from my initial deposit, will have been to make the total supply of currency in the hands of the public go (up, down) by _____, to make the total amount of checking deposits go (up, down) by _____', to make M-1B go (up, down) by _____, and to make M-2 (go up by _____, go down by _____, stay the same).

2. Show what happens as a direct result of each of the following transactions by filling in the appropriate number for that transaction in the balance sheet. Each balance sheet should represent the *change* in total assets and total liabilities of all banks. In each case, suppose that the required reserve ratio on checking deposits is 20 percent, and on all other deposits is 10 percent. Each transaction should be considered separately from all the others.

  A. Someone puts $25,000 of currency into a checking deposit.
  B. Someone makes a cash withdrawal of $100,000 from a noncheckable savings account, in order to hold the money in the form of currency.
  C. Someone switches $200,000 from a checking deposit to a noncheckable savings deposit.
  D. A bank lends $40,000 to someone who holds the proceeds of that loan in the form of currency.
  E. A bank lends $100,000 to someone who uses that $100,000 to pay off a loan to someone who puts the $100,000 into a noncheckable savings deposit.

Balance Sheet A

Change in assets		Change in liabilities	
Loans	_____		
Total reserves	_____		
		Checking deposits	_____
Required reserves	_____		
		Savings deposits	_____
Excess reserves	_____		

Balance Sheet B

Change in assets		Change in liabilities	
Loans	_____		
Total reserves	_____		
		Checking deposits	_____
Required reserves	_____		
		Savings deposits	_____
Excess reserves	_____		

Balance Sheet C

Change in assets		Change in liabilities	
Loans	_____		
Total reserves	_____		
		Checking deposits	_____
Required reserves	_____		
		Savings deposits	_____
Excess reserves	_____		

Balance Sheet D

Change in assets		Change in liabilities	
Loans	_____		
Total reserves	_____		
		Checking deposits	_____
Required reserves	_____		
		Savings deposits	_____
Excess reserves	_____		

Balance Sheet E

Change in assets		Change in liabilities	
Loans	_____		
Total reserves	_____		
		Checking deposits	_____
Required reserves	_____		
		Savings deposits	_____
Excess reserves	_____		

Essay Questions

1. What do you suppose would happen if the Federal Reserve abolished all reserve requirements?

2. Most deposits with commercial banks are now covered by Federal Deposit Insurance. Thus, if your bank finds itself unable to meet your request to withdraw the money that you have deposited with it, you can collect your deposit from the Federal Deposit Insurance Corporation. Since the institution of the FDIC, there has not been a major bank panic in the United States. Why do you suppose this has been the case?

3. It has been argued that the existence of near-money makes it more difficult for banks to predict their deposits and withdrawals than if these near-money did not exist. Why do you suppose this is the case? (Hint: Consider what happens to banks' deposits and withdrawals when savings and loans associations begin offering higher interest rates on their deposits.)

4. It has also been argued that the existence of a federal funds market helps to make the monetary system more stable. See if you can fill in some of the details of this argument. (Hint: Over any given week do you think it is easier to predict the deposits and withdrawals of a particular bank or of the banking system as a whole?)

5. In what sense do bankers "create money"? How can this be reconciled with the view, often expressed by individual bankers, that they don't create money, they just lend out the money that is deposited with them?

6. Suppose that banks hold no excess reserves, but that everybody holds half of his or her money in the form of bank deposits and half in the form of currency. In this case, what is the maximum expansion of bank deposits following a new deposit of A dollars?

*7. Many people think that in the future most payments will be made through an electronic transfer system. That is, when you buy something from a store, instead of paying with cash or a check, the store will use a remote computer terminal to transfer money instantaneously from your account to theirs. How would the institution of such an electronic transfer system affect the amount of money that people wish to hold in the form of currency? How would it affect the total amount by which bank deposits would expand following the deposit of some new currency into a bank account?

*8. Recall the three different roles of money. For each role, can you think of another item besides money that also serves this role in specific cases?

*9. Banks often find it difficult to predict how much money is going to be deposited or withdrawn from their accounts in any given day or any given week. Which do you think they find easier to predict: deposits and withdrawals of demand deposits, or deposits and withdrawals of savings deposits? Why? How is this connected to the fact that banks historically have tended to hold more reserves against demand deposits than against the same amount of savings deposits?

Answers

True-False Questions: **1** T **2** F **3** F **4** T **5** F **6** T **7** F **8** F **9** T **10** T **11** T **12** F
Multiple-Choice Questions: **1** b **2** c **3** c **4** d **5** a **6** a **7** c **8** d **9** d **10** a **11** c **12** d **13** a **14** d
Exercises:

1a 100,000; 20,000; 80,000; down; 100,000; up; 100,000; not changed; not changed; **b.** down; 80,000; stay unchanged; down; 80,000; up; 80,000; up; 16,000; up; 64,000; stayed the same; increased by 80,000; up; 80,000; increased by 80,000; **c.** down; 100,000; up; 500,000; up; 400,000; go up by 400,000.

2. Balance Sheet A

Change in assets			Change in liabilities	
Loans		0		
Total reserves		25,000		
			Checking deposits	25,000
Required reserves	5,000			
			Savings deposits	0
Excess reserves	20,000			

Balance Sheet B

Change in assets			Change in liabilities	
Loans		0		
Total reserves		−100,000		
			Checking deposits	0
Required reserves	−10,000			
			Savings deposits	−100,000
Excess reserves	−90,000			

Balance Sheet C

Change in assets			Change in liabilities	
Loans		0		
Total reserves		0		
			Checking deposits	−200,000
Required reserves	−20,000			
			Savings deposits	+200,000
Excess reserves	+20,000			

Balance Sheet D

Change in assets			Change in liabilities	
Loans		40,000		
Total reserves		−40,000		
			Checking deposits	0
Required reserves	0			
			Savings deposits	0
Excess reserves	−40,000			

Balance Sheet E

Change in assets			Change in liabilities	
Loans		100,000		
Total reserves		0		
			Checking deposits	0
Required reserves	+10,000			
			Savings deposits	100,000
Excess reserves	−10,000			

CHAPTER 11
The Federal Reserve and the Tools of Monetary Policy

Learning Objectives

After you have studied this chapter in the textbook and the study guide, you should be able to

Identify the three major tools of monetary policy

Describe how each of these tools works

Explain how the Federal Reserve System is organized

Explain how open market operations by the Fed affect interest rates and the money supply

Show why a "fall in interest rates" means the same thing as a "rise in security prices"

State why the discounting procedure of the Federal Reserve System might reduce the effectiveness of open market operations

Explain why the discounting procedure may promote economic stability

Explain why large changes in reserve requirements can be very disruptive

Explain how margin requirements affect the stability of the stock market

Define moral suasion, and explain why it is less effective as a tool of monetary policy in the United States than in Britain or Canada

Describe how federal deposit insurance makes the economic system more stable

Explain what "backs up" our money supply

Argue the cases for and against returning to the gold standard

CHAPTER HIGHLIGHTS

This chapter describes how monetary policy is conducted. The three major tools of monetary policy used by the Fed (Federal Reserve) are: (1) open market operations, (2) changes in the discount rate, and (3) changes in required reserve ratios.

The United States is divided into 12 Federal Reserve Districts, each with its own Federal Reserve Bank. Each of these banks has a president and nine directors. Coordinating this system of banks is the Board of Governors of the Federal Reserve System (known as the Federal Reserve Board) in Washington, whose seven members are appointed to 14-year terms by the President (subject to congressional confirmation). The Chairman of the Federal Reserve Board is also appointed by the President, with a 4-year term.

The Board has the power to change reserve requirements, within limits set by Congress. For example, the required reserve ratio is 3 percent on the first $25 million of checking accounts of an individual bank, and the Board can set the ratio between 8 and 14 percent on checking accounts in excess of $25 million. On large nonpersonal time deposits it can vary from 0 to 9 percent. Discount rates may vary from district to district. Changes are proposed by the regional Federal Reserve Bank, subject to approval by the Board. Open market operations are conducted by the New York Federal Reserve Bank under the direction of the Federal Open Market Committee, which consists of the seven members of the Board and the presidents of five of the district banks, one of which is always the New York Federal Reserve Bank.

Open market operations involve purchases or sales by the Fed of government securities in the open market. The Fed operates in the market for these securities in the same way as a private firm, except that when the Fed buys securities it creates the money to pay for them and when it sells securities it destroys the money that is received in the sale. An open market purchase of securities by the Fed has three main effects: (1) It increases the money supply, (2) it increases the reserves that banks are able to loan out, and (3) it lowers interest rates on securities. All three effects operate in reverse with an open market sale.

Increases in the discount rate can be used to make banks less willing to make loans. Commercial banks usually borrow from the Fed only when their reserves are temporarily low. When the cost of this borrowing is raised, they can protect themselves against having to borrow so often by lending out fewer of their excess reserves. The problems with the discounting procedure (the procedure whereby the member banks borrow from the Fed) are two-fold. First, it introduces "slippage" into open market operations. Even when the Fed is conducting open market sales, trying to reduce the level of bank reserves, banks can maintain their reserves by borrowing. Second, it can provide a "hidden subsidy" to banks. This occurs whenever the banks are able to borrow from the Fed at a rate lower than the rate at which they could borrow elsewhere. However, the discounting procedure can also make the banking system more stable because it provides member banks with a "lender of last resort" in the event of difficulties.

Changes in reserve requirements are very potent. They operate directly on the deposit multiplier discussed in the previous chapter. When the required reserve ratio is increased, banks are forced to curtail their loans. This can have drastic consequences, as in the 1930s, when large increases in reserve requirements were responsible for prolonging the Great Depression. The Fed now tries to avoid such errors. Recent changes in reserve requirements have been small.

There are two minor tools of monetary policy:

1. Selective credit controls have been implemented. An example is margin requirements on stock-market transactions. The purpose of margin requirements is to prevent excessive speculation from causing a financial crisis as in the stock-market crash of 1929.

2. Moral suasion is sometimes exercised. An example is the "voluntary" restraint on banks' foreign lending in the mid-1960s.

When the Fed purchases securities on the open market, it creates money "out of thin air." Our money is not backed by gold. Dollar bills retain their value because they are scarce and are accepted by sellers of goods and services. The acceptability of demand deposits is reinforced by the FDIC, which ensures that bank deposits can be converted into cash. Ultimately, the only thing that "backs" our money is the Fed's determination not to create it so fast that it becomes worthless.

Many of those who are not very impressed by the Fed's determination in this sense have called for a return to the gold standard, under which the quantity of bank reserves would be linked to the quantity of gold in the system. The main problem with such a proposal is the fragility of a system of money built like an "inverted pyramid" on gold (see Figure 11-4 in the textbook). Any sudden increase or decrease in the supply of gold to the banking system will cause a "multiplied" change in the stock of money. Such large changes can occur just when you don't want them. For example, massive withdrawals of gold from the U.S. banking system by frightened depositors in the early 1930s contributed to the greatest monetary collapse of our history, just when a stimulus to aggregate demand was badly needed.

IMPORTANT TERMS

Open market operation The purchase or sale by the Fed of government securities in the open market.

Discount rate The interest rate at which the Fed lends to member banks.

Federal Reserve Banks The operating arms of the Fed. There is one in each of the 12 Federal Reserve Districts.

Federal Reserve Board The coordinating agency of the Federal Reserve System, consisting of seven members appointed by the President.

Federal Open Market Committee (FOMC) A committee consisting of the seven members of the Federal Reserve Board and the presidents of five of the Federal Reserve Banks, which meets monthly to decide how the Fed's open market operations are to be conducted. (All 12 presidents of the regional Federal Reserve Banks attend the FOMC but only five are voting members at one time.)

Treasury bill A short-term government security, often bought or sold in open market operations. It usually matures (the loan is repaid) 90 days after it is issued.

Prime rate A bank's publicly announced interest rate for short-term loans.

Perpetuity A bond with an infinite term to maturity. In other words, a perpetuity is a promise to pay a certain sum of money every year from now until the end of time. (See Box 11-1.)

Coupon A coupon payment on a bond is the regular payment of interest (usually made semiannually or quarterly).

Present value The present value of a stream of future returns is the amount that the ownership of that stream of returns is worth on the market today. (See Box 11-1.)

Moral suasion The Fed uses moral suasion when it exhorts bankers to refrain from certain actions or encourages them to take others.

Selective credit controls Restrictions imposed by the Fed upon transactions in particular credit markets.

Margin requirement A requirement limiting the amount that can be borrowed to buy shares. It stipulates the maximum percentage of a stock purchase that can be financed with borrowed money.

Legal tender An item (such as a dollar bill) is legal tender if it must be accepted by a creditor as payment of a debt.

Federal Deposit Insurance Corporation (FDIC) An agency of the federal government that ensures deposits in a national bank or other member of the FDIC up to $100,000.00 per deposit.

Gold standard The historical system under which paper currency was convertible at a fixed price into gold. (More details will be given in Chapter 18.)

True-False Questions

T (F)   1. Changes in reserve requirements are the most commonly used tool of monetary policy.
(T) F   2. The Federal Reserve System was established in the twentieth century.
T (F)   3. There are eight Federal Reserve districts.
T (F)   4. Open market operations are carried out entirely at the discretion of the Chairman of the Fed.
(T) F   5. The discount rate may vary from one Federal Reserve district to another.
T (F)   6. An open market sale by the Fed causes bank reserves to rise.   *Contracts*
T F   7. An open market purchase by the Fed causes security prices to rise.
T (F)   8. An increase in interest rates means the same thing as an increase in security prices.
T (F)   9. A treasury bill is legislation required to change reserve requirements.
T F   10. Under the discounting procedures of the Federal Reserves System, the Federal Reserve Banks have no choice but to lend whatever amounts the member banks want to borrow at the existing discount rate.
T F   11. The discounting procedure involves a hidden subsidy to commercial banks whenever the treasury bill rate is less than the discount rate.

Multiple-Choice Questions

1. The most commonly used tool of monetary policy is
   (a) Open market operations
   (b) Changes in reserve requirements
   (c) Moral suasion
   (d) Selective credit controls

2. An open market sale by the Fed of $800 million paid for out of someone's checking account will cause
   (a) Bank reserves to increase by as much as $800 million

   (b) Bank reserves to decrease by as much as $800 million
   (c) Excess bank reserves to decrease as much as $800 million
   (d) (a) or (b) depending upon how it affects interest rates

3. If the Fed undertakes an open market purchase and the seller of the security is a commercial bank, then
   (a) Bank reserves will increase by as much as if the

seller had been a private corporation that holds no currency

(b) Bank reserves will increase by less than if the seller had been a private corporation that holds no currency

(c) Excess reserves will change by less than if the seller had been a private corporation that holds no currency

(d) Excess reserves will be unaffected

4. A sudden increase in required reserve ratios, unaccompanied by an expansion of bank reserves, will lead to

(a) An increase in interest rates and in the supply of money

(b) An increase in interest rates but a decrease in the supply of money

(c) A decrease in interest rates and a decrease in the supply of money

(d) A decrease in interest rates but an increase in the supply of money

5. The voting membership of the Federal Open Market Committee consists of

(a) All Federal Reserve Board members and all Federal Reserve Bank presidents

(b) All Federal Reserve Board members and some Federal Reserve Bank presidents

(c) Some Federal Reserve Board members and all Federal Reserve Bank presidents

(d) Some Federal Reserve Board members and some Federal Reserve Bank presidents

6. The Federal Reserve Board has how many members?

(a) 5   (c) 9

(b) 7   (d) 12

7. When the discount rate falls below the treasury bill rate, some commercial banks will be tempted to

(a) Increase their holdings of excess reserves

(b) Sell their treasury bills in order to pay off their loans from the Fed

(c) Call in loans in order to lend to the Fed

(d) Borrow from the Fed to buy treasury bills

8. The discounting procedure of the Fed is said to create "slippage" in the effects of open market operations because

(a) The discount rate is slipped up too often

(b) The Fed does not grant enough loans to commercial banks when it is selling securities

(c) The Fed allows the commercial banks to replenish their reserves by discounting when it is undertaking restrictive open market operations

(d) The Fed is prevented by law from imposing margin requirements on security purchases

9. In 1936 and 1937 reserve requirements were raised drastically. This action

(a) Promoted a recovery from the Great Depression

(b) Halted the recovery from the Great Depression

(c) Had little effect on the recovery because this tool of monetary policy is not very potent

(d) Would have promoted the recovery if only it had been accompanied by open market sales of treasury bills

10. If a 90-day $100,000 treasury bill sells for $99,000, then the annual interest rate is approximately

(a) 1 percent   (c) 10 percent

(b) 4 percent   (d) 12 percent

11. If a $100 bond which reaches maturity in 2 years pays an annual coupon of $10, then its market price is

(a) More than 100 dollars if the rate of interest exceeds 10 percent

(b) Less than 100 dollars if the rate of interest exceeds 10 percent

(c) Equal to 100 dollars if the rate of interest exceeds 10 percent

(d) Always 100 dollars because its rate of interest by definition always equals 10 percent

12. Which of the following is an example of the Fed's use of "moral suasion"?

(a) Threatening not to grant a license for opening a foreign branch to a bank which makes loans that the Fed does not wish to see made

(b) Persuading buyers in the treasury bill market to part with their securities at the market price

(c) Persuading Congress that the Fed is pursuing good policies

(d) Raising reserve requirements

13. The U.S. dollar is "backed" by

(a) Silver

(b) Gold

(c) The Fed's commitment to prevent the supply from growing

(d) None of the above

14. The gold standard

(a) Reduces the ability of a central bank to pursue an independent monetary policy

(b) Has been strengthened considerably in recent years

(c) Was never used by the United States

(d) Contributes to economic stability if there are unpredictable changes in the flow of gold in and out of the banking system

Exercises

1. Suppose the required reserve ratio on all deposits is 20 percent.

   A. In balance sheets A, show the initial effects of an open market purchase of $10 million of securities by the Fed where the seller is a corporation that deposits the proceeds of the

sale immediately with its bank, which keeps the funds in the form of a deposit with the Fed.

   B. In balance sheets B, show the ultimate effects of the above transaction, assuming that the deposit expansion process continues up to its maximum limit given by the deposit multiplier. Assume that each bank in the process holds all its extra reserves in the form of deposits with the Fed.

C. In balance sheets C, show the initial effects of a decrease in the required reserve ratio from 20 percent to 10 percent, assuming that the banks originally had $100 billion in re-

serves and no excess reserves.

D. In balance sheets D, show the ultimate effects of the change in C, assuming that the deposit creation process continues up to the limit determined by the deposit multiplier and assuming that all reserves continue to be held in the same form as before.

BALANCE SHEETS A

Federal Reserve System		All commercial banks	
Federal government securities _____	Federal Reserve notes _____	Loans _____	Deposits _____
		Total reserves _____	
	Deposits of member banks _____	Required reserves _____	
	Net worth _____	Excess reserves _____	

BALANCE SHEETS B

Federal Reserve System		All commercial banks	
Federal government securities _____	Federal Reserve notes _____	Loans _____	Deposits _____
		Total reserves _____	
	Deposits of member banks _____	Required reserves _____	
	Net worth _____	Excess reserves _____	

BALANCE SHEETS C

Federal Reserve System		All commercial banks	
Federal government securities _____	Federal Reserve notes _____	Loans _____	Deposits _____
		Total reserves _____	
	Deposits of member banks _____	Required reserves _____	
	Net worth _____	Excess reserves _____	

BALANCE SHEETS D

Federal Reserve System			All commercial banks			
Federal government securities _____	Federal Reserve notes _____		Loans _____		Deposits _____	
			Total reserves _____			
	Deposits of member banks _____		Required reserves _____			
	Net worth _____		Excess reserves _____			

2. (This exercise is only for those who have studied Box 11-1.) Consider a $100 bond with an annual coupon of $10. In the table below, fill in the price of the bond under the different assumptions concerning the term to maturity and the rate of interest.

TERM TO MATURITY

Rate of interest	1 year	2 years	Perpetuity
8%	_____	_____	_____
10%	_____	_____	_____
12%	_____	_____	_____

What general proposition is suggested by this example concerning the relationship between (a) the term to maturity of the bond and (b) the size of the effect upon the price of the bond of a change in the rate of interest?

_____
_____
_____
_____.

Essay Questions

1. Suppose that a bank has invested most of its assets in long-term securities that yield a rate of interest just slightly above the rate of interest that the bank is paying on its savings and time deposits. What sort of trouble will the bank run into if other banks now begin offering higher interest rates on their savings and time deposits? Explain how the discounting procedure of the Federal Reserve System would come in handy in this event.

2. The discounting procedure was referred to in the text as a source of "slippage" in open market operations. Name two other potential sources of such slippage, explaining in each case why slippage might occur. (Hint: the answer is in Chapter 10.)

3. Show by means of an example how, if you buy shares on a 50-percent margin, your losses will be increased by 100 percent if prices fall and your gains will be increased by 100 percent if they rise. (Ignore brokerage fees and interest charges.)

4. What are the pros and cons of having a discount rate that fluctuates automatically with the rate of interest on treasury bills, as is the case in some countries?

5. What would the pros and cons be of having the chairman of the Fed appointed for a 14-year term rather than a 4-year term?

6. One of the drawbacks of using fiscal policy to affect aggregate demand is that a change in taxes or in government spending usually requires congressional approval, which may take a long time to obtain. Are the three major instruments of monetary policy also subject to this drawback?

*7. Open market purchase of government securities by the Fed affects bank reserves, interest rates, and the money supply. Explain how each of these individually would affect the level of aggregate demand in the economy.

*8. Some people have suggested that the Fed should pay interest on commercial bank reserves. How would this affect the profits of the commercial banks? The profits of the Federal Reserve System? How do you think this might affect the overall size of the money supply? If the rate of interest on reserves were set equal to the discount rate, would member banks be likely to hold treasury bills? If they did, what could you infer about the "hidden subsidy" discussed in this chapter?

*9. "Holding money is not as risky as holding bonds, because interest rates may change." Do you agree? Explain.

Answers

True-False Questions: 1 F 2 T 3 F 4 F 5 T 6 F 7 T 8 F 9 F 10 F 11 F
Multiple-Choice Questions: 1 a 2 b 3 a 4 b 5 b 6 b 7 d 8 c 9 b 10 b 11 b 12 a 13 d 14 a
Exercises:
1.

BALANCE SHEETS A

Federal Reserve System			All commercial banks		
	Federal Reserve notes	0	Loans	0	Deposits $10 million
			Total reserves	$10 million	
Federal government securities $10 million					
	Deposits of member banks $10 million		Required reserves $ 2 million		
	Net worth	0	Excess reserves $ 8 million		

BALANCE SHEETS B

Federal Reserve System			All commercial banks		
	Federal Reserve notes	0	Loans	$40 million	Deposits $50 million
			Total reserves	$10 million	
Federal government securities $10 million					
	Deposits of member banks $10 million		Required reserves $10 million		
	Net worth	0	Excess reserves	0	

BALANCE SHEETS C

Federal Reserve System			All commercial banks		
	Federal Reserve notes	0	Loans	0	Deposits 0
			Total reserves	0	
Federal government securities 0					
	Deposits of member banks	0	Required reserves −$50 billion		
	Net worth	0	Excess reserves +$50 billion		

BALANCE SHEETS D

Federal Reserve System				All commercial banks			
		Federal Reserve notes	0	Loans	$500 billion		
Federal government securities	0			Total reserves	0	Deposits $500 billion	
		Deposits of member banks	0	Required reserves	0		
		Net worth	0	Excess reserves	0		

2. Table 11-1

Rate of interest	1 year	2 years	Perpetuity
8%	$101.85	$103.57	$125.00
10%	$100.00	$100.00	$100.00
12%	$ 98.21	$ 96.62	$ 83.33

The longer the term to maturity the greater the change in the price of the bond for any change in the interest rate.

PART THREE

GREAT MACROECONOMIC QUESTIONS OF OUR TIME

CHAPTER 12
Monetary Policy and Fiscal Policy:
Which is the Key to Aggregate Demand?

Learning Objectives

After you have studied this chapter in the textbook and the study guide, you should be able to

Identify the links in the chain of events connecting changes in the money supply to changes in aggregate demand (according to the Keynesian view of monetary policy)

Explain how, according to the Keynesian point of view, the rate of interest adjusts so as to equilibrate the supply and demand for money

Describe how the MEI schedule is constructed, and why it is the same thing as the investment-demand schedule

State two major reasons why, according to the Keynesian view, monetary policy may be ineffective

Explain why monetary policy may be more effective in reducing aggregate demand than in increasing it

Explain the chain of events that occurs, according to the monetarist view, when the supply of money exceeds the demand for money (and when the demand for money exceeds the supply of money)

Explain the key propositions of monetarism

Describe how *crowding out* may occur

Explain why it is difficult to settle the Keynesian-monetarist controversy by looking at the facts

State the advantages of the "eclectic" policy of using both monetary and fiscal policy

Explain how the wrong mix of monetary and fiscal policy could reduce the rate of economic growth

CHAPTER HIGHLIGHTS

The controversy studied in this chapter involves the relative strengths of monetary and fiscal policy. On this issue there are two extreme positions (although most economists take an intermediate position between these extremes). One position—which we may call strong Keynesian—maintains that fiscal policy is very important in determining aggregate demand, while monetary policy has little or no effect. The other extreme position—strong monetarism—maintains just the opposite. The chapter is organized around five issues concerning this controversy: (1) the Keynesian view of how monetary policy works (or doesn't work), (2) the monetarist view of how monetary policy works, (3) the monetarist argument that fiscal policy has little effect on aggregate demand, (4) the statistical evidence on the controversy, and (5) the "eclectic" case for using both fiscal and monetary policies.

The Keynesian View of Monetary Policy

According to the Keynesian view, there are three links in the chain of events whereby an open market purchase of securities by the Fed affects aggregate demand. First, the purchase causes interest rates to fall, as discussed in Chapter 11. Second, the lower interest rates induce business firms to plan more investment projects. Third, this increase in investment demand has multiplied effects on the level of aggregate demand as explained in Chapter 8. An open market sale sets off the same chain of events, but with all effects going in the opposite direction.

This chapter goes beyond Chapter 11 in analyzing the first link. The analysis focuses upon the amount of money that people wish to hold; that is, the demand for money. Figure 12-2 in the textbook shows how the demand for money depends upon the rate of interest. The rate of interest measures the opportunity cost of holding wealth in the form of money, rather than in the form of an interest-bearing bond. When the rate of interest falls, the cost of holding money falls, so people are willing to hold a larger quantity. This is reflected in the downward slope of the demand curve in Figure 12-2.

Equilibrium occurs at a rate of interest where the demand for money just equals the supply. But if the supply of money is increased, as for example, through an open market purchase by the Fed, then at the previous equilibrium rate of interest there will now be an excess supply; some people will be holding more money than they wish to at that rate of interest. Their efforts to get rid of this excess supply by purchasing more bonds will drive up the price of bonds. This automatically drives down the rate of interest. The fall in the rate of interest reduces the excess supply of money, by increasing the amount that people are willing to hold (moving down the demand curve). Thus, the rate of interest continues to fall until the excess supply is eliminated.

The second link is also examined in this chapter. Business firms will undertake investment projects as long as the rate of return on such projects is at least as great as the rate of interest. The rate of return may be calculated provided that you know (1) the initial cost of the project, (2) the lifetime of the project, (3) the contribution of the project to annual sales during its lifetime, and (4) the annual operating costs of the project. Given this information on all the potential investment projects in the economy, an economist can construct a schedule showing for every rate of return how much investment can take place until the next best project yields just that rate of return. This is called the *marginal efficiency of investment* (MEI) schedule. It is also the investment-demand schedule, for if the rate of interest is plotted on the vertical axis, then the horizontal distance to the MEI schedule shows how much investment will yield at least that high a rate of return, and will thus be worth undertaking.

According to the Keynesian view, there are two major reasons why monetary policy may be ineffective. (1) The rate of interest may not fall much in the first link, especially if it is already low. Figure 12-5 in the text shows the extreme situation of the liquidity trap, where the rate of interest doesn't fall at all, because of a horizontal money-demand curve. (2) If the MEI schedule is steep, then a change in the rate of interest will have only a weak effect on desired investment in the second link. This second argument is subject to two criticisms: (a) It is difficult to measure the degree of responsiveness of investment demand to the rate of interest. (b) When interest rates rise, this may have a large effect on investment demand even with a steep MEI schedule. This is because bankers may ration credit, in order to limit loans, thus forcing firms to curtail their investment plans for lack of finance (forcing firms off the MEI schedule as in Figure 12-7 in the textbook).

There are three reasons why the effects of monetary policy may be asymmetrical; that is, why restrictive policy may work more strongly than expansive policy.

1. The rate of interest cannot be driven below zero, but there is no limit to how high it can be forced.

2. Banks are forced to reduce their lending when their reserves fall below the required amount. But, no matter how many excess reserves they have, they cannot be forced to expand their lending if they are not inclined to do so.

3. Through credit rationing, banks can force business firms to borrow less than they want. But no one can force them to borrow more.

The Monetarist View of Monetary Policy

The monetarist view can be expressed in terms of the *equation of exchange*: $MV = PQ$. (See important terms below.) This equation must hold true because of the way V is defined. But monetarists then add the proposition that V is stable. Underlying this proposition is a theory involving the demand for money. Suppose that people always wish to hold the fraction $(1/V)$ of their annual income (PQ) in the form of money. If they all find themselves holding more than this, everybody will try to run down excess cash holdings by buying other assets, goods, and services. But one person's expenditure is another's receipts. The excess cash is a "hot potato" that gets passed around. The attempt to get rid of this excess cash stimulates aggregate demand, which will raise P and/or Q. This will continue until people's nominal incomes have risen to the point where they no longer regard their cash holdings as excessive; in other words, until $M = (1/V)PQ$, which is just a rewritten version of the equation of exchange. (Study Figure 12-8 in the text and the surrounding discussion. Then, as an exercise, restate the argument, starting from the situation in which people find themselves holding less money than they wish.)

Five key propositions of monetarism are:

1. The money supply is the most important variable in determining the level of aggregate demand.

2. In the long run, the *real* level of national output, Q, tends toward its full-employment level independently of monetary factors, so that the only long-run effect of a change in M is a change in P.

3. The short-run effect of a change in M is a change in *both* P and Q.

4. If M is stable, then aggregate demand will also be reasonably stable.

5. Therefore, the Fed should aim at keeping a steady rate of growth of M (say, 4 percent) rather than try to vary M in an effort to smooth out the business cycle.

The Monetarist View of Fiscal Policy

Monetarists' reservations concerning fiscal policy are expressed in the notion of "crowding out." When the government spends more or cuts taxes, it normally finances the resulting deficit by borrowing from the public. (If it borrows from the Fed, then the money stock will rise, and a monetarist would consider this monetary policy, not fiscal policy.) The increase in the demand for borrowing tends to raise interest rates, which, as in the Keynesian view of monetary policy, tends to reduce investment demand. How much crowding out occurs depends upon the responsiveness of investment demand to changes in interest rates.

The Evidence

The main statistical evidence consists of studies that measure how closely aggregate demand moves together with monetary or fiscal variables. These studies have generally shown that aggregate demand and the money supply are much more closely related than are aggregate demand and various measures of fiscal policy. However, as Keynesians are quick to point out, when A (the quantity of money) and B (aggregate demand) move together, this does not prove that A *causes* B. Increases in aggregate demand may induce business firms to take out more bank loans, thus causing the money supply to expand. In other words, changes in aggregate demand may be causing changes in the money supply, rather than the reverse. Indeed, there are two more possibilities: that the relationship is purely coincidental (not likely, given the frequency with which it has been observed), or both aggregate demand and the money supply may be influenced by some third variable.

Another kind of evidence involves specific historical episodes. A case in point is the 1968 temporary tax surcharge, which failed to have the restrictive effect predicted by Keynesians at the time. Historical episodes may be cited which undercut either extreme position, whether Keynesian or monetarist.

The Case for Both Monetary and Fiscal Policy

The "eclectic" case can be built around four major points:

1. When we know as little as we do about how the economic system operates, it makes sense to diversify—use some of each kind of policy—rather than putting all our eggs into one policy basket.

2. When any particular policy is relied upon exclusively to restrain aggregate demand, some groups inevitably will be hurt more than others by the necessary cutbacks. Using a combination of restrictive policies is one way of "spreading the pain."

3. Relying exclusively upon fiscal policy to promote expansion may be unwise because government programs that are initially seen as "temporary" have a way of becoming permanent.

4. On the other hand, some economists feel that relying exclusively upon monetary policy to promote expansion may be ineffective because of the above-mentioned asymmetry.

A major problem arises because of the mix of

monetary and fiscal policies adopted. The Fed may be biased toward restrictive monetary policies that reduce investment demand, while the government may be biased toward expansive fiscal policies, which further reduce investment demand. As a result of these two biases, there may be a low rate of investment, and consequently a low rate of growth.

IMPORTANT TERMS

Keynesian The label attached to economists whose analytic framework derives from Keynes' *General Theory*. These economists generally stress the importance of fiscal policy.

Monetarist The label attached to economists who stress the importance of monetary rather than fiscal policy as a determinant of aggregate demand.

Transactions demand for money The willingness of people to hold money because it will be needed to make purchases. This demand depends primarily on the size of national income.

Speculative demand for money The willingness of people to hold money rather than bonds, because they fear that bond prices may fall. This demand depends primarily upon the rate of interest.

Liquidity preference Another term for the demand for money.

Liquidity trap A situation where the money-demand curve is horizontal. An increase in the supply of money results in no change in the rate of interest and thus no change in aggregate demand.

Marginal efficiency of investment (MEI) The schedule or curve that shows the amounts of investment which are expected to yield various rates of return. This represents a demand schedule or curve for investment.

Credit rationing A situation in which bankers restrict the amount that they will lend to their customers, even when these customers are creditworthy and would like to borrow more at the going rates of interest.

Income velocity of money The number of times that the average dollar is used during the year to purchase final output.

Equation of exchange The equation $MV = PQ$, where M denotes the supply of money, V denotes the income velocity of money, P denotes the price level, and Q denotes the level of real output in the economy during the year. V is defined as being equal to PQ/M, therefore, the equation of exchange is a tautology.

Tautology A statement that is true by definition, such as the statement that older people are not so young as younger people.

Crowding out The effect of expansive fiscal policy in reducing the level of investment demand by causing interest rates to rise.

Pure fiscal policy A fiscal policy that leaves the supply of money unaffected. (In other words, changes in taxes or government spending are reflected in changes in the publicly held government debt, and not in changes in the quantity of money.)

True-False Questions

T F 1. Milton Friedman is usually identified as one of the leading monetarists.

T F 2. According to the Keynesian view of monetary policy, an open market purchase of securities by the Fed will usually cause an increase in investment demand.

T F 3. If the demand for investment goods were completely unresponsive to changes in the rate of interest, then the marginal efficiency of investment schedule would be vertical.

T F 4. According to the monetarist view, fiscal policy is less effective the less responsive is the demand for investment goods to changes in the rate of interest.

T F 5. If credit is rationed, business firms may be forced off the marginal efficiency of investment schedule.

T F 6. The transactions demand for money depends primarily upon the rate of interest.

T F 7. The equation of exchange may be regarded as a tautology because of the way velocity is defined.

T F 8. Monetarists are more inclined than Keynesians to believe that the free market system is inherently stable.

T F 9. If the supply of money exceeds the demand for money, then nominal income is likely to fall.

T F 10. A combination of expansive fiscal policy and restrictive monetary policy tends to restrain the rate of economic growth.

Multiple-Choice Questions

1. Which of the following is *not* one of the three major links in the chain of events connecting an increase in the money supply to an increase in aggregate demand according to the Keynesian view?

(a) The increase in the quantity of money causes the rate of interest to fall

(b) An increase in the demand for investment causes the national product to rise

(c) A change in the rate of interest crowds out private expenditures

(d) A change in the rate of interest causes the demand for investment goods to increase

2. According to the Keynesian view, an open market purchase of securities by the Fed will lead to

(a) An increase in the rate of interest and in the level of national product

(b) An increase in the rate of interest but a decrease in national product

(c) A decrease in both interest and national product

(d) A decrease in interest but an increase in national product

3. Which of the following is most likely to decrease as a result of an expansive monetary policy?

(a) National product

(b) The quantity of money demanded

(c) The marginal efficiency of investment

(d) Consumption expenditures

4. Which of the following views do you think is *least* likely to be held by a monetarist?

(a) In the long run, the level of real output tends toward its full-employment amount

(b) The Federal Reserve should vary the rate of growth of the money supply frequently, so as to stabilize aggregate demand

(c) In the long run, changes in the money supply cause proportional changes in prices

(d) In the short run, the money supply is the most important single variable in determining aggregate demand.

5. The income velocity of money

(a) Is defined by the equation of exchange in such a way that it must always be constant

(b) Is believed by Keynesians to be approximately constant

(c) Will be stable if the demand for investment goods is stable

(d) Will decrease when the Fed undertakes open market purchases of securities if the economy is in a liquidity trap

6. According to monetarists, an increase in M will ultimately cause a proportional change in

(a) V

(b) Q

(c) P

(d) $P \times Q$, but the separate effects on P and Q in the long run cannot be predicted with accuracy

7. If some, but not all, of the effect of a cut in taxes is offset through "crowding out," then the cut will lead to

(a) An increase in the rate of interest and in the level of national product

(b) An increase in the rate of interest but a decrease in national product

(c) A decrease in both interest and national product

(d) A decrease in interest but an increase in national product

8. The effects of the 1968 tax surcharge in the United States

(a) Were generally regarded as having confirmed the strong Keynesian view of macroeconomics

(b) Did not produce any decisive evidence, because both monetary and fiscal policy were restrictive at the same time

(c) Were inconsistent with the predictions of strong Keynesians

(d) Involved a smaller decline in aggregate demand than expected by monetarists

9. From the empirical evidence alone we can say that

(a) Aggregate demand is much more closely related to monetary variables than to fiscal variables

(b) Changes in the money supply cause changes in aggregate demand

(c) Changes in aggregate demand cause changes in the money supply

(d) All of the above

10. Which of the following is *not* a point in favor of an "eclectic" policy of using both monetary and fiscal policy?

(a) For institutional reasons there tends to be an expansionary bias to both fiscal and monetary policy

(b) In reality, there is much we don't know about the detailed workings of the economic system

(c) Temporary government programs tend to become permanent

(d) When restrictive policies are called for, the government should try to "spread the pain"

11. If the government simultaneously undertakes an expansive monetary policy and a restrictive fiscal policy, then we can be fairly sure that

(a) The rate of interest will rise

(b) The rate of interest will fall

(c) The level of real output will rise

(d) The level of real output will fall

12. If the government wants to increase the level of real output but leave the rate of interest unaffected, then the only one of the following combinations that can accomplish this goal is

(a) Expansionary monetary policy and expansionary fiscal policy

(b) Expansionary monetary policy and restrictive fiscal policy

(c) Restrictive monetary policy and expansionary fiscal policy

(d) Restrictive monetary policy and restrictive fiscal policy

Exercises

1. In Figure 12-1, the demand curve for money is AB. When the supply of money is OC the equilibrium rate of interest is _____. If the supply of money were now increased to OD, then at the previous equilibrium rate of interest there would now be an excess (demand for, supply of) money.

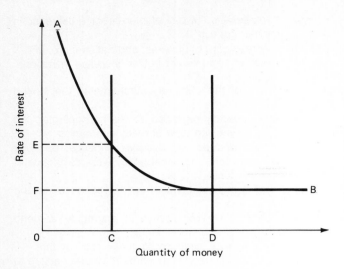

FIGURE 12-1

This would cause bond prices to (rise, fall), which would be reflected in (an increase, a decrease) in the rate of interest. The new equilibrium rate of interest would be _____. If the money supply were increased again beyond OD, the equilibrium rate of interest would (rise, fall, remain unchanged), because the economy would be in a _____.

2a. In Figure 12-2 below, the curves labeled A and B denote two different MEI schedules. Of the two, curve (A, B) is the one in which the demand for investment is least responsive to the rate of interest. According to curve A, when the rate of interest is 10 percent the demand for investment is _____ and when the rate of interest is 5 percent the demand for investment is _____. According to curve B, when the rate of interest is 10 percent the demand for investment is _____ and when the rate of interest is 5 percent the demand for investment is _____. If two economies, A and B, are identical in every respect except that the MEI schedule is given by curve A in economy A and by curve B in economy B, then monetary policy is stronger in economy (A, B), and fiscal policy is stronger in economy (A, B).

2b. Figure 12-3 shows the 45-degree line and the line indicating consumption demand plus government demand for goods and services. In this economy, the multiplier has a value of _____. (Refer back to Chapter 9 if you have trouble). Draw a line indicating total aggregate demand $(C + I + G)$ in economy A, assuming a rate of interest of 10 percent. Do the same assuming a rate of interest of 5 percent. Do the same for economy B, first assuming 10 percent, then 5 percent

2c. If open market purchases by the central bank caused the rate of interest to fall from 10 percent to 5 percent, then the increase in national product in economy A would be _____ and in economy B it would be _____. If government demand for goods and services rose by 150 and the rate of interest remained unaffected by this change, then national product would rise in economy A by _____ and in economy B by _____. But if that increase in government demand caused the rate of interest to rise from 5 percent to 10 percent, then the overall effect of the fiscal policy measure would be to make national product rise by _____ in economy A and by _____ in economy B.

FIGURE 12-2

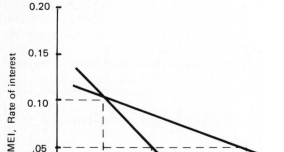
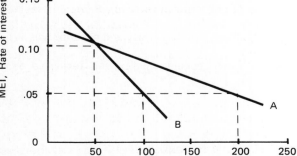

FIGURE 12-3

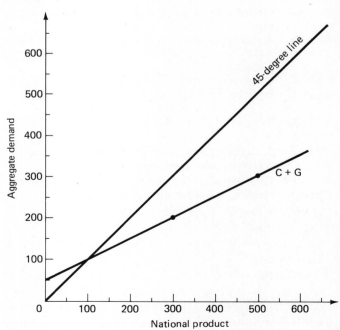

3. Table 12-1 below lists the pertinent data on different investment projects, starting with the most profitable project, *A*, and going down to the least profitable project, *D*. Calculate the marginal efficiency of investment schedule in Table 12-2. (Study footnote 2 of Chapter 12 in the textbook before attempting this question.)

Table 12-1

	Initial cost*	Lifetime of project	Annual* additions to sales	Annual* operating cost	Scrap* value
Project *A*	50	Infinite	20	5	—
Project *B*	25	17 years	6	1	25
Project *C*	15	2 years	7	1	5.55
Project *D*	10	1 year	8	4.5	7

*These data are all expressed as millions of dollars.

Table 12-2

Marginal efficiency of investment (percent per annum)	Quantity of investment (millions of dollars)
_____ 30% 15/50	50
_____ 20% 5/25	75
_____	90
_____	100

Essay Questions

1. Recall the reasons given in the text why monetary policy may have asymmetrical effects. Can you think of a reason why the policy of changing income taxes to affect aggregate demand may also have asymmetrical effects?

2. Evaluate the following statement: "The equation of exchange is completely useless because it is a mere tautology."

3. In the text it was argued that the existence of credit rationing might make monetary policy more powerful. Can you think of any reasons why the existence of credit rationing might similarly alter the effectiveness of fiscal policy?

4. See how many different groups you can identify that would gain more than the average if the government were to undertake an expansive fiscal policy. Which groups would gain the least, or perhaps even lose? Do the same thing for an expansive monetary policy.

5. Economists should keep their political beliefs out of scientific discussions. But this is often difficult when it comes to policy questions. In fact, it is often easy to predict an economist's political beliefs by reading his or her analysis of economic policy. If you were to read two articles on economic policy, one advocating Keynesian policies and the other advocating monetarist policies, which author would you think the more likely to hold the view that the government is interfering too much in private economic affairs? Why?

6. Recall the difficulties standing in the way of getting a precise measure of the responsiveness of the demand for investment goods to changes in the rate of interest. Can you think of similar reasons why it might be difficult to measure the responsiveness of the demand for money to changes in the rate of interest? How would you go about trying to identify this degree of responsiveness?

7. Why might a monetarist be more likely than a Keynesian to believe that the MEI schedule is relatively flat?

*8. The opposite of a liquidity trap would be a situation in which the rate of interest had no effect at all upon the demand for money. Would such a situation be more compatible with monetarist theory or Keynesian theory? Why?

Answers

True-False Questions: 1 T 2 T 3 T 4 F 5 T 6 F 7 T 8 T 9 F 10 T
Multiple-Choice Questions: 1 c 2 d 3 c 4 b 5 d 6 c 7 a 8 c 9 a 10 a 11 b 12 a
Exercises:

1. *OE;* supply of; rise; a decrease; *OF;* remain unchanged; liquidity trap

2. Figure 12-3 completed:

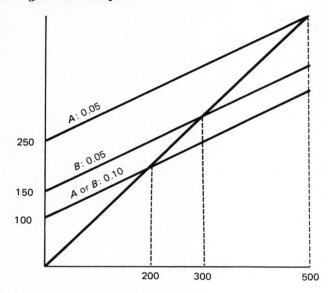

a *B*, 50, 200, 50, 100, *A*, *B*

b 2

c 300, 100, 300, 300, 0, 200

3. Table 12-2

Marginal efficiency of investment (percent per annum)	Quantity of investment (millions of dollars)
30%	50
20%	75
10%	90
5%	100

CHAPTER 13
Aggregate Supply:
How Can Inflation and Unemployment Coexist?

Learning Objectives

After you have studied this chapter in the textbook and the study guide, you should be able to

Explain why the Kennedy-Johnson wage-price guideposts broke down

Present the cases for and against using incomes policies to restrain wage and price increases

Explain why the Phillips curve has shifted up since the late 1960s, according to cost-push theories

Explain why the Phillips curve has shifted up since the late 1960s, according to the accelerationist theory

Describe the differences and similarities between cost-push theories and the Phelps-Friedman theory

Explain the difference between the Phelps-Friedman theory and the theory of Eckstein and Brinner

Show in a Phillips-curve diagram (like Figure 13-13 in the textbook) how a stable aggregate demand promotes a low average rate of unemployment

Explain the arguments both for and against using incomes policies to ease the transition to a lower rate of inflation

Describe three proposals for reducing the natural rate of unemployment

CHAPTER HIGHLIGHTS

This chapter deals with the problems of inflation and unemployment. It covers the following topics: (1) the Phillips curve, (2) wage-price guideposts, (3) cost-push theories of inflation, (4) accelerationist theories of inflation, and (5) major policy issues posed by the problems of inflation and unemployment.

The Phillips Curve

The Keynesian macroeconomics of Part 2 assumed an L-shaped aggregate supply curve (Figure 13-1 in the textbook). According to this view, there can be large-scale unemployment (when aggregate demand is low) or inflation (when aggregate demand is high), but not both. However, the facts do not fit this simple L-shaped function. Indeed, the observations for the past three decades, as shown in Figure 13-3 in the textbook, don't seem to fit any simple pattern. The data for the 1960s do suggest a negative relationship between inflation and unemployment. Such a relationship, as pictured in Figure 13-5 in the textbook, is called a Phillips curve. According to the Phillips curve, high unemployment leads to low inflation. However, the data for the 1970s do *not* seen consistent with a Phillips curve. During this period we had both high unemployment and high inflation.

Wage-Price Guideposts

The Phillips curve suggests that an expansive aggregate demand policy, aimed at reducing the rate of unemployment, would also cause inflation. In order to avoid this side effect, the Kennedy-Johnson administration introduced wage-price guideposts. Specifically, they proposed that (1) prices should not be raised on average, and (2) money wages should not rise by more than the increase in labor productivity in the economy as a whole, estimated in the early 1960s to be 3.2 percent per annum.

These guideposts eventually broke down. Powerful unions in such industries as airlines and construction were able to get wage increases greater than 3.2 percent. And as demand increased, businesses raised their average prices. After inflation started growing it was difficult to persuade workers to accept wage increases within the guideposts when that would result in little or no increase in their real wages.

There are a number of arguments against the use of incomes policies (guideposts and wage-price controls) to restrain wage and price increases:

1. The effectiveness of guideposts may be questioned. In particular, they may put a floor rather than a ceiling on wage increases because any self-respecting union will aim to get at least as much as the guideposts allow.

2. If such policies are effective in restraining prices, they will create excess demands (shortages) of particular goods.

3. Controls infringe upon personal freedom.

4. It is hard to operate an incomes policy equitably. Wage income tends to be easier to control than profits or interest, so labor unions often complain that guideposts and controls discriminate against them. The main argument in favor of incomes policies is that they offer the only hope of achieving both high employment and stable prices.

Cost-Push Theories

An increase in demand-pull inflation is a movement upward to the left along a given Phillips curve, whereas cost-push inflation involves an upward shift of the Phillips curve. As Figure 13-4 in the textbook illustrates, the Phillips curve has shifted upward since the late 1960s. This has given support to cost-push theories, most of which emphasize the dramatic increases in world oil prices in 1973–1974 and in 1979–1980. According to cost-push theories, these increases raised costs, which firms passed on in the form of higher prices. Faced with a higher cost of living, labor unions bargained for higher wages, which pushed the Phillips curve up even further.

Accelerationist Theory

The accelerationist theory of Phelps and Friedman offers a different explanation for this upward shift. It makes the bold claim that the Phillips curve is not even a stable relationship in the long run. To understand this theory, suppose first that the economy has experienced several years of stable prices, and has attained an equilibrium at point G in Figure 13-8 in the textbook. This equilibrium involves a rate of unemployment that could be maintained as long as the government prevents increases in aggregate demand that could cause prices to rise. Wages will be increasing, but this does not disturb the equilibrium as long as productivity is increasing at the same rate.

Now suppose that aggregate demand is increased. In the short run, national output will increase and unemployment will decrease, say to U_T in Figure 13-8. The increase in demand will cause prices to rise at first, moving up to point H on the Phillips curve. But this situation is not stable. The Phillips curve PC_1 reflects wage contracts that were negotiated with the expectation of stable prices. When workers see that prices are actually rising at 2 percent, they will bargain for larger wage increases to catch up with the cost of living. Firms faced with a strong demand for output will settle for higher wage increases, which they will pass on in the form of higher price increases; hence a further increase in inflation. In Figure 13-10, the Phillips curve will shift up to PC_2, reflecting the new contracts negotiated with the expectation of 2 percent inflation. If unemployment remains at U_T this further increase in inflation above 2 percent will cause workers' real wages again to fall short of what they had expected. Thus, they will bargain for still higher wage increases, causing the Phillips curve to shift up again. Thus, as long as aggregate demand keeps rising by enough to keep unemployment at U_T, the Phillips curve will continue to shift up, and inflation will accelerate.

Is there any end to this upward spiral? Yes, but only if the growth in aggregate demand is restrained, so that unemployment increases. For example, suppose that at point H the government were to adopt restrictive policies that cause unemployment to increase back to where it was initially at G. Then the upward shift in the Phillips curve, from PC_1 to PC_2, would permit inflation to remain at 2 percent. The economy would move directly to the right to point N.

The most important implication of the Phelps-Friedman theory is that the long-run Phillips curve is vertical, at the natural rate of unemployment (the rate at G). For example, consider point N. The rate of unemployment, the real wage rate, and all other real variables are the same as they were at G. Prices are rising 2 percent faster at G than N, but in the long run firms and workers both will realize this, and they will negotiate for wages that also rise 2 percent faster. *Real* wages will thus grow at the same rate as they would at G; that is, at the same rate as productivity.

Since all *real* variables will thus be the same at N as they would at the original equilibrium G, then N must also be in a position of equilibrium. Likewise, any point involving the natural rate of unemployment (for example, R or T) is an equilibrium. Joining all these points gives us a long-run Phillips curve that is *vertical*. In long-run equilibrium there can be any rate of inflation, but only one rate of unemployment—the natural rate. If the government were to try keeping unemployment below the natural rate, we have seen how inflation would be higher than expected, causing the short-run Phillips curve to shift up and inflation to accelerate indefinitely. Likewise, a permanently higher rate of unemployment would cause ever-accelerating deflation.

The accelerationist theory is similar to the cost-push theory, because both attempt to explain the upward shift in the Phillips curve. However, they are different because (1) the cost-push theory stresses the role of market power of big unions and corporations, whereas the accelerationist theory stresses the lagged response of worker's expectations; and (2) incomes policies help to control inflation by restraining market power according to cost-push theory, but attack the symptoms rather than

the causes of inflation according to accelerationist theory.

The theory of Eckstein and Brinner is similar in some respects to the Phelps-Friedman theory. The Eckstein-Brinner theory maintains that the long-run Phillips curve is vertical for rates of inflation above 2 or 3 percent, but negatively sloped for lower rates. The key to this theory is the assumption of downward wage rigidity. At any one time, some workers' wages will be falling behind others. Such changes in relative wages are an important part of the market mechanism in an ever-changing economy. At a high rate of inflation (2 or 3 percent or more), this can happen without anyone's money wage having to fall. Workers in industry A may find their wages rising at 8 percent while wages in industry B are rising at 3 percent. The B workers are falling behind, but their money wages are still rising. But at a low rate of inflation this change in relative wages might require, for example, that the wages of A workers rise at 3 percent and the wages of B workers *fall* by 2 percent. If the B workers resist any decline in their nominal wages, then unemployment will result in their industry.

Major Policy Issues

The first major issue is how to maintain a stable aggregate demand. Fluctuations in aggregate demand increase the average rate of unemployment. This is because when inflation rises, the accompanying decrease in unemployment is less than the increase in unemployment that accompanies an equal-size fall in the rate of inflation (Figure 13-13). Thus, maintaining a *stable* aggregate demand is important for maintaining a low average rate of unemployment.

The second issue is how to ease the transition to a lower rate of inflation. If tight aggregate demand policies are used to combat inflation, the economy will move downward to the right along the short-run Phillips curve, thus causing an increase in unemployment. Thus the problem is how to combat inflation without causing large-scale unemployment. One proposal that has been suggested to deal with this problem is to use incomes policies. For example, Okun, Wallich, and Weintraub have put forth *TIP* proposals. These programs would use the tax system to reward firms who successfully resist wage increases by their employees, or to punish firms who don't. Such proposals have rekindled the controversy of the 1960s; in particular, the debate over the effectiveness of incomes policies. Any such policy is designed to make people settle for lower wage and price increases. In other words, it is designed to speed up the downward shift in the Phillips curve that must take place for inflation to be eliminated without high unemployment. However, incomes policies have not met with much success in the 1970s. The 1971 price freeze by Nixon was intended to get us down to a lower rate of inflation, but instead of backing it up with restrictive monetary and fiscal policies, the administration did the reverse. Like Kennedy and Johnson, they tried to stimulate aggregate demand to reduce unemployment and rely on incomes policies to hold down inflation. As a result they kept the symptoms of inflation temporarily under control while aggravating the basic cause, Carter's later efforts at "wishboning" and voluntary guideposts were also unsuccessful.

The third major policy problem is how to reduce the natural rate of unemployment. Since the early 1960s the natural rate seems to have increased from about 4 percent to perhaps as high as 6 percent. Possible explanations include: (1) the increased proportion of teenagers (who have higher than average unemployment rates) in the labor force; (2) the increased generosity of unemployment insurance and welfare, which reduces the pressures on the unemployed to take a job; and (3) minimum wages that prevent unskilled workers (especially teenagers) from acquiring jobs. Five kinds of proposals have been suggested: (1) exempting teenagers from minimum-wage legislation; (2) making unemployment insurance harder to get; (3) reducing discrimination against blacks and others in order to reduce their unemployment rates; (4) instituting training programs to reduce structural unemployment; and (5) using the government as employer of last resort, as suggested in the 1976 version of the Humphrey-Hawkins Bill. Opponents of the employment-of-last-resort idea argue that (a) the cost may be extremely high, and (b) it is difficult to design incentives for people to move out of last-resort employment and into the private sector.

IMPORTANT TERMS

Full employment A situation in which the only unemployment that exists is the kind that cannot be permanently eliminated by an increase in aggregate demand. Full employment was estimated to occur at about 4 percent unemployment in the 1960s, but as high as 6 percent now.

Natural rate of unemployment The "equilibrium" rate of unemployment. The term "natural rate" is used by those who believe that the long-run Phillips curve is vertical.

Frictional unemployment Unemployment caused by workers changing jobs, and by normal delays in finding jobs.

Structural unemployment Unemployment resulting from such things as changes in the location of industry or in the composition of output.

Phillips curve A downward-sloping relationship between the rate of unemployment and the rate of inflation.

Stagflation A situation of high unemployment (*stag*nation) and rapid in*flation*).

Trade-off A choice between two conflicting goals, such as high employment and low inflation.

Labor productivity The average amount produced by a worker in an hour. It is calculated by dividing real output by the number of labor hours used.

Real wage The quantity of goods and services which the wage will buy. It is measured by adjusting the money wage for inflation. For example, if the money wage rises by 5 percent while prices rise by 2 percent, then the real wage has increased by 3 percent.

Wage-price guideposts Rules set up by the government to limit increases in wages and prices.

Jawboning The attempt to enforce wage-price guideposts (or other proposals) by official persuasion or pressure.

Incomes policy A policy aimed at limiting inflation by limiting increases in money wage and in other types of income.

Demand-pull inflation The inflation that occurs when demand is high and eager buyers bid up the prices of goods and services.

Cost-push inflation The inflation that occurs when wages and other costs rise, and these costs are passed along to consumers in the form of higher prices. Also known sometimes as *market power* inflation.

Wage-price spiral The "vicious circle," in which higher wages are justified on the grounds that prices have risen, and higher prices are justified on the grounds that higher wages are being paid.

Money illusion People have money illusion if their behavior changes in the event of a proportionate change in prices and in money income (and in the money value of assets).

Long-run Phillips curve The curve (or line) traced out by the possible points of long-run equilibrium; that is, the points where people have adjusted completely to the prevailing rate of inflation.

TIP Tax-based incomes policy. An incomes policy backed up by tax credits to firms that are successful in holding the line on wages, and/or by tax penalties on those who exceed the guidelines.

Real-wage insurance A guarantee by the government that those who accept government wage-price guidelines will be compensated in the event of an unexpectedly high rate of inflation.

Employer of last resort A government is an employer of last resort if it offers jobs to all those who are unable to find work in the private sector of the economy.

True-False Questions

T F   **1.** There is structural unemployment even when unemployment is at its natural rate.

T F   **2.** During the early 1960s the government estimated the natural rate of unemployment to be about 6 percent.

T F   **3.** Since the 1960s, the Phillips curve has shifted downward on average.

T F   **4.** The wage-price guideposts of the Kennedy-Johnson administration stated that the rate of change of money wages should be equal to that of labor productivity in the economy as a whole.

T F   **5.** One of the problems with price controls is that they tend to produce surpluses in markets where the controls are effective.

T F   **6.** The TIP proposal of Okun was supposed to work by stimulating aggregate demand.

T F   **7.** Cost-push inflation tends to shift the Phillips curve up rather than to cause a movement upward along a given Phillips curve.

T F   **8.** Accelerationists believe that there is only one rate of inflation consistent with equilibrium in the long run.

T F   **9.** According to the Phelps-Friedman theory, we cannot eliminate inflation and have unemployment at its natural rate until the expectations of inflation have been eliminated.

T F   **10.** One of the reasons commonly proposed for explaining the rightward shift in the natural rate of unemployment in the 1970s is the increasing proportion of teenagers in the work force.

Multiple-Choice Questions

1. The Phillips curve is
   (a) L shaped according to the Phelps-Friedman theory
   (b) Vertical in the long run according to cost-push theory
   (c) Vertical in the short run according to the Phelps-Friedman theory
   (d) Vertical in the long run according to the Phelps-Friedman theory

2. Which of the following kinds of unemployment does *not* exist when the rate of unemployment equals its natural rate?
   (a) Frictional
   (b) Aggregate demand
   (c) Structural
   (d) None of the above will exist

3. Since the 1960s
   (a) The short-run Phillips curve appears to have shifted up
   (b) The short-run Phillips curve appears to have shifted to the left
   (c) The long-run Phillips curve appears to have shifted down
   (d) The short- and long-run Phillips curves do not appear to have shifted

4. Which of the following was a policy objective throughout most of the Kennedy-Johnson administration?
   (a) To move to the right of the Phillips curve by using wage-price guideposts
   (b) To use monetary policy in order to reduce inflation
   (c) To stimulate aggregate demand through monetary and fiscal policies
   (d) To shift the Phillips curve by making unemployment insurance benefits harder to get

5. One reason why the Kennedy-Johnson guideposts broke down is that:
   (a) They specified that wages could rise by 7 percent
   (b) They were not voluntary
   (c) A high level of aggregate demand was allowed to persist
   (d) Tight monetary policies contributed to cost-push inflation by raising the cost of borrowing

6. The most promising way of reducing the efficiency loss from a wage-price freeze would be to change the controls to
   (a) Allow prices to rise in high-productivity industries
   (b) Allow prices to rise in low-productivity industries
   (c) Require all prices to rise at the same rate
   (d) Allow no exceptions to the specified rate of change in wages

7. Which of the following events is *least* likely to shift the short-run Phillips curve?
   (a) An increase in aggregate demand, which did not affect workers' expectations of inflation
   (b) A shift in workers' expectations of inflation
   (c) A decision by big unions to take a harder bargaining position
   (d) A successful worker retraining program

8. Which of the following is an assumption of the Phelps-Friedman theory?
   (a) People suffer from money illusion
   (b) In the long run, peoples' expectations will adapt to experience
   (c) There is downward rigidity of nominal wages
   (d) Inflation is caused mainly by unions and monopolies

9. According to the Phelps-Friedman theory, when the rate of unemployment is less than the natural rate
  (a) Inflation will remain constant as long as unemployment is not reduced any further
  (b) Inflation will decrease if unemployment is held constant
  ✓(c) Inflation will be higher than workers had anticipated
  (d) Unemployment will fall if inflation is held constant

10. In Figure 13-1, the natural rate of unemployment is 6 percent. When we are on the Phillips curve labeled PC_1, the expected rate of inflation is
  (a) 0   (c) 6 percent
  ✓(b) 3 percent   (d) 11 percent

11. If you were at point A last year in Figure 13-1 and workers have now revised their expectations, then which of the Phillips curves are you most likely to be on?
  (a) PC_1
  (b) PC_2
  (c) PC_3
  (d) Any of the above, depending upon the rate of inflation

12. Which of the following most accurately describes the Eckstein-Brinner theory of inflation?
  (a) The long-run Phillips curve is vertical
  (b) The short-run Phillips curve is vertical
  (c) The long-run Phillips curve is vertical above an inflation rate of 3 percent
  (d) The short-run Phillips curve is vertical above a rate of inflation of 3 percent

13. Which of the following is likely to cause the highest average rate of unemployment in the long run?
  (a) A variable rate of growth of aggregate demand
  (b) A high rate of growth of aggregate demand
  (c) A reduction in the minimum wage
  (d) A reduction in the fraction of teenagers in the labor force

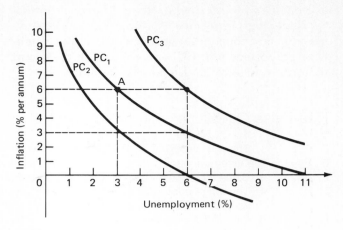

FIGURE 13-1

14. TIP is
  (a) A proposal to restrain demand-pull inflation by reducing aggregate demand
  (b) A policy designed to reduce the natural rate of unemployment
  (c) The policy followed by Nixon in 1971
  (d) A proposal to use the tax system to encourage compliance to guideposts

15. Which of the following would be *least* likely to reduce the natural rate of unemployment?
  (a) Policies that reduce the amount of discrimination against black workers
  (b) Policies that would increase the level of aggregate demand
  (c) A reduction in the generosity of unemployment insurance benefits
  (d) A reduction in the proportion of teenagers in the labor force

FIGURE 13-2

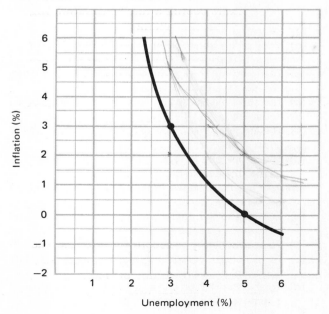

Exercises

1. Figure 13-2, represents the Phillips curve for a year (year one) when the expected rate of inflation was zero. The natural rate of unemployment is __5__ percent, at which rate according to this Phillips curve, the rate of inflation would be __0__ percent. When the rate of unemployment is 3 percent, the rate of inflation would be (more, less) than the expected rate of inflation by __3__ percent. Suppose that during year two the expected rate of inflation was 2 percent. Draw the Phillips curve for year two in the same diagram. In year two if the rate of unemployment is still 3 percent, then the rate of inflation will be __5__ percent.

If, on the other hand, inflation is kept constant at 3 percent, the rate of unemployment will be __4__ percent. If the rate of inflation is kept at 3 percent, then, according to the accelerationist theory the expected rate of inflation will eventually

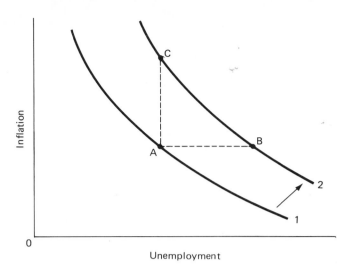

FIGURE 13-3

be ___3___ percent and the rate of unemployment will eventually be ___5___ percent. According to the accelerationist theory, if aggregate demand policies are aimed at keeping the rate of unemployment at 3 percent, the rate of inflation will ___↑___ .

2a. Suppose the economy is initially at point A on Phillips curve 1 in Figure 13-3. Now the curve shifts, so the new one is Phillips curve 2. If policy makers pursue restrictive monetary and fiscal policies that keep inflation from increasing, then unemployment will (increase, decrease) by the amount ___A B___ . If, on the other hand, they keep the rate of unemployment constant by following more expansionary policies, then inflation will (increase, decrease) by the amount ___A C___ .

2b. Suppose this shift in the Phillips curve was caused by workers seeing a rate of inflation higher than they had expected. Then, according to the accelerationist theory, the rate of unemployment at A must have been (higher than, lower than, equal to) the natural rate. Therefore, the attempt by policy makers to go to point C this year will cause the Phillips curve to ___↑ more shift___ next year.

2c. Suppose instead that unemployment was at its natural rate at A, and that this shift in the Phillips curve was caused by an increase in the generosity of unemployment insurance benefits. If there was no change in expectations, then the natural rate of unemployment has (increased, decreased) by the amount _____. In this case, the attempt by policy makers to go to point C this year will cause the Phillips curve to _____

_____

next year.

3. In Figure 13-4 below, the curve labeled P_1 is a short-run Phillips curve of the usual shape, based on an expected rate of inflation of 5 percent. According to this curve, if inflation equals 5 percent every year, then the rate of unemployment will equal ___6___ percent every year. The natural rate of unemployment is ___6___ percent. Suppose that the rate of expected inflation remains constant at 5 percent. Then, if the actual rate of inflation is increased temporarily to 6 percent, the rate of unemployment will (increase, decrease) to ___5___ percent, and if the actual rate of inflation is decreased to 4 percent, the rate of unemployment will (increase, decrease) to ___9___ percent. Therefore, if actual inflation is 6 percent half the time and 4 percent the other half of the time, the average rate of inflation will be (higher, lower, no different) than if the rate of inflation was 5 percent all the time, but the average rate of unemployment will be (more, less) by an amount equal to _____ percent.

FIGURE 13-4

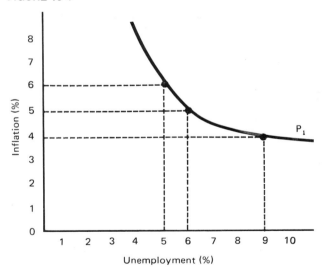

Essay Questions

1. Explain why, according to the accelerationist argument of Phelps and Friedman, the rate of unemployment cannot be maintained permanently *above* its natural rate by tight aggregate demand policies.

2. Most economists agree that the long-run Phillips curve is steeper than the short-run Phillips curve. It is also commonly accepted that politicians, when deciding upon aggregate demand policies, care more about what will happen between now and the next election than the more distant future. Putting these two ideas together, show why politicians may adopt expansive policies (aimed at moving to the left, up the Phillips curve) even when they realize that voters dislike inflation.

3. According to the short-run Phillips curve, if unemployment rises inflation should fall. But in many years unemployment and inflation *both* rise. How would an accelerationist explain this? How would a cost-push theorist explain it?

4. It has been argued that combating inflation with wage-price controls is like trying to cure a fever by using a thermometer that won't register

anything higher than 98.6 degrees. Why? Would this argument be more likely to come from an accelerationist or from someone who subscribes to a cost-push theory? Why?

*5. If you study Figure 13-4 in the text, you will notice that there appear to be loops in the Phillips curve. That is, the time path traced out in this diagram from the early 1950s to the present time seems to be following a clockwise spiral upward and to the right. The text describes why an upward shift in the Phillips curve may occur. Can you think of any reason why these loops might exist? (Hint: This question is related to question **2.**)

Answers

True-False Questions: **1** T **2** F **3** F **4** T **5** F **6** F **7** T **8** F **9** T **10** T
Multiple-Choice Questions: **1** d **2** b **3** a **4** c **5** c **6** b **7** a **8** b **9** c **10** b **11** c **12** c
13 a **14** d **15** b
Exercises:
1 5, zero, more, 3, 5, 4, 3, 5, become more and more rapid

FIGURE 13-2 completed.

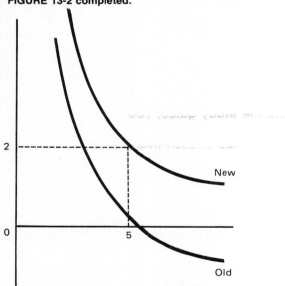

2a. increase, *AB*, increase, *AC*
2b. lower than, shift further up
2c. increased, *AB*, shift further up
3. 6, 6, decrease, 5, increase, 9, no different, more, 1

CHAPTER 14
How Does the Economy Adjust to Inflation?

Learning Objectives

After you have studied this chapter in the textbook and the study guide, you should be able to

Explain why, in the simplest tax-free economy, perfectly anticipated inflation might have no real effects

Explain the difference between the nominal rate of interest and the real rate of interest

Give examples of people who lose from unexpected inflation, and examples of people who gain

Show how graduated-payment mortgages can help prospective house buyers to cope with inflation and high interest rates

Explain how inflation increases the real burden of income taxes

Show how the taxation of nominal interest income gives a tax break to borrowers but penalizes lenders

Describe the effects of the taxation of nominal income on the housing market

Present the cases for and against replacement-cost depreciation

Explain why high inflation tends to "dry up" the long-term bond market, and how variable-interest mortgages help to cope with this problem in the mortgage market

State the pros and cons of wage-indexation

CHAPTER HIGHLIGHTS

In Chapter 13 we began to see how the economy adjusts to inflation. As inflation continues, people learn to anticipate it. For example, unions bargain for wage increases that they hope will compensate for the increase they have come to expect in the cost of living. If the economy has adjusted completely and people's expectations turn out to be accurate, then the inflation need not affect real wages, because the rise in prices may be offset by these wage increases. Nor will it necessarily affect the rate of unemployment, which we have seen may remain at its natural rate as long as inflation is perfectly anticipated.

The Real Rate of Interest

Adjustments like this occur in all markets, not just the market for labor. Among the most important examples are financial markets; markets for loans, bonds, and other financial instruments. We saw how an important feature of adjustment in the labor market was the absence of money illusion: People care about their real wages, not their nominal wages. Likewise, borrowers and lenders in financial markets care about the real rate of interest—the nominal rate of interest adjusted for inflation. They realize that when inflation is 10 percent, then a nominal rate of interest of 10 percent doesn't give them any real return on their investment. An initial $100 will yield $110 a year later, but this won't buy any more when they get it than the $100 could now. The *real* rate of interest will be zero. In general, the real interest rate is (approximately) the nominal interest rate minus the rate of inflation. In this case the 10 percent nominal rate minus the 10 percent inflation rate equals the 0 percent real rate of interest.

Just as perfectly anticipated inflation would leave real wages unaffected, so it would leave the real interest rate unaffected, under ideal circumstances. In the absence of money illusion, the demand and supply of bonds depends not on the nominal rate of interest, but on the real rate. Suppose markets are all in equilibrium to begin with and inflation increases. At first this might make the real rate of interest fall. But equilibrium in the bond market will be restored when the real rate returns to its previous value, for this was the value at which supply equals demand. The nominal interest rate will have risen to compensate for the extra inflation but this will not affect the balance between supply and demand, which depends only on the real rate. (This argument is illustrated in Figure 14-2 in the textbook.)

Unanticipated Inflation

Unfortunately, inflation is seldom anticipated perfectly. The equilibrium rate of interest may compensate lenders for the inflation they expect to occur. But if the actual rate of inflation turns out to be greater than expected they won't be compensated for the unexpected inflation. They will be stuck with the nominal interest specified in the bonds they have bought.

Just as lenders lose from unexpected inflation, so borrowers gain. A family that took out a mortgage at 6 percent 15 years ago now pays back with inflated dollars. (Besides, the size of the mortgage is probably a fraction of the current inflated value of the house.) For this family unexpected inflation has provided a windfall.

The Duration of Debt

Even if the rate of inflation turns out to be what people expected, it can still have real effects. The historical data in Figure 14-4 in the textbook suggest that although nominal interest rates are generally higher during periods of more rapid inflation, nevertheless they do not compensate entirely for increases in inflation. Real rates on short-term government bills fall when inflation increases.

Bonds, mortgages, and other financial instruments usually specify a constant *nominal* payment from one year to the next. If I owe $500 a month on my mortgage and there is 10 percent inflation, then the real value of this payment will decrease by 10 percent each year. In real terms, I will pay more in the first 10 years than I will in the last 10. In this way inflation shortens the "duration" of debt.

Even if inflation turns out as expected, it has real effects on the economy through this shortening of duration. Many families cannot afford a large house now because for the first few years the mortgage would take too much out of the monthly paycheck. But they might be able to afford it if only they could spread those real payments more evenly over time instead of having to pay so much in the first few years. This is what a *graduated-payment mortgage* would allow them to do. It would have the nominal payment start at a lower level and grow over time as inflation proceeds and the paycheck grows. If it were *fully graduated* it would keep the real payments constant over time. Until now graduated mortgages have been virtually nonexistent, but if inflation keeps up in the double digits for long we can expect to see more innovations in this direction.

Taxes and Inflation

Another factor preventing full adjustment to inflation is taxes. Some taxes, like sales taxes, go up in proportion to prices. Thus, the real amount of these taxes is not affected by inflation. But this is not true of income taxes. If your nominal income goes up by 10 percent when there is 10 percent inflation, your real income doesn't change. But your real taxes do. If the 10 percent nominal increase moves you to a higher tax bracket, your taxes are now a higher proportion of the same real income. Furthermore, the real value of your basic exemptions is now reduced. Because the brackets, exemptions, and other dollar measures in the tax code are not indexed, inflation increases the real burden of taxes (at least until Congress cuts taxes to give you back what inflation took away).

Perhaps the biggest real effect of expected inflation is on the taxation of interest income. Suppose you were getting 5 percent on your savings account when no inflation was expected. If you were wealthy, you perhaps paid half this in taxes and kept the other 2½ percent as your *after-tax* real rate of interest. Now, when inflation is expected to be 3 percent, the nominal rate of interest may adjust fully to 8 percent. You haven't really gained anything from this rise in nominal interest; it has just compensated you for the rise in expected inflation. Still, you must pay half of it in taxes. After taxes you now get 4 percent. But after deducting the 3 percent inflation you are left with only a 1 percent after-tax real rate of interest—a drop from the previous rate of 2½ percent.

Just as inflation reduces the after-tax real rate that a lender gets, so it reduces the after-tax real rate that a borrower has to pay. With no inflation you can count the interest on your 5 percent mortgage as a deduction which reduces your taxable income. If you're in a 50 percent tax bracket, you then get half of this interest back as a tax reduction. So your mortgage really only costs you 2½ percent. With inflation at 3 percent, even if the nominal mortgage rate is fully adjusted to 8 percent, you get back half of this in taxes for an after-tax nominal rate of 4 percent. Since inflation reduces the real value of your debt by another 3 percent, your after-tax real mortgage rate is only 1 percent, compared to the previous 2½ percent. Likewise, any business that issues bonds or takes out loans gets a big tax break by declaring all its *nominal* interest as an expense. This encourages businesses to go more heavily into debt during inflation, financing new investments by issuing bonds rather than equity.

Perhaps the biggest impact of this effect on interest rates is on the housing market.:

1. The larger your tax rate, the bigger the advantage of being able to declare this "padded" deduction. Thus, the rich in high tax brackets are especially affected. The result is that inflation particularly encourages the building of large, expensive houses.

2. Since inflation stimulates the demand for all housing to some extent, it also increases the relative price of housing. (This is one reason why, when inflation increases, house prices generally go up even faster than other prices.)

3. As a result, inflation can also raise the real

values of property taxes, many of which are fixed as a proportion of property values.

4. Inflation also decreases the demand for rental accommodation, because renters are not permitted to deduct any of their housing expenses.

5. Inflation has encouraged many previous tenants in big-city apartments to buy their apartments from their landlords as condominiums or cooperatives, in order to qualify for the deduction.

6. By encouraging people to put so much of their saving into housing inflation has put many into an illiquid position. (Houses are a prime example of an asset that cannot be sold at little expense or at predictable dollar values.) It has also diverted much of the nation's saving away from buying the stocks and bonds that finance business investment.

The third major area where real taxes are affected by inflation is through depreciation. As we have seen, a business may choose to deduct a certain fraction of the original cost of a machine as a depreciation expense. But business executives argue that the real cost of wearing a machine out is that a new one will have to be bought. And the new one will cost much more than the old one bought several years ago. Thus, they argue that they should get to deduct a certain fraction of the *replacement* cost. This argument is quite controversial, especially in view of the tax break that businesses already get from declaring nominal interest as an expense.

Inflation and Uncertainty

Another factor that impedes perfect adjustment is uncertainty. Periods of especially *rapid* inflation tend also to be periods of especially *erratic* inflation. Thus, when inflation rises it also becomes harder to predict. As a result, real interest rates also become harder to predict. After you get into a period of rapid inflation the nominal interest rate might adjust so that *according to the best forecasts of inflation* the real interest rate will be the same as before. But these forecasts won't be as reliable as before.

This is one reason why long-term bond markets tend to "dry up" during periods of rapid inflation. Both borrowers and lenders become frightened of entering into long-term commitments with an unpredictable real rate of interest. This is also one reason why you see variable-rate mortgages during rapid inflations in some countries. When inflation changes unexpectedly nominal interest rates on new mortgages will adjust to compensate, at least partially. With a variable rate they will also change on existing mortgages. Thus, before you buy such a variable-rate contract, you have some assurance that the real rate of interest will be protected against unexpected inflation. With a fixed-rate mortgage you have no such assurance; you are exposed to the same kind of real-rate uncertainty that scared people away from the long-term bond market.

Indexed Wages

Indexing wages is one way of helping to adjust to inflation. Rather than specifying a nominal wage and hoping that inflation turns out as expected, a fully indexed contract specifies a real wage and allows the nominal wage to adjust automatically to compensate for inflation.

Indexation of wages can help to reduce uncertainty in labor markets (just as variable-rate mortgages help to reduce uncertainty in the mortgage market). They can also help ease the problems we discussed in the last chapter of going to a lower rate of inflation; when inflation starts falling, wage increases come down automatically instead of waiting for contracts to be renegotiated.

There are, however, two major problems with indexation. First, by making wages respond more quickly to prices, they speed up the wage-price spiral discussed in the previous chapter. Thus, in periods when inflation goes up and down, indexation makes it go even further up and further down; it makes inflation more erratic. Second, when the economy is hit by an external shock like a rise in the price of oil, someone has to pay the price, in the form of a lower real income. By protecting real wages against such price increases, indexation impedes this necessary adjustment.

IMPORTANT TERMS

Nominal rate of interest The rate at which your money grows if invested in an interest-bearing security.

Ex ante real rate of interest To calculate this, you subtract the *expected* rate of inflation from the nominal rate of interest. (The term "real rate of interest" usually means the ex ante rate.)

Ex post real rate of interest The real rate of return that bondholders end up getting, after the fact. This is obtained by subtracting the *actual* rate of inflation from the nominal rate of interest.

Graduated-payment mortgage One on which the money payment rises as time passes, to adjust for inflation. If the money payments rise rapidly enough to keep the real payments constant, then the mortgage is *fully graduated*.

Indexed taxes If taxes are indexed, then tax brackets, exemptions, and other dollar measures in the tax code are by law increased automatically, in the same proportion that the average price level increases. That is, they are tied to a price index (usually the CPI).

After-tax real rate of interest The real return on a bond, after taxes are paid. For example, if the nominal rate of interest is 16 percent, while taxes are 50 percent, and the rate of inflation is 7 percent, the after-tax real rate is 1 percent. (You get to keep 8 percent nominal after taxes, which keeps you just 1 percent ahead of inflation.)

Replacement-cost depreciation A way of calculating depreciation using current replacement costs of buildings and equipment, rather than their actual acquisition costs. Businesses would like to be able to calculate depreciation this way, but the proposal is quite controversial.

Variable-rate mortgage One with a provision for the interest rate to be adjusted periodically in response to changes in market interest rates.

Shared-appreciation mortgage One where the borrower is committed to pay the lender a fraction of the appreciation of the property on which the loan is made.

Indexed wage contract One that contains an *escalator clause* that provides for additional money wages to compensate for inflation (generally as measured by the CPI). The additional wage is often referred to as a *cost-of-living allowance* (COLA).

True-False Questions

T F   1. People who have borrowed large sums generally gain from unanticipated inflation.

T F   2. People who have invested heavily in the bond market generally gain from unanticipated inflation.

T F   3. Historical data for the United States suggest that the real rate of interest on short-term securities falls when inflation rises.

T F   4. Inflation shortens the real duration of most debt contracts.

T F   5. Graduated mortgages allow for periodic renegotiation of the real interest rate.

T F   6. The larger your marginal tax rate, the greater is the incentive provided to you by the taxation of nominal interest to invest in housing.

T F   7. When inflation increases, the price of housing tends to rise faster than the average of other prices.

T F   8. The U.S. tax system is fully indexed.

T F   **9.** A COLA clause in a wage contract provides for a fixed nominal amount to cover the cost of living, no matter what happens to inflation.

T F   **10.** Wage indexation tends to speed up the response of inflation to an increase in aggregate demand.

Multiple-Choice Questions

1. Unanticipated inflation tends to
- **(a)** Confer gains on people who have borrowed
- **(b)** Inflict losses on people who have borrowed
- **(c)** Leave unaffected the real position of people who have borrowed
- **(d)** Confer gains or losses on people who have borrowed, depending upon how large their marginal tax rate is

2. Someone who has just retired is most likely to
- **(a)** Gain from inflation, especially if it was not expected when the family house was sold
- **(b)** Gain from inflation, especially if it was unexpected when the pension was arranged
- **(c)** Lose from inflation, especially if it was unexpected when the pension was arranged
- **(d)** Lose from inflation, especially if everyone had expected it when the family house was sold

3. If the nominal rate of interest is 10 percent and the real rate of interest is 5 percent, then the rate of inflation is
- **(a)** 5 percent
- **(b)** 10 percent
- **(c)** 15 percent
- **(d)** You cannot tell from the information given

4. Inflation has the greatest real effects on the economy when
- **(a)** The tax system is fully indexed
- **(b)** Wages are fully indexed
- **(c)** People have fully graduated mortgages
- **(d)** It is unanticipated

5. During a period of inflation, graduated mortgages
- **(a)** Shorten the real duration of debt
- **(b)** Lengthen the nominal duration of debt
- **(c)** Fix the nominal rate of interest
- **(d)** Make the nominal payments decline over time

6. One reason why inflation makes housing particularly difficult for young families to acquire is that
- **(a)** Inflation makes renting much more attractive for tax purposes
- **(b)** The only kind of mortgages available to them are graduated ones
- **(c)** They are typically in low tax brackets, and therefore find it hard to compete against older, wealthier people, for whom the tax advantages of homeownership are much greater
- **(d)** Inflation tends to reduce after-tax real rates of interest

7. Under a nonindexed tax code, if your nominal income just keeps pace with inflation
- **(a)** Your nominal income taxes stay the same
- **(b)** Your nominal income taxes rise, but just in proportion to your income
- **(c)** Your real income taxes fall
- **(d)** Your real income taxes rise

8. When inflation proceeds rapidly, businesses pay the *least* taxes if they are allowed to compute
- **(a)** Depreciation using historical cost
- **(b)** Depreciation using replacement cost
- **(c)** No depreciation at all
- **(d)** Depreciation using historical cost, but only if there was even more inflation in the past

9. History shows that inflation has been most erratic
- **(a)** When it has been low
- **(b)** During the 10 years after 1954
- **(c)** When it has been high
- **(d)** At all times; there has been almost no change in the variability of inflation over the past five decades

10. During periods of rapid inflation, the real volume of trading on long-term bond markets tends to
- **(a)** Increase, because after-tax real interest rates rise
- **(b)** Decrease, because the predictability of real interest rates decreases
- **(c)** Decrease, because the real rate of interest falls even more than on short-term securities
- **(d)** Go back to its normal level as soon as people get accustomed to a higher average rate of inflation

11. A variable interest rate mortgage provides for
- **(a)** Increasing payments over time, even if there are no changes in market interest rates
- **(b)** Increases in the rate of interest when market interest rates rise
- **(c)** Paying the lender a specified fraction of the capital gains on the house
- **(d)** An interest rate that is tied automatically to the family's income

12. Critics of wage indexation argue that it
- **(a)** Impedes the return to the natural rate of unemployment when the government is using restrictive monetary policies to reduce inflation
- **(b)** Causes inflation to be more erratic
- **(c)** Causes real wages to fall automatically in the event of an increase in the price of oil
- **(d)** Does not work as well as escalator clauses

Exercises

1a. Suppose that by putting $200 into a savings account and keeping it there you can have $220 in a year. At the same time, the CPI goes from 100 to 106. Then the nominal rate of interest is _____ percent, the rate of inflation is _____ percent, and the real rate of return has turned out to be _____ percent. If you had been expecting the CPI to rise only to 104, then the expected rate of inflation was _4_ percent, and the ex ante real rate of interest was _6_ percent.

1b. If you are in a 40 percent marginal tax bracket, then after paying taxes on the interest your savings account will have $_____ in it. Thus, your after-tax nominal rate of interest is _____ percent. Using the date at which you first put your money into the savings account as the base year, the real value of your savings account after paying tax on the interest will be $_____. Thus your after-tax real rate of return will be _____ percent.

2. Figure 14-1 shows the demand and supply of (real) loanable funds, plotted against the nominal rate of interest when no one expects any inflation. The equilibrium nominal rate of interest is _2_ percent. The equilibrium real rate of interest is _2_ percent. In the same diagram, draw in the supply and demand curves that would exist if people all expected 2 percent inflation and the economy had adjusted fully to that expectation. The equilibrium nominal rate of interest is now _4_ percent, and the equilibrium real rate of interest is _2_ percent. The equilibrium real quantity of loanable funds is now (more than, less than, the same as) before.

3. Consider the tax schedule in Table 14-1, which applies for the taxation year 1982:

a. Suppose that during 1982 your income was $10,000. Then you had to pay $_500_ in taxes, and your after-tax income was $_9500_.

b. Suppose that from 1982 to 1983 there is 10 percent inflation, and your pretax income just keeps up with this inflation. Then in 1983 your income before taxes is $_11,000_. Using 1982 as the base year your real income before taxes in 1983 is $_10,000_, which is (more than, less than, the same as) in 1982. If there is no change in the tax schedule, then you owe $_650_ in taxes in 1983. Thus the percentage increase in your nominal taxes is (more than, less

Table 14-1

Income before taxes	Taxes payable
0–$ 5,000	0
5–$10,000	10% of before-tax income in excess of $5,000
10–$15,000	$500 plus 15% of any income in excess of $10,000

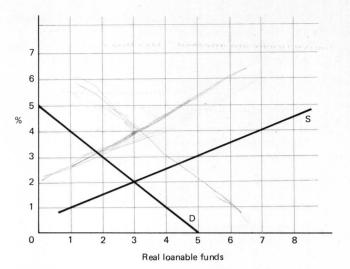

FIGURE 14-1

than, the same as) the rate of inflation. So your *real* taxes have (increased, decreased, stayed the same) and your real after-tax income has (increased, decreased, stayed the same).

c. Show in Table 14-2 what the 1983 tax schedule would look like if there had been a fully indexed system (and no other change since 1982):

Table 14-2

Income before taxes	Taxes payable
0–	0
–$	10% of before-tax income in excess of $_____
–$	_____ plus 15% of any income in excess of $_____

d. If this had been the tax schedule you faced in 1983, you would have paid _____ in taxes. Your after-tax nominal income would have been _____, which is _____ percent (higher, lower) than in 1982. Thus your real after-tax income would have been (more than, less than, the same as) in 1982.

Essay Questions

1. In Chapter 12 we learned that high interest rates discourage investment. In 1980, interest rates were twice as high as they were in 1970. Yet real investment expenditures were just as high. Why? Do investment expenditures depend more closely upon the real interest rate or the nominal interest rate?

2. "Inflation has no real effects. It makes all prices rise in the same proportion. Therefore, no relative prices are affected." Has this been the case in U.S. history? What have been some of the notable exceptions? What kinds of imperfections in our economic system have led to these exceptions?

3. How does inflation affect each of the following groups? Explain your answer, making sure in each case to specify whether you are talking about anticipated or unanticipated inflation.

  A. Young people who are borrowing to finance their university education.
  B. People saving for their retirement through life insurance.
  C. Landlords.
  D. Real estate developers
  E. Interior decorators.
  F. Tax accountants.
  G. People who have decided to wait until they have saved enough to make a 50-percent down payment before buying a house.

4. Explain in detail the differences between graduated mortgages, variable-interest mortgages and shared-appreciation mortgages.

5. Indexation of wage contracts tends to become more common when inflation rises. What does this have to do with the historical fact that rapid inflation tends to be more erratic than less rapid inflation?

6. In 1980 the rate of inflation in Israel was about 130 percent. Why do you suppose that the tax authorities in Israel require you to pay income taxes four times a year? The tax system in Israel is also indexed. Why is there a tendency for people to claim that most of the income they received during the year accrued at the end of the year rather than at the beginning?

7. In Israel many transactions take place using the U.S. dollar as the medium of exchange rather than the Israeli shekel. What do you suppose this has to do with the extremely high rate of inflation in Israel?

8. Because the U.S. tax code is not indexed, unless it is revised the government's real tax revenues go up substantially every year as a result of inflation. Some have argued that this provides an automatic stabilizer for the economy. When inflation rises, how does this tend to affect the size of the government deficit in real terms? What does this tend to do to the level of aggregate demand in the economy? Does this help to reduce inflation, or does it make the problem worse? In what sense does the indexation of the tax system in other countries contribute to economic instability in those countries?

Answers

True-False Questions: 1 T 2 F 3 T 4 T 5 F 6 T 7 T 8 F 9 F 10 T
Multiple-Choice Questions: 1 a 2 c 3 a 4 d 5 b 6 c 7 d 8 b 9 c 10 b 11 b 12 b
Exercises: **1a.** 10, 6, 4, 4, 6
1b. 212, 6, 200, 0
2. 2, 2, 4, 2, the same as

FIGURE 14-1 completed.

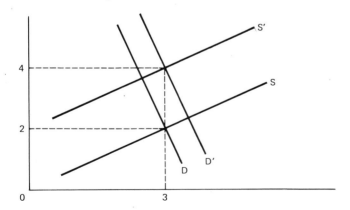

(Both *D* and *S* have shifted up by 2 percentage points.)
3a. 500, 9,500
3b. 11,000, 10,000, the same as, 650, more than, increased, decreased

3c. Table 14-2 completed

0–5,500	0
5,500–11,000	10% of before-tax income in excess of $5,500
11,000–16,500	$550 plus 15% of any income in excess of $11,000

3d. 550, 10,450, 10, higher, the same as

CHAPTER 15
Why Is the Economy Unstable?

Learning Objectives

After you have studied this chapter in the textbook and the study guide, you should be able to

Identify the four phases of the business cycle

State which of the major components of GNP fluctuates most widely over the business cycle.

Describe the stages by which slower growth in sales affects a firm's investment demand

Explain why a decline in investment demand contains the seeds of a recovery

Show how the interaction between the multiplier and accelerator adds to the momentum of a recession or expansion

Explain why the demand for consumer durables is generally less stable than total consumption demand

Describe at least one recent example showing how monetary or fiscal policy has added to economic instability

Identify the three different lags that make it difficult for fiscal and monetary policies to stabilize the economy

Explain how a political business cycle might be generated

Show why the central bank might get caught in a policy trap if it attempts to keep interest rates stable

CHAPTER HIGHLIGHTS

This chapter addresses the question of why business fluctuations occur. As you might guess, there is no single answer; instability has a number of explanations.

The business cycle is divided into four phases: recession, trough, expansion, and peak, as shown in Figure 15-2 in the textbook. The cycle is not regular. No two cycles are of exactly the same length, nature, or severity. Often it is hard to tell, for example, exactly when a recession has ended.

Investment

The percentage changes in investment over the cycle are usually much larger than in any other component of GNP. Thus, much of business cycle theory has been aimed at explaining the fluctuations in investment. Such explanations are based on the acceleration principle, according to which a firm's investment expenditures depend mainly upon the rate of change of its sales. There are four major implications that follow from this principle:

1. The percentage changes in investment tend to be much larger than the percentage changes in consumption. (We already know this as a fact; the accelerator principle offers an explanation of this fact.)

2. A reduction in the *growth* of consumption can cause a *decline* in investment. As a consequence, an unsustainably rapid expansion may lead to a recession.

3. Investment can collapse following even a small reduction in consumption.

4. In order for investment to recover from a decline, the level of consumption does not have to stop falling; it only has to fall more slowly than before. (Thus, a decline in economic activity contains the seeds of a recovery.)

All these points are illustrated by Table 15-1 in the textbook. (It may help to work through the other examples in Problem 15-3 in the textbook and in Exercise 1 below.)

The accelerator principle applies not only to machinery investment, but also to investment in buildings and inventories. However, the rigid relationship between capital and sales shown in the basic accelerator (Table 15-1) is an oversimplification. In fact, there is no rigid relationship between sales and capital in the form of buildings, equipment, and inventories. This is because firms want their capital to vary with their *long-run* sales, not with every little rise or fall in their weekly or monthly sales. As a consequence, a decline in sales affects a firm's investment in three stages:

1. At first, there is little or no effect on production. For a period, the firm is likely to absorb a decline in sales by building up inventories (unsold goods) rather than by changing its production plans for what may turn out to be a temporary sales decline.

2. If the decline persists for some weeks, the firm will begin cutting back production to reduce its inventories, and eventually it will also reduce its new orders for machinery.

3. Finally, as the decline in sales slows down, the firm will increase its new orders for machinery.

The cyclical behavior of investment is affected not only by the accelerator but also by the multiplier. As sales grow more slowly, investment declines (through the accelerator). This tends to make output decline (through the multiplier), which can amplify the initial slowdown in sales. This causes investment to decline even further (again, through the accelerator). In this way, the initial decline in investment expenditures can feed on itself, gathering more momentum.

There are three general conclusions that may be drawn from this discussion:

1. The accelerator principle will probably not turn a temporary drop in consumption into a recession, for the drop may be over before investment expenditures are affected.

2. If a drop in consumption is more than temporary, the interaction of the accelerator and the multiplier can cause a sizable downward movement in aggregate demand.

3. This downward movement cannot persist forever; the decline of consumption will eventually slow down (after all, consumption does not fall continuously toward zero), and (through the accelerator) this will cause investment expenditures to increase.

Consumption

Much of the foregoing applies not only to investment expenditures but also to expenditures on consumer durables. Both investment goods and consumer durables are long-lived assets that are bought with a view to the long-term benefits that they provide. A change in peoples' expectations or in the cost or availability of funds can cause people to delay or advance their purchases of cars, appliances, and so on, and thus contribute to instability in the same way as fluctuations in the demand for investment.

The demand for consumer durables may contribute to instability through something like the accelerator. As incomes fall, people will economize by delaying purchases of durables, thus contributing to the decline. But, like the accelerator, this can also help bring about an eventual recovery of aggregate demand when the worn-out cars and other durables are finally replaced.

Fiscal and Monetary Policies

Earlier chapters showed how fiscal and monetary policies could (ideally!) be used to stabilize the economy. But the present chapter shows how in fact these policies have sometimes contributed to instability. Figure 15-7 in the textbook shows that both monetary and fiscal policies were contractionary prior to the 1969–1970 recession; and again just prior to the 1974–1975 recession. In general, it seems that changes in these policies have been procyclical as often as countercyclical. Three reasons have been suggested for this:

1. There are lags in the operation of policy: a recognition lag, an action lag, and an impact lag, and these lags make it difficult to design policies for the conditions which will exist when they have their effects. Thus, expansive policies aimed at combating a recession may not take hold until the recovery is well advanced, when further stimulus is no longer appropriate.

2. The policymakers' other objectives may conflict with the objective of stabilizing the economy. Proponents of the "political business cycle" theory believe that expansions may be deliberately engineered by politicians just before elections in the hopes of winning votes.

3. The Fed may have fallen into a policy trap in attempting to stabilize the rate of interest. If the economy moves into a recession because of a drop in investment demand, the demand for loans will decrease, and the rate of interest will begin to fall (that is, bond prices will begin to rise). If the Fed is trying to stabilize the rate of interest, it will counteract this fall by selling securities on the open market. But this causes a decline in the rate of monetary growth, which will contribute even further to the developing recession. Some economists believe that the unwillingness of the Fed to adjust its interest rate targets rapidly enough in 1974 contributed to the recession. If the Fed had allowed interest rates to fall more rapidly, and had paid more attention to the rate of growth of the money supply, this recession would probably have been less severe. During the 1940s the reverse happened. The Fed kept interest rates pegged, initially to help finance the war effort. By 1951 they were convinced that this policy was stimulating an already overheated economy. As aggregate demand increased, the rate of interest tended to rise in response to the greater demand for loans. The Fed was counteracting this rise with open market purchases that made aggregate demand increase even more. Their 1951 Accord with the Treasury let them out of this trap by ending their obligation to peg interest rates.

IMPORTANT TERMS

Business cycle   The alternating rise and fall in economic activity.

National Bureau of Economic Research (NBER)   A private research organization which has measured and studied the business cycle. The NBER determines when a recession has occurred.

Recession   The downward phase of the business cycle. It may be defined as a recurring period of decline in total output, income, employment, and trade, usually lasting 6 months to a year, and marked by widespread contractions in many sectors of the economy.

Trough   The low point of a business cycle; the month at the end of the recession phase.

Expansion   The upward phase of the business cycle, occurring after the trough.

Peak   The high point of the business cycle; the month at the end of an expansion, before the succeeding recession.

Seasonal adjustment   Some economic variables have regular seasonal fluctuations. The data on such a variable are seasonally adjusted when these regular seasonal fluctuations have been removed. Thus, seasonally adjusted data reflect the effects of all influences other than the regular seasonal effects. (See Box 15-1 in the textbook.)

Acceleration principle (Also called the *accelerator*), the principle that the *level* of net investment demand depends upon the *change* of consumption demand.

Capital-output ratio   The value of a firm's capital, divided by the amount of its output during a period.

Consumer durable   Any consumer good that can normally be expected to last for over a year—for example, a car, TV set, or refrigerator.

Countercyclical policy   Government policy that has tended to stabilize economic activity. The opposite to this is *procyclical policy*.

Recognition lag   The interval between the time when economic conditions change and the time when the need to take corrective action is recognized.

Action lag   The interval between the time when the need for policy action is recognized and the time when such action is actually taken.

Impact lag   The interval between the time when a policy action is taken and the time when the major effects of the policy actually occur.

Political business cycle A business cycle that is caused by changes in policies aimed at increasing the chances of politicians being reelected.

Treasury–Federal Reserve Accord of 1951 The agreement whereby the Fed was released from its commitment to hold down the rate of interest on government bonds.

True-False Questions

T F   **1.** Business cycles occur regularly every 7 years.

T F   **2.** The last recession was that of 1969–1970.

T F   **3.** The acceleration principle refers to the effect of fiscal policy on economic stability.

T F   **4.** According to the acceleration principle, a decline of sales does not have to come to an end before investment increases; it just has to slow down.

T F   **5.** Because of the lags in investment decisions, even brief declines in aggregate demand are amplified by the accelerator.

T F   **6.** The multiplier eliminates most of the instability caused by the accelerator.

T F   **7.** Consumer durable expenditures vary by a larger percentage amount over the business cycle than do other consumption expenditures.

T F   **8.** The automatic stabilizers discussed in Chapter 9 reduce the magnitude of economic fluctuations.

T F   **9.** The "action lag" refers to the delay before the accelerator comes into action.

T F **10.** The lags in the effect of policy would probably create less of a problem for economic stability if we knew more about how the economic system works.

T F **11.** The major reason why the Fed ran into criticism in connection with the 1974–1975 recession is that it was attempting to stabilize the rate of growth of the money supply rather than stabilize the rate of interest.

Multiple-Choice Questions

1. Which of the following is *not* one of the four phases of the business cycle?
(a) Expansion   (c) Peak
(b) Recession   (d) Inflation

2. Which of the following years is commonly regarded as a peak associated with the most violent business cycle in U.S. history?
(a) 1921   (c) 1933
(b) 1929   (d) 1973

3. Which of the following typically shows the greatest percentage variation over a business cycle?
(a) Consumption   (c) Investment
(b) Government purchases   (d) GNP

4. According to acceleration principle
(a) The change of investment depends upon the change of consumption
(b) The change of investment depends upon the level of consumption
(c) The level of investment depends upon the change of consumption
(d) The level of investment depends upon the level of consumption

5. Suppose that a firm's sales go from 100 to 120 in the first year, and from 120 to 130 in the second year. Then, according to the accelerator principle, the firm's net investment will
(a) Increase in both years
(b) Increase in year two but not necessarily in year one
(c) Increase in year one but not necessarily in year two
(d) Decrease in year two

6. Which of the following is a firm likely to do *first* when faced with a decline in demand?
(a) Lay off workers
(b) Cut production
(c) Reduce investment plans
(d) Wait to see if the decline persists

7. According to the acceleration principle, a decline in investment demand contains the seeds of a recovery because
(a) The decline in sales must eventually slow down, at which time investment will stop falling
(b) Congress will not allow a depression to persist forever
(c) The resulting drop in interest rates will stimulate aggregate demand
(d) The aggregate supply schedule is vertical

8. Monetary and fiscal policies have been
(a) Procyclical during every business cycle in U.S. history
(b) Countercyclical during every business cycle in U.S. history
(c) Procyclical about as often as countercyclical
(d) Only rarely procyclical

9. Prior to the 1969–1970 recession
(a) Both monetary and fiscal policies were contractionary
(b) Monetary policy was contractionary but fiscal policy was expansive
(c) Both monetary and fiscal policies were expansive

(d) Monetary policy was expansive but fiscal policy was contractionary

10. The lag that occurs in the operation of fiscal policy because Congress takes time to approve changes in tax laws is
  (a) An action lag   **(c)** An impact lag
  (b) A recognition lag   **(d)** All of the above

11. The political business cycle refers to
  (a) The shifting trend of opinion for or against big business
  (b) The cycle in economic activity resulting from policies aimed at getting politicians reelected
  (c) The cycle in the fortunes of political parties that is

due to economic events beyond anyone's control
  (d) The cycle in the fortunes of political parties that is deliberately engineered by big business interests

12. Under the terms of the 1951 Federal Reserve–Treasury Accord, the Fed
  (a) Agreed to keep interest rates up
  (b) Agreed to keep interest rates down
  (c) Was released from its obligation to keep interest rates up
  (d) Was released from its obligation to keep interest rates down

Exercises

1. Suppose that a manufacturer of tennis balls wants 5 machines for every 100,000 balls sold in a year. Suppose that the manufacturer starts the beginning of year one with 50 machines and that it replaces 10 machines every year, no matter how many machines it has. Suppose that its annual sales behave as indicated in Table 15-1 below. Fill in the rest of the table. (If you have trouble, refer back to Table 15-1 in the textbook.)

2. Figure 15-1 below shows how real GNP might fluctuate during the course of two consecutive business cycles. The recessions occurred during the time periods _____ and _____; the expansions during the periods _____ and _____. The peaks occurred at _____ and _____, and the troughs at _____ and _____.

3. Suppose the economy is initially at point A in Figure 15-2 below, with the MEC schedule I_1.

Table 15-1

Year	Annual sales (hundreds of thousands)	Desired no. of machines	Net investment	Gross investment
1	10	50	0	_____
2	10	_____	_____	_____
3	12	_____	_____	_____
4	16	_____	_____	_____
5	14	_____	_____	_____
6	14	_____	_____	_____
7	12	_____	_____	_____
8	10	_____	_____	_____
9	9	_____	_____	_____
10	10	_____	_____	_____
11	10	_____	_____	_____

FIGURE 15-1

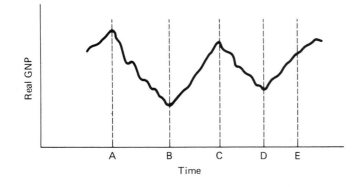

FIGURE 15-2

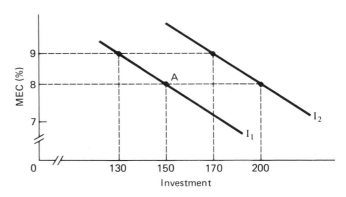

Now suppose that, because of an improvement in business optimism, the MEC schedule shifts to the one labeled I_2.

a. If the central bank allows the rate of interest to rise to 9 percent, then the new quantity of investment demand will be _____. This represents an increase of _____ in investment demand. With an MPC of 0.8 the multiplier will be _____ (for simplicity assume that all taxes are lump-sum). Thus, the change in investment demand will result in a change in equilibrium national product, of the amount.

b. If the central bank pegs the rate of interest at 8 percent the shift in investment demand will cause the demand for bank loans to (increase, decrease). In order to keep the rate of interest constant in the face of this change in demand for bank loans, the central bank will conduct open market (purchases, sales). In this case, the change in investment demand will be _____, causing an increase of _____ in equilibrium national product.

c. The increase in equilibrium national product is greatest when the central bank (allows, does not allow) the interest rate to rise. If there is an inflationary gap to begin with, then this gap will grow fastest when the central bank (allows, does not allow) the interest rate to rise.

Essay Questions

1. In studying such items as GNP and unemployment to determine whether or not a recession has occurred, the NBER looks at seasonally adjusted data. Why wouldn't the seasonally unadjusted data be just as good?

2. If seasonally adjusted real gross national product were constant for several quarters in a row, what would likely happen to the average person's real income? What do you think would happen to the rate of unemployment?

3. Some people have argued that the U.S. economy could never undergo another great depression, because the FDIC would prevent another bank panic like the one in the early thirties, the Fed's margin requirements would prevent speculative indulgence of the sort that preceded the 1929 crash, and the Congress and administration would adjust fiscal policy to combat the downward movement. Do you agree or disagree?

4. Consider your own expenditures on consumption. Do they vary from year to year by more or less than your income? Do they vary from month to month by more or less than your income? From week to week? From day to day? In the light of this, why do you suppose that the percentage changes in consumption demand over the business cycle are generally much smaller than the percentage changes in investment demand?

5. "Because of the interaction between the accelerator and the multiplier, business cycles can be caused by even small fluctuations in the demand for investment goods." Do you agree or disagree? Explain.

6. Why do you think a business firm might not want its production or investment decisions to respond to temporary fluctuations in demand? How can a business firm decide when a fluctuation in demand is temporary and when it is permanent?

7. Suppose that the President were to ask Congress for a reduction in tax rates during each month when the unemployment rate was above 5 percent, and to ask for an increase in tax rates whenever the rate of unemployment was below 5 percent. Do you suppose that this would accomplish the goal of stabilizing the rate of unemployment at 5 percent? Why or why not?

8. In Exercise 3 above, suppose that the initial position (at A) was one of a recessionary gap, rather than an inflationary gap. Would you still say that the central bank was falling into a policy trap by pegging the interest rate at 8 percent rather than letting it rise to 9 percent? Why or why not? What lesson can be drawn from this about policy traps?

*9. According to monetarists, the business cycle is primarily monetary in origin; that is, recessions and expansions are caused principally by decreases and increases in the rate of growth of the money supply. Others feel that it is "real" in origin; that is, that recessions and expansions are caused by decreases and increases in the level of investment demand or some other component of aggregate demand independently of monetary causes. Also, it has been observed that the rate of interest tends to rise during the expansion phase of the business cycle and to fall during recession. Does this fact tend to support the case of the monetarists or of their opponents? Why?

*10. It has also been observed that the money supply generally moves in a procyclical direction. Can you think of a way in which an opponent of monetarism could explain this observation without having to give up his or her "real" explanation of the business cycle? (Hint: Refer back to the section on the statistical evidence in Chapter 12.)

Answers

True-False Questions: **1** F **2** F **3** F **4** T **5** F **6** F **7** T **8** T **9** F **10** T **11** F
Multiple-Choice Questions: **1** d **2** b **3** c **4** c **5** d **6** d **7** a **8** c **9** a **10** a **11** b **12** d

Exercises

1. Table 15-1

Year	Desired no. of machines	Net investment	Gross investment
1	50	0	10
2	50	0	10
3	60	10	20
4	80	20	30
5	70	−10	0
6	70	0	10
7	60	−10	0
8	50	−10	0
9	45	−5	5
10	50	5	15
11	50	0	10

2. AB, CD, BC, DE, A, C, B, D
3. **a.** 170, 20, 5, 100
   b. increase, purchases, 50, 250
   c. does not allow, does not allow

CHAPTER 16
Fine Tuning or Stable Policy Settings?

Learning Objectives

After you have studied this chapter in the textbook and the study guide, you should be able to

Describe the procedures followed in implementing the activist policies of the 1960s

Argue the cases for and against discretionary policies

Explain how "rational expectations" could make inflation accelerate rapidly during a period of expansion, but cause a quick unwinding of inflation in the event of a restrictive policy

Explain why, according to "rational expectations" theorists, systematic demand-management policies are ineffective

Argue the cases for and against the use of policy rules

CHAPTER HIGHLIGHTS

This chapter deals with the controversy over rules versus discretion. The aim is to acquaint you with the arguments and counterarguments put forth by each side in the controversy and with the general points of agreement that have so far resulted.

Discretionary Policy

The case for discretionary policy has origins in Keynes's *General Theory.* The advocates of discretion argue that aggregate demand will tend to be (1) inadequate and (2) unstable, unless fiscal and monetary policies are adjusted periodically. This view

was influential in the early 1960s. During that era, government policy was aimed at (1) estimating potential GNP for the next several years, (2) forecasting where the economy would actually go (and therefore the size of the GNP gap) with different alternative policy settings, and then (3) selecting fiscal and monetary policies which, according to these forecasts, will close the GNP gap in a reasonably short period. In preparing such forecasts, economists use a number of techniques, including the use of econometric models, survey data, and leading indicators.

The case against discretion consists mainly of the following four arguments:

118

1. Economists' forecasting ability is weak, especially in forecasting the lags in government policy. Thus, policy makers can easily overreact to current events, like the panicky helmsman, doing more harm than good.

2. Government policy affects real national output with a lag but it affects the price level with an even longer lag. Because of this, there is an inflationary bias to activist policy. Political decision makers may choose expansionary policies for the short-run benefits of increasing real output, and worry later about the inflationary consequences.

3. Activists may tend to overestimate potential GNP. This can add another inflationary bias, because an activist may strive to attain an unrealistically high level of aggregate demand. (On this point see Figures 16-4 and 16-5 in the textbook.)

4. The use of discretion by government officials reduces individual freedom; we should be as free as possible from government meddling.

Rational Expectations

Another criticism of discretionary policy has arisen recently, based on the theory of *rational expectations*. This criticism is a refinement of the accelerationist argument discussed in Chapter 13. When policy makers try to hold unemployment below its natural rate (at, say, U_T in Figure 16-6 in the textbook), people will increase the rate of inflation that they expect. These expectations will get incorporated into wage contracts and will shift the Phillips curve up, causing inflation to accelerate. The rational expectations critique argues that the increase in expected inflation will occur not just because people *react* to the experience of *past* inflation, but because they *anticipate* the *future* inflation that will be caused by these expansionary policies of the government. Thus, the theory predicts a more rapid acceleration than the argument spelled out in Chapter 13. It also has two important policy implications. First, it argues that the transition to a lower rate of inflation (recall this from Chapter 13) would be eased by a strong, announced, credible policy of limiting the growth in aggregate demand. People would anticipate the effects of this policy, revise downward their expectations of inflation, and hasten the downward shift of the Phillips curve needed to complete the transition. The other policy implication is that systematic policies aimed at stabilizing aggregate demand are ineffective. When people realize that an expansionary policy is likely to be followed, they will anticipate the eventual effects on prices, and this will cause prices to rise quickly, rather than after a long lag. Thus, the increase in aggregate demand takes the form of a price increase rather than an increase in national product. Both these policy conclusions are highly controversial.

Rules

Advocates of rules argue that the best policy is one that follows rules designed to permit the system to function smoothly in the long run rather than to offset short-run fluctuations in aggregate demand. Two commonly advocated rules are: (1) that the Fed be required to make the money supply grow by some fixed amount, say 4 or 5 percent, each year, and (2) that the federal government be required each year to achieve a balanced full-employment budget. (Recall this concept from Chapter 9.)

Neither of these rules has ever been adopted in the United States. Opponents of rules have made the four following arguments:

1. The policy maker is foolish to adopt rigid rules that may become outdated as circumstances change in unforeseen ways.

2. The benefits of stable policy are questionable. There is no guarantee that stable monetary and fiscal policies will lead to stable aggregate demand. Indeed, stable monetary policy, according to one definition of money, will probably lead to *un*stable monetary policy according to other definitions because, for example, M-1 and M-2 follow quite different time paths.

3. The rules that have been advocated may have a bias toward slow growth and high unemployment. For example, the adoption of a rule aimed at producing no inflation may generate too much unemployment in the short run. It may also cause high unemployment in the long run unless the long-run Phillips curve is really vertical.

4. Since no rule is ever really fixed, the attempt to stick to a rigid rule and let the chips fall where they may can actually produce violent swings in policy when the government's resolve finally gives and the rule is broken. An example sometimes referred to is the sudden introduction of wage-price controls by President Nixon in 1971 after 2½ years of trying to stick to a stable policy.

Conclusions

Advocates of rules make their case by referring to the chaotic economic events of the 1970s, especially the rising inflation, which they attribute to overexpansive activist policies in the 1960s. Activists point to the continuous expansion from 1961 to 1969, which they attribute to the same activist policies.

General agreement has emerged on the following two points: (1) Demand management by the government may increase economic instability rather than reduce it, especially because of the unpredictable lags. (2) More attention should be paid to the long-term effects of policy, especially the effects on inflation.

IMPORTANT TERMS

Discretionary policy Monetary or fiscal policy that is changed from time to time according to the judgment of the policy maker.

Policy rules Formulas that prevent policymakers from using their discretion.

Fine-tuning The extreme case of discretionary policy, in which policy is adjusted with the aim of smoothing out even minor fluctuations in aggregate demand.

Potential GNP The amount of GNP that could be produced with full employment.

GNP gap Potential GNP minus actual GNP.

Leading indicator Any variable that tends regularly to reach a turning point (peak or trough) before the economy as a whole changes direction. (New orders for durable goods are an example.)

Labor productivity (Sometimes called just *productivity*.) Total output divided by the number of units of labor input.

Rational expectations Expectations that make use of available information and anticipate the effects of systematic (and therefore predictable) government policies.

True-False Questions

T F 1. Advocates of discretionary policy tend to be more in the Keynesian tradition than are advocates of rules.
T F 2. One rule commonly advocated by monetarists is for the Fed to maintain the same interest rate from month to month.
T F 3. Fine-tuning is not a policy advocated by those in favor of rules.
T F 4. Advocates of discretionary policy often refer to the long expansion of the 1960s as evidence in support of their case.
T F 5. Activists are more inclined than proponents of rules to support restrictive policies.
T F 6. The activist case would be stronger if economists could forecast better.
T F 7. According to the advocates of rules, activists tend systematically to underestimate potential GNP.
T F 8. The fact of rising inflation over the 1970s is often pointed out by critics of discretionary policy as evidence of the inflationary bias of activists.
T F 9. The issue of economic freedom arises in the controversy over rules versus discretion mainly because the more rules we have to obey the less freedom we have.
T F 10. Advocates of rules are more inclined than activists to believe that the long-run Phillips curve is vertical.

Multiple-Choice Questions

1. Forecasts of potential GNP are required mainly for
    (a) Discretionary policies
    (b) Money-supply rules
    (c) Limiting the growth of government spending
    (d) Gradualist policies
2. Which of the following was *not* an integral part of the discretionary policies pursued in the early 1960s?
    (a) Estimating potential GNP
    (b) Forecasting the effects of alternative policy settings
    (c) Selecting policies predicted to close the GNP gap in a brief time
    (d) Predicting the ultimate effects of these policies on inflation
3. Suppose the Council of Economic Advisers forecasts a GNP gap of $50 billion for the coming year under the assumption of no change in government policy (that is, actual GNP *below* potential GNP by $50 billion). Then, an
    (a) Advocate of rules would prescribe an increase in government spending
    (b) Advocate of rules would prescribe a decrease in government spending
    (c) Activist would prescribe an increase in government spending
    (d) Activist would prescribe a decrease in government spending
4. Which of the following is a commonly used tool of forecasting?
    (a) Survey data
    (b) Econometric models
    (c) Leading indicators
    (d) All of the above
5. Which of the following was a period of continuous expansion in the U.S. economy?
    (a) 1929–1944   (c) 1961–1969
    (b) 1951–1959   (d) 1971–1979

6. The most common example of a policy rule advocated by monetarists is to

(a) Make the money supply grow by 4 percent each year

(b) Let the rate of the growth of the money supply during any year equal 4 percent plus the percentage GNP gap of the previous year

(c) Fix the rate of unemployment at its natural rate

(d) Always balance the government budget

7. The institution of a price freeze and simultaneous expansionary policies in 1971 is best cited as an example of

(a) The kind of rule that monetarists advocate

(b) The danger that the policy of gradualism may eventually lead to an even bigger change in policy settings when it is abandoned

(c) The discretionary policies that had been pursued continuously since the early 1960s

(d) A policy that was motivated mainly by long-run considerations

8. Monetarists argue that if it followed a fixed monetary rule, the Fed would

(a) Eliminate economic instability

(b) Reduce economic instability

(c) Increase economic instability

(d) Not affect economic instability

9. Which of the following is *not* a major point in the case against activist policy?

(a) Activists tend to overestimate potential GNP

(b) Activists tend to advocate policies with an expansionary bias

(c) Activists tend to underreact to changes in aggregate demand

(d) Activist policies are contrary to individual freedom

10. Which of the following is *not* a major point in the case against policy rules?

(a) No rule is ever really fixed, anyway

(b) There is a long historical experience of following monetary and fiscal rules in the United States which suggests that they don't work

(c) Rules introduce too much rigidity into policy making

(d) The benefits of following rules are nebulous, as illustrated by the difficulty of choosing the appropriate definition of money

11. Which of the following assumptions does the theory of rational expectations *add* to the accelerationist argument?

(a) People anticipate the effects of future government policies

(b) Peoples' expectations change in response to the experience of past inflation

(c) Unemployment cannot remain below its natural rate without causing peoples' expectations of inflation to increase

(d) The position of the short-run Phillips curve depends upon the expected rate of inflation

12. According to the theory of rational expectations

(a) The long-run Phillips curve is not vertical

(b) Systematic demand-management policies are ineffective

(c) Changes in aggregate demand affect prices only with a long and variable lag

(d) The transition to a lower rate of inflation will take many years to accomplish unless an incomes policy is used

13. The unpredictability of lags is now generally agreed to be a reason why

(a) Monetary policy should follow rules, not discretion

(b) Fiscal policy is preferable to monetary policy

(c) Fiscal and monetary policies may easily increase economic instability

(d) More reliance should be placed on the estimates of potential GNP by the Council of Economic Advisers

14. There is now substantial agreement among economists of all persuasions that

(a) The "rational expectations" critique of activist policy is valid

(b) Policy during the 1960s on the whole was not expansionary enough

(c) During the 1980s governments should be less concerned with lags in the economic system than they were in the 1960s

(d) Policy makers should pay more attention to the long run than they did in the 1960s and 1970s

Exercise

In this exercise you must choose a fiscal policy. See if you can learn from this what kind of problems beset policy makers in the presence of imperfectly understood economic lags.

a. Suppose your advisers tell you that potential GNP is now $990 billion and that it will grow by $60 billion per year for each of the next four years. (All figures are in constant dollars.) Last year (year zero) and the year before, actual GNP was $810 billion and G (the level of government spending on goods and services) was $250 billion. Next, suppose that your advisers tell you that the government spending multiplier is 3, that they do not foresee any lags in the economic system, and that aggregate demand will not change unless G changes. In Table 16-1, chart the behavior of potential GNP, and of actual GNP and the GNP gap under different assumptions about G.

In this example, policy (A, B, C) is the neutral policy of keeping the same level of government spending, policy (A, B, C) is the activist policy of trying to eliminate the GNP gap immediately, and policy (A, B, C) is the "gradualist" policy of eliminating the GNP gap in stages over 4 years.

Table 16-1

	Year 1	Year 2	Year 3	Year 4
Potential GNP	990			
G	250	250	250	250
A. Actual GNP	810	810	810	810
GNP gap	180			
G	310	330	350	370
B. Actual GNP				
GNP gap				
G	280	310	340	370
C. Actual GNP				
GNP gap				

b. Now suppose that your advisers were mistaken. Instead of no lag, the multiplier operates with a 1-year lag, so that any change by one unit in G this year would cause a 3-unit change in GNP *next* year, but no change in GNP *this* year. Then, show the results of the three policies in Table 16-2.

c. Next, suppose that as well as the lag there are shifts in aggregate demand that were unforeseen by your advisers. Suppose that the changes in investment from one year to the next were as indicated in Table 16-3, and that these changes, just like changes in G, affected GNP with a multiplier of 3 and with a 1-year delay. Show in Table 16-4 the outcomes of the three policies.

Table 16-4 shows a potential hazard of activist policies. The activist policy, B, instead of just closing the GNP gap in years 2, 3, and 4, would result in a sizable (recessionary, inflationary) gap. The less active, "gradualist" policy, C, would result in a (smaller, larger) gap. And the best policy in terms of producing the smallest average gap over the years 2 through 4, would be the (neutral, activist, gradualist) policy.

Table 16-2

G	Year 1	Year 2	Year 3	Year 4
A. Actual GNP	810	810	810	810
GNP gap	180			
B. Actual GNP	810			
GNP gap				
C. Actual GNP				
GNP gap				

Table 16-3

	Year 0	Year 1	Year 2	Year 3
Change in investment over previous year	0	+50	+40	+20

Table 16-4

	Year 1	Year 2	Year 3	Year 4
A. Actual GNP				
GNP gap				
B. Actual GNP				
GNP gap				
C. Actual GNP				
GNP gap				

Essay Questions

1. Why can't the government always eliminate the GNP gap by continuing to change government spending as long as the gap persists?

2. Suppose that a 4 percent monetary rule were adopted. Then suppose that the introduction of an electronic transfer system for making payments caused a large increase in the income velocity of money. What would happen to the price level? Could this have been avoided if the rule hadn't been adopted? Can you think of a way to set up a rule that would allow for such contingencies?

3. What is meant by the statement that lending indicators have predicted seven of the last five recessions?

4. Explain why activist policies may have an inflationary bias, compared with those advocated by the proponents of rules.

5. Policy makers have objectives in addition to the major goals of economic policy. They are concerned, for example, about national defense and human rights. How does the presence of these other objectives affect the cases for and against adopting policy rules?

6. Explain why economists who attach a great deal of importance to the long-run consequences of economic policy are more likely to be advocates of policy rules than are those who are more concerned with the short-run consequences.

*7. Some government policy makers tend to be skeptical of the forecasts produced by their economic advisers. Discuss with reference to the experience after World War II in the United States whether or not such skepticism is justified. (Refer to the Appendix to Chapter 9.)

Answers

True-False Questions: 1 T   2 F   3 T   4 T   5 F   6 T   7 F   8 T   9 F   10 T
Multiple-Choice Questions: 1 a   2 d   3 c   4 d   5 c   6 a   7 b   8 b   9 c   10 b   11 a   12 b   13 c   14 d.

Exercise:

a. Table 16-1   A, B, C

Year 1	Year 2	Year 3	Year 4
990	1050	1110	1170
810	810	810	810
180	240	300	360
990	1050	1110	1170
0	0	0	0
900	990	1080	1170
90	60	30	0

b. Table 16-2

Year 1	Year 2	Year 3	Year 4
810	810	810	810
180	240	300	360
810	990	1050	1110
180	60	60	60
810	900	990	1080
180	150	120	90

c. Table 16-4   inflationary, smaller, neutral

Year 1	Year 2	Year 3	Year 4
810	960	1080	1140
180	90	30	30
810	1140	1320	1440
180	−90	−210	−270
810	1050	1260	1410
180	0	−150	−240

CHAPTER 17
Productivity and Growth:
Why Have They Been So Disappointing?

Learning Objectives

After you have studied this chapter in the textbook and the study guide you should be able to

Explain the relationship between total output, total number of hours worked, and labor productivity

Describe what happened to productivity between 1948 and 1966, and what happened during the 1970s

Summarize Denison's conclusions about the sources of growth from 1929 to 1969

Explain why, according to Denison, total output per employed worker fell between 1973 and 1976

Explain why Denison's "unexplained residual" might be attributed, at least in part, to two factors that he may have underestimated

Explain how the objective of economic growth may conflict with other important objectives

Summarize the changes in attitude toward economic growth that have occurred since 1960

Explain the main difference between Keynesian economics and supply-side economics

Explain the idea of an industrial strategy, and state the chief danger of adopting one

Explain how across-the-board tax cuts stimulate growth and productivity, according to supply-side economists

Draw a Laffer curve, and explain why it is shaped the way it is

Explain five ways in which lower tax *rates* might lead to higher tax revenues

Give four reasons why lower tax rates might not, in fact, cause increased growth and higher tax revenues

CHAPTER HIGHLIGHTS

The total output in the economy (Q) is equal to the total number of hours worked (L) times labor productivity (the amount of output per hour worked). Thus, to understand economic growth (the rate at which potential Q grows), we study the changes that have occurred in L and in productivity.

Figure 17-1 in the textbook shows these changes since 1800. During the 1970s, L has grown rapidly. Two reasons for this were (*a*) the rapid increase in population following World War II, and (*b*) the increasing participation of women in the labor force.

But while L was growing, productivity slowed down almost to a halt in the 1970s. Why this happened (and why economic growth slowed down during the 70s) is one of the main topics of this chapter.

The sources of economic growth during the period 1929–1969 have been studied in depth by Edward F. Denison, whose conclusions are summarized in Table 17-1 in the textbook. During this period the average rate of growth was 3.4 percent per annum. The largest single source of this growth was the increase in quantity and quality of the labor force, which accounted for 1.3 percent. Changes in capital, improved allocation of resources, and economies of scale accounted for another 1.2 percent. The remaining 0.9 percent is the unexplained residual that Denison attributes at least partly to advances in knowledge. Perhaps the main conclusion of this study is that growth has many sources. There is no single "key" source overshadowing all the rest in importance.

Table 17-2 in the textbook summarizes Denison's findings on the question of the slowdown in productivity in the 1970s. From 1973 to 1976, output per person employed *declined* at an annual rate of 0.6 percent, despite increases in education. (Denison estimates that this factor alone would have caused a 0.9 percent increase in output per person.) Denison estimates the main causes of this decline to be the reduction in hours worked (accounting for a 0.5 percent decline), changes in the age-sex composition of the labor force (0.3 percent), and increased crime and regulation that diverted resources from producing measurable output (0.4 percent).

Denison's calculations go some way toward explaining the decline. But after taking all the measurable factors into account he still calculates that output per worker should have grown at a 0.1 percent rate. Thus, he was left with an unexplained

negative residual of 0.7 percent! Some think that this large residual arises because Denison underestimated the importance of the 1973–1974 increase in oil prices, which required major changes in the U.S. economy—such as the redesign of the automobile. He may also have underestimated the effects of the slowdown in research and development expenditures during the 1970s. (R and D went from 3.0 percent of GNP in 1964 to 2.3 percent in 1977.)

One question raised by this slowdown in growth is: Why grow? The textbook points out three major costs of growth that must be considered when addressing this question: (*a*) lower present consumption (we must save more if we wish to accumulate more capital); (*b*) environmental deterioration (one way to grow faster is to reduce the regulatory constraints on business designed to protect the environment), and (*c*) less leisure (by working harder we can produce more output, but we may ask if the extra output is really worth the effort).

The chapter briefly discusses the concept of "optimal population"; one that maximizes the output per person in the economy. When population grows, output per head may at first increase because of increased opportunities to exploit economies of scale, but later fall, as the other productive resources of the country become increasingly scarce relative to the growing labor force. The "optimum" occurs somewhere in the middle. But we must be warned against attaching much importance to this concept. Even if more people would depress the standard of living of the existing population, who can say that the new lives are not worth the cost?

Attitudes toward the question of growth have changed a lot in recent decades. The Kennedy administration actively sought to encourage growth to keep ahead of the Russians, as well as to help alleviate poverty. In the 1970s concern with the environment and with our dwindling stock of natural resources led many people to deemphasize the goal of economic growth. The Reagan administration has revived interest in growth as a means to help pay for increased military expenditures and to counteract inflation.

This new concern with growth reflects a major change in macroeconomics. Attention is turning away from the Keynesian concern with aggregate demand, toward aggregate supply. One proposal put forth by supply-side economists is that business and government should cooperate more, with more sensible regulation and less hostility. Such cooperation, they argue, would create a climate in which business could put our productive capacity to more efficient use. Some economists have gone further and have argued that the government should adopt an *industrial strategy* of identifying the most promising industries and encouraging the flow of resources into these industries. Whether such a strategy would reap great dividends, as it has in some Japanese industries, or lead to "lemon socialism" in which the government gets increasingly entangled in unprofitable ventures, as in Italy and Britain, is an open question.

Another proposal of the supply-siders is that taxes should be cut, not, as in Keynesian economics, to stimulate aggregate demand, but to stimulate aggregate supply. The 1978 Kemp-Roth bill, which was defeated in Congress, proposed an annual 10 percent across-the-board cut in income tax rates for three years, as a means of stimulating growth. While this bill was defeated, a similar measure (a 25 percent cut over 3 years) was enacted in 1981. Lower tax rates, it is argued, would reduce the penalty against working and saving, and this increases the supply of labor and capital.

Arthur Laffer has gone so far as to argue that reduced tax *rates* would lead to increased tax *revenues*. Taxable income would expand more than the rate of taxation is decreased. This idea is illustrated by the *Laffer curve* in Figure 17-4 in the textbook. If the income tax rate were zero, then obviously no tax revenues would be raised. If the rate were increased above zero, revenues would start to come in. Thus, at first increased rates would lead to increased revenues. But this couldn't go on forever. By the time the rate had reached 100 percent, revenues would be back to zero, because no one would bother producing income that went entirely to the government. With no income there would be no income taxes collected. Thus, at some point, as the rate was increased, revenues would stop increasing. Beyond this point increased rates cause lower revenues.

Laffer argues that we are indeed beyond this point; the way to increase tax revenues is not to increase tax rates but to decrease them. There are at least five ways that this might work:

1. By encouraging people to work harder. The evidence on this is mixed. Some people work less if paid more because they can now afford more leisure.

2. By reducing the incentive to "do it yourself" (and thus avoid the taxes that the hired hand would have to pay).

3. By reducing the incentive to cheat on taxes by taking part in the underground economy. As we have seen in Chapter 7 the evidence on this is not very reliable.

4. By reducing the incentive to find tax loopholes.

5. By encouraging people to save more.

The last of these items is perhaps the most controversial. Some have argued that lower tax rates won't be effective in stimulating more growth and tax revenues because (a) with more disposable income people will consume more, thereby diverting resources away from the production of capital goods; (b) increased savings will not go to finance new investment if the government has to borrow them in order to pay for the deficits caused by lower tax rates; (c) many have argued that the effect of lower taxes on saving and growth will not be *strong* enough to make a difference; and (d) some have argued that what effects there are will occur only after a lag of many years.

Supply-siders have also pressed for specific tax cuts aimed directly at encouraging investment and saving. Examples include the proposals to make the investment tax credit payable even to firms not earning profits, to shorten depreciation periods, and to exempt interest and dividends from the income tax. The 1981 tax act included a shortening of depreciation periods, and a partial exclusion for interest payments. (The principal interest-rate provisions do not become effective until 1985.)

IMPORTANT TERMS

Productivity By itself, this term usually refers to *labor productivity*; that is, total output of the economy divided by the total number of hours worked.

Economic growth This is measured by the rate at which potential output grows. Defining growth in terms of potential rather than actual output allows us to separate the effects of growth from the effects of the business cycle. (The business cycle causes fluctuations in actual output.)

Technological improvement Inventions, better design of machinery, and better methods of production. This is one of the sources of economic growth.

Supply-side economics The theory that emphasizes supply factors—such as the quantity of capital and the willingness to work—as the principal constraints to growth, rather than the demand factors stressed by Keynesian economics.

Industrial strategy The attempt by government to identify the most promising products for future development and to encourage the flow of resources into these areas.

Lemon socialism Government ownership and support of dying companies. Many fear that an industrial strategy might lead to lemon socialism, as it appears to have done in Italy and Britain.

Laffer curve The curve that shows how tax *revenues* depend upon the *rate* of taxation. As shown in Figure 17-4 in the textbook, revenues rise first as tax rates increase, then fall back again as rates are increased even higher. Supply-side economists like Arthur Laffer, whose name is on the curve, think that the United States is on the backward bending part of the curve, where tax revenues could be raised by *lowering* the rate of taxation.

True-False Questions

T F   **1.** Total output equals total hours worked times labor productivity.
T F   **2.** Labor productivity grew faster in the 1970s than in the 60s.
T F   **3.** Denison found that almost all the economic growth from 1929 to 1969 could be attributed to growth in the quality and quantity of labor input.
T F   **4.** Denison's account of the decline in productivity from 1973 to 1976 left most of the decline unexplained.
T F   **5.** Higher oil prices can contribute to declining productivity even if they do not cause the consumption of oil to fall.
T F   **6.** The Reagan administration has reemphasized the goal of economic growth, partly as a means of helping to pay for increased military expenditures.
T F   **7.** The "optimal population" is the largest one that can be maintained at more than subsistence incomes.
T F   **8.** According to supply-side economists, tax cuts will reduce the supply of labor by allowing people to earn more after taxes while working less.
T F   **9.** The 1981 tax bill included a 25 percent cut in income tax rates.
T F   **10.** According to Laffer, tax rates in 1981 were so high that a cut in tax rates would increase revenues.

Multiple-Choice Questions

1. Labor productivity equals
   (a) Total output divided by the labor force
   (b) Total output divided by the number of hours worked
   (c) Total output divided by the number of manual workers
   (d) The output that can be attributed to labor rather than to any other factor of production
2. During the 1970s the total number of hours worked
   (a) Increased faster than the average since 1900
   (b) Increased slower than the average since 1900
   (c) Stayed roughly constant
   (d) Decreased sharply
3. During the 1970s labor productivity
   (a) Increased faster than the average since 1900
   (b) Increased slower than the average since 1900
   (c) Stayed roughly constant
   (d) Decreased sharply
4. The increase in the growth of labor input during the 1970s can be attributed, at least in part, to
   (a) The sharp increase in population growth following World War II
   (b) The increasing rate of participation of women in the labor force
   (c) both (a) and (b)
   (d) Neither (a) nor (b)
5. The average rate of growth of potential output from 1929–1969 was what percent?
   (a) 0.9   (c) 2.3
   (b) 1.3   (d) 3.4

6. To which of the following does Denison attribute the largest share of economic growth from 1929–1969?
   (a) The quality and quantity of labor input
   (b) The capital stock
   (c) Economies of scale
   (d) Technological improvement
7. According to Denison which of the following did *not* contribute to the decline in output per worker from 1973 to 1976?
   (a) Hours worked
   (b) Legal and human environment
   (c) Education
   (d) Age-sex composition of the labor force
8. Which of the following is *not* one of the major costs of economic growth?
   (a) Less consumption
   (b) Less capital
   (c) Less leisure
   (d) More environmental damage
9. The "optimal population" occurs at what size in Table 17-1 below?
   (a) 100 million   (c) 200 million
   (b) 150 million   (d) 250 million

Table 17-1

Population	Total output
100 million	1,500 billion
150 million	3,000 billion
200 million	3,500 billion
250 million	4,000 billion

10. Supply-side economics differs from Keynesian economics mainly because it
- **(a)** Predicts that tax cuts will cause output to increase
- **(b)** Predicts that tax cuts will cause output to decrease
- **(c)** Predicts that increases in government spending will be more effective than tax cuts as a means of increasing output
- **(d)** Assumes that the effects of tax cuts on output work mainly through aggregate supply, not aggregate demand

11. The main argument *against* adopting an industrial strategy is that
- **(a)** The government is in the best position to predict which industries will be the future "winners"
- **(b)** We should concentrate more on agriculture, less on industry
- **(c)** Such a strategy could develop into "lemon socialism"
- **(d)** It would put us on the upward-sloping part of the Laffer curve

12. Which of the following events is most likely, according to Laffer, following an across-the-board reduction in income tax rates?
- **(a)** Inflation will decrease
- **(b)** Tax revenues will decrease
- **(c)** National output will decrease
- **(d)** The supply of labor will decrease

13. Supply-side economists argue that lower tax rates would facilitate the growth of the capital stock. Which of the following events would be most likely to contribute to this outcome?
- **(a)** The resulting deficits cause the government to borrow more
- **(b)** The extra disposable income induces people to consume more
- **(c)** The resulting deficits lead to greater inflation, and thus more disruption of long-term bond markets
- **(d)** The lower tax rates increase the after-tax real rate of interest, thus increasing the reward to saving

14. Which of the following is *not* one of the ways that lower tax rates might cause higher tax revenues, according to supply-side economists?
- **(a)** People might cheat less on their taxes
- **(b)** People might be encouraged to "do it yourself" more
- **(c)** People might work longer hours
- **(d)** People might not search as hard for tax loopholes

Exercises

1. Fill in the blanks.

a. Denison found that the main factors contributing to economic growth between 1929 and 1969 (other than the unexplained residual which he attributed at least partly to technological improvement) were

_____,

_____,

_____,

and _____.

Over this period, one factor that worked to restrain the growth rate was _____

_____.

b. Two factors that Denison may have underestimated in accounting for the decline from 1973 to 1976 in output per employed worker are _____

and _____.

c. Economic growth first became a major objective of the government under the administration of President _____, who emphasized growth as a means of_____

_____

and _____

_____.

During the early 70s the goal of growth was (reemphasized, deemphasized) because of concern for the _____

and for our dwindling _____.

The Reagan administration has (reem-

phasized, deemphasized) this goal as a means of paying for _____

_____

and of alleviating the problem of

_____.

2a. According to supply-side economists, across-the-board tax cuts will induce people to work (more, less), to engage in (more, less) in nonmarket activities (for example, "doing it yourself"), to cheat (more, less) on taxes, to spend (more, less) time search-

FIGURE 17-1

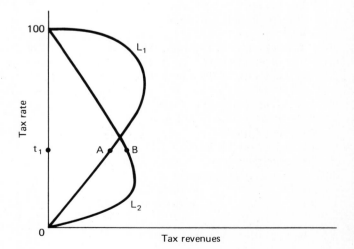

ing for tax loopholes, and to save (more, less).

   b. Critics of supply-side economics argue that following such a tax cut, people with more disposable income will consume (more, less), that governments will have to borrow (more, less), that the effects of lower taxes on increasing saving and growth are (strong, weak), and that these effects will occur (quickly, with a long lag).

3. Curves L_1 and L_2 in Figure 17-1 are two alternative Laffer curves. If the tax rate had been t_1 in 1980, then, according to Laffer we were at point _____ on curve _____, where a higher tax rate would cause tax revenues to (increase, decrease). According to Laffer's critics we were at point _____ on curve _____, where a higher rate would cause tax revenues to (increase, decrease).

Essay Questions

1. In defining economic growth, why do economists usually use potential output rather than actual output?

2. What were the probable causes of the big increases in the growth in labor input during the 1970s? Do you expect these causes to operate throughout the 1980s? What do you think explains the *inverse* relationship between growth in labor input and growth in labor productivity, as shown in Figure 17-1 in the textbook? On the basis of these answers can you make any predictions about what will happen to labor productivity through the 1980s?

3. Recall the concept of "measure of economic welfare" (MEW) discussed in Chapter 7. If this were used rather than GNP in measuring economic growth and productivity, what difference do you think it would make to the historical record as shown in Figure 17-1 in the textbook? How would it affect the costs of economic growth? How do your

answers to these two questions depend upon the way that leisure is treated in MEW?

4. What is optimal about the "optimal population"? Do you think it would be wise for the U.S. government to adopt policies to move toward this population size? Why or why not? What about poorer countries like India or China?

5. Show what would happen in a short-run Phillips curve diagram if income tax rates were reduced, according to Keynesian economics. In particular, would the tax-cut cause a movement along the curve or a shift of the curve? Show what would happen according to supply-side economics. This suggests a supply-side explanation of the rightward shift in the Phillips curve that has occurred since the 1960s. What is it?

6. "The argument that higher tax revenues will result from lower rates depends upon a combination of untested and implausible assumptions about how people will respond." Do you agree or disagree? Defend your answer.

Answers

True-False Questions: 1 T 2 F 3 F 4 T 5 T 6 T 7 F 8 F 9 T 10 T
Multiple-Choice Questions: 1 b 2 a 3 b 4 c 5 d 6 a 7 c 8 b 9 b 10 d 11 c 12 a 13 d 14 b
Exercises:
1a. labor input, physical capital, economies of scale, improvement of resource allocation; hours per worker
  b. increases in energy prices, slowdown in research and development
  c. Kennedy, helping pay to alleviate poverty, keeping ahead of the Russians; deemphasized, environment, stock of natural resources; reemphasized, increased military expenditures, inflation
2a. more, less, less, less, more
  b. more, more, weak, with a long lag
3. B, L_2, decrease; A, L_1, increase

CHAPTER 18
Fixed or Flexible Exchange Rates?

Learning Objectives

After you have studied this chapter in the textbook and the study guide you should be able to

Identify three sources of demand for a country's currency in the foreign exchange market and three sources of supply.

Describe four options available to a government when the demand for its currency shifts to the left (or supply shifts to the right) in the foreign exchange market

Explain why exchange market intervention does not provide a permanent solution to a disequilibrium in the foreign exchange market

Describe the relationship between the gold stock and the money stock under the gold standard

Describe the automatic adjustment mechanism of the gold standard

Explain the shortcomings of the gold standard

Describe how the "adjustable peg" worked

State three major differences between the gold standard and the gold exchange standard

Explain four major problems with the adjustable peg

Describe two proposals that were suggested to improve the adjustable peg

Explain the advantages and disadvantages of a flexible exchange rate

Describe the European monetary system

Explain how the rise in oil prices since 1973 has disrupted international finance

CHAPTER HIGHLIGHTS

This chapter deals with the issue of whether a government ought to regulate the country's exchange rate, and, if so, how. The main topics covered under this general issue are: (1) the mechanics of the foreign exchange market, (2) the gold standard, (3) the adjustable peg system that was organized by the

130

International Monetary Fund (IMF) from 1945 to 1971, and (4) developments in international finance since 1973.

The Foreign Exchange Market

International trade differs from domestic trade because it involves (1) tariffs and other barriers, and (2) different monies (currencies). The exchange rates between the different currencies are determined in the foreign exchange market. In this market the demand for, say, the Canadian dollar, is the amount of Canadian dollars that people wish to acquire in exchange for other currencies. It arises from the demands by foreigners for (1) Canada's exports of goods (like automobiles and newsprint), (2) Canadian services (like hotel accommodation), and (3) Canadian assets (like ownership of Canadian factories and nickel mines). Likewise, the supply of Canadian dollars in the market is the amount that people wish to give up in order to acquire other currencies. It arises from (1) Canada's imports of goods, (2) Canadian demand for foreign services, and (3) Canadian demand for foreign assets.

An exchange rate is the price of one currency in terms of another. An exchange rate may be quoted either way; for example, $1 Canadian = $0.83 U.S. means the same as $1 U.S. = $1.20 Canadian. An equilibrium exchange rate is one at which the amount of currency supplied is equal to the amount demanded.

When demand decreases (shifts to the left), the equilibrium price of a currency falls. In response to this the government has four options: It can (1) let the rate fall, (2) purchase the surplus to prevent the price from falling, (3) try to decrease the supply by direct actions like higher tariffs or exchange controls limiting the amounts of foreign currencies that people can buy, or (4) try to decrease the supply and increase the demand by restrictive monetary and fiscal policies that reduce domestic incomes and prices, thus stimulating exports and reducing imports. If option (2) is chosen and the shift in demand is permanent then some combination of (3) and (4) must also be used or eventually the government will run out of foreign exchange reserves with which to buy up the surplus amounts of its own currency.

The Gold Standard

The gold standard of the nineteenth and early twentieth centuries is an example of a fixed exchange rate system. (That is, a system which fixes the exchange rate within narrow limits.) Under a gold standard the government (1) promises to buy or sell gold freely in exchange for the domestic currency at a fixed *official price*, (2) allows its citizens freely to export and import gold, and (3) should, according to the "rule of the game," allow the country's money stock to rise when there is an inflow of gold into the country and to fall when there is an outflow.

Under this system the exchange rates between any two currencies will be fixed (within limits) by their official prices. For example, suppose the official price of an ounce of gold is $20 U.S. or 4 British pounds. Then for $5 you can buy a quarter of an ounce of gold from the U.S. government, which you can sell to the British government for 1 British pound. The freedom of people to buy and sell gold in this manner will keep the exchange rate close to £1 = $5. (Close, but not exactly at this price, because the gold transactions may involve brokerage fees and shipping costs.)

Under the gold standard, there was an automatic mechanism ensuring that no country would "run out" of gold. If a country had a large deficit in international payments, then gold would be leaving the country to pay for it. If the government obeyed the "rule of the game" this would cause the country's money supply to contract. This would cause a reduction in prices and incomes in the economy. And this in turn would correct the deficit automatically by increasing demand and reducing supply for the country's currency in the foreign exchange market. (That is, option 4 of the previous section would automatically come into play.)

There were three main problems with the gold standard:

1. The automatic adjustment could be quite costly for a country with a payments deficit, because the monetary contraction could cause severe unemployment.

2. The burden of adjustment was unevenly divided between deficit and surplus countries. A surplus country found it easy to break the "rule of the game," and allow its gold reserves to accumulate without increasing its money supply. This "sterilization" of gold forced much or all of the adjustment onto deficit countries.

3. With gold acting as the ultimate monetary reserve, a large superstructure of money was built upon a small base of gold. This meant that any disturbance that caused a "crisis of confidence" could lead to a large flow of gold out of the central bank, thus causing a drop in the money supply and starting a recession.

The Adjustable Peg

The adjustable peg operated as follows:

1. The United States fixed its dollar in terms of gold (at $35 per ounce of gold).

2. Other countries intervened in their foreign exchange markets to fix their exchange rate in terms of the U.S. dollar within 1 percent of the official "par value."

3. Countries with a temporary balance of payments disequilibrium were expected to maintain their fixed exchange rate by running down their reserves (in case of deficit) or allowing their reserves to increase (in case of surplus).

4. These reserves were held in the form of (*a*) gold, (*b*), U.S. dollars, (*c*) a reserve position in the IMF, or (*d*) beginning in 1970, SDRs.

5. Countries faced with a "fundamental" disequilibrium were permitted to change their official par value.

6. Countries were expected not to intervene with trade barriers and exchange controls except under extreme circumstances.

This system was also called the "gold exchange standard." The major differences between it and the gold standard are twofold:

1. Free private ownership of gold was crucial for the gold standard, whereas citizens of the United States and a number of other countries were not allowed by law to own gold under the adjustable peg (except for artistic or other special purposes).

2. The official rates were expected to be "permanently" fixed under the gold standard but not under the adjustable peg.

There were four major problems with the adjustable peg system.

1. It was not clear how to distinguish between a "fundamental" and a "temporary" disequilibrium.

2. If a government attempted to peg its exchange rate when speculators felt there was a fundamental disequilibrium, the speculators often made large profits at the government's expense. For example, when a country had a large balance of payments deficit, speculators would sell its currency in large quantities. The government would have to use its reserves of foreign exchange to buy up the excess supply of its currency, in order to maintain the peg. When the reserves were gone this was no longer possible and the government was forced to devalue. Thus, the speculators were able to sell high (before the devaluation) and buy low (after the devaluation).

3. Surplus countries were reluctant to revalue or to take expansionary measures that might cause inflation. As a consequence, deficit countries believed that they had to bear and unfair share of the adjustment burden.

4. The position of the U.S. dollar was somewhat precarious. If the U.S. government maintained a strong payments position (with a surplus or a small deficit), then other countries found it difficult to acquire foreign exchange reserves (most of which were held in the form of U.S. dollars). But if it ran large deficits (thereby providing the other countries with dollars), the holders of the U.S. dollars might fear that the United States would be unable to maintain the convertibility of dollars into gold. This could induce them to sell their dollars for gold, which would deplete the U.S. government's gold reserves, making it even more difficult for the U.S. to maintain the dollar's convertibility. Thus a "run" on the U.S. gold reserves could start, similar in nature to the banking panics of the nineteenth and early twentieth centuries.

Two proposals were suggested to improve this system: (1) the crawling peg, which would permit gradual changes in the official rate (par value) every month to add more flexibility to the system, and (2) wider bands that would allow the actual rate to deviate by more than 1 percent from the official rate. The crawling peg was never introduced among the major industrial countries, but wider bands were adopted in the Smithsonian agreement of December 1971.

Recent Developments

Under the flexible or floating rate system that has been in effect since 1973, a government need not intervene in its foreign exchange market (that is, it may adopt a "clean float"). If so, the exchange rate will equal its equilibrium value. But most countries have adopted a "dirty float," by buying and selling in the market to influence exchange rates.

The advantages of a flexible rate are that:

1. It avoids the problems of the other two systems.

2. It allows fiscal and monetary policies to be directed toward the important goal of stabilizing the domestic economy rather than toward maintaining the exchange rate.

The disadvantages are:

1. Changes in exchange rates may disrupt trade.

2. Many of the large fluctuations in exchange rates since 1973 appear to have served no useful purpose.

3. Flexible rates release governments from the discipline of a fixed rate system; that is, from the necessity to follow restrictive policies when the balance of payments is in deficit.

4. Depreciation of the currency adds to inflation by making imports more expensive.

In view of these disadvantages, most of the countries of Western Europe returned in 1979 to a limited form of fixed rate system called the European monetary system (EMS). Under the EMS, each currency is maintained within a range of not more than 6 percent from an official value (relative to the other currencies of the system). It is hoped that this relatively wide range will give the EMS more flexibility than previous fixed-rate systems.

One of the biggest influences on international finance since 1973 has been the increase in oil prices, first in 1973–1974, then in 1979–1980. These increases produced huge current account surpluses for OPEC countries, whose oil export revenues went from $35 billion in 1973 to $290 billion in 1980. Likewise they produced deficits for the other countries. Particularly hard hit were the less developed countries that produce no oil. Many of them have gone far into debt to pay for larger oil bills.

IMPORTANT TERMS

Foreign exchange The money of another country. Also called foreign currency.

Foreign exchange market A market in which one country's currency is bought or sold in exchange for another country's.

Exchange rate The price of one country's currency in terms of another's. A country's exchange rate can be expressed either as the price of foreign currency in terms of the domestic currency, or as the price of the domestic currency in terms of foreign currency.

Tariff A tax imposed upon a foreign good that is imported. Also called a duty.

International payment deficit A country has an international payment deficit when its foreign expenditures exceed its receipts from abroad. In other words, the supply of its currency exceeds the demand for it in the foreign exchange market. The opposite of a deficit is a *surplus*.

Gold standard The pre-World War I system under which the value of a country's currency was fixed in terms of gold.

Rule of the gold standard game The rule that each country should let its money stock rise when its gold stock is rising and fall when its gold stock is falling.

Sterilization Steps by a central bank to cancel out the automatic effects of a deficit or surplus on the country's money supply. This is against the "rule of the gold standard game."

Adjustable peg The system used by most countries in the world from 1945 to 1971.

IMF The International Monetary Fund, set up in 1944 to operate the adjustable peg system.

Par value The official exchange rate (or price of gold) chosen by a country under the adjustable peg system.

Fundamental disequilibrium This term was introduced, but not defined, by the IMF. It might be defined as an international payment deficit or surplus that is not just temporary.

Foreign exchange reserves Holdings by a central bank or government of foreign exchange.

Devaluation The reduction by a country of its currency's par value. An increase is called a *re*valuation.

Speculator Anyone who buys or sells a foreign currency (or any other asset) in the hope of making a profit when its price changes.

SDR Special Drawing Right. A new form of international reserve first issued by the IMF in 1970.

Floating exchange rate The system under which governments do not maintain any particular value for their exchange rate. Also called *flexible* exchange rate.

Clean float The central bank and treasury of a country with a clean float refrain from intervening in the foreign exchange market.

Dirty float Under a dirty float, the central bank or treasury *does* intervene in the foreign exchange market, with the objective of affecting the exchange rate.

Depreciation A decrease in the value of a currency in foreign exchange markets, under a floating exchange rate. An increase is called an *appreciation*.

*The following definitions are from the Appendix:

**Merchandise account* The record of a country's exports and imports of goods.

**Goods and services account* The record of a

country's exports and imports of goods and services.

Current account The record of all international transactions of the residents of a country not involving the acquisition or sale of an asset.

Capital account The record of all acquisitions or sales of foreign assets by domestic residents or of domestic assets by foreign residents.

Official settlements balance The net total of all international transactions except for changes in official reserves

True-False Questions

T F **1.** The demand for British exports is one source of the demand for British pounds in the foreign exchange market.

T F **2.** Foreign purchases of a country's assets constitute one source of demand for the country's currency.

T F **3.** The gold standard was an example of a fixed exchange rate system.

T F **4.** A restrictive monetary policy in a country will shift the supply curve for domestic currency to the right in the foreign exchange market.

T F **5.** Surplus countries had an easier time avoiding adjustment problems than did deficit countries under the gold standard.

T F **6.** If a country under the gold standard increased its money supply when it had a net inflow of gold then it was obeying "the rule of the game."

T F **7.** Under the adjustable peg, a country was expected to change its exchange rate in the presence of "fundamental" disequilibrium.

T F **8.** One of the problems of the adjustable peg was that if the United States restricted the supply of dollars they would experience a balance of payments deficit.

T F **9.** Under the adjustable peg until 1971 countries were expected normally to maintain an exchange rate within 1 percent of par.

T F **10.** The Smithsonian Agreement of 1971 replaced the adjustable peg with a crawling peg.

T F **11.** Special drawing rights were first issued in 1960.

T F **12.** The European monetary system fixes the value of all European currencies in relation to the dollar.

T F **13.** Increases in oil prices have led to current account deficits by nonmembers of OPEC, as a group.

Multiple-Choice Questions

1. Which of the following is *not* a source of demand for a country's currency in the foreign exchange market?
  (a) The exports of that country
  (b) That country's sales of services to foreigners
  (c) That country's demand for official reserves
  (d) Purchases by foreigners of that country's assets

2. Which of the following events would be likely to shift the demand for a country's currency to the right in the foreign exchange market?
  (a) A restrictive monetary policy in that country
  (b) A restrictive monetary policy in other countries
  (c) An increase in that country's demand for imports
  (d) A devaluation

3. An increase in the demand by foreigners for British assets will cause
  (a) The demand for pounds to shift to the right in the foreign exchange market
  (b) The pound to appreciate under a flexible exchange rate
  (c) A reduction in Britain's balance of payments deficit under a fixed exchange rate
  (d) All of the above

4. Under the gold standard, an increase in the American demand for imports was most likely to cause
  (a) An increase in the exchange value of the U.S. dollar
  (b) An increase in the outflow of gold from the United States

  (c) A decrease in the official price of gold
  (d) An increase in the U.S. money stock

5. Which of the following was *not* a part of the gold standard?
  (a) Governments had to intervene in foreign exchange markets to peg their exchange rates
  (b) Governments had to ensure convertibility between their currencies and gold at the official price
  (c) The money supply was supposed to vary in the same direction as the stock of gold in each country
  (d) Private citizens were free to import or export gold

6. Under the automatic adjustment mechanism of the gold standard an outflow of gold causes
  (a) A reduction of the money stock and a decrease in the balance of payments deficit
  (b) A reduction of the money stock and an increase in the balance of payments deficit
  (c) An increase in the money stock and a decrease in the balance of payments deficit
  (d) An increase in the money stock and an increase in the balance of payments deficit

7. Which system allows a government the greatest freedom to direct its monetary and fiscal policies toward the goal of domestic stabilization?
  (a) The gold standard
  (b) The gold exchange standard
  (c) A crawling peg

(d) A flexible rate system

8. Which of the following was *not* a problem with the gold standard?
 (a) The burden of adjustment was placed more heavily upon the deficit than on the surplus countries
 (b) The adjustment mechanism could be costly in the short run, especially for deficit countries
 (c) It was a potential source of monetary instability in the member countries
 (d) Exchange rates were never changed

9. Which of the following was true under the gold standard?
 (a) It was legal for U.S. citizens to own gold for most purposes
 (b) Exchange rates were adjustable
 (c) Governments were not required to buy or sell gold
 (d) Gold coin was the only medium of exchange

10. Which of the following statements about the workings of the adjustable peg is *not* correct?
 (a) A country could adjust its exchange rate in the presence of a fundamental disequilibrium.
 (b) The IMF was set up to provide funds to countries facing temporary payments deficits.
 (c) Countries were expected to impose exchange controls when faced with fundamental disequilibrium.
 (d) The IMF could make a loan to a deficit country contingent upon that country taking restrictive monetary and fiscal policy measures.

11. If, under the adjustable peg, a country (other than the United States) increased the official domestic price of its currency in terms of the dollar, this was called
 (a) Devaluation
 (b) Revaluation
 (c) Depreciation
 (d) Appreciation

12. Under a clean float, the depreciation of a currency causes
 (a) A decrease in that country's exports
 (b) An increase in the domestic price level
 (c) An increase in that country's balance of payments deficit
 (d) None of the above

13. The maximum width of the bands in the European monetary system is
 (a) 1 percent
 (b) 2 percent
 (c) 6 percent
 (d) 10 percent

14. Increases in oil prices seem to have caused the most severe balance-of-payments deficits in
 (a) OPEC countries
 (b) Developed countries with little oil production
 (c) Developed countries with large production
 (d) Underdeveloped countries with little oil production

Exercises

1. The data in Table 18-1 describe the demand and supply for pounds in the foreign exchange market.
 a. The equilibrium exchange rate is _____ dollars per pound, or _____ pounds per dollar. The equilibrium quantity of pounds transacted in the market is _____, and the equilibrium quantity of dollars transacted in the market is _____. Plot the supply and demand curves in Figure 18-1 and label the demand curve D_1.
 b. If the demand for pounds decreased by £20 million at each exchange rate, the equilibrium exchange rate would be _____ dollars

FIGURE 18-1

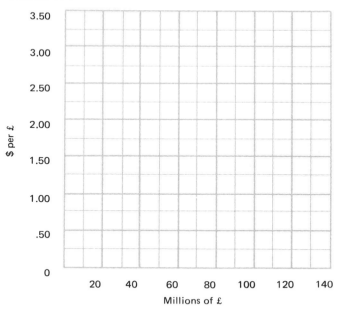

Table 18-1

Exchange rate ($ per £)	Amount demanded (millions of £)	Amount supplied (millions of £)
1.25	100	40
1.50	90	50
1.75	80	60
2.00	70	70
2.25	60	80
2.50	50	90
2.75	40	100

per pound. Plot the new demand curve in Figure 18-1 and label it D_2. The equilibrium quantity of pounds transacted would be £_____ and the equilibrium quantity of dollars transacted would be $_____. If the rate was held fixed by the government at its *previous* equilibrium value Britain would now have a balance of payments (surplus, deficit) of £_____ or $_____.

2a. Which ones of the following would be likely to increase a country's balance-of-payments deficit under a fixed exchange rate?

(i) A sudden increase in the rate of open-market purchases of securities by the central bank

(ii) A rightward shift in the demand curve for the country's exports

(iii) An increase in interest rates in other countries

(iv) An increase in that country's disposable income that caused residents to demand more imported goods

(v) A devaluation.

b. Which ones of the above would lead to a revaluation of the country's currency under a clean float? _____.

3.[1] Fill in Table 18-2 to show how each of the following sets of transactions would affect the current and capital accounts of the United States (putting a "+" to indicate that the surplus would be increased, a "−" if the surplus would be decreased, or a "0" if it would be unaffected).

A. A U.S. resident receives dividends from shares that he already owns in a foreign company, and converts the dividends into U.S. dollars.

B. A U.S. resident receives dividends as in **A** but uses his receipts to pay for an imported car.

C. A U.S. resident receives dividends as in **A** and **B** but uses the receipts to buy more shares of the same company.

D. A French company buys a U.S.-manufactured computer, paying for it by exchanging some of the francs in its bank account for U.S. dollars.

E. The French company buys the computer but pays for it with some of the earnings of its branch plant in Texas.

F. The French company buys the computer but pays for it by selling bonds to U.S. residents.

Table 18-2

	Current Account	Capital Account
A		
B		
C		
D		
E		
F		

[1] Only for those who have studied the Appendix to Chapter 18.

Essay Questions

1. Suppose that, under the adjustable peg, the government of Britain announced that it was going to devalue the pound by 10 percent in three days. How would this affect the demand and supply for pounds Sterling today? What would happen to the official reserve holdings of the British government? Would there be much risk in speculating today in the market for pounds? Why would the British government probably not be able to wait for three days?

2. In early 1969, there was a public controversy between the German central bank (which wanted a revaluation of the mark) and the German government (which didn't). What effect do you think this controversy had on exchange markets? On the operation of German monetary policy? Why do you think the central bank took the public position which it did?

3. Under the adjustable peg system, some countries felt that it was unfair for the United States to be able to benefit from being (virtually) the only country whose currency was held as reserve by other countries. This benefit is commonly referred to as "seignorage." In what sense does seignorage actually benefit the United States? Hint: Suppose that your friends were all willing to lend to you on the basis of your IOUs which they would then pass back and forth among each other to settle their debts from time to time. How would you benefit?

4. Suppose you are a U.S. importer of British cloth. You have just succeeded in selling $2 million worth of cloth to a U.S. customer for delivery in 6 months, and you do not want to buy that cloth from your supplier in England until just before your promised delivery date. Otherwise, you would have to store the cloth at great cost. Your supplier in England has promised to sell you the cloth at that time at a cost of 900,000 pounds including shipping, handling, and insurance. The exchange rate right now is $2.00 per pound so that if it stays the same for 6 months you will realize a profit on this deal of $200,000. What will happen to your profit if the pound appreciates between now and then? What if the pound depreciates? How could you eliminate the risk of making a loss if there was a forward market in pounds? (In a forward market, you can contract now to buy or sell pounds at a future date, at a price determined now.)

5. "Any event which would tend to increase the deficit of a country under a fixed exchange rate system would tend to depreciate its currency under a clean float." Do you agree? Why or why not?

6. Explain why it is easier for a country to sterilize the reserve changes resulting from a balance of payments surplus than from a balance of payments deficit.

7. How does the gold standard impose a discipline upon central banks and governments that are inclined to pursue inflationary policies? What are the advantages of such discipline? The disadvantages?

8. Suppose that all banks were required to keep 100 percent reserves of gold. Would this remove any of the problems with the gold standard? Explain.

9. "Under the adjustable peg, when the United States pursued inflationary policies, it exported inflation to the rest of the world. But under the present floating rate, the other countries can choose not to import inflation from the United States. Instead, they can allow their currencies to appreciate with respect to the U.S. dollar." Do you agree? Why or why not?

*10. In what sense is it true that a country under a floating exchange rate always has an automatic way of eliminating balance of payments deficits or surpluses? Why then do some countries still have balance of payments deficits under a floating exchange rate?

Answers

FIGURE 18-1 completed

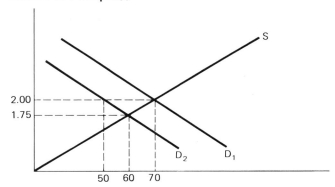

2a. i, iii, iv; **b.** ii

3. Table 18-2 completed

	Curr acct	Cap acct
A	+	0
B	0	0
C	+	−
D	+	0
E	0	0
F	+	−

PART FOUR

MICROECONOMICS: Is Our Output Produced Efficiently?

CHAPTER 19
Demand and Supply:
The Concept of Elasticity

Learning Objectives

After you have studied this chapter in the textbook and the study guide, you should be able to

Define elasticity of demand and elasticity of supply

Explain the limited connection between the elasticity of a demand or supply curve and the flatness of the curve

Explain how a shift in the supply curve alters total expenditure on a good, depending on the elasticity of demand

List four factors that increase the elasticity of demand for a good

List three factors that increase the elasticity of supply for a good

Explain how the inelasticity of the world demand for oil helped the members of OPEC (the Organization of Petroleum Exporting Countries) to increase their export earnings drastically between 1973 and 1980

Describe the special economic problems of agriculture

Show how the causes of these special problems are illuminated by the concept of elasticity

CHAPTER HIGHLIGHTS

In this chapter we begin a detailed study of microeconomics. It carries on from the supply and demand analysis of Chapter 4. In that chapter, it was argued that demand curves generally slope down and supply curves generally slope up, but nothing was said about how steep or flat those slopes might be. For many important applications of supply and demand theory, we need to know something about the steepness or flatness of the curves or, more precisely, the related (but different) concept of *elasticity*.

When the supply curve of a good shifts to the right, the equilibrium slides down the demand curve. In the process, (a) demanders buy more of the good, but (b) they pay a lower price per unit. Whether they end up paying more or less in total for the good depends upon which effect is larger, (a) or (b). This, in turn, depends upon the shape of the demand curve. For example, if the demand curve is almost vertical, then—as you can see by drawing your own diagram—there will be a drop in price but almost no increase in quantity, with the likely effect that demanders end up paying less for the good. Likewise, if the demand curve is almost horizontal, the price will not fall much but the quantity demanded will increase, so that the amount paid will increase.

We say that the demand curve is *elastic* if, in the above example, total expenditure on the good rises. It is *inelastic* if total expenditure falls. The *elasticity of demand* is defined as the percentage change in quantity divided by the percentage change in price. Demand is elastic if the elasticity is greater than one (in absolute value) and inelastic if the elasticity is less than one. As an exercise, what is the elasticity of demand if the demand curve is vertical? _____. If it is horizontal? _____.

Thus, elasticity measures the responsiveness—or flexibility—of demanders when confronted with a price change. If demand is elastic, then a 10 percent decrease in price causes demanders to respond by increasing the amount demanded by more than 10 percent. This is why demanders end up spending more on the good. If demand is inelastic, demanders may increase their purchases, but not by 10 percent. In this case, demanders end up spending less on the good. In the borderline case where the elasticity of demand equals one, demanders increase the amount demanded by exactly 10 percent, with the result that they spend the same amount of money on the good, buying 10 percent more goods at a price per good of 10 percent less.

There is an important fallacy to avoid. The concept of elasticity was introduced with a reference to the steepness or flatness of a demand curve. However, elasticity and flatness *are not the same thing*. For example, one curve may be flatter than another without having a greater elasticity. An example of this is given in Figure 19-3 in the textbook. However, there is one limited but important case where elasticity does reflect flatness. If two demand curves pass through the same point, then the flatter demand curve is also more elastic.

The elasticity of supply is similarly defined as the percentage change in the quantity supplied divided by the percentage change in price, as you move along the supply curve. Once again, this is a measure of the responsiveness or flexibility of suppliers when confronted with a price change. The supply curve is *elastic* if the elasticity of supply is greater than one or *inelastic* if the elasticity of sup-

ply is less than one. As in the case of demand, the elasticity of supply and flatness are related only in a limited sense. If two supply curves pass through the same point, the flatter one is also the more elastic. But if the two curves do not intersect, this is not necessarily so.

The elasticity of demand for a commodity tends to be greater (1) if it is a luxury rather than a necessity; (2) if it is a large item in demanders' budgets rather than a small one; (3) if it has close substitutes—that is, if it is not irreplaceable; (4) if we are considering its long-run demand curve rather than its short-run curve. The elasticity of supply tends to be greater (1) if the commodity is not perishable and has a low cost of storage, (2) if it has close substitutes in production, (3) if we are considering the long-run supply curve rather than the short-run curve. Perhaps the most important of all these items are those referring to the short run versus the long run. It stands to reason that if people are given a longer time to adjust to a change in price, they will do more adjusting than if they are only given a short time in which to adjust. Try to provide a similar explanation for each of the other items mentioned in this paragraph.

The text discusses two important applications of the concept of elasticity. The first of these is the pricing decision of OPEC (the Organization of Petroleum Exporting Countries). The world demand for oil appears to be quite inelastic. The oil revenues of OPEC members rose dramatically between 1973 and 1980, while the price of oil increased more than tenfold. If demand had been elastic, OPEC's revenues would have fallen as a result of the price increase.

The other important application deals with the special problems of agriculture. In agriculture we find (1) a highly inelastic demand curve; (2) a highly inelastic supply curve (at least in the short run); (3) large year-to-year fluctuations in the short-run supply curve, depending upon the state of the harvest from one year to the next; (4) a great deal of technological change in recent decades, which has produced large rightward shifts in the supply curve; and (5) relatively little rightward shift in the demand curve over the same period, because as incomes increase over time, people don't spend much of the increase on food. Items (1) to (3) have given rise to large fluctuations in prices and incomes. You can see why this has happened by drawing very steep demand and supply curves and shifting the supply curve back and forth. Notice how the equilibrium price responds very sharply to the shifts in the supply curve. Since the demand curve is inelastic and is staying put while the supply curve shifts, any increase in price is accompanied by a rise in farm incomes (the amount spent on agricultural products) and any reduction in price is accompanied by a reduction in farm incomes. Items (4) and (5) have contributed to a downward trend in agricultural prices. This, too, can be seen by constructing demand and supply curves. Because the supply curve has shifted to the right by more than the demand curve, the price has declined. (Note, however, that some experts think that item (4) is a thing of the past—that we are headed for a future of more and more limited increases in supply. Be sure you can show in a diagram how this slowdown of the rightward shift in supply can reverse the downward trend in prices.)

The concept of elasticity can be put to many different uses. To keep it simple, just remember this rule: Whenever a change occurs that produces a given shift to the right or left in demand or supply, the resulting change in price will be larger, the smaller is the elasticity of either supply or demand.

IMPORTANT TERMS

Total revenue The amount of money received by the sellers of a product. This also equals the amount of money spent by demanders on the product (except for sales taxes and other minor items).

Elasticity of demand The percentage change in quantity demanded divided by the percentage change in price, obtained by comparing two points on a demand curve. If the elasticity is greater than one we say that the demand curve is elastic; if it is less than one we say that it is inelastic.

Elasticity of supply The percentage change in quantity supplied divided by the percentage change in price, obtained by comparing two different points on the same supply curve. If this elasticity is greater than one, we say that the supply curve is elastic; if it is less than one, we say that the supply curve is inelastic.

*Income elasticity of demand A measure of the effect a change in income has on the quantity demanded. It is defined as the percentage change in quantity demanded divided by the percentage change in income. This is negative for an inferior good.

*Cross elasticity of demand A measure of the effect the price of good X has on the demand for good Y. Cross elasticity is defined as the percentage change in the quantity of Y divided by the percentage change in the price of X. This is positive if X and Y are substitutes, or negative if they are complements.

True-False Questions

T F   1. The elasticity of demand is the same thing as the flatness of the demand curve.

T F   2. The concept of elasticity applies only to the demand curve, not to the supply curve.

T F   3. If we go from one point to another on an elastic demand curve, then total revenue and price move in opposite directions.

T F   4. The elasticity of supply is greater in the short run than in the long run.

T F   5. If the supply curve is a straight line through the origin, then the elasticity of supply is equal to one.

T F   6. If the government were to pay companies the costs of storing inventories, this would probably make supply more elastic.

T F   7. With this subsidy for storing goods an increase in demand would have an even greater impact on price.

T F   8. If demand for food had been more responsive to rising incomes there would not have been such a pronounced downward trend to food prices.

T F   9. A technological change that shifts the supply curve to the right will normally cause the equilibrium price to fall.

T F   10. A technological change that shifts the supply curve to the right will cause total revenue to fall if demand is elastic.

Multiple-Choice Questions

1. When there is rightward shift in the supply curve, total revenue
   (a) Must rise
   (b) Must fall
   (c) Will rise only if the demand curve is elastic
   (d) Will rise only if the supply curve is inelastic
2. If a 1 percent change in price produces a 10 percent change in the quantity demanded, the elasticity of demand is
   (a) 10
   (b) 1
   (c) 0.1
   (d) 0.01
3. Suppose that when the price of oil is $30 a barrel, 40 million barrels are demanded per day, but when the price is

$40 a barrel, only 35 million are demanded. Then the demand for oil is
   (a) Elastic
   (b) Inelastic
   (c) Unit elastic
   (d) Upward sloping

4. If one demand curve is steeper than another, then the first curve is
   (a) More elastic than the other
   (b) Less elastic than the other
   (c) More elastic than the other if they intersect
   (d) Less elastic than the other if they intersect

5. When there is a rightward shift in the demand curve, total revenue
   (a) Must rise
   (b) Must fall
   (c) Will rise only if the demand curve is elastic
   (d) Will rise only if the supply curve is inelastic

6. The straight-line supply curve in Figure 19-1 below is
   (a) Elastic
   (b) Inelastic
   (c) Unit elastic
   (d) Infinitely elastic

7. Suppose that cement producers will offer to sell 13 million tons if the price is $30 per ton, or 20 million if the price is $40. Then the elasticity of supply is
   (a) 0
   (b) Between 0 and 1
   (c) 1
   (d) Greater than 1

8. The demand for a commodity will tend to be *less* elastic when
   (a) The commodity is a luxury
   (b) The commodity has several close substitutes
   (c) We are considering the long-run demand curve, not the short-run curve
   (d) The commodity is a small item in most buyers' budgets

FIGURE 19-1

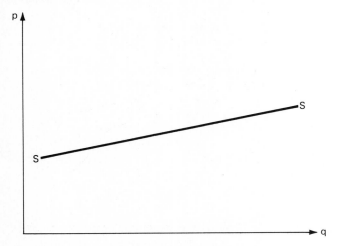

9. The fact that wheat has straw as a joint product
   (a) Makes its supply more elastic
   (b) Makes its supply less elastic
   (c) Makes its demand more elastic
   (d) Makes its demand less elastic

10. When the demand curve shifts to the right, the rise in price is greatest if
   (a) Demand is elastic and supply is elastic
   (b) Demand is elastic and supply is inelastic
   (c) Demand is inelastic and supply is elastic
   (d) Demand is inelastic and supply is inelastic

11. If a change in people's attitudes toward nutrition makes them want to buy twice as much whole wheat bread at any given price, then the price of whole wheat bread will be unaffected if
   (a) The elasticity of demand is zero
   (b) The elasticity of supply is zero
   (c) The elasticity of supply is infinite
   (d) Any of the above

12. Suppose that the minimum wage is above the market-clearing wage. Suppose it is increased further by Congress. Then the total income earned by workers
   (a) Must fall
   (b) Must rise
   (c) Will fall only if the demand for labor is elastic
   (d) Will fall only if the supply of labor is elastic

13. If the supply curve for apples shifts to the left
   (a) The rise in price will be greater in the short run than in the long run
   (b) The rise in price will be less in the short run than in the long run
   (c) The rise in price will be the same in the long and short runs
   (d) The price will fall in the short run and rise in the long run

14. Food prices would be more stable if
   (a) The demand for food were not so elastic
   (b) Food products were more easily storable
   (c) The supply of food were not so elastic
   (d) The weather was more variable

15. The long-term decline in agricultural prices in the United States might be reversed if
   (a) There was a decline in the rate of technological progress in agriculture
   (b) There was a decline in the rate of population growth throughout the world
   (c) There was a decline in the price of fertilizers
   (d) There were several years of good weather and therefore of bountiful crops throughout the world

*16. The burden of a commodity tax is borne entirely by demanders
   (a) If demand has infinite elasticity
   (b) If demand has zero elasticity
   (c) In any case under perfect competition
   (d) If supply has zero elasticity

*For those who have studied Box 19-2.

Exercises

1a. Consider the supply curves in Figure 19-2. At point A the elasticity of curve S_1 is (less than, equal to, more than) unity; the elasticity of S_2 is (less than, equal to, more than) unity, and that of S_3 is (less than, equal to, more than) unity.

1b. Consider point B on S_2. If a straight line drawn from this point through the origin represented a fourth supply curve, its elasticity would be (less than, equal to, more than) unity. Thus, the elasticity of S_2 at B is (less than, equal to, more than) unity. What can you say, then, about the elasticity of S_2 at any point on the curve? _____

Likewise, what can you say about S_3? _____

2a. In Figure 19-3, the elasticity of the supply curve S_1 is (smaller, larger) than that of S_2 at A. Suppose that, in either case, the supply curve shifts to the right by the amount AB (to S_1' and S_2', respectively). Then, if the demand curve is D_1, the fall in price with S_1' is (smaller, larger) than with S_2' and the rise in quantity is (smaller, larger) with S_1' than with S_2'.

2b. Still referring to Figure 19-3, the demand curve D_1 is (less, more) elastic than D_2. When S_1 shifts to S_1' the fall in price with demand curve D_1 is (smaller, larger) and the rise in quantity is (smaller, larger) than with D_2.

2c. In Figure 19-4, the elasticity of the demand curve D_1 is (smaller, larger) than that of D_2. Suppose that, in either case, the demand curve shifts to the

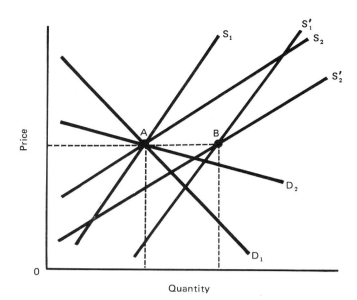

FIGURE 19-3

right by the amount AB (to D_1' and D_2', respectively). Then, if the supply curve is S_1, the rise in the price with D_1' is (smaller, larger) than with D_2', and the rise in quantity is (smaller, larger) with D_1' than with D_2'.

2d. Still referring to Figure 19-4, the supply curve S_1 is (less, more) elastic than S_2. When D_1 shifts to D_1', the rise in price with supply curve S_1 is (smaller, larger) and the rise in quantity is (smaller, larger) than with S_2.

FIGURE 19-4

FIGURE 19-2

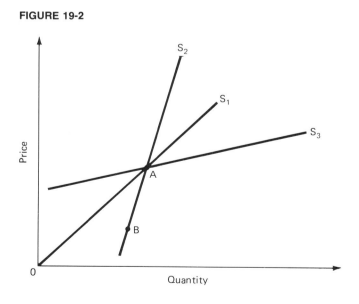

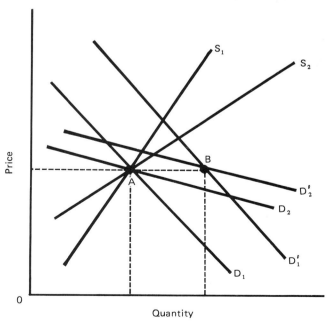

3a. The data in Table 19-1 describe hypothetical demand and supply curves for apples. Plot these curves in Figure 19-5. The equilibrium price of apples is $_____ per bushel, and the equilibrium quantity is _____ million bushels. When the price rises from $10 to $20, the percentage change in price is[1] _____; the percentage change in quantity demanded is _____; the elasticity of demand is _____; the percentage change in quantity supplied is _____; the elasticity of supply is _____.

3b.[2] Suppose now that the government requires the buyers of apples to pay a sales tax of $10 per bushel. (You may assume that initially there were no sales taxes at all.) When the buyers now pay $15 per bushel, the sellers receive only $_____ per bushel. Thus, according to Table 19-1, they will supply _____ million bushels. Fill in the rest of Table 19-2.

Table 19-2

(1) Price per bushel paid by demanders (including tax)	(2) Amount per bushel received by sellers	(3) Millions of bushels supplied
$10	$ 0	0
15		
20		
25		

Plot the new supply curve in Figure 19-5. The new equilibrium price (paid by demanders) is $_____, and the new equilibrium quantity is _____. Of the $10 per bushel paid in sales tax, the sellers are paying $_____ and the demanders are paying $_____.

3c. Draw a straight-line demand curve passing through the point (P = 15, Q = 15) which is less elastic than the one already drawn. If this new demand curve were to replace the old demand curve, the equilibrium price before the imposition of the tax would be[3] _____, the equilibrium quantity before the tax would be _____, the equilibrium price after the tax would be _____, and the equilibrium quantity after the tax would be _____ than with the old demand curve. With the new demand curve, the amount of tax paid by the demanders would be _____ and the amount paid by suppliers would be _____ than with the old demand curve.

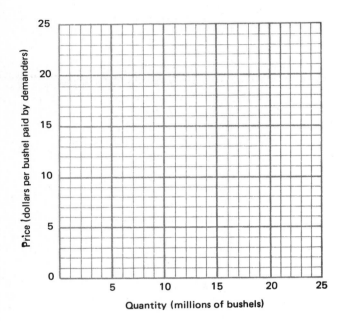

Quantity (millions of bushels)

Table 19-1

Price per bushel	Millions of bushels demanded	Millions of bushels supplied
$ 5	25	5
10	20	10
15	15	15
20	10	20
25	5	25

[1] *Note on computing elasticities* (see footnote 2, page 423 in the textbook): When one is measuring the percentage change in a variable (price, quantity, or income) in order to compute an elasticity, a small problem always arises. Should the change in the variable be expressed as a percentage of its original value or as a percentage of its new value? It turns out that you get a different measure of elasticity depending upon which of these you choose. Since there does not seem to be any obvious reason for choosing one rather than the other, economists use an average of the two. This is how you should compute the elasticities in this exercise. For example, if the price rises from $6 to $10, the percentage change in price is not 4/6 (100) = 75, nor 4/10(100) = 40, but 4/8(100) = 50. (8 is the average of 6 and 10.)

[2] This exercise is mainly for those who have studied Box 19-2. But it should be helpful even to those who haven't.

[3] For this and all subsequent questions in this exercise, answer "higher," "lower," or "no different."

Essay Questions

1. At the end of the Chapter Highlights, the following general rule is given: The smaller the elasticities of supply and demand, the larger the changes in equilibrium prices resulting from shifts in supply and demand. Is it possible to state a similar rule with respect to equilibrium quantities? (Hint: See Exercise 19-2 above.)

2. Why might farmers sometimes cheer for poor crops? (Hint: Refer back to Box 19-3.) Do you suppose that U.S. farmers would cheer more if the crop failure occurred in the United States rather than elsewhere in the world? Why or why not?

3. Over the past 50 years, the number of domestic servants in the United States has fallen drastically. Do you think this is because of the price and availability of labor-saving household appliances? Or is it due to rising wages in other occupations? Or do both factors play a role? Explain how each affects the supply the demand for domestic help.

4. Suppose that a monopoly (single seller) discovered that the demand for its cars was inelastic. Would it then raise its price or lower it? Why?

***5.** It has been argued that stores issue trading stamps to discriminate against people who cannot be bothered collecting, licking, and redeeming the stamps. These people end up paying a higher price for their purchases than those who use the stamps, because only the users receive a "discount" in the form of the items purchased with stamps. Suppose you were the owner of a large chain of stores and you wanted to engage in this kind of price discrimination. (That is, raising the price to nonusers, lowering it to users.) What would happen to your total revenue if the demand by users were elastic and the demand by nonusers inelastic? What would happen to your total revenue if the demand by users were inelastic and the demand by nonusers elastic?

Answers

Chapter Highlights: zero, infinite
True-False Questions: **1** F **2** F **3** T **4** F **5** T **6** T **7** F **8** T **9** T **10** F
Multiple-Choice Questions: **1** c **2** a **3** b **4** d **5** a **6** a **7** d **8** d **9** b **10** d **11** c **12** c
13 a **14** b **15** a **16** b
Exercises:
1a. equal to, less than, more than
b. equal to, less than. It is inelastic at any point. It is elastic at any point
2a. smaller, larger, larger
b. less, larger, smaller
c. smaller, larger, larger
d. less, larger, smaller
3a. $15, 15, 66⅔, 66⅔, 1, 66⅔, 1

Table 19-2

(1)	(2)	(3)
$10	$ 0	0
15	5	5
20	10	10
25	15	15

b. 5, 5, 20, 10, 5, 5
c. no different, no different, higher, higher, higher, lower

CHAPTER 20
Demand and Utility

Learning Objectives

After you have studied this chapter in the textbook and the study guide, you should be able to

Show how the market demand curve is constructed by adding up the individual demand curves

Define marginal utility

Explain the principle of diminishing marginal utility

Describe the condition that must be fulfilled for a consumer to be in equilibrium

Explain the relationship between an individual's demand curve and marginal utility curve

Explain why consumer surplus exists

Show why consumer surplus is measured by the area inside the shaded triangle in Figure 20-4 in the textbook

Explain how the concept of consumer surplus can be applied, as in the case of the Florida freeze

Explain the time cost of a product, and how this enters into the condition for consumer equilibrium

CHAPTER HIGHLIGHTS

We have seen that in many cases a successful application of supply and demand theory requires detailed information concerning the elasticities of supply and demand as well as knowledge about what factors are likely to produce shifts in the curves and how large those shifts will be. In the absence of precise information of this sort, we can often proceed on the basis of informed guesses. For example, we can be confident that a rise in the price of margarine will produce a significant rightward shift in the demand curve for butter, even if we don't know how large this shift will be. Our ability to make such informed guesses depends upon our understanding of the factors underlying the supply and demand curves. The present chapter takes a first look at the factors underlying the demand curve.

The first and most obvious point to note concerning the demand curve is that it is simply the sum of all the individual demand curves, as illustrated in Figure 20-1 in the textbook.

Underlying the individual demand curves are the two basic concepts introduced in Chapter 2—scarcity and choice. In particular, each individual must decide how much of one scarce item (money) to give up for the purpose of acquiring another scarce item (the particular good in question). How do buyers make this choice? Experience has shown that a good working assumption is that they make the choice *rationally*, in the light of their own self-interest.

This brings us to the important concept of *marginal utility*, which is the increase in well-being (utility) that the individual would derive from being able to consume just one more unit of the good in question. In a first course, we measure the utility gain in terms of money, even though this is not a perfect yardstick.

The principle of diminishing marginal utility states that as a consumer buys more and more of a good, the utility acquired from one more unit will eventually fall. This implies that the individual will purchase just that amount of the good that makes our rough measure of marginal utility equal to the price. If the consumer were to buy less than this amount, marginal utility would be greater than price. For example, in Figure 20-4 in the textbook, if the individual were to buy only 2 units, marginal utility would be 17 and price 10. In this situation, it would clearly be in the consumer's interest to purchase more because the cost of buying another unit (the price) is less than the gain (marginal utility). As an exercise, go through the same logic to show why, if more than this optimal amount were purchased, the consumer would be better off purchasing less.

It follows that the demand schedule is (approximately) the same thing as the marginal utility schedule. For example, suppose that, according to the marginal utility schedule, the marginal utility is 3 (in units of money) if the quantity purchased is 50. Then—obviously—if the price equals 3, the individual will want to purchase 50.

An important idea introduced in this chapter is that of *consumer surplus*. Consumer surplus is the extra benefit received by buyers because they are purchasing in a free market at a single price. Suppose that the price of some good is $3.00 and that your demand for that good is 50 units. Then you are paying $150.00 in order to consume 50 units. Now suppose that the market is taken over by some "exploiter" who will not let you freely choose any quantity at the going price. Instead, the exploiter gives you an all-or-nothing choice. Either you pay $200.00 for those 50 units, or you'll get nothing. When faced with this choice, you may actually decide to pay the extra $50.00 in order to keep consuming the good. Why? Because of diminishing marginal utility. The fiftieth unit of the good is worth just $3.00 to you, but the first unit was worth a lot more than that. Therefore, the utility you get from the entire purchase exceeds the $150.00 you were paying; the difference is consumer surplus. As you can see in Figures 20-4 and 20-5 in the text, consumer surplus is measured diagrammatically by the total area inside the "triangle" formed by the demand curve, the price axis, and the horizontal line indicating the price of the good.

The concept of consumer surplus is applied in the textbook to the case of the 1977 Florida freeze. Notice how Figure 20-6 allows us to compare the gains to producers with the losses to consumers in order to arrive at the overall effect on society as a whole. This is made possible by our (admittedly imperfect) practice of measuring all gains and losses in terms of money.

This case illustrates an important *fallacy of composition* (that is, arguing that what applies to an individual also applies to all individuals taken together). Any individual farmer whose own crops were damaged was worse off than if those crops had survived; but, taken together, all farmers were *better* off. Because demand was inelastic, the increase in price more than compensated for the reduced sales.

Another important idea introduced here is that the cost of a good to a consumer includes not just its price but also the time spent using the good, as well as the time spent shopping for it. It is helpful to keep this in mind when trying to understand, for example, why fast-food chains are so much more popular in North America than in other countries. Every hour spent eating is an hour that might have been spent earning income. In many of these other countries, people's wages are lower. Since they can't earn as much with their time, it is not as costly to them to spend an hour or two over a leisurely lunch.

IMPORTANT TERMS

Utility The benefit or satisfaction ultimately derived from goods.

Marginal utility The *additional* utility derived

from one more unit of a good. This can be measured (although only approximately) in dollar terms.

Diminishing marginal utility As more and more of a good is consumed, a point is eventually reached where marginal utility falls.

Consumer equilibrium A situation in which the marginal utility of each good just equals its cost. The cost includes not just the price but also the time

cost. A consumer who is not in such an equilibrium is not maximizing utility.

Time cost The time spent shopping for a good and using it.

Consumer surplus The difference between the total utility derived from a good and the amount paid for it.

True-False Questions

T F 1. The market demand curve is the vertical sum of the individual demand curves.

T F 2. The reason why a demand curve slopes down is that ultimately each consumer's marginal utility begins to fall as the individual consumes more.

T F 3. The height of the individual demand curve measures the total utility derived from that good.

T F 4. If a consumer buys too much of a good, marginal utility falls below the cost of the good.

T F 5. When the price of a good falls, the consumer surplus that an individual receives from that good will rise as a result.

T F 6. In the special case where the individual's demand curve is perfectly vertical, that individual receives no consumer surplus from the good in question.

T F 7. The Florida freeze discussed in the text would not have affected the amount of income received by Florida farmers if the elasticity of demand for their crops had been equal to one.

T F 8. The Florida freeze would not have resulted in any overall loss to the nation if the elasticity of demand had been equal to one.

T F 9. When the cost of time is taken into account, then the consumer equilibrium condition should read (approximately): marginal utility = price + marginal time cost.

T F 10. Time-saving devices are more prevalent in low-wage countries than high-wage countries.

Multiple-Choice Questions

1. Which of the following is true *because of* the principle of diminishing marginal utility?
  (a) If the price increases, producers will offer to sell more
  (b) If people decide they want to buy more of a good, this will cause its price to fall
  (c) Some people buy expensive goods just to impress their friends and relatives
  (d) If the price of a good falls people will usually buy more of it

2. The market demand curve is
  (a) Flatter than any of the individual demand curves
  (b) Steeper than any of the individual demand curves
  (c) Flatter than some but steeper than others
  (d) Steeper or flatter; you can't tell in general

3. Consumer equilibrium requires the price of a good (with no time cost) to equal its
  (a) Total cost
  (b) Total utility
  (c) Marginal utility
  (d) Average utility

4. "Diminishing marginal utility" means that as more of a good is purchased, eventually
  (a) The benefit from an extra unit decreases
  (b) The benefit from an extra unit increases
  (c) The total benefit derived from the good decreases
  (d) None of the above

5. If the marginal utility of a good is 5 (measured in money) and its price is 6, then utility is not maximized because
  (a) The consumer is buying too much of the good and its marginal utility is higher than it ought to be
  (b) The consumer is buying too much of the good and its marginal utility is lower than it ought to be
  (c) The consumer is buying too little of the good and its marginal utility is higher than it ought to be
  (d) The consumer is buying too little of the good and its marginal utility is lower than it ought to be

6. Suppose that Table 20-1 indicates the total utility received by a consumer from consuming various amounts of clothing.

Table 20-1

Units of clothing consumed	Total utility
0	0
1	1
2	4
3	6
4	7

Then
  (a) Marginal utility is diminishing no matter how much clothing is consumed
  (b) Marginal utility in consuming the second unit is greater than the first

(c) Marginal utility is highest with the fourth unit of consumption

(d) When the price rises the quantity demanded will also rise

7. Consumer surplus is measured by a "triangle" whose sides are

(a) The demand curve, the vertical axis, and the horizontal axis

(b) The demand curve, the vertical axis, and the horizontal price line

(c) The demand curve, the horizontal axis, and the vertical line at a distance from the origin equal to the quantity consumed

(d) None of the above

8. Suppose two individuals, facing the same market price, purchase the same quantity. The individual with the larger elasticity of demand will have

(a) Less consumer surplus

(b) More consumer surplus

(c) The same amount of consumer surplus

(d) More or less, depending upon the elasticity of supply

9. The marginal utility of a particular good depends not only upon the amount consumed of that good but also on the amount consumed of other goods. For example, suppose the amount of butter consumed increases while the amount of margarine remains constant. Then

(a) Marginal utility of butter rises and marginal utility of margarine rises

(b) Marginal utility of butter rises and marginal utility of margarine falls

(c) Marginal utility of butter falls and marginal utility of margarine rises

(d) Marginal utility of butter falls and marginal utility of margarine falls

10. Suppose that the amount of bread consumed increases but the amount of butter remains constant. Then

(a) Marginal utility of bread rises and marginal utility of butter rises

(b) Marginal utility of bread rises and marginal utility of butter falls

(c) Marginal utility of bread falls and marginal utility of butter rises

(d) Marginal utility of bread falls and marginal utility of butter falls

11. Which of the following is a time cost of consuming restaurant meals?

(a) The time spent searching for a restaurant with a good menu

(b) The time spent waiting for a table

(c) The time spent eating the meal

(d) All the above

Exercises

1. Suppose that a consumer's total utility from haircuts is given by Table 20-2. Fill in the column giving the marginal utility of each additional haircut. Suppose that the price of a haircut is $2.00. Then fill in the column giving the total yearly cost of haircuts. Next, fill in the column giving the difference between total utility and total cost. This difference is maximized when the consumer buys _____ haircuts per year. Therefore, the consumer will demand _____ haircuts per year at $2.00 per haircut. At this quantity the marginal utility of the last haircut during the year is (more, less) than the price, and the marginal utility of one more haircut would be (more, less) than the price.

If the price is $1.00 per haircut, the equilibrium condition ("marginal utility equals price") is satisfied when _____ haircuts are demanded, and also when _____ haircuts are demanded. What possible reason could there be for the fact that the marginal utility of the seventh haircut is negative? Can you think of any way in which the consumer could be induced to buy seven haircuts per year?

Table 20-2

Number of haircuts per year	Total utility of haircuts (in dollars)	Marginal utility of haircuts	Total cost per year of haircuts at $2.00 each	Total utility minus total cost at $2.00 each
0	0	0.00	_____	_____
1	1.00	_____	_____	_____
2	6.00	_____	_____	_____
3	10.00	_____	_____	_____
4	13.00	_____	_____	_____
5	15.50	_____	_____	_____
6	16.50	_____	_____	_____
7	16.25	_____	_____	_____

2a. In Figure 20-1, suppose that the relevant supply curve is the one labeled S_1, and ignore for the time being the one labeled S_2. Then the equilibrium price will be OB and the equilibrium quantity will be _____. The total revenue received by producers will be equal to the area _____. The total amount paid by demanders will be equal to the area _____. The total utility enjoyed by demanders of this good will be equal to the area _____, and the consumer surplus will be equal to the area _____.

2b. Now, suppose that, as a result of some technological improvement, the supply curve shifts out to the one labeled S_2. After this shift, the equilibrium price will be _____, the equilibrium quantity will be _____, the revenue received by producers will be _____, the amount paid by demanders will be _____, the total utility enjoyed by consumers will be _____, and the consumer's surplus will be _____.

2c. As a result of this change in supply, the net gain to consumers is measured by the area _____, while the producers lose the area _____ but gain the area _____. Therefore, the overall gain to the nation is measured by _____.

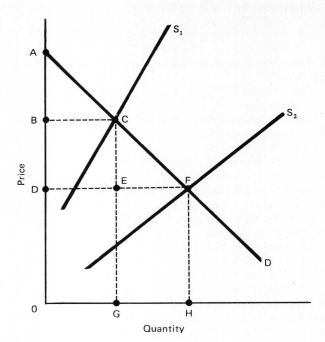

FIGURE 20-1

Essay Questions

1. No matter how you look at it, it's obvious that people derive more utility from the water in the world than they do from all the diamonds in the world. Yet diamonds cost far more than water. Adam Smith tried to explain this apparent paradox simply by noting that value in exchange did not always reflect value in use. Can you give an explanation by noting that the price of water reflects its *marginal* utility, but that its value to us depends upon the *total* utility that it provides? Do you suppose that diamonds would be more expensive than water if water were as scarce as diamonds? What role does diminishing marginal utility play in the explanation of this paradox?

2. To judge by the amount of time spent, most people seem to derive more utility from watching television than from going to movies. Yet they will pay $3 or $4 to go to a movie when they could stay home and watch television for nothing. Is this consistent with utility theory?

3. When Henry Ford invented the mass production of automobiles, what effect do you suppose this had on the typical marginal utility schedule for horse-drawn carriages? What do you suppose it did to the price of horse-drawn carriages? To the elasticity of demand for carriages?

4. In Box 19-2, it was pointed out that when a tax is put on a commodity, the heavier burden is borne by people in the least flexible (more inelastic) situation. Is it true that the greater the consumer surplus enjoyed by demanders of a good the heavier the burden they will have to bear of any new tax? Explain.

5. Heroin addicts find that the more they consume the more they want. Does this contradict or illustrate diminishing marginal utility?

Answers

Exercises: **1.**

Table 20-2

Marginal utility	Total cost	Total utility Minus total cost
$0	$0	$0
1.00	2.00	−1.00
5.00	4.00	2.00
4.00	6.00	4.00
3.00	8.00	5.00
2.50	10.00	5.50
1.00	12.00	4.50
−0.25	14.00	2.25

5, 5, more, less, 1, 6

2a. *OG, OBCG, OBCG, OACG, ABC*

2b. *OD, OH, ODFH, ODFH, OAFH, ADF*

2c. *DBCF, DBCE, GEFH, GCFH*

CHAPTER 21
Costs and Perfectly Competitive Supply

Learning Objectives

After you have studied this chapter in the textbook and the study guide, you should be able to

Explain the difference between the short run and the long run

State and explain the law of (eventually) diminishing returns

Explain the distinction between fixed and variable costs, showing why there are no fixed costs in the long run

Define marginal cost

Describe the equilibrium condition that must be satisfied by any profit-maximizing firm

Show why the condition "price = marginal cost" must be satisfied by the profit-maximizing firm in perfect competition

Explain, using a diagram, why average cost equals marginal cost when average cost is at a minimum

Demonstrate why the short-run supply curve of a perfectly competitive firm is its marginal cost curve (above its average variable cost curve)

Explain the distinction between accounting costs and economic costs

Show how a short-run production function can be seen as one row of a long-run production function

Show in a diagram how long-run and short-run average cost curves are related to each other by an envelope relationship

Define "economies of scale" and explain why they do not violate the law of diminishing returns

Define perfect competition

State the two conditions under which an industry's long-run supply curve is perfectly elastic, explaining why

Define producer surplus and explain why it exists

Show how producer surplus can be measured in a diagram

154

CHAPTER HIGHLIGHTS

Just as the previous chapter took a look at what underlies the demand curve, so this chapter looks at what underlies the supply curve. Once again, the assumption of rational self-interest is involved. In this case, we assume that producers supply whatever amount will give them the greatest possible profit.

In order to understand a firm's profit-maximizing behavior, we consider a simple example where the firm produces only one product using just two kinds of input: labor and capital. We first consider how the firm behaves in the *short run*, when there is no time to vary the amount of capital input, and labor is the only variable input. The short-run production function, as illustrated in Table 21-1 and Figure 21-1 in the textbook, shows how output varies as the quality of labor input is increased. The slope of this production function is the marginal product of labor—the extra output obtained from hiring one more unit of labor. (The concept of slope was explained in Appendix 1A in this Study Guide.) According to the law of (*eventually*) *diminishing returns*, the marginal product must eventually decrease as more and more labor is hired.

Since the quantity of capital cannot be varied in the short run, the costs of capital already in place cannot be avoided. Thus they are called *fixed costs* (overhead costs). If more output is produced in the short run, more labor must be used. Thus, the costs of the labor input are called *variable costs*; they vary with the amount produced. The sum of fixed and variable costs is *total costs*. Figure 21-2 in the textbook shows how total costs vary with the amount produced. The slope of this total cost curve is *marginal* cost—the extra cost of producing one more unit.

The general rule for any firm to follow in maximizing its profits is to produce an amount such that marginal cost equals marginal revenue—the extra revenue obtainable from producing one more unit of output. For if marginal cost (MC) were less than marginal revenue (MR) the firm could increase its profits by producing more. The extra revenue (MR) from one more unit would exceed the extra cost (MC); thus profits, the difference between revenue and costs, would increase. Likewise, if MC were greater than MR the firm could increase profits by producing less.

The perfectly competitive firm takes the price of its output as given. Its MR is just the price (P). For example, if it sells apples at $2 a basket, then each extra basket sold produces $2 extra revenue. Thus, the profit-maximizing rule for a perfectly competitive firm is to set MC = P.

This is not the *only* rule. The firm must first decide whether or not to produce at all. It will produce as long as it can generate enough revenue to pay its *variable* costs, for then it will have something left over to help cover its fixed costs. Even if the firm's revenues fall short of *total* costs this will be better than shutting down and having to pay all the fixed costs out of pocket. Thus, the firm must also obey the role of producing only when its price (revenue per unit) exceeds its average variable cost (variable costs per unit).

This implies that the perfectly competitive firm's short-run supply curve will be that part of its MC schedule lying above its AVC (average variable cost) schedule, as shown in Figure 21-5 in the textbook. At any price above $20 in this diagram, the firm can obey the first rule by producing an amount such that MC = P, and P will exceed AVC. At any lower price there is no level of output at which P > AVC; thus the firm shuts down. The point where the MC and AVC schedules intersect shows the lowest price possible before the firm shuts down. This is called the *shutdown point*.

(Box 21-2 in the textbook explains the general rule that as long as marginal cost is less than average cost, average cost is falling. This follows from the commonsense observation that if you add to a collection something that costs less than the average in the collection, this addition lowers the average. Likewise, if marginal cost exceeds average cost the average is rising. It follows that if you have a U-shaped average cost curve, like the ones we usually draw, it lies above the MC curve at first, while AC is falling; it lies below the MC curve when AC is rising, and therefore it must intersect the MC curve when AC has just stopped falling and is about to start rising (at point *H* in Figure 21-5). In other words, the AC and MC curves intersect at the minimum point of the AC curve.)

Another important concept is that of economic cost as opposed to accounting cost. The difference is that the economist considers many implicit costs that are ignored by the accountant, such as the wages that the owner of a firm could have made if he or she had taken some other job, and the interest income that the owner could have earned by investing the same capital elsewhere. The interest income that could have been earned is called the firm's *normal profit*. The general principle is that the economist tries to take into account all *opportunity costs* (that is, what factors of production could be earning elsewhere). Thus, normal profits are a *cost*. When economists speak of "profit" they are referring to additional profits above and beyond this. Such "above-normal" profits are important for the operation of the market system because they act as a signal to attract resources into profitable uses.

Now let us turn to the long run, in which all inputs, including capital, may be varied. The long-run production function gives the amount of output that can be produced by various combinations of capital and labor. Table 21-5 in the textbook shows how it can be represented by a grid with the quantity of labor varying from column to column and capital varying from row to row. A short-run production function corresponds to just one row of this grid, with the amount of capital held fixed.

The long-run average cost curve (LAC) is shown in Figure 21-6 in the textbook. For each different quantity of capital (each row of the grid in Table 21-5), there is a different short-run production function and thus a different short-run average cost curve (SAC). In the long run, the firm is free to choose its capital and labor inputs. Whatever amount it produces it will choose the least costly combination of inputs. It does this by using the amount of capital corresponding to the lowest of all SAC curves at that level of output (for example, SAC_c for output q_1 in Figure 21-6 in the textbook). The choice of how much labor to use is then determined by that row of the production function as the amount required to produce the given level of output. Thus, the LAC is the "envelope" curve that just touches the lowest SAC at each level of output.

In the short run, MC eventually rises because of the principle of diminishing returns. Since each additional worker (eventually) produces less additional output, each additional unit of output (eventually) requires more additional labor, and hence costs more. But this doesn't necessarily happen in the long run. When you increase all factors in proportion you may get more than a proportional increase in output. If so, LAC is falling, and we say the firm enjoys economies of scale. Economies of scale could persist over the entire range of production. This might appear to violate the principle of diminishing returns but it doesn't; remember, diminishing returns occur when you hold some factors fixed. It is because you hold, say, the number of machines fixed that the marginal product of workers will eventually diminish. But if every time you add a new worker you also add a new machine the workers' marginal products might never fall. (This is illustrated in Figure 21-7 in the textbook.)

To discuss the long-run supply curve of a perfectly competitive industry we need to complete a definition. So far we have defined perfect competition by the condition that everyone is a price taker.

This condition is most likely to hold if (a) there are many buyers and sellers, and (b) the product is standardized. But perfect competition also requires that firms be free to enter the industry without facing any. Consider two cases:

Case A
(Figure 21-8 in the textbook) Assume that all inputs are standardized and the industry is small. In this case the long-run industry supply curve is perfectly elastic at a price equal to the minimum of each firm's LAC curve. At this price firms would produce at their break-even points, earning just normal profits. At any higher price, supernormal profits would be earned, inducing more firms to enter (which they are free to do). The extra supply of the new firms would cause the price to fall down the market demand curve. This process would continue until the price was back to the minimum LAC and the new entry ceased. Thus, the increased demand would be satisfied by more firms producing at the same price. Likewise, at any lower price, losses would drive firms out of business (they are free to leave too) until the resulting contraction in supply brought the price back up. Thus, no matter how much was demanded, the price would be the same in the long run.

Case B
(Figure 21-10 in the textbook) Next, suppose that the industry is large. To meet an increase in demand, firms must hire more inputs. This might cause such a large rightward shift in the demand curves for these inputs that they would become significantly more expensive. Thus the LAC curves in the industry would shift upward. A new long-run equilibrium would again involve each firm at its minimum LAC. But this would now be a higher price than before. The increase in demand would result in a higher price; thus the supply curve must be upward-sloping. The same would happen if the inputs were not standardized, so that as more output was produced, new firms would be forced to use less productive inputs. In this case, new firms would incur higher costs. To draw them into the industry a higher price would be required.

An important concept introduced in this chapter is that of "producer surplus." This is any return to producers in excess of their costs. As explained in Figure 21-11 in the textbook, the increase in producer surplus when the price increases is the area between the two prices to the left of the MC schedule. Study this explanation until you can reproduce it on your own. Note the similarity of producer surplus to the concept of consumer surplus studied in the last chapter.

IMPORTANT TERMS

Short run The time period over which the firm cannot vary its capital stock.

Long run The time period over which the capital stock is variable.

Short-run production function The relationship between the amount of variable factors used and the amount of output that can be produced, when the amount of capital is constant.

Marginal product The marginal product of a factor of production is the extra output that the firm can produce by hiring an extra unit of that factor.

Law of (eventually) diminishing returns A factor's marginal product must eventually decline; that is, if more of the factor is employed while other factors are held constant, the marginal product of that factor must eventually fall.

Fixed costs Costs that do not vary as output increases. Also called "overhead" or "sunk" costs.

Variable costs All costs that aren't fixed but that vary with the amount produced. In the long run, all costs are variable.

Total cost The sum of both fixed and variable costs.

Average cost Total cost per unit produced.

Average variable cost Variable cost per unit produced. In the long run, since all costs are variable, average cost equals average variable cost; but in the short run, average cost exceeds average variable cost by an amount equal to average fixed cost.

Marginal cost The increase in total cost resulting from an increased output of one unit.

Marginal revenue The increase in total revenue from the sale of one more unit. In the present chapter, where we assume that the firm is a price taker, marginal revenue equals the market price.

Break-even point The point at which the marginal cost curve intersects the average cost curve. This is the point at which the firm would just make a zero profit.

Shut-down point The point at which the marginal cost curve intersects the average variable cost curve. If the price falls below this, the firm will shut down its operations even in the short run.

Opportunity cost The opportunity cost of an input is the return that it could earn in its best alternative use. Compare this definition with the one given in Chapter 2.

Economic cost This equals explicit accounting cost plus the implicit opportunity costs that are not considered by accountants. See Table 21-2 in the textbook.

Normal profits The income that the firm could expect to receive if it were to invest its capital elsewhere. Normal profits are actually considered to be part of economic cost because they represent the opportunity cost of the firm's capital.

Economic profit (Also called above-normal profit) Total revenue minus economic cost. These are profits that arise in addition to normal profits.

Long-run production function The relationship that shows the maximum output that can be produced with various combinations of all the different inputs.

Economies of scale Economies of scale exist if doubling *all* inputs more than doubles the firm's output. With economics of scale the long-run average cost will usually be falling. (As explained in Figure 21-7 in the textbook, the firm can face both economies of scale and diminishing returns at the same time.)

Perfectly competitive industry One in which there are many buyers and sellers of a standardized product, with none having any influence over its price, and with new firms free to enter without facing barriers like having to buy a license.

Producer surplus Any return to producers in excess of their opportunity costs.

True-False Questions

T F   1. Fixed costs are usually less than overhead costs.
T F   2. Short-run marginal cost rises because of economies of scale.
T F   3. The law of diminishing returns applies to a situation in which only one factor is varied, the others remaining constant.
T F   4. The firm will produce something in the short run as long as the market price is above the intersection of marginal cost and average variable cost.
T F   5. If a competitive firm is producing more than the profit-maximizing amount, then price is greater than marginal cost.
T F   6. The competitive firm's short-run supply curve is that part of its short-run marginal cost curve that lies above its average fixed cost curve.
T F   7. For every amount of capital, there is a different short-run supply schedule.
T F   8. In the long run there are no variable costs.

T F   **9.** The law of diminishing returns is a result of economies of scale.
T F   **10.** The long-run shutdown point and break-even point are the same.
T F   **11.** Economic profit is generally larger than normal profit.

Multiple-Choice Questions

1. Fixed costs are
  (a) Fixed only in the long run
  (b) All costs that are not variable
  (c) Part of normal profits
  (d) All the above
2. If total costs are rising, then marginal cost must be
  (a) Rising
  (b) Falling
  (c) Positive
  (d) Above average cost
3. The short-run supply curve slopes upward because of
  (a) The law of eventually diminishing returns
  (b) Economies of scale
  (c) The upward slope of the marginal cost curve
  (d) (a) and (c)
4. If average cost exceeds marginal cost, then
  (a) Average cost must be rising
  (b) Average cost must be falling
  (c) Marginal cost must be rising
  (d) Marginal cost must be falling
5. Long-run average cost
  (a) May fall if there are economics of scale
  (b) Always exceeds average revenue
  (c) Is drawn under the assumption that the firm's capital stock is fixed
  (d) Is rising if there is diminishing marginal productivity
6. If the current market price falls short of the minimum point on all firms' long-run average cost schedules, then
  (a) Firms will be dropping out of the industry
  (b) No firm will be producing, even in the short run
  (c) There must be economies of scale in the industry
  (d) Most firms will be expanding their capital stock
7. Michael Merchant left his job, which paid $18,000 per year, and invested $300,000, which he could otherwise have invested at 10 percent per annum, to start a hardware store. His accounting profits for the first year of operation were $52,000; therefore, his economic profits were
  (a) 0
  (b) $4,000
  (c) $30,000
  (d) $52,000
8. In Figure 21-1 the shutdown point is
  (a) S   **(c)** U
  (b) T   **(d)** X

FIGURE 21-1

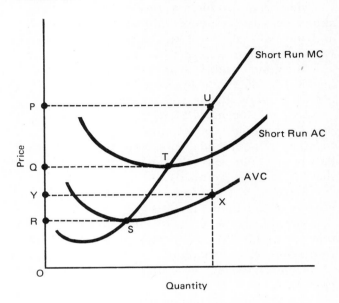

9. In Figure 21-1 the break-even point is
  (a) S
  (b) T
  (c) U
  (d) X
10. When the price rises from OQ to OP in Figure 21-1, the firm's producer surplus rises by the area
  (a) PUXY
  (b) PUSR
  (c) QTSR
  (d) PUTQ
11. For a perfectly competitive firm, marginal revenue is
  (a) Greater than the price of its output
  (b) Less than the price of its output
  (c) Equal to the price of its output
  (d) Greater or less, depending on the elasticity of the market demand curve
12. In the short run, the perfectly competitive firm's break-even point occurs at a
  (a) Higher quantity than the shutdown point
  (b) Lower quantity than the shutdown point
  (c) Lower price than the shutdown point
  (d) (a) and (c)

Exercises

1. In Figure 21-2, the curve labeled SMC denotes the firm's short-run marginal cost schedule, the one labeled SAC its short-run average cost schedule, and the one labeled AVC its short-run average variable cost schedule.
  a. If the price equals OP_1, then the quantity

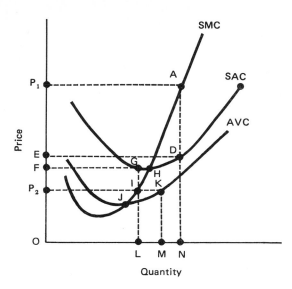

FIGURE 21-2

supplied will be _____, total revenue will be _____, average cost will be _____, total cost will be _____, and economic profit will be _____.

b. If the price equals OP_2, then the firm will supply the quantity _____, total revenue will be _____, average cost will be _____,

total cost will be _____, and economic profit will be _____.

c. The break-even point is _____, and the shutdown point is _____.

2. Table 21-1 describes the amounts of factor input that a firm would need to produce various amounts of output (*a*) assuming that the firm has 5 units of capital, and (*b*) assuming that the firm has 10 units of capital.

The firm uses only 2 factors: labor and capital. The cost of labor is $100 per unit and the cost of capital is $1,000 per unit. Then to produce, say, 3 units of output with 5 units of capital costs a total of $19,000; that is, $5,000 in fixed costs (5 units of capital at $1,000 per unit) plus $14,000 in variable costs (140 units of labor at $100 per unit). This is indicated in Table 21-2. Fill in the rest of this table.

3. Table 21-3 describes a firm's short-run costs. Fill in the missing parts of the table. When the price equals $55, the firm's profit maximizing output is _____, and its producer surplus is _____. When the price equals $75, the firm's profit maximizing output is _____, and its producer surplus is _____. Of all possible prices, the lowest that would induce this firm to produce a positive amount of output in the short run is _____, and the lowest that would enable the firm to avoid suffering a loss in the short run is _____.

Table 21-1

5 units of capital			10 units of capital		
Output	Capital	Labor required	Output	Capital	Labor required
0	5	0	0	10	0
1	5	40	1	10	35
2	5	70	2	10	60
3	5	140	3	10	100
4	5	225	4	10	150
5	5	325	5	10	230
6	5	450	6	10	330

Table 21-2   **a.**   **b.**

Output	Total cost	Fixed cost	Variable cost	Average cost	Average variable cost	Marginal cost	Total cost	Fixed cost	Variable cost	Average cost	Average variable cost	Marginal cost
0				___	___	0				___	___	0
1												
2												
3	19,000	5,000	14,000	6,333	4,667							
4												
5												
6												

Table 21-3

Output	Fixed cost	Variable cost	Average cost	Average variable cost	Marginal cost	Total revenue if price equals $55	Economic profit if price equals $55	Total revenue if price equals $75	Economic profit if price equals $75
0	30	0	_____	_____	0				
1	30	90							
2	30	120							
3	30	170							
4	30	240							
5	30	320							

Essay Questions

1. Economists usually draw average cost curves as being U-shaped. What would it mean if the short-run average cost curve always sloped up (that is, did not initially slope down)? What would it mean if the long-run average cost curve always sloped up? Would it be possible for the long-run average cost curve always to slope down? Explain.

2. The textbook states that the implicit costs considered by economists—but not accountants—are opportunity costs. Explain why even those costs that the accountant does consider are opportunity costs.

3. Explain: If a firm is on its long-run supply curve then the combination of capital and labor that it is using to produce this amount of output costs less than any other combination which could alternatively be used to produce the same amount of output. Illustrate with a diagram.

4. Recall the definition of "externality" from Chapter 5. Do the various measures of cost that have been discussed in this chapter include those costs which are external to the firm? Why or why not? If you think not, then how would the cost curves of a public utility burning coal and creating air pollution shift if this external cost were taken into account?

5. Consider the cost curves for a firm with a fixed amount of capital. Is it possible for price to equal marginal cost at more than one level of output? How? In such circumstances, which of these different output levels will be chosen by the profit-maximizing firm? Why? Following this line of reasoning, prove that a firm's short-run supply curve can never be downward sloping.

Answers

True-False Questions: **1** F **2** F **3** T **4** T **5** F **6** F **7** T **8** F **9** F **10** T **11** F
Multiple-Choice Questions: **1** b **2** c **3** d **4** b **5** a **6** a **7** b **8** a **9** b **10** d **11** c **12** a
Exercises: **1a.** *ON, OP₁AN, OE, OEDN, EP₁AD*
     b. *OL, OP₂IL, OF, OFGL, − P₂FGI;*
     c. *H, J*

2.

Table 21-2

					a.							b.	
Output	Total cost	Fixed cost	Variable cost	Average cost	Average variable cost	Marginal cost	Total cost	Fixed cost	Variable cost	Average cost	Average variable cost	Marginal cost
0	5,000	5,000	0	____	____	0	10,000	10,000	0	____	____	0
1	9,000	5,000	4,000	9,000	4,000	4,000	13,500	10,000	3,500	13,500	3,500	3,500
2	12,000	5,000	7,000	6,000	3,500	3,000	16,000	10,000	6,000	8,000	3,000	2,500
3	19,000	5,000	14,000	6,333	4,667	7,000	20,000	10,000	10,000	6,667	3,333	4,000
4	27,500	5,000	22,500	6,875	5,625	8,500	25,000	10,000	15,000	6,250	3,750	5,000
5	37,500	5,000	32,500	7,500	6,500	10,000	33,000	10,000	23,000	6,600	4,600	8,000
6	50,000	5,000	45,000	8,333	7,500	12,500	43,000	10,000	33,000	7,167	5,500	10,000

3. 0, −30, 4, 30, 56 2/3, 66 2/3

Table 21-3

Output	Fixed cost	Variable cost	Average cost	Average variable cost	Marginal cost	Total revenue if P=55	Profit if P=55	Total revenue if P=75	Profit if P=75
0	30	0	___	___	0	0	−30	0	−30
1	30	90	120	90	90	55	−65	75	−45
2	30	120	75	60	30	110	−40	150	0
3	30	170	66⅔	56⅔	50	165	−35	225	25
4	30	240	67½	60	70	220	−50	300	30
5	30	320	70	64	80	275	−75	375	25

CHAPTER 22
Perfect Competition and Economic Efficiency

Learning Objectives

After you have studied this chapter in the textbook and the study guide, you should be able to

Explain why the condition "marginal cost = marginal benefit" is necessary for allocative efficiency

Explain why perfect competition results in allocative efficiency when there are no externalities

Explain how perfect competition tends to promote technical efficiency, but not necessarily dynamic efficiency.

Describe two possible shortcomings of the competitive system that may arise even if the system is efficient

Explain how speculators may produce the same kind of effect as a government price-stabilization scheme

Demonstrate why the area of the "triangle" illustrated in Figure 22-3 in the text is an appropriate measure of the efficiency loss of a departure from perfect competition

CHAPTER HIGHLIGHTS

You sometimes hear it said that we should learn to cooperate more with each other rather than compete. But the economist will say that, on the contrary, competition is often the best method of ensuring harmony. This is the message of Adam Smith's "invisible hand" (recall our discussion of this in Chapter 1). Each of us in pursuing our own self-interest is led by market forces (as if by an invisible hand) to promote the interests of others as well. The purpose of this chapter is to show how this can happen through the operation of perfectly competitive markets, as well as to point out some of the possible shortcomings of such markets.

The basic idea is that, under ideal conditions, perfectly competitive markets will produce an efficient outcome. Consider first the concept of *alloca-*

tive efficiency, defined in Chapter 1. This requires the marginal cost of any activity to equal its marginal benefit—otherwise, there would be a net social gain from changing the level of the activity. For example, if the marginal cost of producing wheat is less than the marginal benefit, then increasing the production of wheat will provide a net gain. How can this equality of marginal cost and marginal benefit be achieved? One way is by allowing the level of the activity to be determined in a perfectly competitive market. As we saw in Chapter 20, consumers in pursuing their self-interest will consume to the point where their marginal benefit (marginal utility) equals the market price. As we saw in Chapter 21, firms pursuing their self-interest will produce to the point where marginal cost equals the market price. Therefore, marginal benefit equals marginal cost, because they both equal the market price; the perfectly competitive outcome is therefore efficient. This result depends upon perfect competition because the argument in Chapters 20 and 21 assumed that firms and consumers took the market price as given, and this is only true under pefect competition.

This is the bare bones of the argument. But it involves two crucial assumptions that may or may not be true in any actual situation. The first is that the marginal utility that consumers take into account equals the marginal benefit to society as a whole. In many cases this may be true. I'm the only one that benefits from my magazine subscription. But in other cases there may be external benefits. For example, my home improvements may benefit the entire neighborhood. The marginal social benefit of my improvements includes not just my own marginal utility. It also includes my neighbors' marginal utilities. Since I don't take the neighbors' benefits into account there is no reason to suppose that my private decisions will lead to a socially efficient outcome.

The second crucial assumption is that the marginal cost to the firm reflects the marginal cost to society. This will not be the case if there are any external costs, such as those borne by the people downstream when a chemical manufacturer dumps pollutants into a river.

In short, the argument that the perfectly competitive market leads to allocative efficiency is valid only if there are no external costs or benefits. What happens if there are such externalities is the subject of Chapters 26 and 27.

Perfect competition also tends to promote *technical efficiency*. Technically inefficient firms, whose costs are above, rather than on their AC curves, aren't likely to survive competition with lower cost, technically efficient firms.

The situation is different with respect to *dynamic* efficiency. The perfectly competitive firm is not in a good position to spend resources on discovering innovations that generate economic growth. As we shall see in more detail in Chapter 25, it lacks the financial resources and economies of scale that facilitate this kind of activity.

Moreover, efficiency isn't everything. There are problems that the perfectly competitive market doesn't solve. One is how the nation's income should be distributed. Perfect competition provides no answer here; the reason is that for every possible distribution of income there is a different perfectly competitive equilibrium. Each of them is efficient. The economist has no objective way of comparing these different efficient outcomes. This is an important point: Make sure you can explain it using Figures 22-1 and 22-6 in the textbook.

Another possible drawback of the competitive system is that it may aggravate the problem of economic instability, especially when production decisions must be made in the light of expectations concerning future prices. These expectations may be unstable, as in the case of the cobweb cycle discussed in Box 22-4. The starred sections of the chapter discuss how these problems might be reduced by private speculators or by government price-stabilization schemes. If private speculators make accurate forecasts they will tend to iron out fluctuations in the market by selling off their holdings when the price is high, thereby keeping the price from rising even higher, and by buying more when the price is low, thereby keeping the price from falling even lower. Furthermore, a speculator who makes poor forecasts tends to go out of business (although perhaps not if the speculator manages to corner the market, and therefore is able to *choose* the price). Government price-stabilization schemes in agricultural products work in a similar way by buying from farmers when the price is low and selling on the open market when the price is high.

If efficiency is promoted by the automatic forces of a perfectly competitive market, then an efficiency loss will generally result whenever those forces are interfered with. How big is this loss? Figure 22-3 in the textbook shows how it can be measured by the area of the "triangle" formed by the supply and demand curves between the actual (inefficient) output level and the perfectly competitive (efficient) output level. This "triangle" will appear again in many of the following chapters. Be sure you understand why it is an appropriate measure of this efficiency loss.

IMPORTANT TERMS

Allocative efficiency An activity is allocatively efficient if it is run at a level where marginal cost equals marginal benefit.

Efficiency loss The loss, measured in dollars, of producing at a level that isn't efficient. You should understand how to measure such a loss by the "triangle" illustrated in Figure 22-3 in the textbook.

*The paradox of value The paradox that many things which provide a great deal of total utility, such as water, have a smaller market value than other commodities that provide very little total utility, such as diamonds. To resolve this paradox you have to understand that the market value (price) reflects marginal utility, not total utility.

*Pareto optimum This is a term used to describe an outcome that is economically efficient. A situation is Pareto-optimal if it is impossible to make anyone better off without making someone else worse off. Clearly, if someone *can* be made better off without hurting someone else, there is a dead-weight loss in the system; in other words, the outcome isn't efficient.

*Cobweb cycle The fluctuation of prices that results when a high price this year encourages producers to bring more to the market next year, causing a low price next year. This encourages producers to bring less to the market the following year, causing a high price then, and so on. This is also sometimes called the "hog cycle."

*Speculation The activity of buying and selling commodities with a view to profiting from future price changes. This tends to help stabilize movements in prices as long as speculators make reasonably good forecasts.

*Cornering a market This is buying up enough of the commodity to become the single (or at least dominant) seller, and thus acquire the power to resell at a higher price.

True-False Questions

T F   **1.** Perfect competition prevails in most markets in the U.S. economy except for agricultural markets.

T F   **2.** The equality of marginal cost and marginal benefit is required for technical efficiency.

T F   **3.** Under perfect competition, the marginal social benefit of producing a good will exceed the typical buyer's marginal utility if there are external benefits.

T F   **4.** Producers disregard external costs because they are not required to pay for them.

T F   **5.** Suppose that the government imposes a maximum price that can be charged for some good with no externalities that is sold in a perfectly competitive market. Then, if the maximum price is below the equilibrium price, the marginal benefit from producing that good will exceed the marginal cost.

T F   **6.** An economically efficient outcome is one with the best distribution of income.

T F   **7.** Smith's invisible hand tends to guide everyone toward the amount of income that he or she deserves.

T F   **8.** The perfectly competitive outcome is dynamically efficient if there are no externalities.

T F   ***9.** One of the drawbacks of the perfectly competitive system is that it allows resources to be devoted to the socially unproductive activity of speculation.

T F   ***10.** The only objective of government agricultural price supports is to stabilize agricultural prices and consumption.

Multiple-Choice Questions

1. Which of the following is *not* required in order to have perfect competition?

(a) There are many buyers and sellers.

(b) There are no externalities.

(c) The product is standardized.

(d) There is a high degree of mobility of firms into and out of the industry.

2. In a perfectly competitive market that yields an efficiency loss

(a) There are few buyers and sellers

(b) There are externalities

(c) The product is not standardized

(d) There are barriers to entering the industry

3. If a firm was prevented from entering an industry because of failure to obtain a governmental license, then the industry

(a) demand curve would overstate MU_S

(b) demand curve would understate MU_S

(c) supply curve would overstate MC_S

(d) supply curve would understate MC_S

4. For an efficiency loss to occur, the marginal social benefit must be

(a) Greater than marginal social cost

(b) Less than marginal social cost

(c) Greater or less than marginal social cost

(d) Equal to marginal social cost

5. In Figure 22-1 the efficiency loss from producing the amount *OA* is the area
  (a) *CFGI*
  (b) *IGJ*
  (c) *IHJ*
  (d) *OEJ*

6. If more than the efficient amount of output of some good is produced, then
  (a) Marginal benefit will be higher than in the efficient situation and marginal cost will be higher than in the efficient situation
  (b) Marginal benefit will be lower and marginal cost will be lower than in the efficient situation
  (c) Marginal benefit will be higher and marginal cost lower than in the efficient situation
  (d) Marginal benefit will be lower and marginal cost higher than in the efficient situation

7. A technological breakthrough that reduces the marginal cost of producing fertilizer will
  (a) Increase the efficient level of fertilizer production
  (b) Decrease the efficient level of fertilizer production
  (c) Leave the efficient level of fertilizer production unchanged
  (d) Change the efficient level of fertilizer production but not in a predictable direction

8. This same technological breakthrough in fertilizer production will
  (a) Increase the efficient level of corn production
  (b) Decrease the efficient level of corn production
  (c) Leave the efficient level of corn production unchanged
  (d) Change the efficient level of corn production but not in a predictable direction

9. A shift in people's tastes that makes them prefer corn flakes more and oatmeal less will
  (a) Increase the efficient level of oat production
  (b) Decrease the efficient level of oat production
  (c) Leave the efficient level of oat production unchanged
  (d) Change the efficient level of oat production but not in a predictable direction

10. Prices in the market system
  (a) Serve as a "rationing device" to decide who gets to consume how much of a scarce good
  (b) Serve as a device to decide which producers will survive in the market
  (c) Act as a signal to direct resources toward the production of goods in increasing demand
  (d) All the above

*11. According to the cobweb theory analyzed in Box 22-4
  (a) If this year's price is higher than the equilibrium price (the price at *E*), then next year's price will be too
  (b) If this year's price is higher, then next year's price will be lower

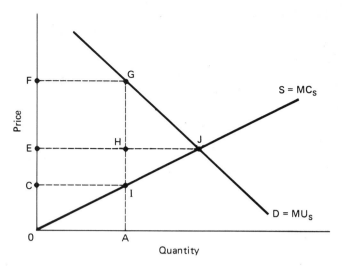

FIGURE 22-1

  (c) If this year's price is higher, then next year's quantity will be lower than the equilibrium quantity
  (d) Producers are making accurate forecasts

*12. Private speculators
  (a) Will likely profit if they reduce the fluctuations in price arising from the "hog cycle"
  (b) Thrive best when their actions cause prices to fluctuate by even more than they would in the absence of speculation
  (c) Can make a profit only if they succeed in cornering a market
  (d) Are more likely to be active in markets for highly perishable commodities than in markets for goods that can be stored for long periods of time at little cost

*13. Government programs aimed at raising farm prices above their free-market levels on average
  (a) Do so at the expense of price stability
  (b) Are successful only if the demand for farm goods is elastic
  (c) Tend to benefit poor farmers at the expense of rich ones
  (d) Raise farm incomes at the expense of economic efficiency

*14. One reason why water sells for less than champagne is that
  (a) Not many people can afford champagne
  (b) Given the choice between water and the same amount of champagne, everyone would choose champagne
  (c) The market mechanism fails to deal adequately with the paradox of value
  (d) Champagne has a higher cost of production than water

Exercises

All these exercises involve computing consumer and producer surpluses. You should review these concepts and their graphical measurement in Chapters 20 and 21 before proceeding.

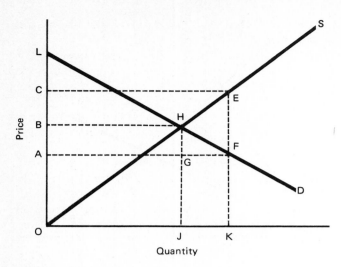

FIGURE 22-2

1. Figure 22-2 above shows the supply and demand for a particular grade of wheat in a particular year in a perfectly competitive market in Chicago.

a. The equilibrium price is _____, the equilibrium quantity is _____.

b. Now suppose that the government, instead of allowing the market to operate freely, buys all the wheat directly from the farmers, offering them a guaranteed price of *OC*. Therefore, the amount supplied will be _____. As a result of this government intervention, producer surplus has gone (up, down) by the amount _____. Shade in this area in the diagram.

c. Suppose that the government, after buying this wheat, now sells it all on the market for whatever price it will fetch. This price will be _____. As a result of this government intervention, consumer surplus has gone (up, down) by the amount _____. Shade in this area in the diagram.

d. If we just considered the change in the sum of consumer and producer surplus (the two shaded areas), we would conclude that there has been a net gain to the economy as a result of the government's intervention. However, the government has made a loss on these wheat dealings which the taxpayers must pay for. The total amount that the government paid for the wheat equals _____ and the total revenue that the government received for selling the wheat equals _____, so its loss equals _____. If we deduct this taxpayer loss from the gain in consumer plus producer surplus we conclude that the government's action resulted in a net (gain, loss) to the economy which equals _____.

e. Alternatively we could have arrived at the same conclusion by noting that the intervention raised output from the perfectly competitive amount _____ to the amount _____, thus resulting in an efficiency loss measured by the triangle _____.

2. The purpose of this exercise is to demonstrate the social benefit that can be produced by the existence of markets. Figures 22-3 and 22-4 represent the markets for a manufactured good in Florida and Texas.

a. Suppose that initially there was no trade between the two states; that is, no market in which people from one state could trade with people from

FIGURE 22-3

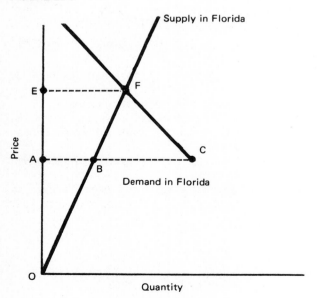

FIGURE 22-4

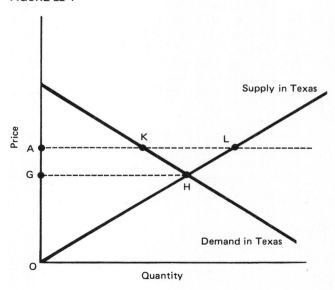

the other. Then the equilibrium price in Florida would be _____ and the equilibrium price in Texas would be _____.

b. Next, suppose that a group of traders organized a market in which Texans could trade with Floridians. Suppose that there were no transportation costs or any other kind of cost to separate the markets of the two states. Then there would in fact be only one market that included both states. A single equilibrium price would be established such that the total amount supplied in the two states was just equal to the total amount demanded in the two states (suppose no other states are involved). Therefore, the excess of supply over demand in one state must equal the shortfall in the other. In Figures 22-3 and 22-4 this equilibrium price equals OA. At that price Florida has an (excess, shortfall) of supply

equal to _____, and Texas has an (excess, shortfall) of supply equal to _____.

c. As a result of allowing trade between the two states, consumer surplus in Florida has gone (up, down) by the amount _____, producer surplus in Florida has gone (up, down) by the amount_____; so the sum of consumer and producer surplus in Florida has gone (up, down) by the amount_____.

d. Consumer surplus in Texas has gone (up, down) by the amount _____, producer surplus in Texas has gone (up, down) by the amount _____, and the sum of consumer and producer surplus in Texas has gone (up, down) by the amount _____. These two triangles provide estimates of the gains to the two states from creating a market between the two states.

Essay Questions

1. According to the economist's theory of how markets work, the butcher provides you with meat in an economically efficient manner, not because the butcher hates to see you go hungry but because he or she is interested in making as large a profit as possible. But if the butcher is interested in maximizing profit, will he or she not then be led to exploit the consumers of meat by charging a price far in excess of the cost of the meat? If this were done, would the results be economically efficient? Why would the butcher not be able to do this under perfect competition? Does the invisible hand lead to an efficient level of output in the case of a good sold by a monopoly? Explain.

2. In Exercise **2** above who would be the gainers and who would be the losers from the opening up of trade between the two states? What sorts of arguments do you suppose the losers might propose in favor of a government prohibition of such trade? How could these arguments be countered?

Can you imagine any way in which the gainers might compensate the losers? Would the total gain in each state be enough so that after such compensation everybody could end up a gainer?

3. Suppose someone were to argue that the excess of total benefit over total cost resulting from wheat production was far greater than the excess of total benefit over total cost in the production of household appliances, but that for efficiency there should be an increase in the production of household appliances and not wheat. Is this possible? Explain why or why not with a diagram.

4. Argue the case that perfect competition tends to promote at least two different kinds of efficiency.

***5.** Show how a speculator who is also a poor forecaster will tend to amplify the fluctuations in the market price. Show why this speculator won't stay in business long.

Answers

True-False Questions: **1** F **2** F **3** T **4** T **5** T **6** F **7** F **8** F **9** F **10** F
Multiple-Choice Questions: **1** b **2** b **3** c **4** c **5** b **6** d **7** a **8** a **9** b **10** d **11** b **12** a **13** d **14** d
Exercises:
1a. *OB, OJ* **b.** *OK*, up, *BCEH* **c.** *OA*, up, *ABHF* **d.** *OCEK, OAFK, ACEF*, loss, *HEF* **e.** *OJ, OK, HEF*
2a. *OE, OG* **b.** shortfall, *BC*, excess, *KL* **c.** up, *AEFC*, down, *AEFB*, up, *BFC* **d.** down, *AKHG*, up, *ALHG*, up, *KLH*

CHAPTER 23
Monopoly

Learning Objectives

After you have studied this chapter in the textbook and the study guide, you should be able to

Explain four reasons why monopolies exist

Illustrate the situation of a natural monopoly in a diagram

Explain why the condition "marginal revenue = marginal cost" must be satisfied by the profit-maximizing monopoly

Show in a diagram why a monopoly generally produces less than the economically efficient level of output

Describe the two types of government policy toward natural monopolies

Explain how marginal cost pricing works

Show how price discrimination may sometimes be beneficial

CHAPTER HIGHLIGHTS

The last chapter discussed the ideal case of perfect competition. This one discusses the pathological case of monopoly—where there is just one seller. It deals with the questions of (1) why monopoly exists, (2) how a monopoly chooses price and quantity, (3) why monopoly is undesirable (usually!), (4) the effects of government policies directed toward monopoly, and (5) how a monopoly may practice price discrimination.

Why Monopoly Exists

Monopolies exist for any or all of the following reasons: (1) the monopoly may possess something valuable that no potential competitor can acquire (for example some talent, property, or patent); (2) the government may have created the monopoly by making competition illegal, as with the post office; (3) there may be a *natural* monopoly; or (4) the existing sellers may have *colluded*—agreed to act in cooperation rather than competition.

The case of natural monopoly is perhaps the

most important. It exists whenever there are economies of scale (recall this from Chapter 21) that would not be exhausted by a large number of firms in competition. In other words, a single firm's average cost curve might continue to fall until its output became about large enough to supply the entire industry (see Figure 23-1 in the textbook).

How a Monopoly Chooses Its Price and Quantity.

A monopoly, just like a perfectly competitive firm, maximizes profit by choosing the level of output where its marginal revenue (MR) equals its marginal cost (MC). But whereas the perfect competitor's MR equals the market price, the monopoly's MR is *less than* the market price. This is because the perfect competitor faces a horizontal demand curve but the monopoly's demand curve slopes downward to the right. When a perfect competitor sells one more unit the price stays the same. His extra revenue is just the market price. When a monopoly sells one more unit the price doesn't stay the same. It falls. Thus the monopoly's extra revenue (MR) is the market price that it receives from selling an extra unit, *minus* the loss it incurs because selling an extra unit lowers the price it receives for all the other units.

In other words, the monopoly's MR curve lies below its demand curve, and consequently it intersects the MC curve at a smaller output, as you can see in Figure 23-5 in the textbook. Thus, the monopoly exploits its advantage by reducing its output. By making the product scarce it keeps the price high.

Like the perfectly competitive firm, the monopoly produces where MR = MC only if it is able to cover its costs. This requires that the demand curve overlap the AC curve—as in Figure 23-4 in the textbook.

Why Monopoly Is (Usually!) Undesirable

Figure 23-5*b* in the textbook shows that the monopoly's profit-maximizing level of output (where MC = MR) is less than the efficient level (where MC = P). Thus a monopoly generates an efficiency loss. This loss is the main disadvantage of monopoly. But a complete verdict on any particular monopoly must also consider such other items as the technical inefficiency that may exist because there is no competition to force the monopoly to keep up the struggle against rising costs, and the transfer of income from consumers to the monopoly resulting from the monopoly's higher price. Whether this transfer is desirable or undesirable is largely a matter of value judgment, because there is no objective way of comparing one person's gain with another's loss.

Government Policies Toward Monopoly

Antitrust policies should be used to break up or prevent monopolies other than the "natural" kind. But in the case of a natural monopoly it usually makes sense to keep the monopoly, with its cost advantages, but control it one of two ways: (1) by controlling the monopoly's price, or (2) by nationalizing the industry (having the government buy it). The first of these is analyzed in this chapter. The rule that guides most price regulation is to set the price that would exist if the industry were perfectly competitive; that is, the price where the demand curve intersects the marginal cost curve. This government policy is called "marginal cost pricing." Because the monopoly must take this regulated price as given, it therefore acts like a perfect competitor—a price taker. The result is an efficient outcome. However, regulation may (*a*) reduce the firm's incentive to control costs (since higher MC will result in a higher regulated price) or (*b*) prevent the firm from making enough profit to stay in business. In case of (*b*), Box 23-2 in the textbook shows how the efficiency loss of monopoly may be reduced by a compromise regulation that sets price equal to AC instead of to MC; or how the efficiency loss may be eliminated altogether if the MC rule is followed, but the firm is given a subsidy to keep it in business.

Price Discrimination

So far we have assumed that the monopoly charges a single price to all consumers. But it will usually find it more profitable if different customers can be charged different prices—that is, if a higher price is charged to customers who are willing and able to pay it. Such price discrimination may be beneficial if it allows the monopoly to make enough profits to stay in business when it would otherwise go bankrupt.

IMPORTANT TERMS

Natural monopoly This occurs when the average cost of a single firm falls over such an extended range of output that one firm can produce the total quantity sold at a lower average cost than could two or more firms.

Market power A firm has market power if it is able to influence the market price (and thereby increase its profit).

Marginal revenue The change in total revenue resulting from a one-unit increase in output. For the perfect competitor marginal revenue (MR) equals price, whereas for the monopoly MR is less than price.

Price discrimination The practice of charging different prices to different customers for the same good. This is one method by which a monopoly might increase its profits.

Marginal cost pricing The policy of regulating a monopoly's price by setting it at the level where the monopoly's MC curve intersects the market demand curve.

***Theory of second best** The theory of what constitutes an efficient level of output in one industry when the level of output in other industries is not efficient (perhaps because of monopoly in some of the other industries). See Box 23-1 in the textbook.

***Average cost pricing** The policy of regulating a monopoly's price by setting it at the level when the monopoly's AC curve intersects the market demand curve.

***Producer's association** An organization designed to allow the firms in a perfectly competitive industry to behave collectively like a monopoly, by setting quotas that restrict production. These associations tend to break down because of the incentive for individual firms to cheat by exceeding their assigned quotas (although not if the government cooperates and gives the quotas the force of law).

True-False Questions

T F   **1.** The term monopoly includes the situation in which the government operates the only firm in an industry.
T F   **2.** A monopoly's marginal revenue is less than the market price.
T F   **3.** An unregulated profit-maximizing monopoly will set a price equal to marginal cost.
T F   **4.** A natural monopoly might have a rising MC curve at the profit-maximizing output.
T F   **5.** The elasticity of the monopoly's demand curve is less than that of the demand curve faced by the firm in perfect competition.
T F   **6.** The monopoly exercises its market power primarily by influencing the position of the demand schedule.
T F   **7.** With no externalities an unregulated monopoly will produce more than the economically efficient level of output.
T F   ***8.** According to the theory of second best, if all other industries are unregulated monopolies it may be efficient for this industry to produce less than the level of output that would exist under perfect competition.
T F   **9.** The monopoly that can practice price discrimination will make more profits than the single-price monopoly with the same costs and the same demand curve.
T F   **10.** The desire by the owner of a firm to enjoy "a quiet life" rather than to maximize profits is one important reason why monopoly might involve technical inefficiency.

Multiple-Choice Questions

1. A successful voluntary producers' association would best be classified as
  (a) A monopoly arising from exclusive ownership of something
  (b) A legal monopoly
  (c) A natural monopoly
  (d) A collusive monopoly

2. A monopoly's marginal revenue is
  (a) Always positive
  (b) Always above average cost
  (c) Equal to the height of its demand curve
  (d) Less than the height of its demand curve

3. Which of the following probably has the most market power?
  (a) A perfectly competitive firm
  (b) A monopoly that is forced to obey a marginal-cost pricing rule
  (c) An unregulated monopoly
  (d) A firm thinking of entering a currently monopolized industry

4. The firm illustrated in Figure 23-1 below is in what kind of industry?

FIGURE 23-1

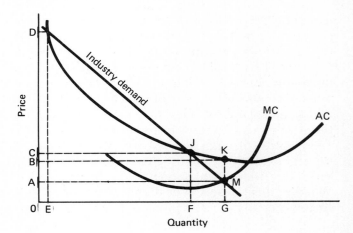

(a) Perfect competition (c) Natural oligopoly
(b) Natural monopoly (d) Collusive monopoly

5. A marginal-cost pricing rule would force the firm in Figure 23-1 to set the price

(a) *OA*   (c) *OC*
(b) *OB*   (d) *OD*

6. Under a marginal-cost rule, if no subsidy were granted the firm in Figure 23-1 would

(a) Eventually shut down
(b) Produce the quantity *OE*
(c) Produce the quantity *OF*
(d) Produce the quantity *OG*

*7. In Figure 23-1, the minimum subsidy required to keep the firm in business under a marginal-cost rule would be

(a) *OG* × *GK*
(b) *OF* ×*FJ*
(c) *OG* × *MK*
(d) No subsidy would be required

8. Which of the following is true of both the monopoly and the perfect competitor?

(a) Price will be no greater than marginal cost
(b) Price will equal average cost
(c) Marginal revenue will equal marginal cost, regardless of average variable cost
(d) Marginal revenue will equal marginal cost, as long as the price is high enough to cover average variable cost

9. Regardless of the number of other firms in the industry, a firm's demand curve indicates its

(a) Marginal revenue   (c) Average revenue
(b) Marginal cost   (d) Average cost

10. If a monopoly's marginal revenue exceeds marginal cost it will want to

(a) Decrease production
(b) Increase production
(c) Leave production unchanged
(d) Close down

*11. Which of the following makes the largest profit? (Assume that the monopolies are identical in all respects except those explicitly mentioned.)

(a) The unregulated monopoly charging a single price
(b) The unregulated, price-discriminating monopoly
(c) The monopoly subject to a regulation that enforces marginal cost pricing
(d) The monopoly subject to a regulation that enforces average cost pricing

*12. Which of the following policies might allow the survival of a monopoly whose average cost curve is always above its demand curve?

(a) Average cost pricing
(b) Marginal cost pricing
(c) Marginal cost pricing combined with subsidization
(d) Forcing the monopoly to charge the same price to all customers, but letting the monopoly choose the price

13. If a monopolized industry is not a natural monopoly then the principles of this chapter suggest that efficiency would best be served by a policy that

(a) Breaks up the monopoly so as to promote more competition
(b) Subsidizes the monopoly
(c) Leaves the monopoly unregulated
(d) Allows the monopoly to remain but imposes marginal-cost pricing

14. Which of the following can definitely be shown to result when a monopoly sets a price above MC and earns positive profits?

(a) An undesirable transfer of income
(b) A desirable transfer of income
(c) A gain of technical efficiency
(d) A loss of allocative efficiency

Exercises

1a. The monopoly described by Figure 23-2 will, if unregulated, produce the amount _____, charge the price _____, and make a profit equal to _____.

1b. The efficiency loss of this output level would be _____. If the monopoly were regulated according to an average cost pricing scheme its price would be _____, its output would be _____, and its profit would be _____. The efficiency loss of this level of output would be _____.

1c. If it were regulated according to a marginal cost pricing scheme its price would be _____, its output would be _____, its profit would be _____, and the minimum amount of lump-sum subsidy required to keep the monopolist in business would be _____. The efficiency loss of this level of output would be _____.

FIGURE 23-2

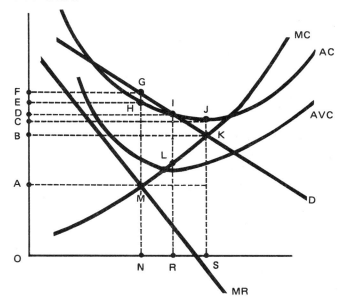

2. A monopoly has the demand and total cost figures shown in Table 23-1. Fill in the rest of this table, ignoring for the time being the last three columns.

2a. The monopoly's fixed cost is _____. It will choose to produce a level of output equal to _____ and charge a price equal to _____. Its maximum attainable profit is _____.

2b. Suppose that, in an attempt to capture some of this monopoly's profits for the general taxpayer's benefit, the government were to impose a lump-sum tax of $5. This tax may be regarded by the monopoly as a fixed cost, because it must be paid no matter how much output is produced. After the imposition of this tax, the monopoly's fixed cost is _____. Fill in the third-last column (1) indicating the monopoly's after-tax profit. After the imposition of the tax the monopoly will choose to produce an amount of output equal to _____ and to charge a price equal to _____; and its maximum attainable

after-tax profit will be _____.

2c. Suppose that instead of a lump-sum tax the government decides to impose a 50 percent excise tax on the monopoly's output. In other words, the monopoly must now pay to the government 50 percent of its total revenue (before tax). In this case the monopoly's fixed cost is _____. Fill in the second-last column (2) showing the monopoly's net (after-tax) total revenue, and the last column (3) showing its net profit under the excise tax. In this case the monopoly will choose to produce an amount of output equal to _____, and to charge a price equal to _____; and its maximum attainable after-tax profit will be _____. The amount of excise tax collected from this monopoly will be _____.

2d. From the point of view of economic efficiency the (lump-sum, excise) tax is preferable. From the point of view of maximizing the amount of tax revenue collected from the monopoly, the (lump-sum, excise) tax is preferable.

Table 23-1

P	Quantity demanded	Total revenue	Marginal revenue	Total cost	Average cost	Marginal cost	Profit	(1) Net profit with lump-sum tax	(2) Net total revenue with excise tax	(3) Net profit with excise tax
$10	0	$	$0	$2	$___	$0	$	$	$	$
8	1	8		3						
6	2			6						
4	3			11						
2	4			18						

Essay Questions

1. Suppose that the government decides to prevent the merger of the only two firms in an industry, even though that merger would result in a reduction in costs of production in that industry because of the elimination of wasteful duplication. Defend the position that this government action is warranted on the grounds of economic efficiency. Defend the position that it is not warranted on the grounds of economic efficiency.

2. What do you suppose would happen to expenditure on research if the government always taxed away the monopoly profits that firms earned from their patented research results? With this in mind, do you think the government should tax the profits of a natural monopoly differently from the profits of a monopoly based on the exclusive possession of patents?

3. Explain carefully what is wrong with the following statement. "If the industry demand curve lies below a monopoly's average cost curve, then on the grounds of economic efficiency it is a good thing for the monopoly to go out of business because demanders aren't willing to pay enough for the good to cover the cost of producing it."

4. It has been argued by some that the American Medical Association is a collusive monopoly, because it restricts the output of medical services by controlling the licensing of medical schools. How does this restriction affect the cost of medical services? What unfavorable consequences might there be if the government were to allow completely free entry into the medical profession—that is, allow anyone, with or without training, to practice medicine? In view of this, (a) defend the position that the medical profession's collusive monopoly has been beneficial to the economy and (*b*) defend the position that the monopoly has been harmful.

5. A monopoly might find it profitable to expand output even if this had the effect of reducing its price and increasing its costs per unit of output. How could this possibly make sense?

6. Recall our discussion of the elasticity of demand from Chapter 19. If a monopoly's demand function is elastic then what happens to its total revenue as output increases? In this case what can be said about the monopoly's marginal revenue? In the case where the market demand function is inelastic what can be said about marginal revenue? In view of this explain why a monopoly that has discovered that its demand curve is inelastic would want to change its output.

*7. In a perfectly competitive market if the demand curve shifts to the right the quantity produced in that industry will rise. Show how this might or might not be the case in a monopolistic industry depending upon how the shift in the demand curve affected the elasticity of demand.

*8. If a monopoly were a *perfect* price discriminator then for each unit sold it would charge the maximum attainable price. That is, it would charge a price so high for each unit that none of its consumers would be left with any consumer surplus whatsoever. (Each customer would pay the maximum amount he or she could be made to pay.) What is the monopoly's MR? Its equilibrium price and quantity? Show that in this case the standard efficiency loss resulting from monopoly would actually disappear! How does this illustrate the conflict that often exists between efficiency and equity?

Answers

True-False Questions: 1 T 2 T 3 F 4 T 5 T 6 F 7 F 8 T 9 T 10 T
Multiple-Choice Questions: 1 d 2 d 3 c 4 b 5 a 6 a 7 c 8 d 9 c 10 b 11 b 12 c 13 a 14 d
Exercises: **1a.** *ON, OF, EFGH* **b.** *GKM, OD, OR,* zero, *ILK*
      c. *OB, OS,* minus *BCKJ, BCJK,* zero

2.

Total revenue	Marginal revenue	Total cost	Average cost	Marginal cost	Profit	(1)	(2)	(3)
$ 0	$ 0	$ 2	$−	$0	$ −2	$ −7	$0	$ −2
8	8	3	3	1	5	0	4	1
12	4	6	3	3	6	1	6	0
12	0	11	3⅔	5	1	−4	6	−5
8	−4	18	4½	7	−10	−15	4	−14

a. 2, 2, 6, 6; **b.** 7, 2, 6, 1; **c.** 2, 1, 8, 1, 4; **d.** lump sum, lump sum

CHAPTER 24
Markets Between Monopoly and Perfect Competition

Learning Objectives

After you have studied this chapter in the textbook and the study guide, you should be able to

Explain the distinction between oligopoly and monopolistic competition

Give two reasons why oligopoly may arise

Describe the kinked demand curve diagrammatically

Explain why the kinked demand curve would discourage an oligopolist from changing price frequently

Explain the concept of price leadership and its connection with collusion

Give three examples of non-price competition

Describe two possible barriers to entry

Summarize the case for advertising and the case against

Explain why the OPEC cartel succeeded in raising prices without imposing production quotas

Explain why the monopolistic competitor earns no supernormal profits in the long run

CHAPTER HIGHLIGHTS

The last two chapters dealt with the extreme cases of perfect competition, with many price-taking firms, and monopoly, where there is only one firm. This chapter deals with markets between these extremes, where firms are not price takers and there is more than one firm. There are two basic forms of such markets:

1. *Oligopoly:* the case of "few sellers." This is typical of much large-scale manufacturing that is dominated by giant corporations.

2. *Monopolistic competition:* In this case there are many sellers but each firm can raise its price at least a little without losing all its sales to rivals. Because the firm's product is differentiated from its rivals, some customers will continue to buy the product even if it costs a little more. This is true of some manufacturing industries in the United States that are not dominated by giant corporations.

This chapter discusses how these two forms of "imperfect competition" might come about, what principles govern the behavior of firms, and why either form of market organization might be regarded as desirable or undesirable. It also discusses the very important case of the OPEC oil cartel.

First, consider oligopoly. How many sellers is "a few"? This depends on the industry's concentration ratio—the fraction of sales going to the few (usually four) leading firms. Oligopoly exists if this concentration ratio is "high." An oligopoly can arise either because of natural oligopoly, where the lowest cost way of satisfying market demand is with a small number of firms, or because some firms grow large enough to obtain market power (some influence over price).

Because there are few clear-cut principles governing the behavior of oligopolists, the theoretical analysis in this chapter is much less straightforward than in earlier chapters. But the following points are important:

1. There is a tendency for oligopolists to collude—to act like a monopoly so as to maximize the total profits available to the industry as a whole. However, there is also a tendency for collusive arrangements to break down because of the incentive for each member to produce more than its assigned quota. (If any single member was to do this it could increase its own profits because at the quota output its price would exceed its marginal cost.)

2. When the oligopolistic firm chooses its price and output, it must take into account the possible reaction of its rivals—something that need not even be considered by the monopolist (with no rivals) or the perfectly competitive firm (whose rivals don't even notice it). This sort of complicated decision-making is what makes the theory of oligopoly so difficult.

3. Some think that the typical oligopolistic firm faces a kinked demand curve. If it raises its prices its rivals won't. Instead they'll hope to capture some of its sales. But if it lowers its price the rivals *will* follow suit to avoid being undersold. As Figure 24-6 on page 553 of the textbook explains, this inhibits the oligopolistic firm from changing its price except in extreme circumstances. However, many think that the kinked demand curve is not a very realistic theory.

4. Some oligopolies seem to operate by a pattern of *price leadership* in which one firm takes on the role of being the first to announce price changes, on the understanding that other firms will follow suit. This sort of "gentleman's agreement" has often been criticized as a collusive arrangement. The price leader may set the price just as a monopolist would.

5. Rather than undertake potentially destructive price competition many oligopolies favor various forms of non-price competition such as packaging, product differentiation, and advertising. But advertising may involve wasteful competition, distort people's values, and mislead consumers. (In defense of advertising it has been argued that it helps to make consumers well informed, that it supports the communication industry and that it helps to promote product quality by making firms fearful of losing the goodwill that they achieve through advertising.)

6. Oligopolies often succeed in erecting barriers to entry against new competition. Advertising may serve as a barrier to entry by creating in customers' minds a favorable image of the existing firms, which is hard for new firms to overcome. But the most important barrier to entry may be economies of scale that leave room for only a few low-cost firms in the industry.

OPEC

An important example of a collusion oligopoly is the international oil cartel, OPEC. This cartel succeeded in quadrupling oil prices in 1973–1974, and again doubling them in 1979–1980. Their collusive agreement has not come apart, despite the lack of enforceable quotas on its members. The textbook lists six reasons:

1. The international oil companies do not want to damage relations with their OPEC suppliers by switching to other member countries that are "cheating."

2. These companies are further discouraged from switching by the special chemical properties that make it difficult for a refiner to substitute oil from different sources.

3. Because of the low elasticity of demand for oil, the large price increases have made many OPEC members wealthy enough to resist the temptation to cheat.

4. These price increases have been reinforced by a rightward shift in demand for oil that apparently occurred in the early 1970s.

5. Noneconomic factors like the 1973 war with Israel have helped the solidarity of the group.

6. The Saudis, whose large reserves give them a longer time-horizon and therefore a greater interest in moderating the price increases, have been willing to cut back their production by whatever is necessary to maintain the cartel's price, even when all the other members are producing as much as they like.

Monopolistic competition presents few of the problems that characterize oligopoly. Its main drawback is that it results in prices greater than marginal cost. Like a monopolist, the monopolistic competitor faces a downward-sloping demand curve. Thus it quotes a higher price, and produces a smaller output than a perfectly competitive firm. However, this does not necessarily imply inefficiency. Lower output by each firm means there will be more firms to satisfy total market demand. Thus the consumer can choose from a wider range of differentiated products. This wider choice may more than make up for the lower output of each firm. Moreover, although the firm in monopolistic competition does have some influence over its price, it cannot use this market power in the long run to earn supernormal profits. Whenever existing firms start earning supernormal profits, new firms will enter, reducing the demand for existing firms' products, until all supernormal profits have been eliminated. In other words, in the long run the monopolistic competitor's demand curve will be just tangent to its AC curve. (See Figure 24-7 in the textbook.)

IMPORTANT TERMS

Oligopoly A market dominated by only a few sellers.

Concentration ratio A measure of oligopoly—usually the proportion of an industry's sales going to the four largest firms.

Natural oligopoly One that arises because of economies of scale. It occurs when a firm producing at minimum average cost is large enough to satisfy a significant fraction of total market demand.

Product differentiation The ability of firms to distinguish their product from those of their rivals. Such differentiation may be real or fancied.

Cartel Formal agreement among firms to collude in setting prices and/or in determining market shares.

OPEC The Organization of Petroleum Exporting Countries. This is the international oil cartel formed in late 1973.

Kinked demand curve The demand curve that may face oligopolists. It has a kink in it at the current price because rivals will respond to the oligopolist's price reductions by cutting their prices, but they will not respond to the oligopolist's price *increases* by raising their prices. (See Figure 24-6 in the textbook.)

Price leadership The practice in some oligopolistic industries of having one firm announce its price changes first, on the understanding that other firms will follow suit.

Barrier to entry Anything that makes it difficult for new firms to enter an industry to compete against existing firms. Some barriers, like advertising, are "created" (artificial); but some are natural, like economies of scale.

Monopolistic competition A market in which (*a*) there are many firms, and (*b*) each seller's product is differentiated from those of the others. The demand curve facing the individual seller is quite elastic, but not completely so.

True-False Questions

T F 1. The minimum point on the AC curve lies further to the right for a natural monopoly than for a natural oligopoly (assuming the same market demand curve in each case).

T F 2. In monopolistic competition there is always product differentiation.

T F 3. The oligopolist's market power allows it to choose its price without having to worry about its rivals' reactions to its decision.

T F 4. The OPEC oil cartel has not broken down, partly because noneconomic factors have helped to keep the members together.

T F 5. The kinked demand curve arises mainly in monopolistic competition.

T F 6. The theory of the kinked demand curve doesn't predict at which price the kink will occur.

T F 7. A price leader is often suspected of being the manager of a tacit cartel arrangement.

T F   **8.** Monopolistic competitors earn supernormal profits in the long run.
T F   **9.** Economies of scale may constitute a natural barrier to entry in an industry.
T F   **10.** Barriers to entry are rare or nonexistent in monopolistically competitive industries.

Multiple-Choice Questions

1. The concentration ratio usually measures the share of the industry sales going to the top
  (a) 1 firm   **(c)** 10 firms
  (b) 4 firms   **(d)** 20 firms

2. The Boeing Aerospace Company is a
  (a) Monopolist
  (b) Oligopolist
  (c) Monopolistic competitor
  (d) Perfect competitor

3. The oligopolist is sometimes referred to as a
  (a) Price taker   **(c)** Price searcher
  (b) Price maker   **(d)** Quantity taker

4. The efficiency loss that collusion imposes upon the nation results mainly from
  (a) The incentive for each firm to cheat by exceeding its quota
  (b) The transfer of income from customers to the sellers that collude
  (c) The resulting restriction in the industry's output
  (d) The unwillingness of other sellers to follow the price leader

5. A "kinked" demand curve would
  (a) Encourage frequent price changes
  (b) Discourage frequent price changes
  (c) Exist only for a price leader
  (d) Discourage non-price competition

6. According to the theory of the kinked demand curve
  (a) The kink is in the market demand curve, not the firm's individual demand curve
  (b) The kink in one firm's demand curve will occur above the price being charged by other firms
  (c) The firm believes that its rivals will follow suit if it raises its price
  (d) None of the above

7. The practice of price leadership
  (a) Makes tacit collusion difficult to detect
  (b) Is most common in monopolistic competition
  (c) Does not occur in markets with product differentiation
  (d) Is a device that is used only in perfect competition

8. Non-price competition
  (a) Is often engaged in by oligopolists who fear that price-competition might be mutually destructive
  (b) Is practiced by the firm in perfect competition
  (c) Is practiced only by monopolies
  (d) Is an effective way to stimulate aggregate demand during a recession

9. Heavy expenditures on packaging a product do *not* constitute
  (a) A barrier to entry
  (b) Non-price competition
  (c) A means of enforcing production quotas
  (d) A means of product differentiation

10. Advertising
  (a) Is generally agreed to be an efficient way to promote full employment
  (b) Helps to finance our communications industry
  (c) Does not exist in oligopolistic industries
  (d) Is only done for shoddy products

11. The unusual feature of the OPEC cartel is that it has
  (a) Successfully raised prices without imposing production quotas on its members
  (b) Not stayed together for very long
  (c) Produced so little revenue for its members
  (d) Raised the price of its output, in the face of an elastic market-demand curve

12. Product differentiation by a firm occurs
  (a) Only in perfect competition
  (b) Only in monopoly
  (c) In monopolistic competition and some oligopolies
  (d) In all market structures

13. In the long run the firm in a monopolistically competitive industry will
  (a) Face a perfectly elastic demand curve
  (b) Produce more than the amount that would minimize average cost
  (c) Produce less than the amount that would minimize average cost
  (d) Produce a quantity such that marginal revenue exceeds marginal cost

Exercises

1. Figures 24-1, 24-2, and 24-3 depict three alternative short-run situations that might face a firm in monopolistic competition. The short-run cost curves (AC, AVC, MC) are identical in each situation, but the demand curves (D_1, D_2, D_3) and thus the marginal revenue curves (MR_1, MR_2, MR_3) are different in the three situations.

In Figure 24-1 the firm will produce the amount _____, charge the price _____, and earn the amount of profits _____. In Figure 24-2 the firm will produce the amount _____, charge the price _____, and earn the amount of profits _____. In Figure 24-3 the firm will produce the amount _____, charge the price _____, and earn the

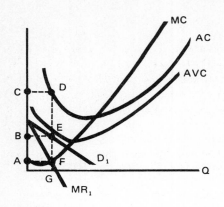

FIGURE 24-1

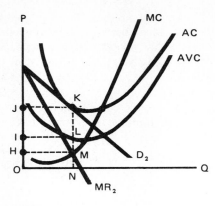

FIGURE 24-2

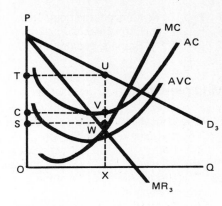

FIGURE 24-3

amount of profits _____. Of the three diagrams the one that depicts a situation of long-run equilibrium in the industry is Figure _____.

2. In Figure 24-4 the oligopolist and all its rivals are currently charging the price P and produc-

FIGURE 24-4

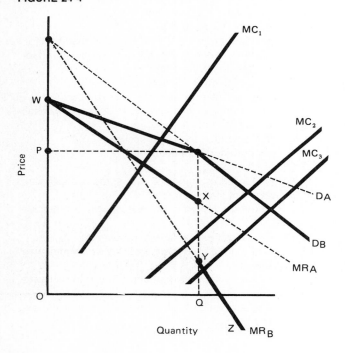

ing the quantity Q. It faces the kinked demand curve that consists of the segment of D_A above the price P and the segment of D_B below the price P. The respective marginal revenue curves are MR_A and MR_B.

a. If it increases output beyond Q, its MR curve follows (MR_A, MR_B). But if it decreases output below Q, its MR curve follows (MR_A, MR_B). Therefore the complete MR curve is (MR_A, MR_B, $WXYZ$).

b. If its MC is MC_1, then it will charge a price that is (more than, less than, the same as) P; and will choose a quantity that is (more than, less than, the same as) Q.

c. If its MC is MC_2, then it will charge a price that is (more than, less than, the same as) P; and choose a quantity that is (more than, less than, the same as) Q.

d. If its MC is MC_3, then it will charge a price that is (more than, less than, the same as) P; and choose a quantity that is (more than, less than, the same as) Q.

e. If MC is MC_2 we now see from a different point of view why the kinked demand curve results in a stable price. For if MC_2 shifted up, but still intersected the horizontal segment XY, then the firm would (raise, lower, leave unchanged) the price. And if MC_2 shifted down, still intersecting XY, it would (raise, lower, leave unchanged) the price.

Essay Questions

1. Suppose you observe an industry over a period and notice that during any day the price at which one firm is selling is identical to the price at which all of the other firms are selling. Is this what you would expect to observe if the firms were acting competitively? Is it what you would expect to observe if they were acting collusively in a secret car- tel? Can you therefore use this bit of evidence to support the argument that a cartel exists? What other sort of evidence would you look for in order to support such an argument? What sort of evidence would you look for in order to support the contrary argument that the firms are behaving competitively?

2. What sort of products would you expect to be advertised most heavily? In what sort of industries would you expect advertising to play the greatest role?

3. Some advertisements on television tell you absolutely nothing about the specific products being sold by a firm. Instead, they tell you why the people in the firm are likable, or how the country would suffer if the firm didn't exist. Why do firms engage in such advertising? What would be the gains and losses to the economy as a whole if such advertising were prohibited by law?

4. Explain why an oligopolistic firm facing a kinked demand curve will be unlikely to change its price. (It may help to refer to Exercise 2 above.)

5. How does the monopoly know what the market demand curve looks like? If it doesn't know already, how could it try to guess? In what sense is this problem of estimating the firm's demand curve more difficult for an oligopoly than for a monopoly? Will a firm be more likely to keep its price stable if it can only guess its demand curve than if it *knows* its demand curve? Explain.

6. Would firms in an industry with a high concentration ratio be more or less likely to engage in collusive activity than those in an industry with a low concentration ratio? Why? In determining wheather collusion is likely, what other factors would you take into consideration? How would you measure them?

*7. Carefully criticize the following statement: "All industries are monopolistically competitive, because (*a*) every firm's product is differentiated from every other firm's product at least a little bit, and (*b*) no matter how much market power a firm has, its demand curve will be affected by the prices that are charged by other firms in the economy."

Answers

True-False Questions: 1 T 2 T 3 F 4 T 5 F 6 T 7 T 8 F 9 T 10 T
Multiple Choice Questions: 1 b 2 b 3 c 4 c 5 b 6 d 7 a 8 a 9 c 10 b 11 a 12 c 13 c
Exercises:
1. 0, undefined, minus the fixed cost, *ON, OJ,* 0, *OX, OT, CTUV,* 24-2
2a. MR_B, MR_A, *WXYZ* **b.** more than, less than
  c. the same as, the same as; **d.** less than, more than
  e. leave unchanged, leave unchanged

CHAPTER 25
Government Regulation of Business

Learning Objectives

After you have studied this chapter in the textbook and the study guide, you should be able to

Identify and briefly describe the three legislative acts that form the cornerstone of federal antitrust policy

Explain why it might be advantageous to have large-sized firms

Show how economic efficiency might be promoted by a policy of allowing natural monopolies to exist but using antitrust policies to break up other monopolies

Explain why this policy would have to be supplemented by a policy of regulating the prices of the natural monopolies

Explain why cutthroat competition and collusion are so difficult to control

Give several reasons why "market-structure" regulation tends to act in the interest of the firms being regulated rather than in the consumers' interest

Explain why it is often easier for an industry to act like a cartel if it is regulated

Explain how former Civil Aeronautics Board (CAB) regulations affected the interests of (*a*) passengers on long trunk routes, (*b*) passengers on small-city routes, (*c*) established airlines, and (*d*) the nation as a whole

Identify and briefly state the purpose of the major regulatory agencies listed in Table 25-1 in the textbook

Explain why benefit/cost analysis of quality regulation often requires us to attach a price tag on human life

Give three examples of the efficiency cost of regulations

CHAPTER HIGHLIGHTS

The focus of the last three chapters has been on the behavior of business enterprises under various conditions. This chapter focuses on the role of the government in regulating business.

Antitrust

The first category of regulations consists of antitrust laws. The main laws that underlie the government's antitrust policy are: (1) The Sherman Antitrust Act (1890), which made collusion illegal; (2) the Clayton Act (1914), which banned, for example, interlocking corporate directorships, corporate takeovers that would eliminate competition, and tying contracts that force someone to buy a whole product line or nothing; and (3) the Federal Trade Commission (FTC) Act (1914), which established the FTC to prevent "unfair competition"—in particular, business mergers that would violate the Sherman or Clayton Acts. The text mentions the examples of the Robinson-Patman Act (1936) and the Miller-Tydings Act (1937) to show how some government laws actually work in *opposition* to the spirit of the antitrust legislation.

The primary objective of antitrust legislation is to avoid the problems of monopoly and oligopoly. The main tactic in pursuing this objective has been to enact and enforce legislation aimed at limiting the size of enterprises. But this carries a cost, for size has advantages:

1. Large firms can better afford Research and Development (R and D) expenditures, which contribute to economic growth by generating technological improvements and substantial spillover benefits. (Large firms also have more incentive to undertake R and D expenditures, because their market power allows them to keep many of the benefits of resulting inventions for themselves.)

2. The prospect of acquiring market power in the future can induce even small enterprises to invest in R and D.

3. Large firms may enjoy economies of scale that would not be exhausted by smaller firms, especially in the case of "natural monopoly" described in Chapter 23.

Since economies of scale can be so important, a good policy for promoting efficiency would be to allow monopolies to form whenever they are "natural," and rely on antitrust policy to break up "unnatural" monopolies. The problem with this policy is that despite its cost advantage a natural monopoly will produce the efficiency loss that we studied in Chapter 23 if left unregulated. Consequently, the policy needs to be supplemented by price regulation of natural monopolies. As we have seen, this sort of regulation is imperfect. Thus in practice it might even make sense to break up a natural monopoly, despite its economies of scale, as a way of eliminating all these problems of regulation.

Another tactic of antitrust policy, besides limiting the size of enterprises, is that of ensuring fair competition. In particular, much antitrust policy is designed to prevent cutthroat competition: pricing below costs in order to drive competitors out of business. The problem with this objective is that it is never clear whether prices are below costs because the firm is trying to starve out its competitors, or because it is just trying to make the best out of a weak market. (Remember that even under perfect competition a firm might continue to operate with a price less than average cost as long as it is covering average variable cost.)

A third tactic is to prevent firms from colluding to "cartelize" an otherwise competitive industry. But collusion, like cutthroat competition, is difficult to establish in the courts. For example, the fact that all firms in an industry are charging the same price is hardly enough to establish that there has been a conspiracy to fix prices. After all, this uniformity of prices is just what you would expect to see even if the market were perfectly competitive.

Other Regulations

Let's turn now from antitrust policy to other forms of regulation of business enterprises. These fall into three categories: (*a*) regulation of natural monopolies; (*b*) regulation of market-structure in industries that are by their nature more competitive; and (*c*) quality-of-life regulation of health, safety, and working conditions. Natural monopoly regulation has already been discussed in Chapter 23, so this chapter deals with the other two categories.

Market-Structure Regulation

The textbook discusses this kind of regulation mainly in terms of the example of the airlines industry, which has been regulated since 1938 by the Civil Aeronautics Board (CAB), even though it is not a natural monopoly.

As in many other cases, the regulation of this industry has been more in the interests of the firms being regulated than in the consumers' interests.

The reasons for this include: (1) the friendships that naturally develop between the regulatory officials and industry executives; (2) the fact that regulated firms are often the only source of technical information for the regulatory agency, and (3) the fact that the firms find it in their interests to spend large sums of money arguing their point of view with the agency, whereas very few consumers find it worthwhile to organize and present the opposing viewpoint.

The CAB clearly tended to cartelize an otherwise competitive industry. It did this by restricting entry into particular air routes, and by regulating the price. This form of "public-cartel" is actually more effective than a real cartel, of the sort described in Chapter 24, because (a) being run by a government agency it is exempt from antitrust legislation, and (b) having the individual firms' "quotas" imposed by force of law eliminates the problem that so often destabilizes other kinds of cartels—the problem of firms cheating by overproducing. Individual firms responded, predictably, to this prohibition on direct competition by engaging in non-price competition—offering more inflight services, more frequent flights, etc. Like any good cartel manager the CAB reacted to this by expanding the scope of its regulation to cover these non-price items—right down to the allowable size of sandwiches.

The textbook includes an overall assessment of the effects of the CAB. First, it reduced overall efficiency by restricting the total amount of air travel. As for the transfer effects, there was a "cross-subsidization" transfer from the passengers on the longer trunk routes to small-city travelers. That is, the CAB required the airlines to provide small-city service even in cases where it was not profitable, as a price for having the trunk routes. Finally, the airlines themselves received a transfer, in the form of above-normal profits, as a result of the high prices. But this transfer was lessened considerably by the non-price competition that reduced airline profits.

In recent years the airlines have been substantially deregulated. In 1978 Congress passed the Airline Deregulation Act, empowering the CAB to dismantle most of its regulations and open the industry up to competition. As expected, the immediate effect of deregulation was to reduce price and increase quantity (number of passengers). It also resulted in severe financial difficulties for many of the airlines not efficient enough to survive the intensified competition. Finally, it drew into the industry many new firms whose entry had previously been prohibited by the CAB.

Unfortunately, Congress has not quite provided economists with a controlled experiment. As dereg-ulation was taking place jet fuel prices doubled, and a recession curbed the demand for air travel. Thus it is not clear how much of the financial plight of some of the airlines is attributable to deregulation and how much to these other factors.

Quality-of-Life Regulation

This differs from market-structure regulation in two major ways. First, most such regulatory agencies cut across all industries rather than being focused on one particular industry. Second, the regulations in this case are clearly *not* in the self-interest of the firms that are being regulated. Business enterprises complain vociferously about having to comply with the regulations of such agencies as the Occupational Safety and Health Administration (OSHA), the Environmental Protection Agency (EPA), and others.

In this section of the textbook there are two major things for you to learn. First, you should study Table 25-1 in the textbook to learn the names and the basic functions of some of the most important regulatory agencies. Second—and this is what we will concentrate on in the *Study Guide*—you should find out how benefit/cost analysis might be used to evaluate the net contribution made by each quality-of-life regulation.

Regulations to make air cleaner, jobs safer, cars more reliable, etc., obviously have significant benefits, in terms of better health, safer workplaces, less dangerous transportation, etc. But they may also have significant costs. If there is only one principle you learn in economics it should be that not everything with a significant benefit is worth undertaking; the benefit must also outweigh the cost. The purpose of benefit/cost analysis is to perform just such a benefit/cost test.

You might think that the first thing Congress would do when considering a regulation would be to perform such a benefit/cost analysis. Unfortunately this is not the case. In some recent legislation it is expressly stated that regulations must be enforced *regardless* of their cost. One approach that does at least take costs into account is the requirement that a regulation must be cost-effective; i.e., that there must be no cheaper way of achieving the same benefits. Unfortunately this criterion stops short of a full benefit/cost test because it does not ensure that the cost is less than the benefit.

This reluctance of Congress to weigh the benefits against the costs can probably be attributed, at least in part, to the fact that one of the benefits of most quality-of-life regulation is the saving of lives. To weigh this benefit against the costs of achieving it is to attach a price tag to human life. No politician wants to be accused by the electors of being so cold and calculating. But in fact, such a price tag does get placed on life one way or another, even if no one wants to admit it. We all take a chance with our lives every time we cross the street. By doing this we are saying that staying on the same block all your life is too high a price to pay for the extra safety it would achieve. Regulation forbidding anyone to cross the street would undoubtedly save lives, but by our own actions we have decided that the cost would be too great; that our lives are not worth that much! To do a proper job of benefit/cost analysis we have to decide just how much they are worth. To learn more about how economists have approached this difficult topic, read Box 25-4 in the textbook.

Partly because of this problem of putting a price on life, the benefits of quality regulation are hard to estimate. The costs are only a little easier. They come in three sorts: (*a*) the payment of the operating costs of the agencies, (*b*) the costs incurred by the firms in complying with the regulations, and (*c*) the efficiency costs of the regulation. The last category includes such items as the time delays imposed by the Food and Drug Administration (FDA) which prevent new, potentially life-saving drugs from coming on the market until after years of testing. They also include the business ventures that do not get undertaken because the entrepreneurs were discouraged by the thought of all the regulatory paper work that would be involved. Finally, they also include the output lost because funds have been diverted away from investments that would have increased productivity and growth, to investments in safety and antipollution equipment.

Important Terms

Cutthroat competition   Pricing below costs in order to drive competitors out of business.

Price leadership   The practice in some oligopolistic industries of having one firm announce its price changes first, on the understanding that other firms will follow suit. Such a practice is sometimes suspected of being a form of "tacit" or silent collusion, in which the price leader tries to maintain the same price that a cartel would set if it were legal.

Interlocking directorate   This exists when a director sits on a board of two or more competing firms. The Clayton Act of 1914 outlawed interlock-

ing directorates designed to lessen competition.

Tying contracts (sometimes called *full-line forcing*) Contracts which require purchasers to buy other items in a seller's line in order to get those they really want. These, too, are prohibited by the Clayton Act.

Fair trade contracts   Contracts under which the manufacturer of a name-brand good could fix the price that retail stores charge the public. These were exempted from antitrust legislation by the Miller-Tydings Act of 1937, but the exemption has now ended.

Horizontal merger   The union of firms in the same competing activity. This would be the case if, as now seems likely, Chrysler were bought up by some European auto manufacturer.

Vertical merger   The union of a firm and its supplier. This happened, for example, when the shoe retailer T. R. Kinney merged with the shoe manufacturer Brown Shoe Co. (Since Kinney was also a shoe manufacturer this was both a vertical and a horizontal merger.)

Conglomerate merger   The union of firms in unrelated activities. This almost happened when American Express, a credit card firm, tried to take over McGraw-Hill, the company that publishes this book.

Natural monopoly regulation   Setting the price that can be charged by a natural monopoly like an electric power company or a telephone company.

Market-structure regulation   Regulation of the price and entry conditions in a naturally more competitive industry, such as the nation's trucking firms.

Quality-of-life regulation   Regulation of health, safety, and working conditions.

Cross-subsidization   This happens when a regulated industry is forced to continue unprofitable operations along with its profitable ones. The result is that the customers of the unprofitable operations, who buy at less than cost, are in effect subsidized by the customers of the profitable operations, who buy at more than cost. For example, under former CAB regulations small-city passengers were subsidized by trunk-route passengers.

Benefit/cost analysis   This involves estimating both the benefits and costs of a program.

Benefit/cost test   The requirement that the benefits of a program be at least as great as its costs.

True-False Questions

T   F   **1.** Some of the advantages of economies of scale would be lost if antitrust policies were to break up a natural monopoly.

T F **2.** Large firms with market power are in a better position to undertake R and D expenditures than smaller more competitive firms.

T F **3.** Cutthroat competition exists whenever a firm sells at less than cost.

T F **4.** Collusive price-setting arrangements by the firms in an unregulated industry are illegal.

T F **5.** Market-structure regulation is imposed only on natural monopolies.

T F **6.** The CAB kept the price of air travel on trunk lines higher than it would have been with free entry.

T F **7.** Since the powers of the CAB have been curtailed, almost all established airlines have had higher profits.

T F **8.** Quality-of-life regulation usually favors the interests of the regulated firms over the interests of the consumers.

T F **9.** The Environmental Protection Agency is empowered to impose regulations only after it has been shown that they can pass a benefit/cost test.

T F **10.** The time delays imposed by the Food and Drug Administration on the introduction of new, potentially life-saving drugs constitute one of the efficiency costs of quality regulation.

Multiple-Choice Questions

1. Which of the following is legal?
(a) Interlocking directorates designed to lessen competition
(b) Tying contracts
(c) Cross-subsidization
(d) Mergers that act in restraint of trade

2. Which of the following Acts has the effect of lessening competition rather than increasing it?
(a) Robinson-Patman (1936)
(b) Celler-Kefauver (1950)
(c) Sherman (1890)
(d) Clayton (1914)

3. The main purpose of having antitrust policy limit the size of firms is to
(a) Allow economies of scale
(b) Maintain safety standards
(c) Prevent prices from falling too low
(d) Avoid the welfare loss from reduced competition

4. Which of the following is *not* one of the ways antitrust policy tries to promote competition?
(a) Preventing mergers that act "in restraint of trade"
(b) Market-structure regulation in industries with many firms
(c) Prosecution of executives of companies suspected of price-fixing arrangements
(d) Prohibition of tying contracts

5. Under ideal conditions the goal of efficiency would best be pursued by a policy of
(a) Breaking up all monopolies
(b) Breaking up natural monopolies and leaving the other monopolies unregulated
(c) Breaking up natural monopolies but regulating the rest
(d) Regulating natural monopolies and breaking up the rest

6. The practice of price leadership
(a) Makes tacit collusion difficult to detect
(b) Is practised by monopolies
(c) Is practised only under perfect competition
(d) Is used primarily in cutthroat competition

7. Which of the following is *not* one of the main categories of regulation?
(a) Quality of life   (c) Bureaucratic
(b) Antitrust   (d) Market structure

8. Market-structure regulation would be *even more* likely to favor the interests of firms over those of consumer if
(a) Conflict of interest-laws were more strictly enforced to prevent the friends of the executives in a firm from working for the agency regulating it
(b) Consumers had more of an interest in organizing to present their case to the regulatory agencies
(c) Regulatory agencies would rely more on the technical expertise of the experts working in the industry rather than outside "experts" with no first-hand knowledge
(d) Regulatory agencies would permit freer entry into the regulated industries

9. A cartel organized by a regulatory agency is easier to operate than a cartel in an unregulated industry because in the regulated industry
(a) The quotas are imposed by law and the executives are immune from prosecution
(b) The firms are free to engage in non-price competition
(c) The interests of the public are being served when the industry is regulated
(d) Regulated firms are not forced to cross-subsidize the consumers of unprofitable lines

10. Before deregulation the CAB conferred a net gain upon
(a) The established airlines and the nation as a whole
(b) The nation but not the airlines
(c) The airlines perhaps, but not the nation
(d) Neither the airlines nor the nation

11. Although the CAB restricted entry into particular routes, nevertheless the airlines did engage in substantial
(a) Price competition
(b) Non-price competition
(c) Cutthroat competition
(d) Quantity limitations to ensure high capacity utilization

12. The deregulation of airlines in 1978 caused
(a) Airfares to decrease
(b) The volume of air travel to decrease
(c) A decrease in entry of new airlines
(d) An increase in cross-subsidization of small-city routes

13. Which of the following agencies is primarily responsible for enforcing clean air and water standards?

(a) OSHA (c) CPSC
(b) NHTSA (d) EPA

14. Which of the following is a "market structure" agency rather than a "quality of life" agency?
(a) FDA (c) ICC
(b) NLRB (d) MESA

15. Economic efficiency would best be served if no quality-of-life regulation were passed unless it could be shown that
(a) It had a signficant benefit
(b) It had no cost
(c) Its benefit exceeded its cost
(d) It was cost effective

16. When using benefit/cost analysis economists

(a) Avoid having to place a value on human life
(b) Attach a zero value to a human life
(c) Implicity attach an infinite value to human life
(d) None of the above.

17. Which of the following is best classified as an efficiency cost of quality-of-life regulation (rather than a direct administrative cost or a cost of complying with the regulations)?
(a) The salaries of the FDA officials
(b) The higher cost of cars as a result of required antipollution devices
(c) The lives saved by seatbelt legislation
(d) The investment lost because of firms having to divert their funds into buying expensive safety equipment

Exercises

1a. Suppose that the total cost for any firm producing widgets equals the fixed cost of $2 million plus a variable cost equal to $4 for every widget produced. Thus the marginal cost of producing widgets is always (constant, increasing, decreasing), and average cost is always (constant, increasing, decreasing.) The widget industry is a _____.

1b. Suppose a firm were allowed to operate as a monopoly under a marginal cost-pricing regulation. Then its price would be $_____. Suppose the firm sells 2 million units at this price. Its cost per unit would be $_____. The taxpayer would have to pay a total subsidy of $_____ to keep the firm in operation.

1c. If the industry were broken up in to two separate firms, each with the same cost structure as before, and each firm were to produce half of this quantity, then the cost per unit would be _____, which is (more than, less than, the same as) before. The loss per unit would now be (higher, lower, no different) than before, so the total subsidy required to keep the industry alive would be (higher, lower, no different) than before.

1d. As a result of breaking up this monopoly, the firms would, after the subsidy (gain, lose, be unaffected), the consumers would (gain, lose, be unaffected), and the taxpayers would (gain, lose, be unaffected). Thus the nation as a whole would (gain, lose, be unaffected). What important principle is il-

lustrated by this hypothetical example? _____
_____
_____.

2. Suppose that someone in the OSHA found a method of reducing the noise level in automobile plants by 50 percent, but that OSHA would have to hire 100 officials at $30,000 each to impose a regulation forcing firms to use this method. Moreover, suppose that it would cost the car companies a total of $97 million to put the method into effect, and that it would also discourage new investment into the automobile industry, resulting in a further loss of $100 million in output to the nation. Fill in Table 25-1 showing the itemized costs of the regulation

Table 25-1

Direct Administrative Costs - $		million
Compliance Cost - $		million
Efficiency Cost - $		million
Total Cost - $		million

Suppose that the only significant benefit would be the saving of 100 lives from reduced stress on the auto workers. Then if we placed an infinite value on human life, the regulation would obviously pass a benefit/cost test. Would it pass if you placed a value of $1 million on each life? _____. What is the lowest price you could attach to a life for the regulation to just pass the benefit/cost test? _____.

Essay Questions

1. Describe the three main legislative acts in antitrust policy and show how they relate to one another.

2. What are the possible advantages to society of having large-sized firms?

3. What is lost when natural monopolies are

subjected to antitrust actions? How is this problem avoided when a policy of price regulation is used instead?

4. What is the difference between cutthroat competition and "fair" competition? Why is cutthroat competition so hard to identify in practise?

5. Evaluate the following FTC ruling on mergers:

"... proof of violation [of the antitrust laws] consists of ... evidence showing that the acquiring firm['s] ... over-all organization gives it a decisive advantage in efficiency over its small rivals." In the matter of Foremost Dairies, Inc., 60 FTC. 944, 1084 (1962).

Does this judgment protect competition or existing competitors regardless of their inefficiency? Do you agree that it tries to make economies of scale illegal?

6. Why does quality-of-life regulation tend to be less in the interest of the regulated firms than market-structure regulation?

7. What would the main differences have been in the airline industry between 1938 and 1978 if the CAB had operated then as it does now?

8. Why do you suppose the unions representing truck drivers tried so hard to prevent the trucking industry from being deregulated?

9. Does the reluctance of politicians to attach a dollar value to a human life impart a bias toward too much quality-of-life regulation or too little? Explain why.

10. Using the time delays imposed by the FDA as an example, show how the efficiency costs of regulation often get too little consideration because they are not as obvious as many of the benefits.

11. Show by reference to the same FDA how the value of human life may have to be taken into account in calculating the costs of regulation as well as the benefits.

Answers

True-False Questions: **1** T **2** T **3** F **4** T **5** F **6** T **7** F **8** F **9** F **10** T

Multiple-Choice Questions: **1** c **2** a **3** d **4** b **5** d **6** a **7** c **8** c **9** a **10** c **11** b **12** a **13** d **14** c **15** c **16** d **17** d

Exercises: **1a.** constant, decreasing, natural monopoly **1b.** $4, $5, 2 million **1c.** $6, more than, higher, higher **1d.** be unaffected, be unaffected, lose, lose. From the point of view of efficiency natural monopolies should be regulated but not broken up

2.

Table 25.1

Direct	3
Compliance	97
Efficiency	100
Total	200

No, $2 million

CHAPTER 26
Problems of the Environment:
Pollution and Congestion

Learning Objectives

After you have studied this chapter in the textbook and the study guide you should be able to

Explain why pollution is an externality

Explain why perfect competition does not lead to efficiency when pollution is present

Measure diagrammatically the efficiency loss due to pollution, as in Figure 26-2 in the textbook

List several reasons why it is often costly to reduce pollution

Show why the marginal cost of having pollution should equal the marginal cost of reducing pollution

Show why we should not attempt to eliminate pollution entirely

Explain why the tax on pollution should just equal the marginal cost of pollution

Indentify the two major legislative acts designed to control pollution in the United States

Give several reasons why the United States government's antipollution policy has been unsatisfactory

Explain how recycling reduces the damage of pollution

State why the problem of traffic congestion is similar to that of pollution

CHAPTER HIGHLIGHTS

You may think that environmental pollution has little to do with economics. But this chapter attempts to show that pollution can be seen as an economic problem—one that involves many of the principles that you have already encountered in this book. The basic objectives of the chapter are to show how economic analysis can shed light on the following questions:

1. What is pollution?

2. Why is it a problem that even a perfectly competitive market cannot deal with efficiently?

3. What principles should guide our antipollution policy?

4. What policies have actually been used in the United States, and how successful have they been?

Let us deal with each of these questions in turn.

What is Pollution?

Pollution is an externality. It is a cost to society resulting from our economic activites of production and consumption. But the cost is external because it isn't paid for by those responsible for it. For example, when someone's clothes are soiled by smoke from a factory chimney, the factory owner doesn't have to pay the cleaning bill.

A Failure of the Invisible Hand

When there is an externality like pollution, the classical analysis of the "invisible hand" is no longer valid. The conclusion in Chapter 22 that perfect competition results in economic efficiency depends on the assumption that the marginal cost to producers (MC) equals the marginal cost to society (MC_S). But when there is an external cost then MC is *less* than MC_S. The difference is the marginal external cost (MC_E). (This is illustrated in Figure 26-1 in the textbook.) Efficiency requires that we equate price with MC_S (at E_2 in Figure 26-2). But under perfect competition with no government intervention, producers would equate price with MC (at E_1). This means that the level of output under perfect competition (Q_1 in Figure 26-2) exceeds the efficient level (Q_2). The efficiency loss from this failure of the "invisible hand" can be estimated by the same sort of measurement that we used in Chapter 22: the triangle formed by the demand curve and the marginal social cost curve. (In Chapter 22, we used the triangle formed by the demand curve and the *supply* curve, because the supply curve was, by assumption, the same as marginal social cost.) Be sure you understand why efficiency can be measured by this triangle. It may help to refer back to the discussion surrounding Figure 22-3 in Chapter 22 of the textbook.

Antipollution Policies: Principles

The basic principle that *should* underlie any antipollution policy is that producers should be made to pay the external cost caused by their pollution. If they were forced to pay MC_E as well as MC, then they would equate price to $MC_E + MC = MC_S$, and efficiency would be restored. How can we force them to do this? Make them pay a tax for their pollution.

Another principle is that reducing pollution is costly; indeed, if pushed far enough it may even be more costly than having pollution. Examples of the cost of reducing pollution include the following: (*a*) Pollution-control devices like those now included in new cars add to the price of goods. (*b*) Costs of pollution control reduce profits of companies that pay them. (*c*) Because of reduced profits, firms may not invest as much; the result is lower growth and productivity. (*d*) Less profits may also lead to layoffs or lower wages in hard-hit industries. (*e*) Firms may have to cut back on production to control pollution, and this lost production is a cost to society.

Because of the costs of reducing pollution, it follows that pollution should not be eliminated entirely (except in extreme cases). Instead it should be reduced just to the point where further reductions would cost more than they are worth. That is, to the point Q_3 where the marginal cost of reducing pollution (MCR) equals the marginal cost of having pollution (MCP) as shown in Figure 26-4 in the textbook.

Often the best way of doing this is to set a tax on pollution equal to the MCP. Producers would then be given the proper incentive to reduce pollution by an efficient amount. For they would equate their MCR to this tax (as in Figure 26-3) and hence to the MCP.

Antipollution Policies: Our Experience

In the United States, the government has not taxed polluters. Instead, it has imposed limits on pollution. These limits have been set up largely by the Clean Air Act and the Water Pollution Control Act; they are enforced by the Environmental Protection Agency (EPA). The government has also relied upon another method—subsidizing the purchase of pollution-control equipment. On the whole, these programs have resulted in a substantial reduction in pollution, but most economists believe that the programs have not been successful in promoting efficiency, for the following reasons:

1. The limits in some cases have been too restrictive, in other cases too loose, because the EPA has tended to disregard the cost of reducing pollution.

2. No satisfactory method has been found for allocating these limits among different firms. The idea that all firms should face the same restrictions has an immediate appeal, but it doesn't make much sense when reducing pollution may be much more expensive—and result in more unemployment—for some firms than for others. Under a pollution tax the firms that can cut back pollution at least expense would automatically cut back by more (see Exercise 3).

3. The use of limits has encouraged many firms to engage the government in costly legal actions to try to gain exemption from the limits.

4. In some cases, the government has been forced to back down from its standards when firms claimed to be unable to meet them.

5. The government has failed to ensure that the pollution-control equipment it has subsidized is used effectively.

6. This pollution-control equipment has been of the "end-of-pipe" variety, which may have discouraged firms from finding more fundamental and perhaps more effective cures for pollution (like using inputs that are less polluting). Again, a pollution-tax would be better because it would give firms not only the incentive to cure pollution, but also an incentive to find the cheapest cure (see Exercise 4).

In addition, there are two other important ideas in this chapter. First, recycling can play a role in reducing the amount of pollution by converting what would otherwise be polluting wastes (such as empty beer cans) into usable commodities that don't pollute. This idea is illustrated by Figure 26-6 in the textbook. Next, you should understand that the problem of traffic congestion is similar to that of pollution. In congestion, as in pollution, there are external costs. When a driver decides to join the traffic on the highway, he or she does not take into account the cost of the extra congestion that the other drivers must face as a result. In other words, this cost to other drivers is an external one. Just as pollution problems can be dealt with by using taxes, so one way of dealing with congestion is to impose highway tolls during rush hours. But once again, as in the case of pollution, the critical question is how large should the tax or toll be? This is by no means an easy question to answer.

IMPORTANT TERMS

Internal cost The cost that is paid by a producer. Also called private cost.

External cost The cost not paid by the producer, but by someone else. Also called neighborhood cost, or cost spillover. Examples include costs of pollution and congestion.

Social cost The total cost to society. It is the sum of internal and external costs.

The marginal cost of reducing pollution The cost of reducing pollution by one more unit.

Marginal cost of having pollution The cost that would result from allowing one more unit of pollution.

"End-of-pipe" treatment The policy of reducing pollution by capturing the polluting agents, such as smoke, just before they enter the environment, rather than undertaking more fundamental and perhaps more effective steps such as changing over to different production processes that produce less pollution in the first place.

Recycling Using materials again rather than throwing them away. This can reduce pollution and preserve natural resources.

True-False Questions

T F **1.** The costs of pollution are external costs only if the firm causing the pollution is taxed for them.

T F **2.** Marginal external cost equals marginal social cost minus marginal private cost.

T F **3.** The main task of the Environmental Protection Agency has been to collect the taxes that the government has imposed to discourage pollution.

T F **4.** Reducing pollution can slow down economic growth.

T F **5.** If pollution taxes accurately reflect the external costs of pollution then legal limits on pollution activities are not also needed in order to achieve economic efficiency.

T F **6.** The efficiency losses from pollution arise only when markets are not perfectly competitive.

T F **7.** The use of taxes rather than limits as an antipollution policy would allow the market to determine how much each firm will be permitted to pollute.

T F **8.** Without government intervention, the marginal cost of having pollution would be zero.

T F **9.** The appropriate tax on pollution can be determined even if the policy maker has no idea of the size of the marginal cost of having pollution.

T F **10.** The most important similarity that economists recognize between pollution and congestion is that both are caused by automobiles.

T F **11.** Subsidizing the use of public transportation would be similar to taxing private transportation in the sense that both policies would raise the cost of using private compared to public transportation.

Multiple-Choice Questions

1. During the 70s, the Environmental Protection Agency concentrated on
    (a) Setting limits on the amount of output that can be produced by polluting firms
    (b) Setting limits on the amount of pollution that can be caused by a firm or its products
    (c) Imposing taxes on the output of polluting firms
    (d) Imposing taxes on a firm depending upon the amount of pollution that it causes or that its products cause

2. The higher prices that we pay for products that must now meet tougher pollution standards
    (a) Exist only because firms have enough market power to make consumers pay for reducing pollution
    (b) Would be entirely avoided if the government levied pollution taxes on firms instead of imposing limits
    (c) Are just one example of the cost of reducing pollution
    (d) Show that our pollution standards are too high for efficiency

3. If the production of some good causes pollution, then in a free competitive market
    (a) More than the economically efficient amount of the commodity will be produced
    (b) The marginal benefit of the commodity will be more than the marginal social cost
    (c) The marginal benefit of the commodity will be less than the marginal private cost
    (d) None of the above

4. The imposition of a tax on the output of firms in a polluting industry will result in an economically efficient amount of output
    (a) No matter how big the tax
    (b) Only if the tax rate is greater than the marginal private cost of production
    (c) Only if the tax rate equals the marginal benefit of producing the commodity
    (d) Only if the tax rate equals the marginal external cost of production

5. The efficiency loss from a polluting good
    (a) Is zero if the good is produced in a perfectly competitive market
    (b) Could conceivably be zero if the good was produced by a monopoly that was restricting its output
    (c) Is measured by the "triangle" formed by industry demand and supply
    (d) Is always reduced by a limit on production, regardless of how severe that limit may be

6. The recycling of wastes
    (a) Can reduce the rate of depletion of natural resources
    (b) Will be attempted by private business firms only if taxes are imposed upon the amount of waste that they produce
    (c) Is always economically efficient, no matter how costly it is
    (d) Causes pollution

7. The ideal amount of congestion would occur if a toll were set
    (a) That eliminated congestion
    (b) That equated the marginal costs of driving in rush-hours and off-hours
    (c) Equal to the marginal external cost of traveling
    (d) Equal to the marginal benefit of driving

8. Which of these is an external cost?
    (a) The extra gas that a motorist uses if he drives now rather than waiting until the road is less crowded
    (b) The extra gas that he causes others to use because the road will be more crowded if he drives now rather than waiting
    (c) The damage to his car if he runs into a retaining wall because he is driving too fast
    (d) The fine he must pay if he is caught speeding .

9. Which of the following antipollution policies was *least* used by the federal government in the 1970s?
    (a) Limits on pollutants that firms may discharge
    (b) Limits on pollutants that products may discharge
    (c) Taxes on pollutants that products may discharge
    (d) Subsidies for pollution-control equipment

10. Airplanes flying low over houses near airports cause "noise-pollution." The principles of this chapter suggest that the best policy would be to
    (a) Rely on the "invisible hand" to take care of the problem
    (b) Impose a tax on each airline depending on the total amount of noise it creates in the affected neighborhoods
    (c) Prohibit specific flights, to be determined by the EPA
    (d) Require all planes to have a particular noise-abatement device installed

11. If many firms are causing pollution in an industry then the least-cost way of reducing it is to
    (a) Force all firms to cut back by the same amount of pollution
    (b) Force larger cutbacks on the larger firms
    (c) Force larger cutbacks on the firms with the lower MCR's
    (d) Let the firms with the highest profits take most of the responsibility for cutting back

12. A firm faced with a pollution tax will equate this tax to its
    (a) Marginal cost of reducing pollution
    (b) Marginal cost of production
    (c) Subsidy for pollution-control equipment
    (d) Marginal revenue

13. The best way of achieving "cost-effectiveness" in reducing auto-emissions would be to
    (a) Tell auto companies what kind of pollution-control devices to put in cars
    (b) Impose an annual tax on car owners depending upon how much pollution was caused by their cars
    (c) Rely on the market, and allow consumers to decide whether or not to buy pollution-control devices as options with their cars
    (d) Fine auto companies whose new cars did not comply with industrywide standards set by the EPA

14. Taking no action against pollution
  (a) Is always efficient
  (b) Would be efficient if the marginal cost of having pollution were zero
  (c) Would be efficient if the marginal social cost of production exceeded the marginal private cost
  (d) Would be efficient if all markets were perfectly competitive

Exercises

1. Figure 26-1 represents the market for a good the production of which causes pollution
  a. If the market is perfectly competitive, the level of output will equal _____, the market price will equal _____, the marginal social cost will equal _____, and the marginal external cost will equal _____.
  b. If the commodity produces no external benefits, then the optimal level of output will equal _____. This output would be attained under perfect competition if the firms were faced with a tax rate equal to _____. Without this tax, the efficiency loss will equal _____. With this tax the market price will equal _____.
  c. Suppose that the good were produced by an unregulated monopolist. Then the level of output (with no tax) would equal _____, the market price would equal _____, and the efficiency loss would equal _____.
  d. Assume that the marginal external cost is constant—i.e., that the lines MC_S and $MC_{industry}$ are parallel, with $LM = HK = IJ$. Then suppose that the government imposes the same tax on the monopolist that it earlier charged to the perfect competitors. In this case, the monopolist will produce an amount of output equal to _____, it will charge a price equal to _____, and the efficiency loss will be equal to _____. Thus a per unit tax on a polluting *monopolist* (will, will not) necessarily lead to greater efficiency.
2. In Figure 26-2, the curve labeled MCR represents the marginal cost of reducing pollution, and the one labeled MCP_1 represents the marginal cost of having pollution. For the time being you may ignore the one labeled MCP_2.
  a. The economically efficient quantity of pollution equals _____. In the absence of any pollution tax, the quantity of pollution will equal _____, the value of MCR will equal _____, the value of MCP will equal _____, and the efficiency loss will equal _____. The economically efficient amount of pollution will result if firms are charged a tax equal to _____ per unit of pollution.

FIGURE 26-1

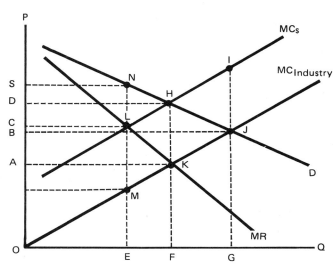

  b. Now suppose that the marginal cost of having pollution is represented by MCP_2 instead of MCP_1. Then the economically efficient amount of pollution will result if firms are charged a tax equal to _____ per unit of pollution.

FIGURE 26-2

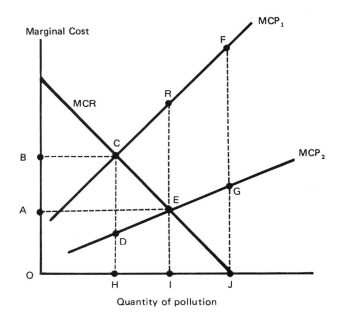

c. Suppose now that the marginal cost of having pollution is really represented by MCP_1 but that the government makes a mistake and estimates it to be represented by MCP_2. Suppose that the government sets the tax rate on pollution (calculated in the last paragraph) which is optimal if the pollution cost is MCP_2. Then the quantity of pollution will equal _____, which is (more, less) than the economically efficient amount; the MCR will equal _____; the true MCP will equal _____; and the efficiency loss will equal _____. Thus we (may, may not) conclude that, if the government underestimates the problem, it will take inadequate action to counter it (that is, set too low a pollution tax).

3a. Figure 26-3 shows the MCR curves of two smoke-polluting firms. Reducing smoke-pollution is less costly for firm (A, B). Suppose each firm is presently required by law to limit its output of smoke to 10 units. Now suppose that a government official decides, after reading this *Study Guide*, to impose a pollution tax instead of limiting each firm's smoke. If he sets the tax at $6 per unit of smoke, then firm A will produce _____ units and B will produce _____. The firm with the higher MCR has (increased, decreased) its pollution and the one with the lower MCR has (increased, decreased) its.

b. Firm A's total pollution-reduction costs have (increased, decreased) by[1] _____ units, while firm B's costs have (increased, decreased) by _____. Thus total pollution-reduction costs ($A + B$) have (increased, decreased, stayed the same), while total amount of pollution by the two firms (increased, decreased, stayed the same). Therefore, the tax is (more, less) efficient in keeping down costs than the previous limits on pollution.

4a. Suppose that a company can produce a car that runs on regular gasoline or one that runs on a newly invented fuel that reduces the emission of pollutants by 50 percent. Unfortunately the car using the new fuel costs $200 more to construct. Consumers do not care which fuel a car uses; if given the choice they will buy the car with the lower purchase price. So, with no regulations the car company will build the car using (gasoline, new fuel). Suppose it is also possible to install a pollution control device on all its cars, which also reduces emissions by 50 percent but costs $250.

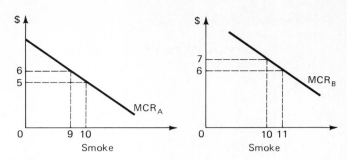

FIGURE 26-3

Again, consumers do not care whether or not a car has this device. Then the company will build the car using (gasoline, new fuel), and (with, without) the device. Even though the cars will pollute the atmosphere the car companies don't take this into account because this is an (external, internal) cost.

b. Now suppose a government agency wants to cut back auto emissions by 50 percent. So it requires the company to install the pollution control device. The company will now build cars using (gasoline, new fuel), but with the device, and the cost to society of the resulting reduction in pollution is $_____ per car. Suppose instead that the agency requiring the device just told the company to cut back by 50 percent on the emissions from its cars, leaving it up to the company to decide how to do this. Then the cost to the company of complying with this requirement would be $_____ per car if it installed the device, or $_____ per car if it switched to the new fuel. Therefore, it would choose the (device, new fuel). In this case the cost to society of the reduction in pollution would be $_____ per car.

c. In this example the policy of telling the company *how* to reduce pollution is (more, less) costly than the policy of just telling them to do it, by $_____ per car. If instead the agency had told the company to do it by making cars that use the new fuel, the cost to society would be (more than, less than, the same as) the cost of just telling them to do it. What general rule does this suggest about the relative cost of telling companies to comply and telling them how to comply?

_____

_____

_____.

[1] You should interpret the MCR at any point as the cost of reducing smoke by one more unit below that point. Thus, for example, the cost to A of reducing smoke from 9 to 8 is $6.

Essay Questions

1. "One advantage of the use of taxes rather than limits to control pollution is that the former policy harnesses the forces of the marketplace to help find an efficient solution, whereas the latter policy does not." Explain this statement.

2. In some cities there is a fine for smoking in elevators in a public building. Do you think that this is an example of the use of taxes or of limits to control pollution?

3. What arguments can be made for government subsidies to support the use of public transportation? What arguments can be made against such subsidization? In what kinds of cities are the arguments for subsidies likely to be stronger than those against? In what sorts of cities are the arguments against likely to be stronger than the ones for?

4. In what sense is a policy of subsidizing firms for recycling materials equivalent to taxing firms according to the amount of waste that they produce?

5. By reference to Figure 26-4 in the textbook, explain the circumstances in which economic efficiency could be promoted by not levying any tax at all upon a particular kind of pollution. How would your answer be different if you took into account the costs involved in collecting the tax?

6. "In an unregulated market, the deposit on returnable beer bottles will be too small for economic efficiency." Explain.

7. Consider the last question of Exercise 4. Why is it generally assumed that, in selecting the least-cost method private firms will do a better job than government agencies. How would the general rule suggested by this example change if the *production* of the new fuel caused pollution, just like the *use* of gasoline? In this case what policies would you recommend?

8. Explain how the concept of externality is illustrated by the following quotation from the nineteenth-century economist J. H. von Thunen: "In time of war we have no hesitation in sacrificing one hundred men in the bloom of their years to save one cannon. In a hundred men at least twenty times as much capital is lost as is lost in one cannon. But the production of the cannon is the cause of an expenditure of the state treasury, while human beings are again available for nothing by means of a simple conscription order. . . . When the statement was made to Napoleon, the founder of the conscription system, that a planned operation would cost too many men, he replied: 'That is nothing. The women produce more of them than I can use.' "

9. In recent years a large Canadian distillery has paid a subsidy to the Toronto Transit Commission which has enabled anyone to travel free on the Toronto subway system on New Year's Eve. Explain carefully how this subsidy has helped to promote economic efficiency by internalizing an external cost. Why do you suppose that the subsidy was offered by a distillery rather than by a tobacco company?

*10. Some economists maintain that all external costs are a result of society's failure to assign property rights to individuals and to defend them. For example, if my factory pollutes the air above your house, then I am using a valuable commodity (namely the air above your house) without having to pay for it, because it doesn't belong to you. If our laws were changed so that anyone who owned a house also owned all the air above that house, then I would have to persuade you to sell me the right to use your air before I could pollute it. Explain how, if the law were changed in this way, the emission from my factory would no longer be an external cost according to the definition that we have given in this chapter. Suppose that I had managed to persuade everyone in the neighborhood except you to sell me the right to pollute their air. Explain how that would put you in a position to take undue advantage of me when we were bargaining over what price I should pay for the right to pollute your air. What other problems can you imagine would arise if this solution to the problem of pollution were to be attempted. Show how this same analysis applies to the case of water pollution.

*11. The textbook mentioned that some cities have tried to reduce the problem of traffic congestion by reserving special fast lanes on throughways for cars with, say, more than two passengers. Explain carefully what you think the costs of such a proposal might have been.

*12. Defend or criticize the following statement, "If the government taxes the amount of wastes dumped by firms into a lake in order to control pollution, then some water pollution will still occur because some firms will still dump their wastes and pay the tax. If this happens then economic efficiency can only be attained if the government spends all the tax revenues that it collects in this way on repairing the damage caused by these wastes."

Answers

True-False Questions: 1 F 2 T 3 F 4 T 5 T 6 F 7 T 8 F 9 F 10 F 11 T

Multiple-Choice Questions: 1 b 2 c 3 a 4 d 5 b 6 a 7 c 8 b 9 c 10 b 11 c 12 a 13 b 14 b

Exercises: **1a.** *OG, OB, GI, IJ* **b.** *OF, KH, HIJ, OD* **c.** *OF, OD, O* **d.** *OE, OS, LNH*, will not

2a. *OH, OJ*, zero, *JF, CFJ, OB* **b.** *OA* **c.** *OI*, more, *IE, IR, CRE*, may

3a. A, 9, 11, increased decreased **b.** increased, 5, decreased, 6, decreased, stayed the same, more

4a. gasoline, gasoline, without, external **b.** gasoline, 250, 250, 200, new fuel, 200 **c.** more, 50, the same as, telling them to comply can never cost more than telling them how, although it might cost the same if the agency happens to pick the least-cost method

CHAPTER 27
Public Goods

Learning Objectives

After you have studied this chapter in the textbook and the study guide, you should be able to

Explain the difference between public goods and private goods

Explain why perfect competition does not produce an efficient quantity of goods with external benefits

Measure, in a diagram, the efficiency loss resulting from the private provision of goods with external benefits, as in Figure 27-1 in the textbook

Construct the marginal social benefit curve in a diagram, starting with the individual marginal utility curves (a) for a public good, and (b) for a private good

Explain why the "free-rider" problem makes it hard to estimate the marginal social benefit of a public good

Show why efficiency requires a good to be subsidized at a rate equal to the marginal external benefit

Give several reasons for believing that government expenditure decisions may not be economically efficient

Explain the concept of "option demand" and state its significance for public goods

CHAPTER HIGHLIGHTS

The last chapter dealt with external *costs*. This chapter deals with external *benefits*; that is, benefits that are enjoyed by others, above and beyond the internal benefits enjoyed by the buyers of a good. (As you might expect, social benefit is the sum of both external and internal benefits.) With external benefits, perfect competition will produce an

inefficient outcome. Why? Because marginal cost will be equated to marginal private benefit (utility) rather than to marginal social benefit. As illustrated by Figure 27-1 in the textbook, the market will produce too little of such a good.

Public Goods

A public good may be defined as an extreme case of a good with external benefits—where the amount of benefit that an individual gets from the good is just as great if someone else buys it as it is if he or she were to buy it. That is, the individual cannot be excluded from enjoying it. For example, you get the same benefit from cleaner air, whether or not you help to pay for antipollution measures. That is not true of a private good. You can't enjoy a movie or a restaurant meal unless you pay for it.

Inefficiency of Private Markets

Not all goods with external benefits are provided by the government. Some, such as home improvements, are produced privately although, as we have seen, too little is produced. The reason for insufficient output can be traced back to the problem of the "free rider." For example, if you live in a nice neighborhood and fail to keep your house and garden in good repair, you are taking a "free ride" on other people's efforts. One solution is for some enterprising private agent to "internalize" the external benefit by forming a large group, merging the producers with the beneficiaries. That is what a developer does who buys all the houses in a block. When the developer makes improvements in one house this raises the value of the neighboring houses. The developer who owns them all captures all the benefits.

This free-rider problem is most extreme in the case of a public good. In this case, as Figures 27-2 and 27-3 in the textbook illustrate, the marginal social utility of the good is the *vertical* sum of the individual MU curves, not the usual horizontal sum. Thus, any project, such as the flood-control dam in the text example, whose marginal cost is less than the sum of those marginal private benefits, is worth undertaking. But the enterprising agent who tried to internalize the benefits by forming a large group out of the beneficiaries would have to collect these private benefits from the individuals concerned. The agent would somehow have to find a way of getting these individuals to reveal their MUs. But each individual, realizing that as long as the project goes ahead he or she can't be excluded from enjoying the benefits, would have an incentive to take a free ride by understating his or her MU, in hopes of getting the benefits while paying little or none of the costs. If every individual did this, the agent wouldn't be able to collect enough to finance the project.

Principles of Effective Policy

When a private good has external benefits the free market may not be able to internalize the externality. But the government might be able to do so, by offering a subsidy to consumers or producers.

The important principle here is to set a rate of subsidy just equal to the marginal external benefit. (Make sure you can show why. If in doubt refer back to Figure 27-1 in the textbook.)

With a public good the authorities must go further and decide themselves how much (if any) to produce. In principle, they ought to produce the amount such that $MC_S = MU_S$. But how to estimate MU_S? We have seen that because of the free-rider problem, people will not reveal their MUs if they think their answer will affect their pocketbooks. On the other hand, if you tell them that the project will come out of the general tax revenues, and be paid more or less equally by all, they will have a tendency to exaggerate their MUs, in hopes of getting a project that others will pay for (again taking a free ride).

In view of this free-rider problem, the authorities must generally estimate MC_S and MU_S not by asking the people affected, but by benefit-cost analysis, in which they estimate the benefit by first trying to predict what effect the provision of the good would have on different producers and consumers and then trying to put a dollar value on these effects. A big problem that is encountered by benefit-cost analysis of a public good—like a flood-control dam, for example—is that one of its effects may be to cause the saving (or the loss) of human lives. In this case, one is faced with the extremely difficult problem of how to attach a dollar value to a human life. (Recall our discussion of this problem from Chapter 25.)

Other Problems with Government Expenditure Decisions

Because benefit-cost analysis is so imperfect, its use is no guarantee that public decision-making will be efficient. Such decision-making may run into the following problems:

1. Private projects are terminated if their usefulness ends, because they start losing money. Public projects are often *irreversible* because (a) no politician wants to admit that a project might have been a mistake (whereas private firms ignore sunk costs), and (b) there is no natural check like bankruptcy to force termination.

2. People vote for projects when they vote for politicians, thus giving the politicians some incentive to satisfy their demands by undertaking useful projects. But political votes are not so specific as are the economic votes that people cast when deciding what to buy with their money. Thus, the incentive to satisfy people's demands is less. You may be able to sell a voter your public goods, even if he or she doesn't much like them, because the voter likes your other policies. In the marketplace the voter can be more specific, buying some of a company's products but not others.

3. Special interest groups can exert an inordinate influence on public decision-making. If you have no particular interest in a dam, it probably doesn't pay you to oppose it, even though it adds to your taxes a little. But those directly affected have an obvious incentive to lobby for its construction. Thus, a few large benefits can outweigh many small costs politically, even if they don't economically.

4. Politicians are mainly interested in projects whose benefits are obvious (for who will pay in votes for something they don't understand) and immedate (if the benefit doesn't occur before the next election it may be too late for the politician). By contrast, the market could provide long-term, less obvious benefits as long as the people who did understand were willing to pay the cost. Thus, there is a tendency for government decision-making to degenerate into *crisis* decision-making (taking obvious actions for short-run gains).

5. Once policies are formulated by politicians they must be implemented by bureaucracies. There is a constant tendency for bureaus and their budgets to expand, and for the bureaus to become technically inefficient, because they are not subject to the check of economic losses and the threat of bankruptcy.

Finally, there is the important idea that the environment can be treated as a public good. Just as pollution of the environment should be taxed, so its protection should be subsidized. This is especially true in the case of the preservation of endangered species, the social usefulness of which may not be obvious until we think of it in terms of an *option demand*.

IMPORTANT TERMS

External (spillover) benefit The benefit derived from a good by those who do not produce it or use it.

Public good A good from which people derive the same amount of benefit, whether or not they own it.

Internal private benefit The benefit from a good derived by the person who owns that good. These are usually the only benefits that are considered by households and firms in making their decisions.

Benefit-cost analysis The technique of estimating the dollar value of the different costs and benefits that are likely to result from a particular government policy.

Option demand The demand to have a good not because you want to use it but because you want it available just in case you might want to use it in the future. This appears to be the nature of the demand for some public goods, such as the preservation of a particular wildlife species.

True-False Questions

T F **1.** External benefits are generated by a firm that voluntarily installs an emission control device in its factory smokestacks.

T F **2.** Generally speaking, the private market produces too large quantity of goods with external benefits.

T F **3.** Generally speaking, the private production of a good with external benefits results in marginal cost being less than marginal social benefit.

T F **4.** To promote economic efficiency, the government could just as easily tax the use of a good with external benefits as subsidize its production.

T F **5.** The reason why private firms can't be relied on to produce a public good is that they would internalize the external benefits.

T F **6.** The marginal social benefit curve of a public good can be constructed as the horizontal sum of the individual demand curves.

T F **7.** You cannot be excluded from enjoying the benefits of a public good even if someone else pays for it.

T F **8.** If you want to use benefit-cost analysis, you may have to choose some method for attaching a dollar value to human life.

T F **9.** If people pay for a public good depending on their share of the benefits, they will tend to understate their benefits.

T F **10.** When benefits are easily identified and costs obscure, the government tends to provide too little of the good.

Multiple-Choice Questions

1. Which of the following is the purest example of a public good?

  (a) National defense
  (b) Smoking in an elevator
  (c) Vaccination against smallpox
  (d) Coal

2. Which of the following is the purest example of a private good?

  (a) Home improvements   **(c)** Fresh air
  (b) Coffee   **(d)** Courtesy

3. Private provision of a good with external benefits may be efficient if

  (a) The good is subsidized .
  (b) The good is taxed
  (c) The good is neither taxed nor subsidized
  (d) The good is subsidized when its price is low and taxed when its price is high

4. The marginal social benefit of a good with external benefits is

  (a) Greater than the marginal private benefit
  (b) Less than marginal private benefit
  (c) Equal to marginal private benefit
  (d) Any of the above, depending upon the price

5. The marginal social benefit curve is the *vertical* sum of the individual marginal utility curves

  (a) In the case of a private good
  (b) In the case of a public good
  (c) In the case of any good with external costs
  (d) In the case of any good, whether or not it produces external benefits

6. To achieve economic efficiency, the per-unit subsidy to a good with external benefits should equal the

  (a) Marginal social benefit of the good
  (b) Marginal private benefit of the good
  (c) Marginal social cost of the good
  (d) None of the above

7. If the government produces more than the economically efficient amount of a public good

  (a) The marginal social benefit of that good will exceed the marginal social cost
  (b) The marginal social benefit of that good will equal the marginal social cost
  (c) The efficiency loss involved in producing that amount may be as much as the efficiency loss from allowing the private market to provide the good
  (d) Marginal social benefit will equal marginal private cost

8. When the government subsidizes a good with external benefits

  (a) The outcome may be efficient if the subsidy is paid to the consumers of the good rather than the producers
  (b) The amount of production of the good will be less than the economically efficient amount if the subsidy is too large
  (c) The same result could be achieved if the government were to put a limit on production of the good

  (d) The same result could be achieved with a tax on the good instead of a subsidy

9. Which of the following is *not* a possible way of internalizing the external benefit of a good?

  (a) Subsidizing production of the good
  (b) Imposing a price ceiling
  (c) Merging the producers and consumers into one large group
  (d) Subsidizing the use of the good

10. A major problem of benefit-cost analysis is that

  (a) It can be used only by private firms
  (b) The benefits of a project are usually obvious but the costs can't be measured at all
  (c) It always ends up with estimated benefits exceeding the estimated costs
  (d) It may require a dollar value to be attached to human life

11. Suppose you voted for Carter in 1980 because you thought his foreign policy was preferable to Reagan's, even though you thought that Reagan's economic policies were sounder. Then this illustrates the problem that

  (a) Public expenditure decisions are hard to reverse
  (b) Special interest groups have an inordinate influence on public decisions
  (c) Bureaucrats are not subject to the normal check of bankruptcy
  (d) Political votes are not as specific as those in the marketplace

12. Many economists have argued that our farm subsidy programs are inefficient—that what farmers gain is less than what consumers lose as a result of higher food prices. But these programs continue. According to the principles explained in this chapter, which seems the most likely explanation?

  (a) Food is a public good
  (b) Farmers' special interests are politically stronger than the consumers' general interest
  (c) Consumers do not adequately recognize the benefits of good food and must be forced to pay for them through taxes
  (d) Farmers have more votes than nonfarmers

13. Which of the following best illustrates the tendency of governments toward crisis decision-making?

  (a) The tendency for welfare programs to expand
  (b) The commonly observed tendency for municipal governments to wait until several bad accidents have occurred at an intersection before installing traffic signals
  (c) The inordinate influence of gun lobbyists
  (d) The Clean Air Act

14. Which of the following is usually true of government bureaucracies?

  (a) They suffer immediate cutbacks in their grants when they expand beyond the efficient scale
  (b) The lack of profit motive means that bureaucrats will consider only the public interest rather than their own narrowly defined self-interest

(c) Bureaucrats try to expand their departments because this gives them greater power and influence

(d) On the whole, they tend to provide too small a quantity of public goods, for the same reasons that any competitive industry produces too little of a good with external benefits

Exercises

1. Figure 27-1 describes a perfectly competitive market for a good that provides external benefits, with the supply curve S and the demand curve D.

a. In an unregulated market, the quantity that is produced is _____ and the market price is _____. If the marginal social benefit curve is MU_S and there are no external costs of producing the good, (for the time being, ignore the curve labeled MC_S), then the economically efficient quantity is _____, and the marginal external benefit is _____.

b. The efficiency loss from relying upon the private market for the provision of this good is _____. The government could eliminate this efficiency loss by offering, to producers of the good, a subsidy of the amount _____ per unit of the good.

c. Now suppose that the good involves external *costs* as well as external benefits. (An example would be a dam that provides flood control to farmers downstream but that floods out farmers upstream.) Let the curve labeled MC_S represent the marginal social cost of producing the good. Then the efficient amount of production of the good would equal _____. At that level of production, the marginal external cost would equal _____ and the marginal external benefit would equal _____. With no tax or subsidy, the private market would produce (more, less) than the economically efficient amount and the efficiency loss would equal _____. This efficiency loss could be eliminated if the government were to (tax, subsidize) the production of the good at a rate equal to _____ per unit.

2. Figure 27-2 shows Mr. A's and B's marginal private benefits (MU_A and MU_B) from a public good (a waste-treatment plant). In Figure 27-2c show the marginal social benefit, under the simplifying assumption that A and B are the only members of society affected by the project.

3a. Suppose that there are 1,000 farmers affected by a proposed dam. Each of them would receive a benefit of $1,000. Then the social benefit of

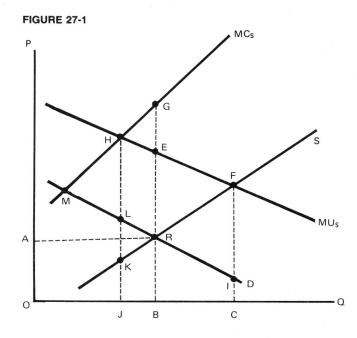

FIGURE 27-1

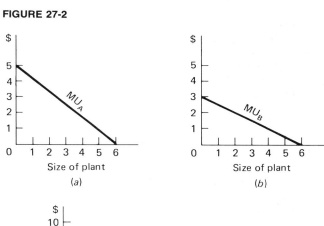

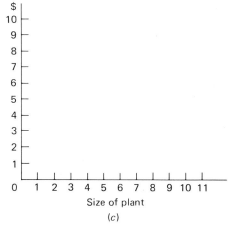

FIGURE 27-2

the dam is $ _____ . If the dam costs $500,000, it (is, is not) worth building.

b. Suppose you are one of these farmers. The government tells you it is going to go ahead with the dam, and intends to tax farmers according to how much each says the dam will be worth to him or her. If you tell the truth it will cost you $ _____ . If you say $2,000 it will cost you $ _____ . If you say no benefit it will cost you $ _____ . You will have an incentive to (understate, overstate, reveal accurately) how much it is worth to you.

c. Suppose instead the government says that if it goes ahead with the dam it will tax the 5 million inhabitants of your state 10 cents each to finance it—but whether or not it goes ahead depends on whether the sum of private benefits exceeds $500,000. If it goes ahead, you will have a net gain (value to you of the dam minus your taxes) of $ _____ . You will maximize your chances of getting this gain if you (understate, overstate, reveal accurately) your benefit. If the dam cost $1,500,000 instead of $500,000, the dam (is, is not) worth building. In this case, the tax per person is 30 cents, so the net gain to each farmer from the dam is _____ , and each farmer has an incentive to (understate, overstate, reveal accurately) his or her benefit. If every farmer stated that his or her gain would be $2,000, the government would estimate the social benefit to be $ _____ and (would, would not) build the dam. This would be (efficient, inefficient).

Essay Questions

1. Explain carefully whether or not each of the following might be considered to be a public good.
a. The United States Olympic Team
b. Your telephone
c. Driver safety lessons
d. Television programs

2. If you ask people to reveal how much they would benefit from a public good they will be unlikely to tell the truth. If you ask them to reveal how much they would be damaged by the production of a good involving external costs, will they tell you the truth? Why or why not? How will their answer be affected if you tell them that the production will be financed out of the government's general tax revenues? If you tell them that those who are damaged the most will pay the least?

3. Zero-based budgeting is the practice of evaluating every government program anew each year, as opposed to the current practice of taking the existing programs as given and evaluating potential new projects. Explain how the adoption of this practice might help to keep down the cost of government expenditures.

4. Many industries pay lobbyists to influence regulatory agencies, congressional committees, and other government agencies and officials in Washington. These lobbyists spend a lot of time promoting the idea that their industry is a source of external benefits. Why would the firms in an industry pay lobbyists to do this?

5. Criticize the following statement: "The government should not be providing money for vaccination programs. If people are unwilling to pay the full cost without subsidy, then vaccinations fail the market test and should not be provided at all."

6. Explain what is wrong with the following statement: "You can rely upon the government to provide you with the goods you want at a reasonable price just as much as you can rely upon private business firms. The reason is that the party in power wants you to be pleased with what it provides so that you will vote for it in the next election, just as a private business firm wants you to be pleased with what it provides so that you will buy the product again."

7. It has been argued that every time the government spends more money, it provides a great deal of benefit to a small number of people and a very small cost to a large number of people (namely, taxpayers). Explain how this might cause government spending to grow.

*8. In Essay Question **10** of the previous chapter, it was pointed out that, according to some economists, all external costs are the result of society's failure to allocate and enforce property rights. Using the same reasoning, could it be argued that this is also the source of all external benefits?

Answers

True-False Questions: **1** T **2** F **3** T **4** F **5** F **6** F **7** T **8** T **9** T **10** F
Multiple-Choice Questions: **1** a **2** b **3** a **4** a **5** b **6** d **7** c **8** a **9** b **10** d **11** d **12** b
13 b **14** c

Exercises: **1a.** *OB, OA, OC, IF* **b.** *REF, IF* **c.** *OJ, KH, LH*, more, *HGE*, tax, *KL*

2.

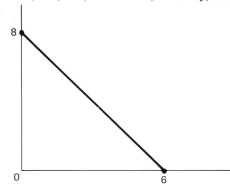

3a. 1 million, is **b.** 1,000, 2,000, 0, understate

c. 999.90, overstate, is not, 999.70, overstate, 2 million, would, inefficient

CHAPTER 28
The Gains from International Trade

Learning Objectives

After you have studied this chapter in the textbook and the study guide, you should be able to

Identify the three main sources of gain from international trade

Give an example showing how international trade can result in an increase in the variety of available products

Explain the difference between comparative advantage and absolute advantage

Explain why countries export those commodities for which they have a comparative advantage

State two reasons why international trade is analogous to technological change

Measure diagrammatically the efficiency gain from international trade as in Figures 28-6 and 28-7 in the textbook

Explain why this efficiency gain can be estimated by comparing the changes in producer surplus and consumer surplus that result from international trade

Identify who gains and who loses from international trade in a specific good, explaining why

CHAPTER HIGHLIGHTS

The purpose of this chapter is to introduce some of the fundamentals of the theory of international trade. The chapter shows how the residents of a country may gain from being allowed to trade with residents of other countries. These gains arise from three principal sources: (1) increased competition,

(2) economies of scale, and (3) comparative advantage.

Increased Competition

If there is no international trade, each producer sells in a market that includes only buyers in a single country. A market of this size may be a natural oligopoly or even a natural monopoly. With international trade each producer now sells in a much larger market that includes buyers from all over the world; moreover, these sales are made in competition with other producers in other countries. Thus, international trade moves us closer to perfect competition, and one of the reasons why we gain from international trade is that this move reduces the efficiency loss resulting from *im*perfect competition. This is illustrated in Figure 28-1 in the textbook.

Economies of Scale

We saw in Chapter 3 that with economies of scale the people in a country can gain if each specializes in the production of one or a few goods. The same principle applies to people in different countries. With no international trade each country must produce a little of everything because it must be self-sufficient. With international trade each country can produce a lot of some things, and purchase the rest of what it wants from other countries. The cost of the goods that we produce ourselves may be reduced through the economies of scale that result from large-scale production. Likewise, the price of the goods that we buy from other countries may be reduced because they too enjoy economies of scale.

Not only are costs reduced, variety may be increased. For example, because of international trade, someone buying a car in the tiny European country of Liechtenstein can choose among Fords, Volkswagens, Datsuns, and many others that are produced elsewhere. Without international trade, the consumer wouldn't have this choice. He or she would have to buy a car produced in Liechtenstein. But these automobile manufacturers would not all produce in Liechtenstein. The market is so small (the population of Liechtenstein is less than 30,000), that they could not *all* sell enough cars there to cover their fixed costs. At best, there would be only one producer.

Comparative Advantage

To understand *comparative* advantage, you must first understand *absolute* advantage. To take an example, America has an absolute advantage over Europe in producing food if food can be produced using fewer inputs in America than in Europe. In the example of Table 28-2 in the textbook, food can be produced using only half as many inputs (workers) in America as in Europe. In other words, America has an absolute advantage in food if its *input* cost of food is lower. By contrast, American has a comparative advantage in food if its

opportunity cost of food is lower; that is, if producing food requires a smaller sacrifice of other goods than it does in Europe. Both absolute and comparative advantages refer to the cost of production. The difference is in how this cost is measured. For absolute advantage you measure it in inputs. For comparative advantage you measure it in other outputs (specifically, the other outputs forgone).

Comparative advantage depends upon absolute advantage in the following way: America would have a *comparative* advantage in food in three different cases:

1. If America had an absolute advantage in food and Europe had an absolute advantage in clothing.

2. If America had an absolute advantage in both food and clothing, but the absolute advantage were greater in food than in clothing.

3. If Europe had an absolute advantage in both food and clothing, but the absolute advantage were greater in clothing than in food.

Case 1 is illustrated in Table 28-2 in the textbook. Europe's opportunity cost of food is 4 units of clothing. This is so because to produce a unit of food requires one worker, but that worker could have produced 4 units of clothing. On the other hand, America's opportunity cost of food is only 1 1/2 units of clothing. The reason is that producing a unit of food in America requires only one-half a worker (because each worker produces 2 units). But this "one-half worker" could have produced 1 1/2 units of food (because each whole worker produces 3 units). Thus, the opportunity cost of food is higher in Europe than in America. In other words, America has a comparative advantage in food. As an exercise, try going through the example of Table 28-3 to show why America also has a comparative advantage in food in case 2.

Even if there are no economies of scale, but instead there are constant costs (i.e., average costs are constant), then each country will gain by specializing in producing those goods for which it has a comparative advantage. The gain arises because trade allows a country to acquire more cheaply the goods in which it does *not* have a comparative advantage. Why produce these goods at home—where their opportunity cost is high—when they can be purchased from another country where their opportunity cost is low? This gain from trade is illustrated by the examples of Tables 28-2 and 28-3 in the textbook.

In addition to this, there is one analogy and one technique that you should be sure to learn from this chapter. The analogy, illustrated by Figure 28-5 in the textbook, is between international trade and technological change. Both allow a country to consume a combination of goods lying beyond its current production possibility curve, and both can be the source of troublesome unemployment that may have to be endured in the short run in order to realize gains in the long run.

The technique you should learn is the method of measuring the efficiency gain from international trade in a commodity. To put it the other way around, this is also the efficiency loss from *not* permitting international trade in the commodity. The efficiency gain from exporting a commodity comes from being able to sell to foreigners at a price above the domestic cost of production (or above the domestic marginal utility of consumption). The gain from importing a commodity comes from being able to buy at a price below the domestic cost of production (or below the domestic marginal utility of consumption). Be sure that you understand why the "triangle" measures of Figure 28-6 and 28-7 in the textbook can be used to estimate these gains. Be sure too that you understand (in Figure 28-8) how this triangle measure is also exactly what we get if we compare changes in consumer and producer surplus that result from international trade. As a check on your understanding, you should be able to use this alternative analysis to confirm the triangu-lar measure of the benefit resulting from an export of wheat (first shown in Figure 28-6). This comparison of how producers and consumers are affected is important for understanding the conflict of interest between them in questions of international trade. In turn, this is important for understanding the problems that have hindered efforts in the United States to formulate sensible policies toward international trade.

IMPORTANT TERMS

Economies of scale A situation in which average cost falls as more is produced. These constitute one source of the gains from international trade.

Comparative advantage A country's comparative advantage is the good that it can produce relatively cheaply; that is, at lower opportunity cost than its trading partner. (Remember that the opportunity cost of a good is the quantity of other goods that must be sacrificed in order to produce another unit of the good.) This is a further source of gain from international trade.

Absolute advantage A country has an *absolute* advantage in any good that it can produce using fewer inputs than its trading partner. This is similar to comparative advantage except that it defines the advantage in terms of *input* cost rather than opportunity cost.

True-False Questions

T F 1. By allowing international trade in a commodity we can possibly make a natural monopoly now face some competition.

T F 2. Suppose that after the introduction of international trade the producers of good X in the United States end up producing less than before because of the competition from foreign producers. Then, even if the United States as a whole gains from its international trade in *all* commodities, it loses from its trade in X.

T F 3. International trade will make new products available to American consumers only if there are economies of scale.

T F 4. Even if a country has no absolute advantage it can have some comparative advantage.

T F 5. Every country has an absolute advantage in something.

T F 6. Economies of scale may exist even if production possibility curves are the same in all countries.

T F 7. Gains from trade come from each country specializing in those goods in which it has an absolute advantage.

T F 8. As a general rule, a country will gain from international trade if it exports those goods for which it has a relatively low opportunity cost of production.

T F 9. If a country exports oranges, then consumers of oranges in that country probably lose from having international trade in oranges.

T F 10. If a country imports oranges, then producers of oranges in that country probably gain from having international trade in oranges.

T F 11. International trade allows a country to *consume* a combination of goods lying outside its current production possibility curve.

T F 12. International trade allows a country to *produce* a combination of goods lying outside its current production possibility curve.

Multiple-Choice Questions

1. Boeing was able to cover the costs of producing the first "jumbo jet" in the 1970s, the 747, because they could sell it not only to domestic U.S. airlines but also to several foreign airlines. This provides us with an example of
   (a) How a natural monopoly can be made to act more competitively with international trade
   (b) A transfer from domestic consumers as a result of international trade
   (c) An increase in the variety of goods made available by international trade when there are economies of scale
   (d) None of the above

2. Which of the following is *not* a principal source of gains from international trade?
   (a) Comparative advantage
   (b) Absolute advantage
   (c) Economies of scale
   (d) Increased competition

3. International trade in a good
   (a) Moves many industries closer to perfect competition
   (b) Guarantees that domestic producers will act as price takers
   (c) Reduces the amount of competition faced by domestic producers
   (d) Lowers all domestic prices

4. Under international trade we export those goods for which we have a relatively low
   (a) Input cost   (c) Accounting cost
   (b) Wage cost   (d) Opportunity cost

5. International trade results in an increased availability of goods especially if
   (a) There are economies of scale
   (b) International trade gives some producer a monopoly in the world market
   (c) There are increasing costs in the long run
   (d) National governments impose tariffs

6. Suppose Canada and the United States produce only two goods: newsprint and machinery, and use only one factor of production, labor. Suppose that in both countries production is subject to constant costs and that the production possibilities are given by Table 28-1

Table 28-1

	Output per worker in the U.S.	Output per worker in Canada
Machinery	7	5
Newsprint	8	4

Then Canada has
   (a) A comparative advantage in machinery
   (b) A comparative advantage in newsprint
   (c) An absolute advantage in machinery
   (d) An absolute advantage in newsprint

7. In the situation described in the previous question, the U.S. has

   (a) A comparative advantage in machinery
   (b) A comparative advantage in newsprint
   (c) An absolute advantage in machinery
   (d) (b) and (c)

8. In question 6, suppose that international trade is allowed between Canada and the United States in machinery and newsprint, following a period in which no such trade has been permitted. Then unemployment may result in the short run in the industry producing
   (a) Newsprint in the U.S.
   (b) Newsprint in Canada
   (c) Machinery in the U.S.
   (d) (b) and (c)

9. According to the theory of international trade discussed in this chapter
   (a) Every American citizen gains from international trade
   (b) As a general rule, international trade in a good will benefit both producers and consumers of that good
   (c) As a general rule, producers lose but consumers gain from international trade
   (d) There is an efficiency gain to the United States from allowing international trade

10. India has a comparative advantage in activities that require a great deal of labor because
   (a) People work longer hours in India
   (b) Labor is a relatively abundant factor of production in India
   (c) Minimum wage laws ensure that many Indians are working in factories
   (d) Output per worker is high in India

11. American car manufacturers face a more elastic demand curve as a result of European and Japanese imports, because buyers can substitute them for American cars if American prices go up.
   (a) Increased competition
   (b) Comparative advantage
   (c) Economies of scale
   (d) Absolute advantage

12. International trade is like technological progress because they both
   (a) Allow us to consume beyond the boundaries of the current production possibility curve
   (b) Benefit everyone
   (c) Reduce unemployment
   (d) Can occur only if there are economies of scale

13. In Figure 28-1, suppose that international trade lowers the price of the good from *OA* to *OB*. Then the resulting increase in consumer surplus equals the area
   (a) *ACE*   (b) *DEF*   (c) *AEDB*   (d) *AEFB*

14. Under the same assumptions the resulting decrease in producer surplus equals the area
   (a) *ACE*   (b) *BCF*   (c) *AEDB*   (d) *AEFB*

15. Under the same assumptions the resulting efficiency gain to America equals the area
   (a) *DEF*   (b) *DGE*   (c) *EJF*   (d) *HDFI*

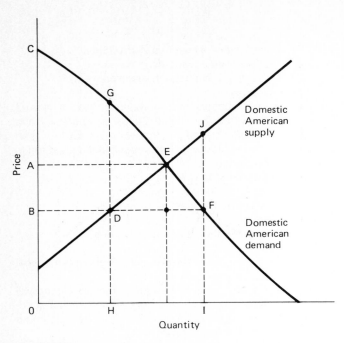

FIGURE 28-1

Exercises

1. Suppose that Figures 28-2 and 28-3 represent the markets for shoes in England and Spain.

  a. Without international trade the price in England would equal _____ and the quantity produced in England would equal _____; the price in Spain would equal _____ and

the quantity produced in Spain would equal

_____.

  b. With international trade (assuming that there are no other countries involved) the single price at which the total demand (English demand plus Spanish demand) equals

FIGURE 28-2

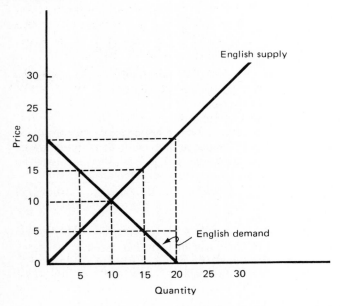

FIGURE 28-3

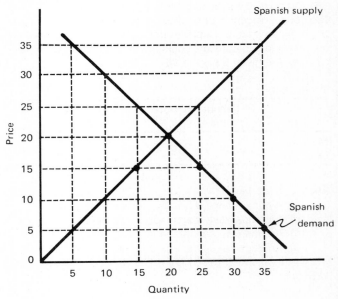

the total supply is _____. At that price English demand equals _____ and English supply equals _____; Spanish demand equals _____, and Spanish supply equals _____. In this situation (Spain, England) will export the amount _____ of shoes.

2. In Figure 28-4, *D* is the demand curve for a good in the United States market alone; MR is the corresponding marginal revenue curve that a firm would face if it were able to monopolize this market. But for now assume that this industry is perfectly competitive, with MC being its supply curve. Also assume that there are no externalities.

  a. Suppose initially that there is no international trade in the good. Then the amount _____ will be produced and the market price will equal _____. Suppose now that international trade is introduced, and that it results in a price equal to *OC*. Then consumption of the good in the United States will equal _____, production of the good in the United States will equal _____, and the difference between these amounts equals _____, which will be the amount of the good that the United States (exports, imports).

  b. As a result of allowing international trade in this good, producer surplus in the United States has gone (up, down) by the amount _____ and consumer surplus in the United States has gone (up, down) by the amount _____; therefore the net efficiency (gain, loss) to the United States equals _____.

  c. Suppose next that there is no international trade in the good and that the market in the United States is an unregulated monopoly. The monopolist will produce the amount _____ and will charge the price _____. Suppose now that international trade is introduced and that as a result the firm that used to have a monopoly in the United States is forced to behave as a perfect competitor. Suppose as before that with international trade the market price will equal *OC*. Then consumption of the good in the United States will equal _____, production of the good in the United States will equal _____, and the difference between these two amounts equals _____, which will be the amount of the good that the United States (exports, imports).

  d. As a result of allowing international trade in this good the total revenue received by the producer in the United States has gone from _____ to _____, so the net gain in total rev-

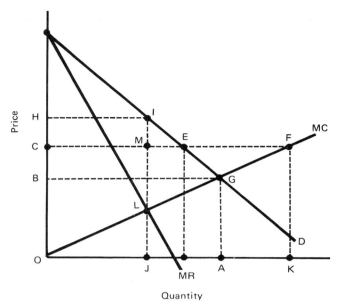

FIGURE 28-4

enue equals the rectangle _____ minus the rectangle _____.

  e. But the producer's cost increases by the four-sided figure _____; thus the net gain to the producer equals the triangle _____ minus the rectangle _____. At the same time, consumer surplus (rises, falls) by _____; thus the net gain to the country (the net gain to conumers plus the net gain to the producer) equals the area of the figure _____. Shade in this area.

  f. Trade in this case brings two efficiency gains: the standard gain that results even in a world of perfect competition, shown by area _____ (like area *ABC* in Figure 28-6 in the textbook), *plus* a gain because trade ends monopoly abuse—shown by area _____ (like the red area in Figure 23-6*a* in the textbook). Both gains make up the shaded area _____.

  g. Does this illustrate a special case in which it is *possible* for international trade in a specific commodity to benefit both the consumers and the producers of that commodity? _____.

3a. This exercise is designed to help you understand comparative advantage. Suppose that for country *A* each acre of land will produce 100 bushels of wheat or 30 bushels of corn, whereas for country *B* each acre of land will produce 40 bushels of wheat or 20 bushels of corn. Suppose that each country has 4,000 acres. Fill in Table 28-2, giving the production possibilities for *A* and *B*.

Table 28-2

A's Production Possibilities		B's Production Possibilities	
Thousands of bushels of wheat	Thousands of bushels of corn	Thousands of bushels of wheat	Thousands of bushels of corn
0		0	
100		40	
200		80	
300		120	
400		160	

3b. Plot the PPCs for the two countries in Figure 28-5.

3c. Country _____ has an absolute advantage in producing corn; country _____ has an absolute advantage in producing wheat; country _____ has a comparative advantage in producing corn; and country _____ has a comparative advantage in producing wheat. Suppose that country A devoted all its land to producing corn, and B devoted all its land to producing wheat. Then A would produce _____ thousand bushels of corn and B would produce _____ thousand bushels of wheat.

3d. Suppose, furthermore, that they were then to trade with each other at the price of 10 bushels of wheat for every 4 bushels of corn. Then if residents of B wanted to consume 120,000 bushels of wheat, they could sell 40,000 bushels of wheat (this is the excess of 160,000 production over 120,000 consumption). They could sell this for 16,000 bushels of corn (remember every 10 bushels of wheat trades for 4 bushels of corn), which they could also consume. This is shown in Table 28-3.

Under these assumptions, we have just seen that country B could possibly consume the combination of 120,000 bushels of wheat and 16,000 bushels of corn. This is illustrated as point X in Figure 28-6. Fill in the rest of Table 28-3. Plot the resulting consumption possibilities in Figure 28-6 and join them with a smooth curve labeled B_1.

3e. Under the same assumptions about specialization and prices, fill in A's consumption possibilities in Table 28-4 and plot them in Figure 28-6, joining them with a smooth curve labeled A_1.

3f. Now, suppose that A were to devote all its land to the production of wheat and B to devote all its land to the production of corn. Then _____ bushels of wheat and _____ bushels of corn would be produced. Once again, suppose that the coun-

FIGURE 28-5

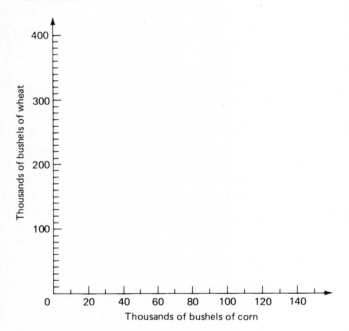

Table 28-3

B's CONSUMPTION POSSIBILITIES*				
Consumption of wheat	Production of wheat	Sales of wheat	Purchase of corn	Consumption of corn
160	160			
120	160	40	16	16
80	160			
40	160			
0	160			

*In thousands of bushels.

tries trade corn for wheat at the price of 4 bushels of corn for 10 bushels of wheat.

3g. Fill in the consumption possibilities of each country in Table 28-5 and 28-6 and plot them in Figure 28-6, labeling the resulting curves A_2 and B_2, respectively.

3h. Why does A_2 lie to the northeast of A_1 and B_2 to the northeast of B_1?

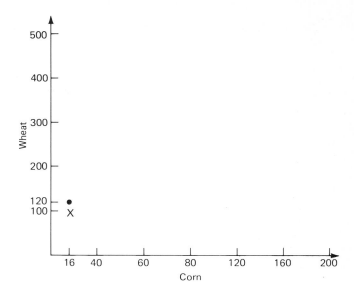

FIGURE 28-6

Table 28-4

A's CONSUMPTION POSSIBILITIES*

Consumption of corn	Production of corn	Sales of corn	Purchase of wheat	Consumption of wheat
120	120	___	___	___
80	120	40	100	100
40	120	___	___	___
0	120	___	___	___

*In thousands of bushels.

Table 28-5

A's CONSUMPTION POSSIBILITIES*

Consumption of wheat	Sale of wheat	Consumption of corn
400	___	___
200	___	___
0	___	___

*In thousands of bushels

Table 28-6

B's CONSUMPTION POSSIBILITIES*

Consumption of corn	Sale of corn	Consumption of wheat
80	___	___
40	___	___
0	___	___

*In thousands of bushels.

Essay Questions

1. Every year, the United States imports a great number of Hondas, Volkswagens, Toyotas, and so forth. Why do you suppose that so many of these cars are produced in other countries, and shipped across the ocean, rather than being produced in the United States? Who in the United States gains from having these cars imported? Why? Who loses? Why?

2. "If the United States is to take full advantage of the gains from trade that arise from eco-nomies of scale then it cannot hope to achieve the goal of self-sufficiency in all commodities. In fact, it must become dependent upon other countries." Explain why this is true, and why it is even more true for Sweden. What are the costs to the United States of trying to become self-sufficient in satisfying its needs for oil and other sources of energy? What are the benefits of self-sufficiency? Do you think, on the whole, that it is a good idea to pursue this goal in the case of oil? In general, for other products as well? Do you think that complete self-sufficiency in all goods would be possible? If so, at what cost?

3. The figures in Table 28-1 in the textbook show that the United States imports a large volume of automobiles and parts, but it also exports a large volume of them. Why do you suppose it does both? How would your answer be different if the United States had not signed a free-trade agreement in automobiles with Canada?

4. Show how we can gain from international trade because it may induce firms to eliminate technical inefficiency.

5. The textbook showed that when we import a specific good our consumers gain at the expense of our producers. Does this mean that all individuals gain at the expense of all business firms? Explain. Can you think of any reason why the leaders of the United Steelworkers of America, who represent the individuals working in the steel industry, argue vigorously that the government should take steps to limit the amount of steel imported into the United States?

6. As a rule, producers of a good lose when it is imported and consumers of a good lose when it is

exported. Yet Washington is full of professional lobbyists who argue successfully for continued government restrictions on imports, whereas hardly anyone ever argues for government restrictions on exports. How do you suppose that this is connected with the basic fact that most of us earn our living in one particular industry, but consume products from *most* industries?

*7. Carefully evaluate the following statement: "If marginal costs rise with the amount produced, then there is no gain from engaging in international trade because the country that ends up exporting a good has to produce more of it. This means that its marginal cost, and accordingly its price, will be higher than without international trade. In other words, international trade makes goods more expensive."

*8. In the example given in Table 28-3 in the textbook, can you tell what the specific price of food will be in terms of clothing when these items are traded between Europe and America? What extra information would you need to answer this? What information *does* the table give you about this price?

Answers

True-False Questions: **1** T **2** F **3** F **4** T **5** F **6** T **7** F **8** T **9** T **10** F **11** T **12** F
Multiple-Choice Questions: **1** c **2** b **3** a **4** d **5** a **6** a **7** d **8** d **9** d **10** b **11** a **12** a
13 d **14** c **15** a
Exercises: **1a.** 10, 10, 20, 20 **b.** 15, 5, 15, 25, 15, England, 10
2a. *OA, OB, CE, CF, EF,* exports **b.** up, *BCFG,* down, *BCEG,* gain, *EFG* **c.** *OJ, OH, CE, CF, EF,* exports **d.** *OHIJ, OCFK, JMFK, CHIM* **e.** *JLFK, LMF, CHIM,* rises, *CHIE, LIEF,* **f.** *EGF, ILG, IEFL,* **g.** yes, provided that area *LMF* is greater than area *CHIM*

3a. Table 28-2

A		B	
Wheat	Corn	Wheat	Corn
0	120	0	80
100	90	40	60
200	60	80	40
300	30	120	20
400	0	160	0

3b. Figure 28-5 completed.

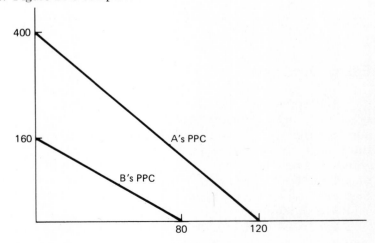

3c. *A, A, B, A,* 120, 160

3d. Table 28-3

160	160	0	0	0
120	160	40	16	16
80	160	80	32	32
40	160	120	48	48
0	160	160	64	64

3e. Table 28-4

120	120	0	0	0
80	120	40	100	100
40	120	80	200	200
0	120	120	300	300

3f. 400, 80

3g. Table 28-5

400	0	0
200	200	80
0	400	160

Table 28-6

80	0	0
40	40	100
0	80	200

Figure 28-6

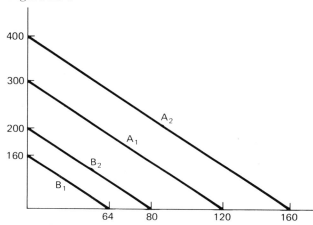

3h. Because in the case of A_2 and B_2, each country specialized in producing the commodity for which it has a comparative advantage, which is more efficient than the alternative of producing according to comparative *dis*advantage.

CHAPTER 29
Tariffs and Other International Trade Issues

Learning Objectives

After you have studied this chapter in the textbook and the study guide, you should be able to

Explain the noneconomic reasons for having tariffs

State three fallacious economic arguments for protection, explaining why they are fallacious

State five economic arguments for protection that may sometimes be true, and the difficulties with each of them

Describe the four major events affecting the course of international trade that occurred in 1947, in the late 1950s, in 1967, and in 1979

Explain why multinational corporations exist

Explain the pros and cons of multinational corporations (MNCs)

CHAPTER HIGHLIGHTS

This chapter discusses tariffs and other trade restrictions. It deals with (1) the reasons commonly given for having trade restrictions, (2) the history of trade policy in the United States and elsewhere, and (3) multinational corporations.

Arguments for Protection

Many trade restrictions exist for economic reasons. But often the reason is purely political. The loss that results from allowing a good to be imported is felt very heavily by the few people who specialize in producing that good and whose jobs are threatened by the competition of imports. These people will often vote for a politician who promises to restrict such imports. As we saw in the last chapter, the benefits from allowing a good to be imported are greater than these losses. But these benefits are typically spread among the many people that consume that good. Although every consumer benefits a little bit, few consumers benefit enough to vote against a politician who proposes to restrict such imports. Trade restrictions rarely make economic sense, but they often make political sense.

There is also a military reason for some trade

restrictions. Some goods are vital for our national defense. Under free trade these goods might not be produced in the United States. If so, the United States would be dependent upon foreign producers in time of war. Protection of such industries by tariffs enables us to supply our own military needs. It thereby contributes to our national security. The problem with this military reason is that it can easily be misused. Almost any industry can make the case that its products are vital for national defense.

The last chapter presented a strong economic argument against trade restriction (that is, for free trade). However, the following economic arguments have often been advanced in favor of trade restrictions. Some of them are fallacious, but some of them contain an element of truth, and merit serious consideration.

1. "Buy American because it keeps our money at home." This argument is fallacious. When you buy Japanese goods your money does indeed go to the Japanese. But it comes back when the Japanese buy our exports. The Japanese want our goods, not our money.

2. "We can't compete with cheap foreign labor." This argument is also fallacious. Foreign labor may be less expensive because it is less productive. We can compete with cheap foriegn labor in goods for which we have a comparative advantage. We can't compete when we don't have a comparative advantage.

3. "Tariffs should be tailored to equalize costs at home and abroad." This too is a fallacious argument. According to the theory of comparative advantage, we gain from international trade because of the *differences* in costs between different countries. Tailoring tariffs to equalize costs would just eliminate trade, and all the gains it provides.

4. "If we buy steel from Pittsburgh rather than Japan, employment will rise in Pittsburgh rather than Japan." There is a grain of truth in this argument. Restricting the imports of steel from Japan may stimulate employment in Pittsburgh, at least in the short run. However, there are two problems. First, Japan may retaliate with her own restrictions. If we both attempt to cure our unemployment through "beggar-my-neighbor" policies we will both be worse off from losing the gains from trade. Second, Japanese competition helps us keep costs and prices down in American industries. If American steel workers did not feel that their jobs were threatened by Japanese competition, they would be less restrained in their wage demands. This is a good example of the benefit we derive from trade through increased competition—a benefit we would lose if our industries were protected.

5. "Restricting trade will diversify a nation's economy." This may be true for some countries. Trade may lead a country to specialize in producing just a few goods. If world prices drop for these few goods, the country will suffer from having put all their eggs in one basket. But don't forget that world prices can also rise—the OPEC countries who produce almost nothing but oil have hardly been suffering as a result of their specialization. Furthermore, a country as large as the United States will always produce such a large variety of goods that lack of diversification is unlikely ever to become a serious problem.

6. "We need to protect our infant industries." This argument is sometimes valid. Without the motherly protection of trade restrictions, some of our industries may never reach the size where they can realize the economies of scale necessary to compete in world markets. The difficulties with this argument are threefold. (*a*) Infant industries never seem to grow up. They typically continue to demand protection, and no government wants to lose votes by cutting the apron strings. (*b*) Even if an industry were to "grow up," it might still not be able to compete effectively. This is always difficult to determine in advance. (*c*) If the infant industry really does have a promising future, then you have to wonder why private lenders are unwilling to lend it enough money to survive until maturity.

7. "Restricting imports may reduce the price we have to pay for them." This may make sense if the United States demands so much of a good that by cutting back its demand it can significantly reduce the world price of that good. However, if other big countries see the United States doing this, they will likely take the same attitude and restrict their imports. If so, the gains from trade will shrink.

8. "Restricting imports may reduce our vulnerability to a cutoff in foreign supplies." Cutbacks in oil exports by OPEC countries in the 1970s made clear the force of this argument. But in most commodities the risk of being cut off is minimal, because if one country stops supplying us we can usually turn to other countries.

History of Trade Policy

The history of trade policy in the Western world has been one of falling tariffs. However, the fall has not been steady. The highlights of this history are illustrated in Figure 29-1 in the textbook. The most important events to remember are the following. In 1947 the United States and 22 other countries signed the General Agreement on Tariffs and Trade (GATT), in which they agreed to have multilateral negotiations to lower tariffs. In the late 1950s the European Economic Community (EEC) was formed with the objectives of (1) free trade between all its members, (2) a common tariff against all goods coming in from outside the EEC, and (3) other measures of economic cooperation. In 1967 the GATT countries completed the "Kennedy Round" of negotiations by agreeing to cut their tariffs on average by about 35 percent. In the 1970s there was some backsliding from the spirit of the Kennedy Round. In particular, many countries began raising non-tariff barriers (NTBs), such as import quotas. But in 1979, a second GATT Treaty was signed, following the "Tokyo Round" of negotiations, which cut tariffs by about another third, and provided regulations to limit NTBs.

The Multinational Corporation (MNC)

The most important thing to understand about MNCs is why they exist. There are several reasons.

1. A company can reduce transportation costs by producing goods in several countries, rather than producing them all in the United States and then shipping them abroad.

2. A company with operations in many different countries is in a position to realize the comparative advantages of each of these countries.

3. A company with operations in many different countries is not so vulnerable to political pressure from any one country; that is, if the company feels that the government in one country is taxing it too heavily or imposing regulations that are too costly, then it can switch some of its operations to other countries.

4. The MNC is in a good position to exploit economies of scale. For example, the technological improvements it discovers in one country can be transferred easily to its operations in other countries.

5. One reason for producing goods in a foreign country rather than producing them in the United States and exporting them is the existence of tariffs in the foreign country. For example, a number of U.S. companies have set up branch plants in Europe to produce there, and have thus avoided the European tariff. (If they had produced here and shipped to Europe instead, they would have had to pay the European tariff at the border.)

The world economy has benefited from the development of MNCs in three ways: (1) the MNC has helped to reduce transportation costs. (2) It has promoted the gain to all countries from international trade by its ability to realize comparative advantages in different countries. (3) It has also helped to raise standards of living in many countries around the world by transmitting technological knowledge across borders.

However, many people think that the MNCs now have too much power over governments. How this power can be abused is illustrated by scandals in which executives of Lockheed paid large bribes to government officials in other countries.

IMPORTANT TERMS

Tariff A tax imposed on imported goods as they enter a country.

Non-tariff barrier (NTB) Any other government regulation that restricts trade, such as a quality regulation that reduces the amount which a country imports, or a quota.

Quota A limit on the amount of a good that can be imported into a country.

Trade restriction Any tariff or non-tariff barrier that reduces the volume of international trade.

Protection The policy of shielding industries within a country from the competition of imports by means of trade restrictions.

"Beggar-my-neighbor" policy The policy of using trade restrictions to reduce unemployment. If such a policy is successful, it transfers the unemployment problem to another country.

Infant industry An industry that has not yet reached the size at which it can exploit enough economies of scale to compete in world markets without some assistance.

Terms of trade The price in terms of our exported goods that we pay for our imported goods. In order to improve the U.S. terms of trade, some people advocate the use of trade restrictions on goods for which the U.S. demand is a large part of world demand.

Bilateral negotiations Negotiations involving only two countries, as opposed to *multilateral* negotiations that involve many countries.

GATT The General Agreement on Tariffs and Trade. This was signed in 1947 by the United States and 22 other countries. It involves multilateral negotiations to reduce trade restrictions.

EEC The European Economic Community. The common market in Europe formed in the late 1950s by Germany, France, Italy, Holland, Belgium, and Luxembourg, and later joined by Britain, Ireland, Denmark, and Greece.

Kennedy Round The series of multilateral negotiations between GATT countries initiated by President Kennedy in the 1960s and concluded by the worldwide tariff reduction of 1967.

Tokyo Round A further series of multilateral GATT negotiations ending with the 1979 Treaty that limited NTBs and further reduced tariffs.

Multinational corporation (MNC) A large corporation with its head office in one country and subsidiaries in other countries.

True-False Questions

T F 1. When a good is allowed to be imported, the domestic loss of producer surplus usually exceeds the gain in consumer surplus.

T F 2. When a good is allowed to be imported, the domestic loss of producer surplus often creates more political pressure than does the gain in consumer surplus.

T F 3. One of the strongest arguments for trade restrictions is that it keeps us from losing our U.S. dollars to foreigners.

T F 4. If the U.S. government were to do nothing about our unemployment problems, this would constitute a "beggar-my-neighbor" policy.

T F 5. If the United States were to increase restrictions on imported cars, that would tend to increase employment in Detroit.

T F 6. A country whose exports are heavily concentrated in one commodity is exposed to risk from adverse movements in its terms of trade.

T F 7. It is usually easy to tell in advance whether an infant industry will be able to compete successfully without assistance once it has matured.

T F 8. The purpose of GATT is to provide for bilateral negotiations in which countries will agree to lowering their tariffs.

T F 9. Stiff safety standards that must be met by imported goods constitute a non-tariff barrier.

T F 10. Multinational corporations tend to impede the international spread of technological knowledge.

T F 11. European auto tariffs reduce production in Europe by Ford and GM subsidiaries.

Multiple-Choice Questions

1. Because we gain from international trade through increased competition, comparative advantage, and economies of scale
   (a) There is usually an efficiency gain from having tariffs
   (b) There is usually an efficiency gain from having NTBs
   (c) There is usually an efficiency loss from having tariffs
   (d) Consumers gain from import restrictions, at the expense of producers

2. An increase in the tariff on importing a good into the United States will cause
   (a) A decrease in the U.S. price and in the quantity consumed in the United States
   (b) A decrease in the price but an increase in the quantity consumed
   (c) An increase in both price and quantity
   (d) An increase in price and decrease in quantity

3. An increase in a tariff will cause
   (a) An increase in the quantity imported and in the volume of domestic production
   (b) An increase in imports but decrease in domestic production
   (c) A decrease in both imports and domestic production
   (d) A decrease in imports but an increase in production

4. An increase in a tariff will
   (a) Benefit domestic producers and consumers
   (b) Benefit domestic producers but harm domestic consumers
   (c) Harm both producers and consumers
   (d) Harm producers but benefit consumers

5. The strongest political pressure for trade restrictions usually comes from
   (a) Producers lobbying for import restrictions
   (b) Producers lobbying for export restrictions
   (c) Consumers lobbying for import restrictions
   (d) Consumers lobbying for export restrictions

6. The main problem with the "national defense" argument for trade restriction is that
   (a) Waging war will not always allow us to recover the money lost through international trade
   (b) There is no reason to produce our own weapons unless we have a comparative advantage in producing weapons
   (c) It is difficult in practice to tell which industries are vital for our defense and which aren't
   (d) Domestic armament producers do not have enough political influence to present the argument effectively

7. U.S. tariffs are most likely to increase employment in
   (a) American export industries
   (b) American industries that compete against imports
   (c) Foreign export industries
   (d) Foreign industries that aren't engaged in international trade

8. Because of specialization
   (a) The United States produces only a narrow range of goods and services
   (b) Exports constitute more than a third of U.S. GNP
   (c) We are able to realize the gains from trade that arise from comparative advantage and economies of scale

(d) We tend to vote more as consumers than as producers

9. Which of the following arguments for protection contains at least a grain of economic truth?

    (a) Infant industries may warrant some tariff protection

    (b) The competition of cheap foreign production justifies tariff protection

    (c) Tariffs should be applied to prevent firms in the United States from being undersold

    (d) Tariffs help us to keep our money from leaving the country

10. Quotas

    (a) Are non-tariff barriers

    (b) Do not constitute a trade restriction

    (c) Were eliminated by the 1967 GATT Treaty

    (d) Are reduced when a country applies rigid safety standards on products

11. The quadrupling of oil prices by OPEC countries in 1973–1974 best illustrated the importance of which of the following arguments for trade restrictions?

    (a) We can't compete with cheap foreign labor

    (b) Restricting imports reduces our vulnerability to a cutoff in foreign supplies

    (c) We need to protect our infant industries

    (d) Tariffs should be tailored to equalize costs at home and abroad

12. Trade restrictions on a good can confer a gain on us by improving our terms of trade only if

    (a) U.S. demand for the good is a significant part of world demand

    (b) The U.S. industry is a natural monopoly

    (c) The lower prices that result drive some of our own producers out of business

    (d) Other countries are provoked into doing the same thing

13. The signing of the treaty establishing GATT took place in

    (a) 1934   **(c)** 1959

    (b) 1947   **(d)** 1967

14. The Kennedy Round resulted in an average tariff reduction of about

    (a) 5 percent   **(c)** 25 percent

    (b) 15 percent   **(d)** 35 percent

15. Which of the following countries is *not* a member of the European Economic Community?

    (a) France   **(c)** Greece

    (b) Denmark   **(d)** United States

16. According to the rules of the European Economic Community, each member has

    (a) No tariffs on imports from other members

    (b) No tariffs on imports from nonmembers

    (c) A different tariff on trade with other members

    (d) A different tariff on trade with nonmembers

17. Which of the following is *not* a reason why multinational corporations (MNCs) exist?

    (a) An MNC can arrange its production throughout the world so as to reduce transportation costs

    (b) MNCs can avoid tariffs by producing in the countries in which they sell

    (c) The United Nations provides protection to MNC's that is denied to producers in any single country

    (d) MNCs are in a good position to transfer production from one country to another so as to exploit the different countries' comparative advantages

18. The major problem posed by multinational corporations is that they

    (a) May acquire too much influence over government policies

    (b) Are unable to exploit the gains from comparative advantage

    (c) Do not have economies of scale

    (d) Incur large transportation costs

Exercise

Parts of this exercise cover the same ground as the appendix to the chapter. You will probably be able to do the exercise and to find it helpful even if you are not being asked to study the appendix. If you get stuck you should refer to the appendix for help. Otherwise try to do the exercise on your own.

1. Figure 29-1 represents the domestic supply and demand for a good that is traded internationally

    a. Without international trade the price would equal _____ and the quantity produced would equal _____. If international trade results in a price of *OA*, then domestic production will equal _____, domestic consumption will equal _____, and the country will (import, export) the amount _____. As a result of this international trade, consumer surplus is (more, less) than without trade, by the amount _____, and producer surplus is (more, less) by the amount _____. The

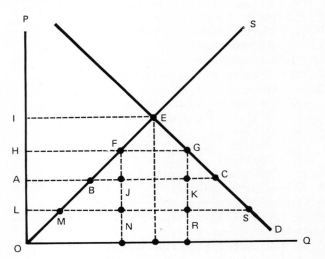

FIGURE 29-1

change in consumer surplus is (more, less) than the change in producer surplus, by the amount _____. Therefore, as a result of international trade there is a net efficiency (gain, loss) to the country, of the amount _____.

b. Now suppose that the government imposes an import quota that restricts imports to no more than the quantity *FG*. (Suppose that the quota rights are owned by foreigners and that they have no effect upon the world price of the good, which remains at *OA*.) Because of the quota, the price in the domestic market will rise to _____. At this price domestic production will equal _____, and domestic consumption will equal _____. The quota (increases, decreases) consumer surplus by the amount _____, and (increases, decreases) producer surplus by the amount _____. The difference between these two changes in surplus is the net (gain, loss) to the nation resulting from the quota, and it equals _____. The gain to the nation remaining from international trade after the quota is imposed equals _____.

c. Instead of a quota suppose that the government imposes a tariff of the amount *AH* on the good. Suppose that this has no effect on the world price of the good. Because of the tariff, the domestic price will equal _____, and the quantity of imports will equal _____. As a result of the tariff, consumer surplus is (more, less) than it would be with free trade by the amount _____, and producer surplus is (more, less) than it would be with free trade by the amount _____. Moreover, the government collects revenues from this tariff, the total amount of which equals _____. Thus, when we take into account the loss to consumers, and the gain to both producers *and* the treasury (taxpayers) the net loss to the nation is the two areas _____ and _____. This loss is (more, less) than the loss from the quota studied in the previous paragraph, by the amount _____.

d. The example of this exercise suggests the general rule that the efficiency loss to a nation from imposing a tariff is (more, less) than the efficiency loss of a quota that results in the same volume of trade, and the difference in these efficiency losses equals the amount of _____.

Essay Questions

1. Why have U.S. presidents been more strongly in favor of free trade than U.S. congressmen? What sorts of states are likely to elect congressmen that favor free trade?

2. Physicians coming from other countries must pass lengthy and difficult examinations before being able to practice medicine in the United States, even if they have already received training in their own country that makes them more qualified than most of the doctors already practicing in the United States. In what sense does this constitute a non-tariff barrier? These examinations are vigorously defended by American physicians who claim that (**a**) they protect the public against unqualified physicians, and (**b**) if we allow free entry of qualified physicians from everywhere else in the world, there will be such an oversupply of physicians here that many of the young Americans graduating from medical school will be unable to find jobs in medicine. What do you think are the strengths and weaknesses of these arguments?

3. The text argued that a country may improve its terms of trade by restricting *im*ports. In 1973 the oil-producing countries of OPEC managed to improve their terms of trade by restricting their *ex*ports. Explain carefully what are the similarities and differences between the "terms of trade" argument for restricting imports and the "terms of trade" argument for restricting exports.

4. Throughout modern history the big increases in trade restriction in the world seem to have occurred during periods of widespread recession. Why do you suppose this has been so?

5. Explain carefully the following statement: "There may be a lot of political pressure on a government to protect an infant industry, but there is even more pressure to keep the protection going once it has been started."

6. Outside the United States, many people think that American-based multinational corporations should be discouraged from setting up operations in their countries because the big decisions that such a company makes will be influenced by its American interests rather than the interests of the country in which it is producing. Analyze the strengths and weakness of this argument.

7. Sometimes American industries demand protection from foreign competition because foreigners have been "dumping" their goods on the United States market. That is, foreigners have been selling their goods in the United States at a price below the price they are charging in their home markets. In what sense does this practice resemble the "cutthroat competition" that sometimes occurs in oligopolistic industries? What are the strengths and weaknesses of the argument that we need tariffs in order to protect our industries against dumping?

Answers

True-False Questions: **1** F **2** T **3** F **4** F **5** T **6** T **7** F **8** F **9** T **10** F **11** F

Multiple-Choice Questions: **1** c **2** d **3** d **4** b **5** a **6** c **7** b **8** c **9** a **10** a **11** b **12** a **13** b **14** d **15** d **16** a **17** c **18** a

Exercise **1a.** *OI, IE, AB, AC,* import, *BC,* more, *AIEC,* less, *AIEB,* more, *BEC,* gain, *BEC* **b.** *OH, HF, HG,* decreases, *AHGC,* increases, *AHFB,* loss, *BFGC, FEG* **c.** *OH, FG,* less, *AHGC,* more, *AHFB, JFGK, BFJ, KGC,* less, *JFGK* **d.** less, tariffs collected

PART FIVE

MICROECONOMICS:
How Income is Distributed

CHAPTER 30
Wages in a Perfectly Competitive Economy

Learning Objectives

After you have studied this chapter in the textbook and the study guide, you should be able to

Explain why a perfectly competitive firm's demand for labor schedule is the same thing as its marginal productivity of labor schedule

State two reasons why the demand for labor curve might shift to the right

Explain why the height of the labor supply curve measures (approximately) the opportunity cost of labor in that market

Explain why the outcome of a competitive equilibrium in the labor market may be socially efficient

Measure diagrammatically the efficiency loss of departing from a perfectly competitive labor market equilibrium

Explain why one cannot jump from the proposition that a perfectly competitive labor market may be socially efficient to the conclusion that a free, unregulated labor market is "best"

Measure in a diagram the total income of labor in a market and the total income of other factors in that market

Show diagrammatically the effects of introducing a minimum wage law into an otherwise perfectly competitive labor market

State the important qualifications to this chapter's analysis of minimum wage laws

CHAPTER HIGHLIGHTS

This chapter deals with the question of how wages are determined under the assumption of perfectly competitive labor markets (*im*perfect labor markets are studied later). This question can be addressed using the same tools of supply and demand that you are already familiar with. For our purposes, someone's wage is just the price of a commodity that is traded in the market. The commodity is labor, the demanders are employers, and the suppliers are workers. The chapter analyses: (1) the demand for labor, (2) the supply of labor, (3) the efficiency of a perfectly competitive equilibrium and how to measure the efficiency loss if the equilibrium is disturbed, (4) the distribution of income between workers and other factors of production, and (5) the effects of minimum wage legislation.

The Demand for Labor

The demand for labor depends upon the marginal productivity of labor (MPL). Under the assumption that a firm sells its output in a perfectly competitive market the firm's MPL is equal to the price of its output times the marginal physical product of labor. The profit-maximizing firm will demand labor up to the point where the MPL is just equal to the wage rate (W). (For if MPL were greater than W the firm could increase its profits by hiring more workers, and if MPL were less than W the firm could increase its profits by hiring fewer workers.) Thus the MPL curve shows how much the firm will hire at each possible wage. In other words, the MPL curve *is the same thing* as the firm's labor demand curve. (The argument here is essentially the same as the one used in Chapter 20 to show that a consumer's marginal utility curve is the same thing as his or her demand curve.)

A firm's demand for labor schedule slopes down because of diminishing returns (recall this concept from Chapter 21). As a firm hires more and more labor (with other factors fixed), it eventually finds that the marginal physical product of labor diminishes.

There are two reasons why a firm's labor demand curve might shift. (1) If the price of the firm's output rises this will shift the MPL up; in other words, it will shift the demand curve. (2) If the firm's marginal physical product of labor shifts up, its MPL and demand curve will also shift. This might occur, for example, because of (a) an increase in the amount of capital employed by the firm, which makes labor physically more productive by providing it with more machinery to work with; or (b) any technological improvement that allows a firm to get more physical output from its workers. (Generally speaking, increased capital equipment and technological change come together, but it is possible for one to occur without the other.)

The market demand curve for labor is just the horizontal sum of the individual firms' demand curves for labor. (Recall how this summation was done at the beginning of Chapter 20.)

The Supply of Labor

The labor supply curve for an industry is derived much like the supply curve for any commodity (as in Chapter 21). The height of the labor supply curve at any point indicates how much must be paid to attract one more worker into the industry. This is (roughly) the wage that the extra worker could earn in another industry. In other words, the height of the labor supply curve is just the opportunity cost of an additional worker.

Efficiency

Social efficiency requires that labor be hired in an industry up to the point where its marginal social cost is just equal to its marginal social benefit. If there are no externalities, then the marginal social benefit equals the MPL (that is, the height of the demand curve) and the marginal social cost is the opportunity cost of labor (that is, the height of the supply curve). In this case, a competitive equilibrium, where supply equals demand, results in a socially efficient level of employment in an industry. This argument is summarized in Box 30-1. Compare it to the similar argument in Chapter 22.

When a labor market has been shifted away from a perfectly competitive equilibrium, the efficiency loss can be measured by the triangle between the demand curve, the supply curve, and the vertical line at the actual quantity of employment, as in Figure 30-7 in the textbook. Remember that this measure is only valid under the twin assumptions of (1) perfect competition, and (2) no externalities. If any of this is not clear, you should review your understanding of Chapter 22.

In summary, a perfectly competitive labor market *may* be socially efficient. However, we cannot go immediately to the conclusion that a free unregulated labor market is "best," for the following four reasons: (1) In an unregulated market, employers may practice unfair discrimination, and thus violate the mobility assumption of perfect competition (see the discussion in Appendix 30-A). (2) In an unregulated market, employers may have market power, thus violating another assumption of perfect competition. (3) There may be externalities. (4) Even if none of these problems arises—and an unregulated labor market is efficient—it may not provide a desirable distribution of income. (The problems involved in dealing with this issue are discussed in Chapter 35.)

The Distribution of Income

The total revenue in an industry is just the sum of the marginal productivities of each worker. In other words, total revenue is just the area under the MPL curve for the industry to the left of the quantity of employment. Of that revenue, the amount going to workers is the quantity of employment times the wage. In Figure 30-4 in the textbook, this is just the rectangular area 2, and the amount going to others (in the form of salaries, rent, interest, and profit) is the triangular area 1 above the equilibrium wage. Notice that this measure of "other" income is defined geometrically in the same sort of way as consumer surplus. It may help to review this measurement technique from Chapter 20.

Minimum Wages

When a competitive labor market is subjected to a minimum wage (above the equilibrium wage), there are four important effects, as illustrated in Figure 30-5 in the textbook: (1) Employment is reduced. (2) The wage received by workers who are still employed rises, so that the overall effect on total labor income is uncertain. If the demand for labor is elastic, labor income will fall, and if the demand for labor is inelastic, it will rise. (According to most estimates it is inelastic, with an elasticity of 0.5 or less.) (3) The amount of income going to other factors of production will definitely decrease, because the triangle under the demand curve has shrunk. (4) There will be an overall efficiency loss. Generally speaking, this will be measured by a triangle, as in Figure 30-7, but when the supply of labor schedule is vertical, it is measured by the four-sided figure in Figure 30-5.

These four effects can be predicted from our theory. There is also an effect that experience has taught us: The unemployment created by minimum wage legislation falls most heavily on teenagers and nonwhites.

There are four important qualifications to this analysis: (1) Even if the minimum wage raises total labor income, workers may not feel that they benefit overall from the change. Even though jobs pay better now, they are harder to find, and hard-pressed employers may no longer offer on-the-job training. (2) The amount of unemployment created will depend upon the comprehensiveness of the minimum wage legislation. In the United States in 1965, 6 to 7 percent of the labor force were in jobs not covered by the minimum wage legislation. (3) There may be an efficiency gain not captured in the diagram if the high wages induce employers to discover new labor-saving techniques. (4) The analysis, as we shall see in the next chapter, depends crucially upon the assumption of perfect competition.

IMPORTANT TERMS

Derived demand   Demand that exists because a good or service is used to produce something else. An example is the demand for labor to produce autos or for land to grow wheat

Marginal physical product of labor   The additional number of units of output that a firm can produce by hiring one more worker.

Marginal productivity of labor   The additional revenue that a firm can earn by hiring one more worker.

Opportunity cost of labor   The opportunity cost of labor in a particular industry is the amount that an additional worker could earn in another industry.

True-False Questions

T F   1. The demand for labor schedule shifts to the right whenever the marginal productivity of labor schedule shifts to the right.

T F   2. If a labor market is always in a competitive equilibrium, then a rightward shift in the labor supply schedule will increase the amount of employment and will reduce the marginal productivity of the last worker hired.

T F   3. If the marginal productivity of labor is less than the wage, a perfectly competitive firm can increase its profits by hiring more labor.

T F   4. The geometric measure of *labor* income using a labor demand curve is identical to the geometric measure of consumer surplus using a consumer demand curve.

T F   5. One effect of an increase in the minimum wage is a decrease in the total income going to factors or production other than labor.

T F   6. An increase in the minimum wage will not reduce economic efficiency if the demand for labor is elastic.

T F   7. Even if there is an external cost to employing labor, a perfectly competitive labor market will still be efficient.

T F   8. The height of the labor supply curve is (approximately) equal to the opportunity cost of labor.

T F   9. A rightward shift in the labor supply schedule in a market may eliminate the inefficiency resulting from a minimum wage in that market.

T F   10. A rightward shift in the labor demand schedule may eliminate the inefficiency resulting from a minimum wage in that market.

Multiple-Choice Questions

1. A perfectly competitive firm's demand curve for labor slopes down because, as the firm hires more, there is
  (a) A decreasing wage
  (b) Decreasing marginal cost
  (c) Diminishing marginal utility
  (d) Diminishing marginal physical productivity

2. Which of the following events is most likely to cause a rightward shift in an industry's demand for labor schedule?
  (a) A decrease in the wage rate in that industry
  (b) A decrease in the amount of capital employed in that industry
  (c) An increase in the price of the output of that industry
  (d) An increase in the work force in that industry

3. If there are no externalities in a labor market and the market is in a perfectly competitive equilibrium, then the height of the labor demand curve at the existing quantity of employment equals
  (a) The marginal productivity of labor
  (b) The opportunity cost of labor
  (c) The marginal social benefit of employing another worker in the industry
  (d) All the above

4. If the labor supply curve is vertical, then a technological improvement that increases the marginal physical product of labor will cause
  (a) An increase in the wage and no change in employment
  (b) An increase in both the wage and employment
  (c) An increase in employment and no change in the wage
  (d) A decrease in the wage and no change in employment

5. Whether or not externalities are present, the socially efficient amount of employment will occur in a labor market if the marginal social cost of employing labor equals
  (a) The marginal productivity of labor
  (b) The marginal social benefit of employing labor
  (c) The wage rate
  (d) The marginal physical product of labor

6. The total area under an industry's demand for labor schedule to the left of the existing quantity of employment equals
  (a) The total revenue received in the industry
  (b) The total income of labor in the industry
  (c) Total profits in the industry
  (d) The income received by other factors in the industry

7. Which of the following is *not* an effect of introducing a minimum wage law in a perfectly competitive labor market with no externalities?
  (a) The quantity of employment falls
  (b) The wage received by employed workers rises

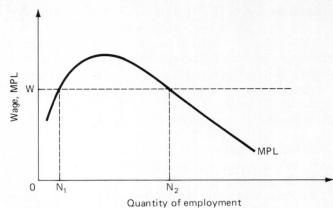

FIGURE 30-1

  (c) The total income of labor rises if the demand for labor is elastic
  (d) There will be an overall efficiency loss

8. It has been commonly observed that the unemployment created by minimum wage legislation is particularly severe among
  (a) Teenagers
  (b) White collar workers
  (c) White workers
  (d) All the above

9. The opportunity cost of labor in an industry
  (a) Is approximately measured by the height of the labor demand schedule
  (b) Is approximately measured by the height of the labor supply schedule
  (c) Decreases as employment in the industry increases
  (d) Is increased for any given quantity of employment when technological change increases the productivity of workers in that industry

10. Suppose that a perfectly competitive firm's marginal productivity of labor (MPL) schedule looks like the one in Figure 30-1. When the wage rate is *W*, the firm will
  (a) Demand the quantity N_1 of labor
  (b) Demand the quantity N_2 of labor
  (c) Be equally satisfied with the quantity N_1 or the quantity N_2 of labor
  (d) Demand some quantity of labor between N_1 and N_2

11. The elasticity of demand for labor is usually estimated to be
  (a) 0.5 or less   **(c)** Between 1.0 and 1.5
  (b) Between 0.5 and 1.0   **(d)** 1.5 or more

*12. The most likely result of discrimination against men in a perfectly competitive market for nurses' labor is
  (a) A decrease in the income received by male nurses
  (b) A decrease in the wages of female nurses
  (c) An efficiency loss
  (d) An increase in employment of male nurses

Exercises

1. Fill in the missing data in Table 30-1 for a hypothetical firm with a given stock of capital, and selling its output in a competitive market at a constant price.

Table 30-1

Number of workers	Total physical output	Marginal physical product	Marginal productivity of labor when price of output equals $10 per unit	Marginal productivity of labor when price of output equals $15 per unit
0	0	—	—	—
1	12			
2	19			
3	24			
4	28			
5	30			

If the wage rate is $55 per worker per day, then the firm will want to hire _____ workers when the price of its output is $10, and _____ workers when this price is $15.

2. Fill in the missing data in Table 30-2 for another hypothetical firm in the same situation, assuming that the wage is $40 per worker per day and the price of output is $5.

Table 30-2

Number of workers	Total physical output	Marginal physical product	Marginal productivity of labor
0	0	—	—
1		10	
2		9	
3		8	
4		7	
5		6	

The firm will be willing to hire no more than _____ workers. With this amount of employment the firm's total revenue will be _____, the total income of labor will be _____, and the income of other factors will be _____.

Plot the labor demand schedule of this firm in Figure 30-2. Draw a horizontal line at the wage rate $40 per worker per day and put a number 1 inside the measure of labor income. Put a number 2 inside the measure of income going to other factors.

3. Figure 30-3 depicts a perfectly competitive labor market with no externalities. The equilibrium wage rate equals _____. The equilibrium quantity of employment equals _____. Suppose the minimum wage equals U. Then the actual quantity of employment will equal _____. Next, suppose the minimum wage equals H. Then the actual quantity of employment will equal _____ and the difference between demand and supply will equal _____. Fill in Table 30-3.

FIGURE 30-2

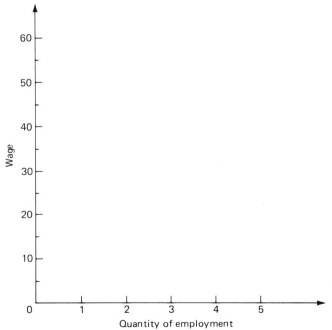

FIGURE 30-3

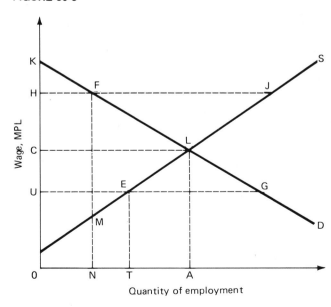

Table 30-3

	Efficiency loss	Total labor income	Income of other factors
No minimum wage			
Minimum wage U			
Minimum wage H			

Essay Questions

1. "The labor demand schedule slopes down for the same reason that the demand curve for a consumer good slopes down." Explain to what extent this is or is not true.

2. List and explain some influences that could shift the labor supply curve in an industry.

3. See if you can list four factors affecting the elasticity of demand for labor, analogous to the four factors affecting the elasticity of demand for a consumer good discussed in Chapter 19.

4. Show by means of a diagram how the effects in a labor market of a minimum wage law can be offset by an employment subsidy; that is, a policy of paying firms a certain amount for each worker they hire.

5. Discuss the relationship between a firm's marginal physical product of labor schedule (MPP) and its short-run marginal cost schedule (MC). Will a shift in MPP shift MC? Why or why not? Is it true that if marginal physical productivity is increasing at first then marginal cost must be decreasing at first? Why or why not?

*6. Would you expect the supply curve for labor as a whole in the United States to be more or less elastic than the supply curve for labor in a particular industry? How would the elasticity of the supply of labor in a particular market be affected by a decrease in the cost of moving from one city to another?

*7. Would you expect labor market discrimination to be more of a problem in a perfectly competitive industry or in a monopolistic industry? Why?

Answers

True-False Questions: 1 T 2 T 3 F 4 F 5 T 6 F 7 F 8 T 9 F 10 T

Multiple-Choice Questions: 1 d 2 c 3 d 4 a 5 b 6 a 7 c 8 a 9 b 10 b 11 a 12 c

Exercises:

1. Table 30-1

W	0	MPP	MPL p = 10	MPL p = 15
0	0	—	—	—
1	12	12	120	180
2	19	7	70	105
3	24	5	50	75
4	28	4	40	60
5	30	2	20	30

2, 4

2. Table 30-2

TPO	MPL
0	—
10	50
19	45
27	40
34	35
40	30

3, 135, 120, 15

FIGURE 30-2

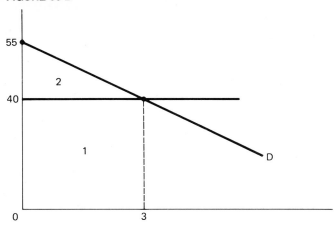

3. *C, A, A, N, HF, FJ*

Table 30-3

O	*OCLA*	*KLC*
O	*OCLA*	*KLC*
FLM	*OHFN*	*KFH*

CHAPTER 31
Wages in Imperfectly Competitive Labor Markets

Learning Objectives

After you have studied this chapter in the textbook and the study guide, you should be able to

Describe how union membership has changed in three distinct periods of U.S. labor history

Identify four important laws in U.S. labor history and state their major provisions

Show in a diagram the effects of introducing a union that succeeds in raising wages in an otherwise perfectly competitive labor market

Explain the effects of introducing a featherbedding agreement into an otherwise perfectly competitive labor market

Describe how unions improve efficiency

Show how the effects of introducing a union into an otherwise perfectly competitive labor market are changed if the market is monopsonistic

Explain why a strike may occur even though no one really gains from it

Identify three ways of averting an imminent strike

Explain why it might not be in the "public interest" to allow unions to develop in the public service

State four reasons why not every worker gets the same wage

CHAPTER HIGHLIGHTS

In real life, many labor markets are not perfectly competitive. This chapter studies what happens when there is *im*perfect competition. The issues discussed are: (1) the history of the labor union movement in the United States; (2) the effects of introducing a union into an otherwise perfectly competitive labor market; (3) the effects of introducing a monopsony (single buyer) into an otherwise perfectly competitive labor market; (4) what happens in a labor market with bilateral monopoly—that is, a union bargaining with a monopsony; (5) the special problems of the market for public service employees; and (6) why wages aren't the same for all workers.

History

Figure 31-1 in the textbook shows that there are three distinct periods in United States labor history:

1. Prior to 1935, union membership was very low. The most important large union, the AFL, was mainly a craft union. Strikes were not an effective union tactic because employers could easily get a court injunction forcing workers back to their jobs. This was ended in 1932 by the Norris-LaGuardia Act, which limited injunctions to protecting property and preventing violence.

2. From 1935 to 1945 union membership grew rapidly, aided by two major events:
   a. The founding in 1936 of the CIO, which favored the development of industrial unions
   b. The Wagner Act of 1935 which
      (1) Made it clear that workers had the right to form a union
      (2) Prohibited various unfair labor practices of employers
      (3) Established the NLRB to control these unfair labor practices and to settle disputes between unions.

3. Since 1945, union membership has fallen steadily as a proportion of total employment. There are four major reasons generally cited for this fall:
   a. Employment in heavy industry, which is highly unionized, has fallen as a proportion of total employment
   b. Much heavy industry has also moved to the relatively nonunionized south
   c. After the recovery from the massive unemployment of the Great Depression, unions no longer had such strong public sympathy and support
   d. During World War II many people felt that unions had used their newly gained power irresponsibly, and this generated some public hostility toward unions.

You should be familiar with two major labor laws of this third period. The first is the Taft-Hartley Act of 1947, which

1. Outlawed closed shops in industries engaged in interstate commerce

2. Outlawed jurisdictional strikes

3. Outlawed the practice of checking off union fees

4. Imposed restrictions on union leaders designed to make them more responsible financially

5. Empowered the President to seek a court injunction forcing strikers to return to work for an 80-day "cooling off" period in the case of a strike that endangers national health or safety

6. In its famous section 14(b), declared that union shops are illegal in any state that decides to pass a right-to-work law.

The other major law is the Landrum-Griffin Act of 1959, which imposed even more financial restrictions upon union leaders and strengthened the power of union members to challenge their leaders in various ways.

The Effects of Unions

A union gives workers a voice in presenting grievances to their employer. It also works with management to establish seniority rules and working conditions. These benefit not only the workers but also the employer, who is able to attract better workers because better jobs are being offered.

But the main objective of a union is to get high wages for its members. (According to recent estimates, unionized workers get 10 to 18 percent higher wages than comparable nonunionized workers.) If a union is established and manages to raise the wage in a previously competitive labor market with no externalities, there are three main effects: (1) Employment in that market falls, (2) incomes of other factors fall, and (3) an efficiency loss is created that can be measured by the usual geometric technique. Study Figure 31-2 in the textbook until you can demonstrate these three effects on your own.

Another objective of a union is to protect its members' jobs, which it does in two ways:

1. It tries to negotiate a shorter work week. This restricts the supply of labor (number of hours worked) without necessarily reducing the number of jobs.

2. It can negotiate a featherbedding agreement. There are three main effects of introducing a featherbedding agreement into a previously competitive labor market with no externalities.
   a. Employment in that market increases
   b. An efficiency loss arises, not just for the usual reason that the quantity of employment differs from the competitive equilibrium quantity, but also because with featherbedding workers may be employed at useless tasks instead of useful ones

c. Job security of members on the union involved may be increased. However, common sense tells us that there are better ways of providing job security.

This analysis of unions may be overly harsh. Unions improve efficiency in at least three ways: First, by giving workers a voice, they allow an alternative to quitting or being fired when a problem arises. Thus, they save unnecessary costs of labor turnover. Second, by improving working conditions they can reduce the tension between workers and employers, and create an atmosphere in which more level-headed decisions can be made. Third, they can, as we shall see, offset the efficiency loss due to market power on the employers' side. (Remember that the efficiency losses discussed earlier apply only when the market would be perfectly competitive in the union's absence.)

Monopsony

A monopsonistic employer tries to exploit its market power by keeping wages below what they would be in perfect competition. If it succeeds, the three main effects will be to (1) reduce employment in that market, (2) create an efficiency loss, and (3) increase the income going to factors of production other than labor. Study Figure 31-3 in the textbook until you can demonstrate these three effects on your own.

Bilateral Monopoly

In many labor markets it is probably most realistic to assume bilateral monopoly. Unfortunately, this case is also the most difficult to analyze. This chapter discusses three issues concerning bilateral monopoly: (1) why the effects of introducing a union may be different when there is a monopsony than when the market is otherwise perfectly competitive, (2) the indeterminancy of the outcome where there is bilateral monopoly, and (3) the problem of strikes.

1. If a union succeeds in raising the wage in a monopsonistic market, the effects may be entirely different than the case of the competitive market that we have already studied. In particular, suppose that after the union has been formed the wage is still below what it would have been in a competitive market. In this case, the union will be simply undoing some of the effects of the monopsony. That is, it will be raising the wage from the low level set by the monopsonist, toward the higher level of perfect competition. In this way the formation of the union will (a) reduce the efficiency loss of monopsony, (b) increase employment, (c) increase the income going

to labor, and (d) reduce the income going to other factors of production. This is illustrated in Figure 31-5 in the textbook.

2. However, there is no guarantee that a bilateral monopoly will produce a wage below the competitive wage. All that we know for sure is that the wage will be no lower than the monopsony wage and no higher than the wage that the union would like to set. Between these two extremes there is no way of predicting exactly where the wage will be. It depends mainly upon the bargaining power of each side. This in turn depends partly on the ability of each to outlast the other in the event of a strike. Thus, the bargaining power of the union depends upon the size of the union's strike fund. The bargaining power of the employer depends upon the size of its inventories of finished goods, which would allow it to continue doing business during a strike, and also upon its ability to survive the delays that would be imposed by a strike.

3. In a sense nobody gains from a strike. The company loses income, which could have gone partly to labor and partly to other factors of production, thus making everyone better off. But strikes occur nevertheless, because (a) each side sees a strike as a means of doing better than the other side's "final offer;" (b) each side may want to demonstrate that even a strike will not make it back down, in order to improve its bargaining power next time around; or (c) breakdowns in communication can be caused by mistakes on either side, preventing agreement from being reached before a strike deadline. (Nevertheless, the average U.S. worker spends less than one day a year on strike).

The main reason why strikes pose an important issue for public policy is spillovers. Strikes can be costly to people not involved in the bargaining, as when a transit strike prevents people from getting to their jobs. There are three main ways of averting a strike when the two sides are unable to reach agreement on their own. (a) The President may seek a Taft-Hartley injunction (see "History" above). The Federal Mediation Service may then help find an agreement during the cooling-off period. (b) Both sides may agree to voluntary arbitration, in which a third party decides upon a settlement that both sides agree in advance to accept. (c) If they don't agree to voluntary arbitration, the government may force them to accept compulsory arbitration.

Public Service Employees

It has been argued that allowing unions to develop in the public service would not be in the "public interest," for the following four reasons:

1. Their strike weapon would be too strong because of the large spillover effects involved.

2. Politicians would find it too easy to give in to the unions, which would mean higher taxes to pay the wage bill.

3. A financially weak government does not have the same bargaining power as a financially weak private employer, because it can't argue that a high wage settlement will force it out of business.

4. Because public service employees now constitute a large bloc of voters, there is an incentive for politicians to try to influence their votes by offering high wages.

Although these problems cannot be denied, nevertheless, workers in the public sector need some defense against a monopsonistic employer (the government). If not a union, what else?

Wage Differences

Wage differences can exist for at least five different reasons: First, *dynamic differentials* can exist temporarily. When new job opportunities open up in an industry, wages must rise temporarily to attract workers from other industries. Eventually, the influx of new workers will bring the wages back down. Second, *compensating* wage differentials give workers more pay for especially hazardous or unpleasant jobs. Third, monopoly or monopsony power may be greater in some labor markets than in others. Fourth, other elements of imperfect competition, like barriers to entry and discrimination, can keep wages artificially high in some jobs. Fifth, those with special talents and skills earn a higher wage because their marginal productivity is higher.

IMPORTANT TERMS

Seniority rules Rules that give preference to those who have been longest on the job. Individuals with seniority are typically the last to be laid off, and the first to be rehired.

Industrial union A union whose members all work in the same industry, or group of industries, although they may belong to different crafts or professions. Examples are the United Auto Workers and the United Mine Workers.

Craft union A union whose members all belong to the same craft or profession, although they may work in different industries. Examples are plumbers' and carpenters' union.

Collective bargaining Negotiations between a union and an employer over wages, fringe benefits, hiring policies, job security, or working conditions.

AFL The American Federation of Labor, formed in the 1880s by Samuel Gompers.

National Labor Relations Act The Wagner Act of 1935 (described under "History").

CIO The Congress of Industrial Organizations, a big union organization that, under the leadership of John L. Lewis, broke away from the AFL in 1936. In 1955 they reunited to form the AFL–CIO.

Closed shop A situation in which an employer can hire only workers who are already union members.

Union shop A situation in which anyone hired by an employer must join the union within some specified period.

Open shop A situation in which employees do not have to join a union.

Right-to-work law A law making closed shops or union shops illegal.

Jurisdictional disputes Conflicts between unions over whose members will do specific jobs.

Checking off The practice of having employers collect union dues by deducting them from workers' paychecks.

Featherbedding Employing labor in superfluous jobs.

Monopsony A market in which there is only one buyer.

Strike fund A sum of money owned by a union for the purpose of supporting its members while on strike.

Injunction A court order compelling someone to refrain from a particular act, as when workers are compelled to end a strike.

Mediation The intervention of a third party to suggest a compromise settlement in a labor dispute. The mediator cannot make any binding recommendations. Also called conciliation. The Federal Mediation Service assists in mediation.

Arbitration Like mediation, except that the recommendation of the arbitrator is binding upon both parties. Even though the recommendation is binding, arbitration is called *voluntary* when both sides agree to call in an arbitrator. *Compulsory* arbitration involves the government forcing both parties to call an arbitrator in.

Dynamic wage differentials Differences in wages that arise because of changing demand or supply conditions in the labor market. They tend to disappear over time as labor moves out of the relatively low wage jobs and into those that pay a relatively high wage.

Compensating wage differentials Differences that may arise if labor views some jobs as less attractive than others. (Employers have to pay a higher wage to fill the unattractive jobs.)

True-False Questions

T F   **1.** Union membership was a higher proportion of total employment in the United States in 1945 than it is now.

T F   **2.** In its early years the AFL was mainly an industrial union.

T F   **3.** The Taft-Hartley Act empowered the President to seek an injunction forcing strikers to return to work for an 80-day "cooling off" period if a strike endangers national health or safety.

T F   **4.** One of the factors contributing to the decline in union membership since 1945 has been the decline in employment in heavy industry as a proportion of total employment.

T F   **5.** The Taft-Hartley Act outlawed closed shops in industries engaged in interstate commerce.

T F   **6.** The Landrum-Griffin Act is also called the National Labor Relations Act.

T F   **7.** If a union succeeds in raising wages above what they would be in perfect competition, this will raise the total income of labor in that market if the demand curve for labor is elastic.

T F   **8.** If a union manages to raise wages, this may not create an efficiency loss if there is a monopsonist employer.

T F   **9.** If employers are seeking to reduce employment (labor hours), then negotiating for a shorter work week is one method whereby a union may attempt to protect jobs.

T F   **10.** Featherbedding is usually an efficient way of increasing job security.

T F   **11.** A company with huge inventories of finished goods has less bargaining power, and therefore will probably have to settle for a higher wage in negotiating with its union, than a company with no inventories.

T F   **12.** Under voluntary arbitration the recommendation of the arbitrator is not binding.

T F   **13.** Dynamic wage differentials tend to go away over time.

Multiple-Choice Questions

1. During which of the following four periods did union membership grow fastest in the United States as a proportion of total employment?

(a) 1915–1925   (c) 1935–1945
(b) 1925–1935   (d) 1945–1955

2. Which of the following acts was legislated first?

(a) Norris-La Guardia   (c) Landrum-Griffin
(b) Taft-Hartley   (d) Wagner

3. Which of the following statements about the Wagner Act is *in*correct?

(a) It outlawed jurisdictional strikes
(b) It established that workers clearly had the right to form a union
(c) It established the NLRB
(d) It prohibited various unfair labor practices of employers

4. Union membership has fallen steadily as a proportion of total employment since 1945, partly because

(a) Employment in heavy industry has increased as a proportion of total employment
(b) The AFL and CIO amalgamated in 1955
(c) Public support for unions declined when the massive unemployment of the Great Depression disappeared
(d) Much heavy industry has moved to the north

5. Which of the following acts outlawed closed shops in industries engaged in interstate commerce?

(a) Norris-La Guardia   (c) Landrum-Griffin
(b) Taft-Hartley   (d) Wagner

6. Which of the following is *most* likely to occur if a union is introduced into a previously competitive labor market with no externalities?

(a) Employment in that market will increase
(b) Incomes of factors of production other than labor will decrease

(c) An efficiency gain will result
(d) Total income to labor will decrease

7. Unionized workers in the United States are estimated to earn wages that are how much larger than comparable nonunionized workers?

(a) 10–18 percent   (c) 40–50 percent
(b) 35–40 percent   (d) 55–73 percent

8. Long apprenticeships

(a) Restrict the supply of labor
(b) Raise union wages
(c) Raise the incomes of union members who have already passed their apprenticeships
(d) All the above

9. Introducing a featherbedding agreement into an otherwise perfectly competitive labor market with no externalities creates an efficiency loss partly because

(a) Job security of the members of the union is reduced
(b) The quantity of employment is less than the competitive equilibrium quantity
(c) Workers may be employed at useless tasks instead of useful ones
(d) All the above

10. Introducing a union into a monopsonistic labor market with no externalities will probably cause

(a) An efficiency loss
(b) An efficiency gain
(c) Neither an efficiency loss nor gain
(d) An efficiency gain if wages have been raised but are still below the perfectly competitive level

11. Which of the following is *most* likely to lead to a high wage settlement?

(a) A large union strike fund
(b) A large stock of inventories held by the employer
(c) Compulsory arbitration
(d) A right-to-work law

12. Which of the following does *not* involve a third party making a decision that is binding on one or both parties to a dispute?

(a) Injunction (c) Voluntary arbitration
(b) Mediation (d) Compulsory arbitration

13. Which of the following is the *best* example of how unions may improve efficiency?

(a) Raising wages above what they would be under perfect competition
(b) Striking against unfair employers
(c) Featherbedding
(d) Reducing labor turnover by giving workers the chance to present their grievances rather than quit or be fired

14. Which of the following is the best example of a compensating wage differential?

(a) The high wages that exist temporarily in a state when the demand for labor suddenly increases there
(b) The high wages you can get if your union succeeds in erecting barriers to entry in your line of work
(c) The high wages you have to pay people risking their lives working as firefighters
(d) The high wages earned by workers with the most seniority

Exercises

1a. Figure 31-1 depicts supply (S) and demand (D) in a perfectly competitive labor market with no externalities. The equilibrium wage equals _____ and the equilibrium quantity of employment equals _____. In perfect competition the income of labor equals _____, and the income of other factors equals _____.

b. Suppose now that a union is formed, which increases the wage to equal *OG*. Then the quantity of employment will equal _____, the income going to labor will equal _____, the income going to other factors will equal _____, and the efficiency loss will equal _____.

c. Now suppose that there is an externality. In particular, the marginal social cost of employment is really indicated by the curve labeled MSC rather than by the supply curve. Then the socially efficient quantity of employment will equal _____. In perfect competition the wage will equal _____, the quantity of employment will equal _____, and the efficiency loss will equal _____.

d. With this externality, if a union is formed to raise wages to *OG*, then the quantity of employment will equal _____ and the efficiency loss will equal _____.

2a. Table 31-1 below depicts the situation in the labor market of an industry with a given stock of capital. Column I indicates the number of workers

FIGURE 31-1

per day and column II indicates total output of the industry. Fill in column III, indicating the marginal physical product of labor, and column IV, indicating the marginal productivity of labor when the output price is $15 per unit. Column V indicates the wage on the labor supply curve. If the market is perfectly competitive, then the wage will equal _____, the amount of employment will equal _____ workers, the total revenue in the industry will be _____, the total income of labor in the industry will equal

Table 31-1

I	II	III	IV	V	VI	VII	VIII	IX
0	0	—	—	0				
1	5	5		2				
2	9			4				
3	12			18				
4	14			30				
5	15			40				

_____, and the total income of other factors will equal _____.

b. Now suppose that all the firms act in the labor market as a single monopsonist. The monopsonist realizes that whatever wage it offers, the total quantity of employment will be determined by the labor-supply curve, and the output price is constant at $15 per unit. Fill in column VI indicating the monopsonist's total revenue, column VII indicating total labor cost, and column VIII indicating the total amount of income to other factors. Suppose that the only other factor is "entrepreneurship." In other words, the income of other factors is all income to the monopsonist. If the monopsonist wants to maximize its income it will hire _____ workers at a wage of $ _____. The monopsonist's marginal factor cost of labor (MFC) is the amount by which labor cost increases whenever the monoposonist hires one more worker. Fill in column IX indicating the monopsonist's MFC. Compare columns IV and IX. What equilibrium conditions does this suggest that governs the employment decision of the monopsonist?

Essay Questions

1. Argue the case that before 1945 Congress tended to support the development of union power but that since 1945 congressional actions have reduced union power.

2. Can you think of any possible legal changes that would improve efficiency by strengthening the powers of unions? Can you think of any that would improve efficiency by weakening their powers? Which of these measures do you think would also be worthwhile on grounds of equity?

3. Chapter 30 showed how an increase in the minimum wage would reduce the amount of employment in a perfectly competitive labor market. Show by reference to Figure 31-3 in the textbook that in a monopsonistic labor market the effect of increasing the minimum wage may be to increase the amount of employment.

4. How would the bargaining power of a union be influenced by a reduction in the cost to its members of leaving town to get another job?

5. Recall the problems of producers' associations discussed in Appendix 23-A. In what sense are these same problems shared by labor unions?

6. What spillovers would probably occur if each of the following went on strike?

a. Municipal garbage workers

b. Air traffic controllers

c. City police

d. Steel workers

e. Doctors

7. Argue the case that public service employees should be allowed to form unions and strike. Argue the opposite case.

8. Is it *possible* for a monopsonist to offer such a low wage that its profit is actually less than what it would be in a perfectly competitive industry? Is it *likely*?

9. In the summer of 1980 the orchestra members of New York's Metropolitan Opera went on strike. Their union thought they had a lot of bargaining power because of the opera's recent financial success. Why might this strengthen the union's bargaining power? Why might that bargaining power also have been strengthened by the knowledge that the opera stood to gain a lot from the nationally televised live performances that were to begin in the fall of 1980? After failing to reach agreement with the union, the management of the opera announced that the whole season would have to be canceled, and offered to refund the tickets already bought. What spillovers would result from a canceled season? Even if there were no spillovers, how does this episode illustrate that there really aren't any gainers from a strike? How does it illustrate how strikes can result from miscalculations? Eventually, one more round of negotiations was undertaken, agreement was reached, and management announced that the season could proceed after all, but with fewer operas than planned. Do you suppose that the first announcement (of cancellation) helped to speed up a resolution of the strike? Why or why not? Why do you suppose management made that early announcement when it turned out not to be true?

Answers

True-False Questions: **1** T **2** F **3** T **4** T **5** T **6** F **7** F **8** T **9** T **10** F **11** F **12** F **13** T
Multiple-Choice Questions: **1** c **2** d **3** a **4** c **5** b **6** b **7** a **8** d **9** c **10** d **11** a **12** b **13** d **14** c
Exercises: **1a.** *OR, OF, OREF, TER* **b.** *OH, OGIH, TIG, IEL* **c.** *OA, OR, OF, ECN* **d.** *OH, ICK*
2.

I	II	III	IV	V	VI	VII	VIII	IX
0	0	—	—	0	0	0	0	—
1	5	5	75	2	75	2	73	2
2	9	4	60	4	135	8	127	6
3	12	3	45	18	180	54	126	46
4	14	2	30	30	210	120	90	66
5	15	1	15	40	225	200	25	80

a. 30, 4, 210, 120, 90 **b.** 2, 4, MPL equals MFC.

CHAPTER 32
Other Incomes

Learning Objectives

After you have studied this chapter in the textbook and the study guide, you should be able to

Explain the concepts of debt capital, equity capital, physical capital, and human capital

Explain why the marginal efficiency of investment schedule is identical to the demand schedule for loanable funds

Show in a diagram the likely effects of imposing an interest rate ceiling upon a perfectly competitive market for loanable funds

Explain why it is a fallacy to suppose that interest rate ceilings necessarily help poor people

State the reasons for believing that investment in human capital may be less than the efficient amount

State the reasons for believing that investment in human capital may be more than the efficient amount

Give two possible reasons why the rate of return on investment in human capital has decreased since 1969

Explain why it is difficult to measure the rate of return on human capital

List five examples of economic rent

Describe the two basic roles played by factor prices in a market economy

CHAPTER HIGHLIGHTS

About one-quarter of national income in the United States does not go to labor. This chapter studies what determines those other incomes, mainly interest, profit, and rent. The specific issues discussed are (1) how the rate of interest is determined in the market for loanable funds, (2) the return to human capital (3) the nature and significance of economic rent, and (4) the role of factor prices in the economic system.

The Rate of Interest

The rate of interest measures the rate at which present goods may be converted into future goods, through "roundabout" methods of production. This

236

rate may be regarded as the price that clears the market for loanable funds. The demand for loanable funds is just the marginal efficiency of investment schedule that we have already encountered in Chapter 12. The supply of loanable funds measures the willingness of savers to part with present income and wait until the loan is repaid. The higher the rate of interest the greater their reward, and the more they are willing to save.

In practice, there is not one rate of interest but many. These differences are accounted for mainly by risk. The greater the risk that a borrower will be unable to repay his or her loan, the higher the rate of interest this borrower will have to pay.

An important issue studied in this section is that of interest-rate ceilings. When the government imposes a ceiling on interest rates in a perfectly competitive loan market with no externalities, there are four main effects: (1) The public saves less because the interest reward for saving has been reduced. Consequently, fewer loans are made and there is less investment. (2) Income is transferred from lenders to those borrowers who are still able to acquire loans. (They now pay a lower rate.) (3) There is an efficiency loss shown by the usual triangle in Figure 32-3 in the textbook. (4) There is a further efficiency loss because the borrowers who are rationed as a result of the ceiling may have been planning to invest in more profitable investment projects than those who are not rationed. Study Figure 32-3 until you can demonstrate these four effects on your own.

It is a fallacy to suppose that interest-rate ceilings necessarily help poor people. The borrowers that are helped by a ceiling may be quite rich, and those who are rationed because of the ceiling may be quite poor.

Normal profits (recall the definition from Chapter 21) are earned by owners of equity capital. Generally speaking, we estimate the amount of normal profit on equity capital as the amount of interest income that the owner could have earned from lending this capital, plus an appropriate allowance for the riskiness of the equity capital.

Human Capital

There are two main forms of investment in human capital: (1) formal education, and (2) apprenticeship, or on-the-job training.

There are three reasons to believe that investment in human capital may be less than the efficient amount:

1. Minimum wage laws tend to discourage employers from giving on-the-job training, because many employers cannot afford to provide an unskilled worker both the minimum wage and an education.

2. Employers are reluctant to provide on-the-job training because trainees may quit and take their skills elsewhere.

3. There are external benefits from human capital, such as when a highly educated scientist discovers a cure for a disease and thereby benefits the entire population.

However, there are two reasons for thinking that there may be overinvestment in human capital: (1) The government subsidizes education, and (2) people may sometimes add to their education not because it makes them more socially productive but because it gives them a "credential" that potential employers insist upon.

The concept of human capital also gives some insight into the problem of discrimination. Workers suffering from discrimination may not be able to invest in human capital in the form of on-the-job training because they can't get the jobs that provide it. They thus remain unskilled, and earn a lower wage—even from firms that do not practice discrimination.

Statistical measurements of the rate of return on education in the United States show that it has fallen since 1969. There are two reasons commonly cited for this: (1) The supply of educated individuals has shifted to the right since 1969, and (2) because of recently declining school enrollments, the demand for teachers has declined.

It is difficult to obtain precise measurements of the rate of return on human capital, because:

1. People who earn a lot tend to have a lot of education and a lot of native ability. It's hard to sort out how much of their higher income is due to each.

2. It is difficult to measure the external benefits of education.

3. It is difficult to estimate the government subsidy to education.

4. It is difficult to tell if education has increased a worker's productivity or simply given him or her a "credential."

5. Not all education is an investment in human capital; some of it is undoubtedly a consumption good.

6. Much of the return to education is in the form of a more satisfying job—a factor that is difficult to measure.

According to recent estimates, the private rate of return to an undergraduate education is between 8 and 10 percent, and the social rate of return may be as low as 4 percent. The private rate of return to acquiring a Ph.D. seems to be only about 2 percent.

Rent

Perhaps the most important thing to understand about rent is that it can be earned not only by land, but also by other factors of production. It is defined as the earnings of any factor above its opportunity cost. The textbook gives five examples of economic rent:

1. The return to agricultural land because of differences in quality.

2. The return to urban land because of differences in location.

3. The income from owning mineral deposits with low extraction costs and high quality.

4. Above-normal profits earned in an industry with barriers to entry.

5. The return to an individual's labor because of a scarce talent.

A person's wage includes (1) the basic wage, (2) the return to his or her human capital, and (3) the rent on the person's special talents. The opportunity cost of the worker's time is the sum of the first two items.

The Role of Factor Prices

Factor prices do more than determine people's incomes. They also help to determine which factors of production will be allocated to which tasks. For example, when labor becomes more scarce, and capital less scarce, wages rise and the cost of capital falls. This encourages firms to substitute capital for labor. While this may be a painful process for the workers "displaced" by automated capital equipment, it is also the source of most of our material progress since the industrial revolution.

IMPORTANT TERMS

Debt capital   Funds that are lent to businesses (or others) to finance the purchase of machinery or the construction of new buildings.

Equity capital   Funds provided by the owners of a business to purchase machinery or new buildings. (These are the funds that don't have to be borrowed.)

Human capital   Skills, training, and education that can be used for producing goods and services.

Marginal productivity theory   The theory that in perfectly competitive factor markets each factor's price reflects its marginal productivity.

Time preference   A preference for consuming now rather than in the future. This is an important factor underlying the supply curve for loanable funds.

Roundabout production   Investment is often described as "roundabout production" (or "indirect production") of consumer goods. Instead of producing consumer goods now, society first produces the capital goods and then uses these capital goods to help produce consumer goods in the future.

Affirmative action program   A program designed to eliminate discrimination by favoring those who have been its victims in the past.

Economic rent   The "surplus" return to any factor of production in excess of its opportunity cost.

Monopoly rent   The above-normal profits accruing to any individual or business because of the possession of monopoly power.

True-False Questions

T   F   **1.** In the United States, labor income is usually about three times as large as the rest of national income.

T   F   **2.** Debt capital and equity capital are two forms of human capital.

T   F   **3.** If the demand for loanable funds is highly elastic with respect to the rate of interest, then the MEI schedule is highly elastic.

T   F   **4.** The efficiency loss of an interest rate ceiling tends to be overestimated by the usual triangular measurement.

T   F   **5.** Above-normal profit is an example of rent.

T   F   **6.** Government subsidization of higher education is one reason why more than the efficient amount of investment in human capital may occur.

T   F   **7.** The fact that many of the benefits of investment in human capital are external is one reason why less than the efficient amount of investment in human capital may occur.

T F   **8.** Minimum wage laws encourage on-the-job training to be substituted for formal education.

T F   **9.** According to most estimates, the social rate of return on investment in an undergraduate education is greater than the private return.

T F   **10.** The fact that workers may quit is one reason why less than the efficient amount of investment in human capital may occur.

Multiple-Choice Questions:

1. Funds that are lent to a business constitute
- **(a)** Debt capital
- **(b)** Equity capital
- **(c)** Human capital
- **(d)** All the above

2. A rightward shift of the MEI schedule would probably
- **(a)** Increase the rate of interest in a perfectly competitive market
- **(b)** Decrease the quantity of loanable funds in a perfectly competitive market
- **(c)** Reduce the efficiency loss imposed by a given interest rate ceiling
- **(d)** Reduce the amount of roundabout production

3. Which of the following is the most likely result of an interest rate ceiling in a perfectly competitive market for loanable funds with no externalities?
- **(a)** A transfer of income from borrowers to some lenders
- **(b)** A transfer of income from rich to poor
- **(c)** A transfer of income from lenders to some borrowers
- **(d)** A reduction in the incidence of credit rationing

4. The normal profit received by a firm on its equity capital
- **(a)** Is usually greater than the interest income that the owners could receive from lending this capital at the risk-free rate of interest
- **(b)** Is usually less than the interest income that the owners could receive from lending this capital at the risk-free rate of interest
- **(c)** Bears no relationship to the interest income that the owners could get from lending this capital
- **(d)** Is zero if the firm is perfectly competitive

5. Which of the following is a factor tending to result in more than the efficient amount of investment in human capital?
- **(a)** Minimum wage laws
- **(b)** The use of "credentials" as a screening device by employers
- **(c)** The fact that workers may quit voluntarily
- **(d)** The external benefits of investment in human capital

6. The social rate of return on investment in human capital
- **(a)** Has been falling since 1969, partly because of the increase in supply of educated workers
- **(b)** Has been increased by the growth in school enrollments in recent years
- **(c)** Is more for someone acquiring a Ph.D. than for someone acquiring an undergraduate degree
- **(d)** Is usually estimated to be much more than the private rate of return

7. Which of the following is *not* a major problem encountered in trying to measure the rate of return on investment in human capital?
- **(a)** Going to school may be a consumption good
- **(b)** The social rate of return on investment may be as low as 4 percent
- **(c)** There are external benefits to investment in human capital
- **(d)** It is difficult to distinguish the separate effects of innate skills and training

8. Other things being equal, an individual will receive a higher wage if he or she
- **(a)** Has invested in human capital in the past
- **(b)** Possesses a rare talent
- **(c)** Is currently receiving on-the-job training
- **(d)** (a) and (b)

9. Which of the following is *least* likely to be an economic rent?
- **(a)** The income from leasing cars
- **(b)** The return to high-quality land
- **(c)** The return to ownership of high-quality mineral deposits
- **(d)** The above-normal profits of a monopolist

10. A leftward shift in the supply curve of unskilled labor is likely to result in
- **(a)** A fall in prices of goods produced mainly by unskilled labor
- **(b)** A fall in wages of unskilled labor, causing less capital to be used in production
- **(c)** A rise in wages of unskilled labor, which induces more labor-saving innovations
- **(d)** An increase in the amount of goods and services produced mainly by unskilled labor

11. Interest ceilings are an ineffective way to help the poor because
- **(a)** There is no guarantee that the gainers from the interest ceilings on the whole are any poorer than the losers
- **(b)** They increase corporate profits
- **(c)** They cause more of societies' resources to be devoted toward producing capital goods instead of consumer goods
- **(d)** The poor save more than the rich

12. An increase in farm price supports will provide the greatest benefit to
- **(a)** Someone who is about to buy a farm
- **(b)** Someone who is about to sell a farm
- **(c)** Someone who sold a farm just before the increase subsidy was announced
- **(d)** Someone who is renting a farm

Exercises

1a. Figure 32-1 depicts a perfectly competitive market for loanable funds with no externalities. The equilibrium rate of interest in this market equals _____ and the equilibrium quantity of loans equals _____. In a competitive equilibrium the interest income received by lenders would equal _____.

b. If the government imposes an interest rate ceiling equal to OM, then the quantity of loans will equal _____, the MEI will equal _____, the excess demand for loans will equal _____, the interest income received by lenders will equal _____, and the size of the efficiency loss will probably be (more, less) than the area _____.

c. If the size of the interest ceiling is OJ then the size of the efficiency loss will be _____.

2a. Figure 32-2 depicts a perfectly competitive market for a factor of production, where D denotes the demand curve and S_1 denotes the supply curve. In a competitive equilibrium, the factor price would equal _____ and the quantity of employment of the factor would equal _____. The income received by the factor would equal _____ and the income received by all other factors would equal _____.

b. Now suppose that a tax is imposed upon income received by this factor, equal in amount to EL per unit of employed factor. This would shift the supply curve up vertically by the amount EL, so that the after-tax supply curve is the one labeled S_1'. With the tax, the equilibrium price paid by the firms for the factor will equal _____, the equilibrium price received, after tax, by the owners of the factor will equal _____, the quantity of the factor employed will equal _____, the after-tax income accruing to owners of the factor will equal _____, the amount of the tax collected will equal _____, the income received by other factors will equal _____, and the size of the efficiency loss will equal _____.

c. Suppose there is no tax. At C the supply curve S_2 is (more, less) elastic than S_1. With supply curve S_2 the equilibrium factor price will be (more, less, no different) than with S_1 and the equilibrium quantity of employment of the factor will be (more, less, no different) than with S_1.

d. With S_2 a tax will shift the supply curve vertically to the one labeled S_2'. With the tax the equilibrium price paid by the firms for the factor will equal _____, the equilibrium

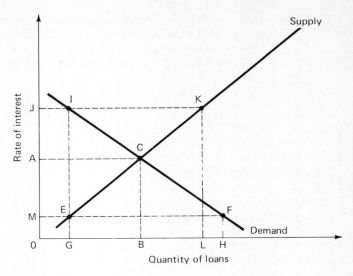

FIGURE 32-1

price received, after tax, by owners of the factor will equal _____, the quantity of employment of the factor will equal _____, the after-tax income accruing to owners of the factor will equal _____, the amount of the tax collected will equal _____, the income received by other factors will equal _____, and the size of the efficiency loss will equal _____.

e. Of the two pretax supply curves, S_1 and S_2, the one which generates the greater tax revenue is (S_1, S_2), the one that produces the smaller efficiency loss from the tax is (S_1, S_2),

FIGURE 32-2

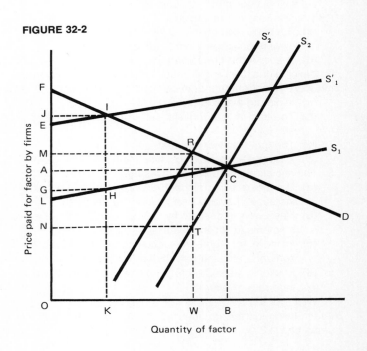

the one for which the tax generates the smaller reduction in employment is (S_1, S_2), the one for which the tax causes the least

reduction in the factor's after-tax income is (S_1, S_2), and the one for which the tax reduces other incomes by less is (S_1, S_2).

Essay Questions

1. The codiscoverers of insulin, Banting and Best, did not become millionaires as a result of their discovery, despite the fact that it has probably saved millions of human lives. What does this suggest about the private and social rates of return to human capital?

2. Name several factors that determine the position of the MEI schedule, explaining in each case how the schedule would be affected, and in what direction, by an increase in that factor.

3. Show how the income of a surgeon is part wage, part return to human capital, and part rent. Which of these components would be increased by the surgeon's efforts to develop more advanced surgical techniques? By the surgeon's decision to work longer hours? How would the rent component be affected if licensing requirements were relaxed so as to permit more people to practice surgery? Explain.

4. Most on-the-job training is job-specific. That is, it is training that is useful only for a particular job, such as selling insurance or operating a crane. Some on-the-job training is also firm-specific. That is, it involves "learning the ropes" of a particular firm's operations. Does the fact that workers may

quit tend to discourage job-specific on-the-job training more or less than it does firm-specific on-the-job training? Does the existence of a minimum wage tend to discourage either kind of on-the-job training more than the other?

5. Recall from Chapter 11 that as interest rates rise the prices of assets fall. Bearing this in mind, show how an increase in the rate of interest affects potential lenders differently from those who have already lent money, especially those who have bought marketable bonds. Show also how it affects potential borrowers differently from those who have already borrowed money.

*6. Suppose that a factor had a totally inelastic supply. What would its opportunity cost be to society? Would it be accurate to classify all its income as rent? What can you say about the efficiency loss that would result from imposing a tax on each firm of a certain number of dollars for each unit of the factor it used?

*7. The textbook sets out several reasons why it is difficult to measure the rate of return on investment in human capital. How many of these reasons also apply to measuring the rate of return on investment in physical capital?

Answers

True-False Questions: 1 T 2 F 3 T 4 F 5 T 6 T 7 T 8 F 9 F 10 T
Multiple-Choice Questions: 1 a 2 a 3 c 4 a 5 b 6 a 7 b 8 d 9 a 10 c 11 a 12 b
Exercises: **1a.** *OA, OB, OACB* **b.** *OG, OJ* (or *GI*), *EF* (or *GH*), *OMEG*, more, *ICE* **c.** O
2a. *OA, OB, OACB, FCA* **b.** *OJ, OG, OK, OGHK, JIHG* (or *EIHL*), *FIJ, ICH* **c.** less, no different, no different **d.** *OM, ON, OW, ONTW, NMRT, MFR, RCT* **e.** S_2, S_2, S_2, S_2, S_2

CHAPTER 33
Natural Resources, Conservation, and Growth

Learning Objectives

After you have studied this chapter in the textbook and the study guide, you should be able to

Describe the two components of marginal cost that underlie the supply curve of a privately owned natural resource

Explain why the outcome of a perfectly competitive market in a natural resource may be socially efficient if the resource is privately owned but not if it is common property

(Optional) Show what happens if more than the maximum sustainable yield is harvested from a population

Explain why simple projections of the use and availability of resources yield misleading predictions

Give three reasons why population growth continues to be rapid in less developed countries despite the scarcity of resources

Present the case in favor of economic growth, and the case against

CHAPTER HIGHLIGHTS

This chapter shows how to apply economic analysis to some important issues concerning our use of the world's resources. These issues are: (1) the efficient use of resources, and how that may be accomplished by a competitive market, (2) the problems of a common property resource, (3) the conservation of nonrenewable resources, and (4) the pros and cons of economic growth.

Efficiency

Consider the supply and demand for a natural resource that is privately owned. The demand curve for this resource will be the marginal productivity schedule of that resource, as with any other productive input. The supply curve is just the marginal cost of providing the resource. This marginal cost has two components: (1) the direct cost of harvesting or extracting the resource, and (2) the cost incurred because the use of the resource now means it will not be available in the future. The sum of these two components of marginal cost is also called the *reservation price* of the resource. In a perfectly competitive equilibrium, the marginal cost of providing the resource would just equal the marginal productivity of using the resource; this would be socially efficient. (This is explained in Figure 33-1 in the textbook.)

Common Property Resources

For the free competitive market to be socially efficient it is important that the resource be privately owned. If it is not—as in the case of a common property resource such as fish—there is reason to suppose that overharvesting will occur, even in a perfectly competitive market. This is because the suppliers will take into account the direct harvesting cost but not the second component of marginal cost—the cost of not having the resource in the future. Figure 33-2 in the textbook shows how much harvesting will occur in this case, and illustrates how a familiar "triangle" can be used to measure the efficiency loss. The tendency for a common property resource to be overharvested is a reason given by some countries for wanting to extend their territorial rights to the waters within 200 miles of their land (the United States did this in 1977).

An optional section of this chapter deals with the concept of maximum sustainable yield. The population growth of a species can be described in terms of a sustainable yield curve as in Figure 33-3 in the textbook, with the size of the population on the horizontal axis and the rate of increase in the population on the vertical axis. Generally speaking, there will be some size of population at which the annual increase is maximized. This maximal increase is called the maximum sustainable yield. It is the highest amount that could be harvested every year without reducing the size of the population. There are two important implications of this idea: (1) If more than the maximum sustainable yield is harvested, then the species will eventually become extinct because we will be extracting more from the population than is being replaced by natural reproduction. (2) If very little harvesting occurs then the population will probably grow beyond the point of maximum sustainable yield. If this happens then it would be inefficient to extract only the sustainable yield. For if more was extracted now, the population would fall toward the point of maximum sustainable yield, which would also permit more to be extracted in the future; in other words, we could extract more now and more later.

Nonrenewable Resources

The big issues concerning nonrenewable resources are whether they will run out, and if so, when? And what can we do about it? Simple projections of present trends point to an eventual doomsday, when rising population overtakes our limited resources. But these simple projections cannot be trusted because they do not allow for the kind of adjustment that the economic system will produce. As a resource becomes more scarce it will also become more expensive. This will create four kinds of adjustment: (1) substitution of other factors of production, (2) substitution of consumer goods that require less of that resource, (3) induced innovation that allows economizing on that resource, and (4) a reduction in the rate of growth of population because of the high cost of raising children. Critics of this economic argument point to the experience of less developed countries, where population growth has continued despite high poverty levels. However, the experience of the less developed countries can be explained by three special factors: (1) With so much poverty people want many children in order to support them in their old age, (2) recent dramatic advances in medicine have produced a sharp decrease in death rates in these countries, and (3) there are religious and social objections to birth control in many of these countries.

Economic Growth

The arguments in favor of economic growth are that it helps to relieve unemployment, it helps in solving the problem of poverty, and it raises not only our incomes but our children's incomes. The arguments against growth are that it depletes our natural resources and contributes to pollution. The main difficulty with the antigrowth argument is that restricting growth is too general a policy to attack these specific problems of resource depletion and pollution.

IMPORTANT TERMS

Reservation price The marginal cost of providing a resource. It includes (1) the cost of harvesting or extraction, and (2) the amount necessary to compensate for the reduction in the resource available in the future.

Sustainable yield curve (Optional) Sometimes called just "the yield curve," this relates the natural annual increase in a species to its population size. This natural annual increase is the sustainable yield. It is the amount that can be extracted and still leave the population size constant.

Maximum sustainable yield (Optional) The large value of sustainable yield on the yield curve. This is the most that can be extracted each year without reducing the population size.

Induced innovations Innovations that result when people turn their minds to finding substitutes for increasingly expensive resources.

Renewable resource One that reproduces itself naturally or that can be reproduced by humans. One that cannot be reproduced is called a nonrenewable resource.

True-False Questions

T   F   1. The height of the supply curve of a privately owned natural resource is its reservation price.
T   F   2. The cost of extracting a resource is more than its reservation price.
T   F   3. For a common property resource, supply is determined by the marginal extraction cost only.
T   F   4. A competitive equilibrium in the market for a privately owned natural resource is generally inefficient.
T   F   5. A competitive equilibrium in the market for a common property natural resource is generally inefficient.
T   F   6. Extension of countries' territorial rights to a 200-mile limit probably increases the size of the inefficiency resulting from the common property nature of fishing.
T   F   7. Handing over a common property resource to a monopolist would probably increase the amount of overharvesting of the resource.
T   F   8. Economists who criticize the simple projections of the "doomsday" approach point to the experience of the less developed countries as an example of how population growth rates are reduced automatically by the scarcity of resources.

The following questions are only for those who have studied the optional section on maximum sustainable yield.

T   F   9. A species whose population size falls below the point of maximum sustainable yield then will become extinct unless its harvest is forbidden, at least temporarily.
T   F   10. If a species is left completely unharvested, then it will grow beyond the size of maximum sustainable yield.

Multiple-Choice Questions

1. The demand curve for a natural resource reflects its
   (a) Reservation price
   (b) Marginal extraction cost
   (c) External benefit
   (d) Marginal productivity

2. Which of the following determines the supply of a natural resource if it is privately owned, but not if it is common property?
   (a) Reservation price
   (b) Marginal extraction cost
   (c) External benefit
   (d) Marginal productivity

3. Which of the following is *not* a common property resource?
   (a) Fish
   (b) Lake water
   (c) Mineral deposits in a privately owned mine
   (d) Timber on unowned property

4. The amount of a common property resource that is harvested tends to be
   (a) Greater than the efficient quantity
   (b) Less than the efficient quantity
   (c) Equal to the efficient quantity

   (d) Greater or less, depending upon the elasticity of demand

5. Which of the following will be greater if a natural resource is privately owned than if it is common property (assuming perfect competition)?
   (a) The price of the resource
   (b) The rate of extraction of the resource
   (c) The size of the efficiency loss associated with extracting the resource
   (d) The quantity demanded

6. Which of the following is *not* an example of a market adjustment that helps us to deal with the increasing scarcity of oil?
   (a) The production of cars that use fuel more economically
   (b) The increased rate of extraction of coal deposits
   (c) Preventing the price of oil from rising
   (d) The move to lower room temperatures in homes

*7. In the free competitive market, as a nonrenewable resource gets depleted
   (a) The quantity demanded increases
   (b) Its marginal productivity falls
   (c) It becomes more expensive

(d) It gets extracted at an increasingly rapid rate

8. If the rate of population growth increased as resources become scarcer, this would most likely

   (a) Help in the adjustment to increasing scarcity
   (b) Induce a more rapid rate of labor-saving innovations
   (c) Cause wages to rise more rapidly
   (d) Lead to intensified efforts to find substitutes for the increasingly scarce resources

9. Which of the following is an argument commonly used in favor of economic growth?

   (a) Unemployment is likely to be less severe in a rapidly growing economy
   (b) Faster economic growth helps to economize on scarce natural resources
   (c) Growth reduces pollution
   (d) Growth is necessary or our children will become far poorer than we are

10. The main problem with the antigrowth argument is that

   (a) The depletion of natural resources is not really a serious problem
   (b) Rapid economic growth is the only sure way to avoid inflation
   (c) Slowing growth is not a specific enough policy to cure any single specific problem
   (d) Growth helps to avoid the pollution problem

*11. The maximum sustainable yield occurs at

   (a) The highest point on the yield curve
   (b) The lowest point on the yield curve
   (c) The point where the yield curve crosses the horizontal axis
   (d) The largest population size possible with no harvest

Exercises

1a. Figure 33-1 depicts a perfectly competitive market for a natural resource. The demand curve is D, the marginal cost of extraction is given by the curve labeled S, and the full reservation price is given by the curve labeled S'. The socially efficient quantity (assuming no external benefits) equals _____, and this quantity will be demanded if the price equals _____. If the resource is privately owned the price will equal _____, the quantity extracted will equal _____, and the size of the efficiency loss will equal _____. This efficiency loss would be eliminated by a tax on extraction equal to _____ per unit.

b. If the resource is not privately owned the price will equal _____, the quantity extracted will equal _____, and the size of the efficiency loss will equal _____. This efficiency loss would be eliminated by a tax on extraction equal to _____ per unit.

2a. In Figure 33-2, D represents the demand curve for a natural resource, S represents the marginal cost of extracting the resource, S' represents the reservation price of providing the resource, and MR represents the marginal revenue curve that

FIGURE 33-1

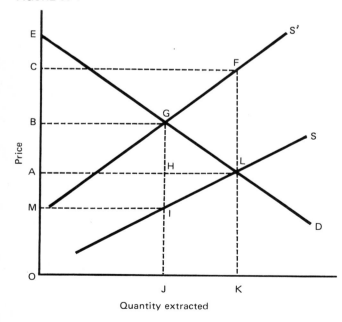

Price / Quantity extracted

FIGURE 33-2

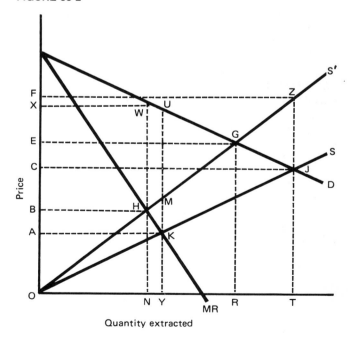

Price / Quantity extracted

would be faced by a monopolist in the market (recall this concept from Chapter 23). The efficient quantity of extraction (assuming no external benefits) equals _____, at which quantity the marginal productivity of the resource would equal _____. If the resource was a common property and the market was perfectly competitive the price would equal _____, the quantity extracted would equal _____, the size of the efficiency loss would equal _____,

and the total cost of the resource to buyers would equal _____.

b. If the resource was now given to a monopolist who exploited its monopoly power to the fullest, it would extract a quantity equal to _____, and set a price equal to _____. The reservation price would equal _____. The size of the efficiency loss would equal _____, and the total cost of the resource to buyers would equal _____.

Essay Questions

1. Explain how the problem of a common property resource is similar to the problem of environmental pollution.

2. How does private ownership help to eliminate the inefficiency caused by a common property resource? Would it be eliminated just as well if ownership were given to a single owner who then had a monopoly? What new problems might be created by allowing the resource to be monopolized? (Hint: see Exercise 2 above.)

3. In what sense have the miracles of modern medicine aggravated the problem of scarce nonrenewable natural resources, especially in less developed countries?

4. In what sense is it difficult for society as a whole to enjoy the cost-saving advantages of economies of scale when some of its resources are nonrenewable:

5. "One of the shortcomings of the market mechanism is that private business interests are concerned, not with the future, but instead with how much profit they can earn right now. We need the government to regulate the rate of extraction of natural resources to protect future generations from being deprived of their rightful share of resources." Do you agree or disagree? Why?

*6. By studying Figure 33-3 in the textbook you can see that if the population of a species is initially above the point of maximum sustainable yield and if people are now harvesting at a rate just large enough to maintain a constant size of population, then by increasing the rate of extraction they can harvest more now *and* more in the future. If the cost of extraction is zero, what is the opportunity cost of raising the rate of extraction in this situation? Is this a case of being able to get something for nothing?

Answers

True-False Questions: 1 T   2 F   3 T   4 F   5 T   6 F   7 F   8 F   9 F   10 T
Multiple-Choice Questions: 1 d   2 a   3 c   4 a   5 a   6 c   7 c   8 d   9 a   10 c   11 a
Exercises: **1a.** *OJ, OB, OB, OJ,* zero, zero **b.** *OA, OK, FLG, GI*
2a. *OR, OE, OC, OT, ZJG, OCJT* **b.** *ON, OX, OB, WGH, OXWN*

CHAPTER 34
Energy

Learning Objectives

After you have studied this chapter in the textbook and study guide, you should be able to

Explain why energy has become a more important problem now than in the 1960s

List the five most important sources of U.S. energy use, stating what percentage is accounted for by each

Describe the short-run emergency measures adopted by the U.S. for coping with oil shortages

List the four broad categories of longer-run response to shortages

Explain the efficiency and transfer effects of allowing the domestic price of oil to rise to the world price

Explain how such a price rise would affect the amounts produced, consumed, and imported in the United States

Describe how the domestic price of oil was controlled before 1979

Describe the practical problems faced by this control scheme

Measure diagrammatically the efficiency loss of keeping the domestic price of oil below the world price, as well as the cost to the government of subsidizing oil imports.

Present the case for raising the domestic price of oil above the world price

Describe the conservation measures adopted by the government when the price of oil was controlled

Explain the pros and cons of using each of the four major sources of energy other than oil

Describe two little-used alternative sources that might become important in the future

CHAPTER HIGHLIGHTS

This chapter focuses on the growing problem of how we will meet our energy needs, now and in the future. This problem was brought to public attention by the more than tenfold increase in the price of oil from 1973 until 1980. Accordingly, the chapter focuses mainly on oil, the source of half the energy used in the United States today, although it also discusses some of the other sources, both actual and potential.

This increase in oil prices and the attendant shortages have led to several problems for the United States. The two periods of the sharpest price increases, 1973–1974 and 1979–1980, were both followed by recessions in the United States. By the late 1970s we were importing about half the oil we consumed; thus, we have become extremely vulnerable to the threat of future cutoffs, like the one imposed during the Arab-Israeli war of 1973. This has led to an increasing danger of U.S. military involvement in the Middle East to protect our oil supplies. Thus, the two main questions dealt with in the chapter are how *have* we coped with the problems caused by these shortages and price increases, and how *should* we have coped.

The measures adopted fall under two headings: Short-Run Emergency Measures, and Longer-Run Responses.

Short-Run Emergency Measures
1. The government plans to build up a *strategic reserve* of 1 billion barrels of oil to keep us supplied in the event of a future cutoff.

2. In 1975 Congress required the President to submit a standby rationing plan to go into effect in the event of a major shortfall. Failure of politicians to agree on a fair scheme for allocating the ration tickets has stalled progress on this.

3. In 1974, 20 countries, including the United States, formed the *International Energy Agency* (IEA) and agreed to share their oil in case any member should suffer at least a 7 percent shortfall. The effectiveness of this agreement has yet to be tested.

Longer-Run Responses
These come under four headings:

1. Limit the growth of GNP. This might help by reducing the demand for energy, but it is too broad and costly a policy to deal effectively with the specific problem of oil scarcity.

2. Conserve more. Many policies are designed to encourage people to use less oil.

3. Increase the domestic production of oil.

4. Develop alternative sources of energy.

The effectiveness of each of these responses depends to a large extent on what happens to the domestic price of oil. So in order to analyze them, we must first analyze the government's policy with respect to the domestic price.

Domestic Price of Oil
In deciding how the U.S. price of oil will be determined, the government has the following policy options:

1. *Allow the domestic price to seek its own level, following a rise in the world price.* Figure 34-6 in the textbook shows what would happen. The domestic price would rise to equal the world price, P_W. In response to this, domestic consumption would fall (as we move back up the demand curve from F to C) and domestic production would increase (as we move up the supply curve from A to B). Thus, both responses (2) and (3) of the last paragraph would be encouraged by this policy. As a result, U.S. imports (U.S. consumption minus U.S. production) would decrease. The rise in oil prices would also encourage the search for less expensive alternatives [response (4)].

Furthermore, the new situation would be allocatively efficient (subject to our usual reservations concerning externalities). The marginal benefit of oil, as measured by the height of the demand curve in Figure 34-6, would equal the marginal cost, as measured by the height of the supply curve. The reason is that both marginal benefit and marginal cost would equal the price, P_W.

This is the policy that President Reagan has now adopted, having accelerated President Carter's plan of 1979. But until mid-1979 the price was not allowed to adjust to the world level. Why not, when there are these advantages? The main concern was *equity*, not efficiency. The rise in price would result in a huge increase in producer surplus, and a corresponding decrease in consumer surplus. (Be sure you can measure these changes in a diagram like Figure 34-6.) Until mid-1979 the government thought this transfer from consumers to producers would be too inequitable to counterbalance the efficiency gain of a price rise. When the price rise was finally allowed, it was accompanied by a windfall-profits tax on oil companies to reduce the size of the transfer.

2. *Keep the domestic price below the world price.* There is a simple way of doing this, and the far more complicated way the government used.

First the simple way:

a. Impose a straightforward price ceiling of, say P_1, below the world price P_W in Figure 34-6. This policy does not provide the benefits possible under policy 1. Specifically, because it does not allow price to rise:

(1) It fails to stimulate the increased production of oil. This results in efficiency loss AHB—the extra cost of buying AD barrels of oil abroad at world price P_W, rather than producing them at home (at the lower cost given by the height of AB).

(2) It fails to encourage conservation. This results in efficiency loss CJF. (This is the extra cost of importing EF barrels of oil at high cost P_W when users of this oil are only getting a benefit equal to the height of FC.)

(3) It involves the government in a costly subsidy of $AHJF$ to those importing the AF barrels of oil. (This is the subsidy necessary to compensate them for the difference between the high cost P_W they incur in buying oil on the world market, and the low price P_1 at which they then have to sell this oil in the United States.)

b. The more complicated approach the government used during the 1970s was the "blended price" system. This was designed to avoid problems (1) and (3). To avoid problem (1) and encourage production, the producers of "new" oil (oil from newly drilled wells) were allowed to charge a higher price. But the price was still kept down on "old oil" from old wells. (Since these wells were already drilled, their output was expected to continue, regardless of price.) To deal with problem (3)—that is, to avoid having to pay a large subsidy on oil imports—the government set the price to oil users between the high price for new oil (and imports) and the low price of old oil.

Ingenious as it was, this scheme involved major difficulties. First, it did not deal with problem (2) above: It was like any other kind of control scheme to hold price down. True, it did reduce the transfer from oil users to oil producers that would otherwise have occurred. However, precisely because it held price down, it failed to stimulate oil conservation.

And there were other practical problems: Refineries, of course, all wanted to buy the low-priced old oil. But this was impossible for coastal refineries that depended on high-cost imports. Accordingly, a system

of "entitlements" was set up to ensure that refineries were given at least a roughly fair treatment (except for the preference given to "small" refineries). Another problem was that the government also became involved in allocating gasoline to filling stations—a policy that contributed to gasoline shortages in several states following the cutbacks at the outbreak of war between Iran and Iraq in 1979. Finally, to make it economical for old, nearly dry wells to be kept in operation, the high price was allowed on oil from "stripper" wells producing less than 10 barrels a day. While this stimulated production from these wells, it also encouraged producers to *decrease* output from wells producing just *over* 10 barrels a day—so as to have them defined as "strippers" and get the world price.

3. *Force the domestic price above the world price.* This last pricing option could be brought into effect by imposing a tariff (or tax) on oil: It would reduce U.S. demand even more than under policy **1**. It has been advocated for three reasons:

a. The United States buys such a large share of the world's oil that reducing U.S. demand would weaken the OPEC cartel and reduce the price we would have to pay for oil on world markets. (Those who have read Box 19-2 will understand that a tariff or tax can *lower* the price OPEC producers receive for oil, while *raising* the price paid by U.S. buyers—with the difference in these two prices being the amount of the tariff.)

b. Each barrel of foreign oil we buy adds to our economic dependency and vulnerability. A tax or tariff would be one way of making U.S. buyers take this extra cost into account, and reduce their purchases.

c. U.S. oil buyers should also pay for the *political* problems created by their large purchases and our resulting dependency on Middle Eastern supplies. [Because of our heavy oil purchases, we are politically (and militarily?) committed to this very unstable and explosive part of the world.]

Conservation Measures

Because conservation was not encouraged by the low domestic price before 1979, other measures were adopted to encourage it: (1) Tax incentives were given for various energy-saving measures such as installing better insulation. (2) Speed limits were reduced to 55 mph. (3) In 1975 the federal government required automakers to almost double the gas mileage of the average car by 1985.

Alternative Energy Sources

Next to oil, the biggest source of U.S. energy consumption is natural gas, which accounts for 25 percent of our energy. Because the price of interstate gas was kept down by controls, we had the same problems as with oil: inadequate production, excessive consumption, and consequent shortages. But in 1978 the controls began to be phased out, and this has helped to stimulate conservation and new discoveries. (We now have very large reserves of natural gas.)

Coal accounts for 18 percent of our energy use. Our reserves are vast (600 times our present annual consumption) but strip-mining creates environmental problems, and underground mining is dangerous. Furthermore, burning coal in power plants pollutes the air.

Nuclear fission satisfies 4 percent of our energy requirements. Concerns over its potential dangers, dramatized again recently by the 1979 accident on Three Mile Island in Pennsylvania, have led to many political and legal complications and costly delays. Since 1974 there has been little growth in the nuclear power industry.

Hydroelectric power accounts for 3 percent of our energy use. The required dams cause flooding which seriously alters the natural environment. But counterbalancing this is the relative safety and cleanliness of this form of power (compared to, say, burning coal). Also, the dams can produce recreational benefit and can be used for flood control downstream. The major problem with this source is finding good new sites for large developments.

Solar energy and nuclear fusion do not yet satisfy a significant amount of our energy requirements, but they may both become important in the future. Solar energy can be used to provide home heat if (1) lots of windows are exposed to the sun; or (2) photovoltaic cells (that generate electricity) or water circulation systems are installed on rooftops. In a more ambitious approach, the French use 10-story mirrors to concentrate the sun's rays for generating electricity.

Nuclear fusion works by combining atoms (instead of splitting them, as in fission) and uses the world's most abundant element—hydrogen—rather than scarce fissionable materials like uranium. It has not yet been used because we have still not discovered how it can produce electricity on balance (it still uses more energy than it provides in return). Even when we discover this, a giant step

will remain: We will still have to reduce its cost to the point where it can compete with other sources of energy.

IMPORTANT TERMS

OPEC (Organization of Oil Exporting Countries) The international cartel, formed in 1965, that raised the world price of oil dramatically between 1973 and 1980.

Strategic petroleum reserves Government stocks, to be held in reserve for use in case of a future cutoff. They help to reduce our vulnerability and dependency on foreign supplies. The government plans to build these reserves up to a total of 1 billion barrels (about half a year's imports).

White rationing A rationing scheme under which the tickets can be sold legally in a "white" market, rather than illegally in the "black" market that arises under other rationing schemes. This kind of rationing scheme is more flexible, because it allows an individual legally to consume more than his or her allotment of tickets, provided he or she is willing to pay the white market price. The standby rationing plan submitted to Congress by President Carter in 1979 included white rationing.

IEA (International Energy Agency) An association formed in 1974 by the United States and 19 other countries, who agreed to share their supplies of oil with any member facing a shortfall of more than 7 percent.

Blended price Under the oil-price controls of the 1970s, sellers received a high price for new oil (oil from newly found wells), and a lower price for their old oil. Buyers paid a blended price in between.

Stripper well An old oil well where production has fallen below 10 barrels a day. In the 1970s oil from such wells was allowed to be sold at the high price, even though it was old oil, as an incentive to keep the wells in operation.

Interstate natural gas Gas produced in one state but consumed in another. Its price used to be controlled, although the controls are now being phased out. The price of *intra*state natural gas, produced and consumed in the same state, was not subject to the same controls.

Nuclear fusion A process in which heat is produced by combining atoms (rather than splitting them, as in nuclear fission). So far we have not learned to control the process and use it economically.

Energy break-even point The point at which we learn to operate a process like fusion so as to create more energy than it uses. We haven't got nuclear fusion to this point yet, let alone to the *economic break-even point*, where we can generate enough excess energy to make the process economically worthwhile.

True-False Questions

T F   **1.** The world price of oil was five times as high in 1980 as in 1973.
T F   **2.** Oil provides roughly half the energy used in the United States.
T F   **3.** Strategic petroleum reserves are the reserves maintained by OPEC countries.
T F   **4.** Allowing the domestic price of oil to rise to the world price encourages conservation of oil.
T F   **5.** Allowing the domestic price of oil to rise to the world price makes us more dependent on foreign supplies.
T F   **6.** The windfall-profits tax of 1980 was designed to reduce the transfer effect of the domestic oil price increase.
T F   **7.** During the 1970s the federal government adopted no measures to encourage conservation.
T F   **8.** Interstate natural gas has been subject to price control.
T F   **9.** Nuclear fission is not yet past the energy break-even point, but nuclear fusion is.
T F   **10.** Hydroelectric power produces no known environmental damage.

Multiple-Choice Questions

1. Which of the following accounts for the largest share of U.S. energy use?
   (a) Coal   **(c)** Natural gas
   (b) Hydroelectric power **(d)** Oil

2. The Emergency Standby Ration Scheme presented to Congress by President Carter in 1979 proposed
   (a) To allow the domestic price to rise to the world price
   (b) A white rationing scheme
   (c) A windfall-profit tax on oil companies
   (d) The distribution of nonmarketable ration tickets

3. Since mid-1979 the U.S. policy with respect to the domestic price of oil has been to
   (a) Allow it to rise to the world price
   (b) Keep it fixed below the world price
   (c) Keep it at some constant fraction of the world price
   (d) Raise it above the world price

4. Before 1979, controls kept the domestic price very low on
   (a) New oil
   (b) Old oil
   (c) Both new and old oil
   (d) Neither new nor old oil

5. An increase in the price of oil encourages increased
   (a) Production of oil
   (b) Conservation of oil
   (c) Use of alternative sources of energy
   (d) All the above

6. Allowing the domestic price of oil to increase to the world price results in
   (a) Efficiency losses through higher costs
   (b) Allocative efficiency
   (c) An increase in the cost of government subsidization of oil imports
   (d) Increased domestic consumption of oil

7. Allowing the domestic price of oil to increase to the world price produces

   (a) A transfer from consumers to producers of oil
   (b) A transfer from producers to consumers
   (c) A gain to both producers and consumers
   (d) A loss to both producers and consumers

8. To alleviate the transfer effect of increased oil prices, the U.S. government in 1980 adopted
   (a) Strategic petroleum reserves
   (b) A 55-mph speed limit
   (c) An emergency standby rationing scheme
   (d) A windfall profit tax

9. In Figure 34-1 below the area *ABC* represents
   (a) The efficiency loss from buying foreign oil at the world price rather than producing it domestically at lower cost
   (b) The efficiency loss from importing oil at the world price even though its marginal benefit was less than that
   (c) The cost to the government of subsidizing oil imports
   (d) None of the above

FIGURE 34-1

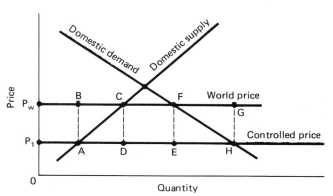

10. In Figure 34-1 the area *FGH* represents
  (a) The efficiency loss from buying foreign oil at the world price rather than producing it domestically at lower cost
  (b) The efficiency loss from importing oil at the world price even though its marginal benefit was less than that
  (c) The cost to the government of subsidizing oil imports
  (d) None of the above

11. In Figure 34-1 the area *DCFE* represents
  (a) The efficiency loss from buying foreign oil at the world price rather than producing it domestically at lower cost
  (b) The efficiency loss from importing oil at the world price even though its marginal benefit was less than that
  (c) The cost to the government of subsidizing oil imports
  (d) None of the above

12. In Figure 34-1 the area *ABGH* represents
  (a) The efficiency loss from buying foreign oil at the world price rather than producing it domestically at lower cost
  (b) The efficiency loss from importing oil at the world price even though its marginal benefit was less than that

  (c) The cost to the government of subsidizing oil imports
  (d) None of the above

13. The fact that a significant reduction of U.S. demand might depress the world price of oil is a point in favor of having a domestic price
  (a) Below the world price
  (b) Equal to the world price
  (c) Above the world price
  (d) Either above or below, depending upon the elasticity of domestic supply

14. Which of the following measures adopted during the 1970s did *not* encourage the conservation of oil?
  (a) Pollution-control standards on cars sold in the United States
  (b) Improved gas mileage requirements on U.S. manufactured cars
  (c) Subsidization of home insulation
  (d) Reduced speed limits on highways

15. The United States has known reserves equal to about 600 years of current annual consumption of
  (a) Coal   **(c)** Natural gas
  (b) Oil   **(d)** All the above

Exercises

1. Fill in the blanks.

a. Three short-run emergency measures adopted by the United States to cope with oil shortages are: _____, _____, and _____.

b. Four broad categories of possible longer-run response to cope with increased scarcity of oil are: _____, _____, _____, and _____.

c. What percent of U.S. energy needs are met by oil _____, natural gas _____, coal _____, nuclear fission _____, and hydroelectric power _____?

d. Until the 1960s U.S. policy was to (tax, protect) domestic oil producers by keeping the domestic price (above, below) the world price and restricting U.S. (imports, exports) of oil.

e. In the 1970s the policy was to keep the domestic price (above, below) the world price. Under this policy what measures were taken to encourage conservation of oil? _____, _____, and _____.

f. From mid-1979 the policy has been to allow the domestic price to (rise to the world price, fall, stay the same). To alleviate the transfer effect of this policy, what measure was adopted? _____.

2a. Under the controlled price in Figure 34-2 below, we would produce the quantity _____, consume the quantity _____, and (import, export) the quantity _____. After letting the domestic price rise to the world price, we would produce the quantity _____, consume the quantity _____, and (import, export) the quantity _____.

b. Allowing the price rise would result in a

FIGURE 34-2

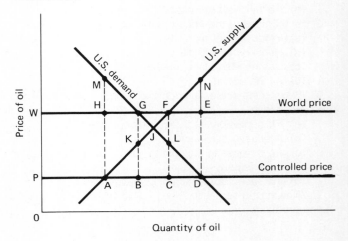

(gain, loss) in consumer surplus, equal to the area _____, and a (gain, loss) in producer surplus equal to the area _____. Thus, the sum of producer and consumer surplus would (increase, decrease) by an amount equal to the area _____ minus the area _____.

c. This price rise also would allow the government to save the amount _____ which it has been paying to subsidize oil imports at the controlled price. Subtract from this the net loss in consumer plus producer surplus calculated above. The result is a net effi-

ciency (gain, loss) to the nation, as a result of the price increase, equal to area *AHF* plus the area _____.

d. As a result of moving to the world price, the efficiency gain from producing at marginal cost rather than importing at the world price equals the area _____. The gain from eliminating consumption of imported oil whose marginal benefit was less than the world price equals the area _____. How does the sum of these two gains compare to the measurement in **c** above of the net efficiency gain to the nation? _____.

Essay Questions

1. "If my brother was hungry and I had a loaf of bread that cost me a dollar he might be willing to pay me two dollars for the loaf, but that really wouldn't be fair. By the same token it is not fair for our oil companies to make excess profits on the oil they sell to us whenever OPEC raises the price. They should be forced to sell what we need at a price corresponding to their costs of production." Which U.S. policy in the 1970s was guided by this sort of philosophy? What is wrong with the argument? (What problems were created by the policy?)

2. "If you raise the price Americans have to pay for oil by taxing it, this will increase conservation. But if you compensate Americans by reducing income taxes or social security taxes they will spend this on oil, thus undoing the conservation." Do you agree or disagree? Why?

3. How have the strict auto emission standards imposed by the EPA during the 1970s affected our efforts to conserve oil? What are the benefits of such policies? In what sense could these benefits have been achieved without damaging the conservation effort if a policy of a higher oil price had been implemented instead of the auto emission standards?

4. In what sense might the increased discoveries of new reserves of natural gas since 1978 have been connected to the government's decision

in 1978 to phase out the price controls on natural gas?

5. "It is easier for governments to deal with the adverse transfer effects of allowing prices to rise than it is to deal with the adverse efficiency effects of preventing them from rising." Show how the U.S. experience with oil could be used to back up this statement.

6. Suppose that before 1979 the United States had been in the situation depicted by Figure 34-2 of Exercise **2** above. Would this have strengthened or weakened the case for raising the domestic price above the world price? Explain.

7. What significant external costs and benefits are associated with the production and use of oil? Of Natural gas? Coal? Nuclear fission? Hydroelectric power?

8. Compare the environmental effects and likely future potential of nuclear fission and nuclear fusion.

9. Which energy source do you think provides the United States with the least dependency on foreign supplies? Which is the safest to produce and use? Which has the greatest potential for being available in the future? In the light of these answers, what do you think Figure 34-4 in the textbook will look like when it is drawn for the year 2077?

Answers

True-False Questions: 1 F 2 T 3 F 4 T 5 F 6 T 7 F 8 T 9 F 10 F

Multiple-Choice Questions: 1 d 2 b 3 a 4 b 5 d 6 b 7 a 8 d 9 a 10 b 11 d 12 c 13 c 14 a 15 a

Exercises: **1a.** strategic petroleum reserves, emergency standby rationing plan, IEA sharing agreement **b.** lower growth, conservation, increased domestic production, development of alternative sources **c.** 50, 25, 18, 4, 3 **d.** protect, above, imports **e.** below, lower speed limits, increased mileage requirements on new cars, subsidized insulation **f.** rise to the world price, windfall profit tax on oil companies

2a. *PA, PD,* import, *AD; WF, WG,* export, *GF* **b.** loss, *PWGD,* gain, *PWFA,* decrease, *AJD, GFJ* **c.** *AHED,* gain, *GED* **d.** *AHF, GED,* they are the same

CHAPTER 35
Income Inequality

Learning Objectives

After you have studied this chapter in the textbook and the study guide, you should be able to

Explain the reasons why some people have more income than others

Describe how the Lorenz curve is constructed and in what sense it measures inequality

Explain why the Lorenz curve possibly exaggerates the degree of inequality

Identify four kinds of government policy that reduce income inequality, and specify which of these accomplishes the most

Explain how the direct effects of transfer programs (in decreasing inequality) may be offset partially by their indirect effects

Show why the outcome of a free-market situation has no special claim to being fair

Show why perfect equality of income is not necessarily fair

Explain two principles for compromising between the extremes of a free market and perfect equality

Show why there exists a conflict between equity and efficiency

CHAPTER HIGHLIGHTS

There are four main issues dealt with in this chapter: (1) why income inequality exists, (2) how much of it exists in the United States, (3) how much of this inequality has been eliminated by government expenditures, transfers, and taxes, and (4) what constitutes a fair method of distributing income.

Why Inequality?

There are at least eight reasons why some people may have more income than others: (1) their greater investment in human capital, (2) a rent earned on some innate ability, (3) greater financial wealth, either because they have inherited it or saved it, (4) greater market power due to membership in a union or possession of some other form of monopoly power, (5) a willingness to work harder or longer hours, (6) discrimination in their favor in the labor market, (7) luck in being in the right place at the right time, and (8) good connections and other benefits of family background. Most of these reasons have been explained in Chapters 30–32. Professor Jacob Mincer recently estimated that 60 percent of the differences in income can be attributed to the first factor on this list—differences in human capital.

How Much Inequality?

In the United States, the poorest 20 percent of families receive less than one-third of 1 percent of the nation's income (before taxes and transfers) whereas the richest 20 percent of families receive half of it. Facts like these are summarized in the Lorenz curve, an important diagrammatic construction that is shown in Figure 35-1 in the textbook. This curve shows the percent of total income received by the poorest 10 percent of families, the poorest 20 percent, and so on. The degree of inequality can be measured by the area between the Lorenz curve and the 45° line. The 45° line is called the "complete equality line." If every family received exactly the same income the Lorenz curve would coincide with this complete equality line. Thus the further away the actual Lorenz curve lies from the complete equality line, the further is the actual situation from the situation of complete equality.

It is important to realize, however, that the Lorenz curve probably overstates the degree of inequality, because it measures current income rather than lifetime incomes. Thus it will depart from the complete equality line even if every family has the same lifetime income. (In any given year, some of these families will be at their peak earning period, while others will have a lower income because of temporary unemployment or because they have just started their very first job.)

The Effects of Taxes and Expenditures on Inequality

The Lorenz curve for family incomes *after* taxes and transfers (Figure 35-2 in the text) shows about one-third less inequality than before taxes and transfers. (That is, the area between the complete inequality line and the Lorenz curve is reduced by a third.) This reduction has been accomplished by (1) taxes, (2) transfers in kind, (3) cash transfers, and (4) social insurance. By far the largest reduction is accomplished by social insurance. Taxes accomplish less equalization than you might

expect. The reason, as we saw in Chapter 5, is that our tax system is not very progressive. Transfer programs have a *direct* effect of reducing inequality. But they have the *indirect* effect of increasing inequality because they reduce the incentives for the poor to find and hold jobs and to stay married. (When a family breaks up the same income is split among two families, lowering the income per family.)

Fairness in Distributing Income

The problem of defining a "fair" way of distributing income can never be answered with complete certainty, because it refers to "what ought to be," not "what is." Nevertheless, reasonable people can agree on two points:

1. The outcome of the free market has no special claim to being fair, because (*a*) there is no way of justifying huge profits to monopolists, and (*b*) even with perfect competition and no externalities we can only say that the market is efficient, not that it "divides the pie" fairly.

2. At the other extreme, complete equality would not be fair either, because some people work harder and longer than others, and some people have more dangerous or odious jobs than others.

The text suggests two principles for compromising between the extremes of a free market and perfect equality:

1. The race should be fair. In other words, we should aim for equality of opportunity rather than equality of reward. For example, we should ensure that no one is denied the opportunity of a formal education because of unfair discrimination. But this doesn't mean that everyone should be awarded a college degree—that should depend on what they are able to make with their opportunity.

2. We should modify the rewards of the game, so that even those at the bottom of the heap are still not impoverished.

As well as these problems of pinning down an acceptable notion of equity there is the conflict between equity and efficiency. To take the extreme case: If everyone was guaranteed an equal income, who would want to fight fires or work the long hours of the hardworking physician?

The ideas of Professor John Rawls are discussed in Box 35-2. Rawls suggests we imagine everyone to be in an "original position" in which no one knows what his or her particular income will be. Then ask what kind of income distribution a reasonable person would choose from behind this "veil of ignorance," knowing that after he or she had chosen a distribution of income he or she would then be assigned by chance to one of the rungs of his or her own ladder.

He argues that everyone would then agree to the "difference principle"; that there should be complete equality in the distribution of income unless there happens to be an unequal distribution that leaves everyone better off. But he gets this conclusion by supposing that everyone would figure that with his or her luck no matter what "income ladder" he or she chose would end up on the lowest rung; so he or she would choose a distribution in which the lowest rung was as high as possible. In other words, he or she would use the "maximin principle" of *max*imizing the *min*imum income he or she could possibly get.

IMPORTANT TERMS

Lorenz curve   The curve that shows the percentage of national income that is received by the poorest 10 percent of families, by the poorest 20 percent of families, and so forth.

Complete equality line   The straight line in the Lorenz curve diagram with slope 45°. The Lorenz curve would coincide with the complete equality line only if all families received exactly the same income in the year of observation.

Social insurance   Any government-run scheme like unemployment insurance or social security where large groups of people are forced to contribute insurance premiums but receive benefits in the event that they become unemployed or retire.

Transfers in kind   Any transfer payments made by the government that are not in the form of cash, but instead are claims to particular commodities, as in the case of food stamps.

*The following terms are important only for those who have studied Box 35-2.

Original position   A situation in which no one knows what his or her income will be, just what the overall distribution of income will be. According to Rawls, one must put oneself in this original position in order to arrive at an acceptable definition of equity.

Difference principle   The principle that income should be equally distributed unless there is some other distribution that makes everyone better off.

Maximin Principle   The principle of choosing the income distribution that maximizes the minimum income.

True-False Questions

T   F   **1.** The poorest 20 percent of families in the United States earn less than 1 percent of national income before taxes and transfers.

T   F   **2.** According to Mincer's study the most important factor in explaining income differences is market power.

T   F   **3.** The Lorenz curve for current income is probably less bowed out than that for lifetime income.

T   F   **4.** Government expenditures, transfers, and taxes have reduced income inequality in the United States by about a third.

T   F   **5.** Income inequality in the United States has been steadily increasing since the early 1960s.

T   F   **6.** One of the reasons that the free-market solution to distributing income is not necessarily fair is the possibility that monopolies may exist.

T   F   **7.** One problem with the ideal of perfect equality of income is that it conflicts with the objective of efficiency.

T   F   **8.** The free-market system under ideal conditions will maximize the total income pie, and will also achieve a fair distribution of that pie.

T   F   **9.** In Rawls's original position you can choose a Lorenz curve, but not your own position on the curve.

T   F   **10.** According to Rawls's difference principle, there should always be exact equality in the distribution of income.

Multiple-Choice Questions

1. According to the study by Jacob Mincer, which of the following is the most important factor in explaining income differentials?
   (a) Rents earned on innate ability
   (b) Financial wealth
   (c) Luck
   (d) Human capital

2. In the United States the richest 20 percent of families get about what percentage of the total national income before taxes and transfers?
   (a) 20 percent
   (b) 35 percent
   (c) 50 percent
   (d) 65 percent

3. The Lorenz curve measures how close the actual distribution is to
   (a) A fair distribution
   (b) Complete equality
   (c) What it was the previous year
   (d) What it would be if all markets were perfectly competitive

4. If the Lorenz curve were a straight line, then
   (a) There would be more inequality of income than there is presently in the United States
   (b) There would be complete equality of incomes
   (c) There would be an equitable distribution of income
   (d) None of the above

5. The Lorenz curve as usually drawn probably overstates the degree of inequality in income distribution because
   (a) It measures inequality in current income rather than in lifetime income
   (b) It measures income rather than financial wealth
   (c) It refers to the incomes of individuals rather than the incomes of families
   (d) It shows that the poorest 20 percent of families get only 20 percent of national income

6. The food stamp program is an example of
   (a) Cash transfers
   (b) A regressive tax
   (c) Social security
   (d) Transfers in kind

7. Which of the following accounts for the largest reduction in income inequality in the United States?
   (a) Taxes
   (b) Transfers in kind
   (c) Cash transfers
   (d) Social insurance

8. Which of the following is an indirect effect of social insurance that increases inequality of earned income per family?

   (a) The incentive to find a job is reduced
   (b) The willingness of the poor to undertake risky ventures is increased
   (c) The average taxpayer is richer than the average recipient of the insurance benefits
   (d) The rich taxpayers who support the program are discouraged from working so hard

9. Which of the following is the most important reason why the free-market solution may not be fair?
   (a) Some people work harder than others
   (b) Some people have more market power than others
   (c) Some people's jobs are more hazardous than those of others
   (d) Some people have invested more than others in human capital

10. Recall from Chapter 2 the distinction between positive and normative economics. Which of the following statements is most accurate?
   (a) Equity and equality are both positive concepts
   (b) Equity and equality are both normative concepts
   (c) Equity is a positive concept and equality is a normative concept
   (d) Equity is a normative concept and equality is a positive concept

*11. According to Rawls's maximin criterion, which of the following income distributions is best?
   (a) Everyone gets $3,000 per year
   (b) Everyone but one person gets $5,000 per year and the other person gets $3,100 per year
   (c) Half the people get $10,000 per year and the other half get $1,000 per year
   (d) Everyone but one person gets $20,000 per year and the other person gets $2,900 per year

Exercises

1. Table 35-1 gives the income distribution of a hypothetical economy, as in panel *a* of Table 35-1 in the textbook. In Table 35-2 below, fill in the cumulative income distribution. (If necessary, review panel *b* of Table 35-1 in the textbook.)

Plot the Lorenz curve in Figure 35-1 and label it L_1. Suppose that the government then taxed away half the income of every family in the top 20 percent of the income distribution and gave it in equal amounts to every family in the lowest 60 percent of the distribution. Fill in the resulting income dis-

Table 35-1

	Lowest 20%	Second 20%	Third 20%	Fourth 20%	Highest 20%
Percent of income	4	6	10	20	60

Table 35-2

	Lowest 20%	Lowest 40%	Lowest 60%	Lowest 80%	Total
Percent of income					

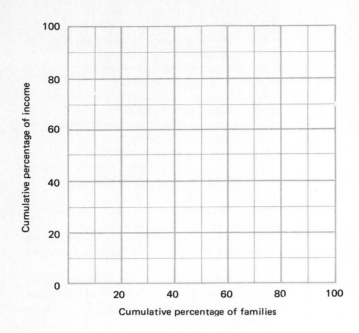

Cumulative percentage of income (vertical axis)
Cumulative percentage of families (horizontal axis)

A. Four families receive $1,100 per year each and the fifth receives $600 per year

B. Four families receive $500 per year each and the fifth family receives $3,000 per year

C. Each family recieves $500 per year

D. Four families receive $1,100 per year each and the fifth family receives $5,600

E. Four families receive $5,000 per year each and the fifth receives nothing

Fill in Table 35-5 giving the total national income according to each distribution:

Table 35-5

Distribution	Total national income
A	
B	
C	
D	
E	

tribution in Table 35-3 and the resulting *cumulative* income distribution in Table 35-4.

Table 35-3

	Lowest 20%	Second 20%	Third 20%	Fourth 20%	Highest 20%
Percent of income					

Table 35-4

	Lowest 20%	Lowest 40%	Lowest 60%	Lowest 80%	Total
Percent of income					

Plot the Lorenz curve for income after taxes and transfers in Figure 35-1 and label it L_2.

2. Consider the five following ways of distributing income among the five families in an economy:

Fill in Table 35-6 for each of the distributions, showing the *cumulative* percentages. (Again, the method is provided in panel *b* of Table 35-1 in the textbook.)

Table 35-6

		Lowest 20%	Lowest 40%	Lowest 60%	Lowest 80%	Total
Percent of income	- A					
	- B					
	- C					
	- D					
	- E					

Draw and label the Lorenz curve for each of these distributions in Figure 35-2. *Indicate in Table 35-7 below the way that these distributions would be ranked according to Rawls's maximin criterion.

Table 35-7

	Distribution
	Best
2d	"
3rd	"
4th	"
5th	"

According to this ranking, does the best distribution have the largest total income? _____. Does it have the least inequality as measured by the Lorenz curve? _____.

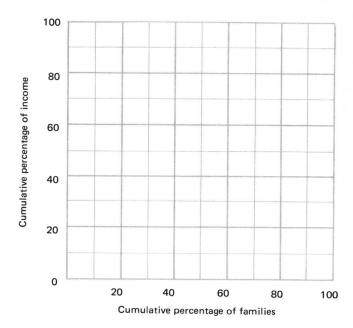

FIGURE 35-2

Essay Questions

1. Some of the ways in which government policy affects the distribution of income are not so obvious as taxes and transfers. How do you suppose that the shape of the Lorenz curve is affected by (a) government's support of higher education, (b) the farm subsidy programs, and (c) the government's support of restrictions to entry into the medical profession?

2. Recall from Chapter 1 the distinction between poverty and inequality. What can you learn about poverty from just studying the Lorenz curve? Explain.

3. Some people feel that no matter how rich we become as a society "the poor will always be with us." Explain why you agree or disagree with this statement, explaining how your answer depends upon the way poverty is defined.

4. The government is able to affect the distribution of income through its taxes and transfers, and we all have an equal vote in choosing the government. In that sense we all have equal opportunity to determine the distribution of income. Why do some people argue that we need more equality of opportunity?

5. Some people believe that all men are self-made men, but most of them have made themselves poor. If they had wanted to make themselves rich they could have done so by saving or by investing in human capital. In what sense is this view correct? In what sense is it misleading?

*6. Marxists believe in the principle "to each according to his needs, from each according to his abilities." Do you agree or disagree? Why or why not? Do you think that this principle would lead to a straight-line Lorenz curve? Why or why not? Explain how a government that tried to put this principle into effect would run into conflict between equity and efficiency.

*7. Is the income distribution which is best according to Rawls's maximin criterion necessarily the one that maximizes total income? Is it necessarily the one that minimizes inequality according to the Lorenz curve? Can it be the one with both the least total income and the greatest inequality? (Hint: refer to Exercise 2 above.)

Answers

True-False Questions: 1 T 2 F 3 F 4 T 5 F 6 T 7 T 8 F 9 T 10 F
Multiple-Choice Questions: 1 d 2 c 3 b 4 b 5 a 6 d 7 d 8 a 9 b 10 d 11 b

Exercise **1.** Table 35-2: 4, 10, 20, 40, 100
Table 35-3: 14, 16, 20, 20, 30
Table 35-4: 14, 30, 50, 70, 100

2. Table 35-5

Distribution	Total national income
A	$5,000
B	$5,000
C	$2,500
D	$10,000
E	$20,000

Table 35-6

	20	40	60	80	Total
A	12	34	56	78	100
B	10	20	30	40	100
C	20	40	60	80	100
D	11	22	33	44	100
E	0	25	50	75	100

Table 35-7

Rank	Distribution
1	D
2	A
3	B
4	C
5	E

no, no

FIGURE 35-2 completed

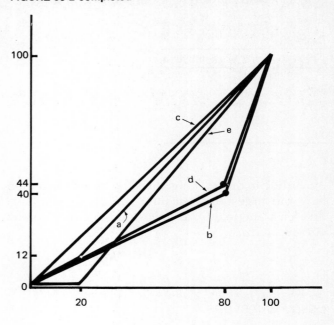

CHAPTER 36
Government Policies to Reduce Inequality:
Can We Solve the Poverty Problem?

Learning Objectives

After you have studied this chapter in the textbook and the study guide, you should be able to
Explain how the poverty line is defined
Explain why the poverty line has been increasing over the years
State the factors that increase the likelihood of a family being poor
Describe four kinds of government policy that attack the causes of poverty
Explain the difference between social insurance and welfare programs, giving examples of each
Argue the case that government welfare programs have been successful
Argue the opposing case
Describe how a negative income tax program would work
Explain why a negative income tax could not simultaneously provide everyone with an acceptable minimum income, preserve incentives, and keep costs down
Explain the theoretical advantages of a negative income tax program
Describe the results of experimental studies with negative income tax schemes
Explain the pros and cons of a wage-subsidy program

CHAPTER HIGHLIGHTS

This chapter discusses: (1) the nature of poverty, (2) government policies that reduce inequality, (3) how successful these policies have been, and (4) the proposal for a negative income tax.

The Meaning of Poverty

The Department of Agriculture estimates the lowest possible cost of feeding a family with a reasonable diet that meets minimal nutrition standards. It then defines the "poverty line" as three times the cost of this diet. In 1981 the poverty line was $8,500 for an urban family of four (lower for a rural family). This poverty line keeps rising every year, for two reasons: (1) inflation makes a given diet cost more each year, and (2) our idea of what constitutes poverty changes over the years.

Studies indicate that a family is more likely to be poor if it is: (1) nonwhite, (2) from the South, (3) large, (4) not well educated, (5) living in the core of a big city, or (6) fatherless. You should be able to explain how each of these factors is related to poverty.

Government Programs

Probably the most significant aspects of government programs to maintain income is their size. From 1965 to 1981 the cost of these programs quadrupled, even after adjusting for inflation. By 1981 this cost was 10 percent of GNP.

Four kinds of government programs attack the causes (as opposed to the symptoms) of poverty: (1) those that subsidize investment in human capital, such as free schooling and CETA subsidies for training unemployed workers; (2) those that aim to reduce unemployment or disability, such as the OSHA program; (3) laws that aim to reduce labor-market discrimination, such as the Equal Pay Act of 1963 and the Civil Rights Act of 1964; and (4) other programs, such as WIN (Work Incentive Program) which subsidizes the training and employment of people on welfare, and also makes it possible for parents to take jobs by providing day-care facilities for children.

There are two categories of programs that attack the *symptoms* of poverty: (1) social insurance programs, such as social security, unemployment insurance, and Medicare. These programs are not designed to cure poverty; they provide benefits to all participants—whether they are poor or not. Nevertheless, they still play an important role in reducing poverty. (2) Welfare programs, specifically designed to alleviate poverty by providing benefits only to the poor. Examples are AFDC (Aid to Families with Dependent Children) and transfers in kind, such as food stamps, public housing, and Medicaid.

Successes and Failures of Welfare Programs

Poverty has been greatly reduced in the twentieth century. By 1980 only one family in 20 fell below the poverty line. In 1929 only half of all U.S. families had this much real income. Some people argue that much of the credit for this is due to our welfare programs. They also argue that these programs have given us an additional "noneconomic"

benefit of knowing that we live in a decent society that provides for the poor. Others argue that government programs have caused as many problems as they have created, for three broad reasons.

First, the complicated array of programs has generated resentment. For example, some recipients complain that they are helped much less than others; indeed some taxpayers who receive no welfare benefits actually have less income than some welfare recipients. Recipients sometimes complain of the arbitrary use of power by welfare workers, and the welfare workers themselves complain about the tangle of bureaucratic rules they must contend with.

Second, the programs have generated much economic inefficiency, through (1) the disincentive effects on taxpayers, who are discouraged from working by the high taxes they must pay to support these programs (although this effect may not be large, there is an additional waste involved insofar as these taxpayers devote more resources and effort in the search for tax loopholes), (2) the disincentive effects on those who *receive* welfare, (they are discouraged from working because on any income they earn they must pay an "implicit tax"—the welfare income they lose as a consequence), and (3) inducing people just above the poverty line (whom the program wasn't intended to support) to quit work in order to qualify for benefits. Figure 36-2 in the textbook illustrates effects 2 and 3.

Third, in addition to these economic costs, these programs raise two severe social problems:

1. They provide fathers with an incentive to leave home. (For example, this will allow their families to qualify for AFDC.) It may be argued therefore that such programs are damaging the family structure of the nation's poor.

2. The incentive for a family to quit work and go on welfare can lead to a weakening of pride and self-respect. Some families have trouble getting off welfare once they have become accustomed to the "culture of poverty."

Negative Income Tax

Many economists have suggested replacing the whole array of existing programs with a negative income tax scheme like the one illustrated in Figure 36-3 in the textbook.

The scheme can be viewed in the following way: To begin with, the government gives every family of four a subsidy of, say, $5,000 per year (more to larger families, less to rural families). Then for every dollar of income that the family earns above this it gets to keep half. (It must pay the other half in taxes.) Thus a family earning $10,000 would just break even; its tax (half of $10,000) would just cancel out the initial subsidy. A family earning more than $10,000 would pay a net tax, but a family earning less than $10,000 would receive a net subsidy; that is, a negative tax. Study Figure 36-3 in the text until this is clear to you.

A negative income tax ought to be more equitable than the present inconsistent array of income maintenance programs. It would guarantee the same minimum income for all. Furthermore, in contrast with the present system, it would ensure that those who earn more by working would get to keep more. The main economic advantage, at least in theory, is that the scheme ought to offer a greater incentive for recipients to find a job. However, the scheme would not be perfect. Like any other antipoverty program it cannot simultaneously attain the three conflicting goals of (1) providing an acceptable minimum income for everyone, (2) preserving the incentive for people to work, and (3) keeping costs down. As an example of how these goals may conflict, suppose the government decides to raise the minimum income (the initial subsidy) level from $5,000 to $6,000 (to better achieve the first goal). This will shift the "income after" line *CQH* in Figure 36-3 in the textbook up by $1,000 throughout its whole length, thus increasing the gray "subsidy gap" that the government must fill. Thus this measure may conflict with objective (3) of keeping costs down.

Unfortunately, the results of experiments in Denver and Seattle suggest that in practice the negative income tax doesn't work very well. In fact it seems to discourage people from working even more than the present welfare system does. It also seems to cause a dramatic rise in marital breakdown. Why these adverse effects arise is not clearly understood. Perhaps it is because the subjects of these experiments had their options (including quitting work and leaving the family with no loss of benefits) clearly explained to them.

The disappointment of these experimental results has led some to suggest the alternative of a wage subsidy that would provide for the poor by increasing their wages. By replacing the tax on earnings with a subsidy it is hoped that this scheme would avoid the work disincentives experienced with the negative income tax; indeed it is hoped that this scheme might in some cases provide a *positive* incentive to go to work. The problem of marital breakdown might be dealt with by making the subsidy larger for a wage earner with more dependents.

The main drawback of such a scheme is that it would remove the guaranteed minimum income of the negative income tax (and of the present system). Thus it would be especially important to "tag" those individuals who, because of age or disability, cannot be expected to work for their financial support. But designing a fair and workable tagging system is extremely difficult.

IMPORTANT TERMS

Poverty Inadequate income to buy the necessities of life.

Poverty line An income equal to three times the minimum cost of an adequate diet, as determined by the Department of Agriculture. In 1981, this was about $8,500 for an urban family of four.

CETA Comprehensive Education and Training Act. This provides federal subsidies for training unemployed workers.

EPA The Equal Pay Act of 1963, which requires that women be paid the same as men for equal work.

Civil Rights Act of 1964 An act outlawing discrimination in hiring, firing, and other employment practices.

OSHA The Occupational Safety and Health Administration, which is responsible for maintaining adequate safety standards in the workplace.

WIN The Work Incentive Program, which subsidizes the training and employment of people on welfare, and also makes it possible for parents to take jobs by providing day-care facilities for children.

AFDC Aid to Families with Dependent Children. Its main thrust is to pay welfare to families not headed by an able-bodied male.

Food stamps Vouchers that provide food for the poor.

Public housing A program under which the federal government pays local governments to clear slums, build houses, and rent these houses to low-income tenants who pay 25 percent of their income in rent, with the federal government paying the rest.

Implicit tax The implicit tax built into a welfare program is the amount of subsidy lost when a family earns another dollar of income.

Culture of poverty A phrase describing the increasing dependency of welfare recipients upon their welfare payments.

Guaranteed income A program in which the government ensures that no one earns less than a certain amount.

Negative income tax A program that guarantees everyone a minimum income and also allows people to retain part of any income they earn.

Tagging The identification of those who, because of age or disability, deserve special support from the government.

Wage subsidy A program for increasing the wages of low-income earners. It is hoped that such a scheme might avoid the work disincentives revealed by the negative income tax experiments.

True-False Questions

T F **1.** In 1980 one American family in 20 was below the poverty line.

T F **2.** The poverty line of 1981 was well below the average real income of 1929.

T F **3.** The increase in the poverty line from year to year is due entirely to inflation.

T F **4.** Families living in the core area of big cities are more likely to be below the poverty line than those living in suburbs.

T F **5.** In 1981 Americans were spending about 10 percent of GNP on income maintenance programs.

T F **6.** None of the federal government's programs attack the causes of poverty; they all merely attack the symptoms.

T F **7.** Giving food stamps to a family may not increase that family's consumption of food even though it uses the stamps.

T F **8.** A subsidy program that gave $3,000 a year to families that earned no income and nothing to families that earned any income at all would involve an implicit tax of over 100 percent.

T F **9.** Under the public housing program low-income tenants pay 25 percent of their income in rent.

T F **10.** The Denver and Seattle experiments showed that a negative income tax provides an even stronger work incentive than expected.

Multiple-Choice

1. In 1981 the poverty line for a *rural* family of four was an annual income of
  (a) Less than $8,500
  (b) $8,500
  (c) Between $8,500 and $11,200
  (d) $11,200

2. The poverty line has risen considerably since the 1920s because
  (a) Productivity has decreased
  (b) Our standards of what constitutes a poverty-line income have risen
  (c) Government welfare programs have been reduced
  (d) Population has expanded

3. Which of the following factors would make it more likely that a family was *above* the poverty line?
  (a) The father has deserted the family
  (b) The family lives in the North
  (c) The family is large
  (d) The family is nonwhite

4. By 1981 income maintenance expenditures in the United States were how many times larger than in 1965 (in real terms)?
  (a) Two
  (b) Three
  (c) Four
  (d) Five

5. Which of the following kinds of government programs relieve only the symptoms of poverty?
  (a) Those that subsidize investment in human capital
  (b) Aid to families with dependent children

  (c) Antidiscrimination policies
  (d) Policies to reduce unemployment and disability

6. Which of the following government programs is designed to attack the causes of poverty?
  (a) WIN
  (b) Social security
  (c) Food stamps
  (d) Public housing

7. Suppose that when a family earns another dollar its welfare benefits are reduced by 25 cents. The implicit tax of this welfare program is
  (a) 20 percent
  (b) 25 percent
  (c) 75 percent
  (d) 125 percent

8. Which of the following is an example of in-kind assistance?
  (a) Public housing
  (b) Food stamps
  (c) Medicaid
  (d) All the above

9. The problem of marital breakdown seems to be aggravated most by which of the following?
  (a) WIN
  (b) CETA
  (c) AFDC
  (d) EPA

10. Under a negative income tax someone who earns more money by working will
  (a) Pay more taxes and have more take-home pay

(b) Pay more taxes and have less take-home pay
(c) Pay less taxes and have more take-home pay
(d) Pay less taxes and have less take-home pay

11. Proponents of a negative income tax argue that when this scheme is adopted other income maintenance programs should
  (a) Remain unchanged
  (b) Be expanded
  (c) Be dropped
  (d) Be expanded or reduced, depending on their cost

12. Experiments with a negative income tax reveal that the incentive to work under the scheme is

(a) Greater than under the present system
(b) Less than under the present system
(c) The same as under the present system
(d) Greater or less than under the present system depending upon where the minimum income level is set

13. Which of the following should offer the greatest work incentive to the very poor?
  (a) No taxes or subsidies
  (b) The present welfare system
  (c) A negative income tax
  (d) A wage subsidy scheme

Exercise

1. Consider the four following tax-subsidy programs:
  a. Every family earning less than $5,000 receives enough subsidy to give it an income of $5,000 after taxes and subsidies. For every dollar earned over $5,000 a family must pay 20-cent tax.
  b. Every family receives a subsidy of $5,000 but then pays a tax of 50 cents for *every* dollar earned.
  c. Every family receives a subsidy of $3,000 but then pays a tax of 30 cents for *every* dollar earned.
  d. Every family receives a subsidy of $3,000 but then pays a tax of 50 cents for *every* dollar earned.

In Figure 36-1 plot the line for each program showing a family's income after taxes and subsidies as a function of its income before taxes and subsidies. For each program indicate in Table 36-1 the marginal tax rates on income earned below $5,000 and on income earned above $5,000. Suppose that the

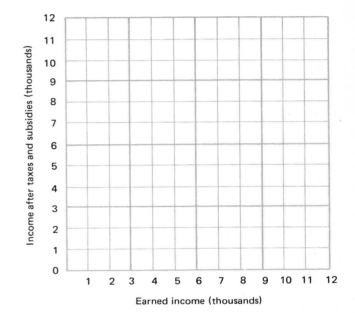

income distribution in the economy is given by Table 36-2.

Table 36-1

Program	Marginal tax rate on income earned above $5,000	Marginal tax rate on income earned below $5,000
A		
B		
C		
D		

Table 36-2

Annual income before taxes and transfers (thousands of dollars)	0	3	5	6	10	15	20	50
Number of families earning this income	1	2	4	4	3	2	1	1

In Table 36-3 fill in the net tax (i.e., tax minus subsidy) paid by each family under each of the programs

In Table 36-4 show the total net taxes collected; that is, total taxes collected minus total subsidy paid, under the assumption that each family *earns* the same, regardless of the program.

Table 36-3

Income (in thousands)		0	3	5	6	10	15	20	50
Net tax of each	A								
family earning	B								
this income	C								
under program	D								

Table 36-4

Programs	Total net taxes
A	
B	
C	
D	

Essay Questions

1. At one point in his unsuccessful presidential campaign in 1972 Senator McGovern proposed sending out a check for $50 to every individual in the country. If this program had been carried out, even with no other change in government programs, in what sense would this have accomplished at least to some extent the benefits of a negative income tax? What would it have done to the federal government's deficit? What would the government eventually have had to do in order to make up for this effect on its deficit? In what sense would this undo the effects of the initial $50 per person?

2. If the main ill effect of AFDC is to encourage fathers to leave home so their families can qualify for welfare, what do you think of maintaining the program but disqualifying any family whose father has abandoned them?

3. Do you think that a negative income tax program would reduce inequality of incomes after taxes and transfers? Do you think it would reduce inequality of incomes before taxes and subsidies? Explain.

4. If the government gave equivalent cash transfers instead of assistance in kind, would the recipients be better off? Why? Why does the government not do so?

5. Why cannot the disincentive effects of welfare programs be overcome simply by requiring welfare recipients to work unless they are disabled?

*6. The textbook mentioned that half of all families in 1929 were below the 1981 poverty line. In what sense is the person on the poverty line in 1981 better off than the person receiving the average income in 1929? In what sense is he worse off?

*7. Our usual definition of the poverty line depends mainly upon the biological fact of life that we need food to live. Argue the case that poverty has little to do with such biological requirements.

Answers

True-False Questions: 1 T   2 F   3 F   4 T   5 T   6 F   7 T   8 T   9 T   10 F
Multiple-Choice Questions: 1 a   2 b   3 b   4 c   5 b   6 a   7 b   8 d   9 c   10 a   11 c   12 b   13 d

Exercise: **FIGURE 36-1 completed.**

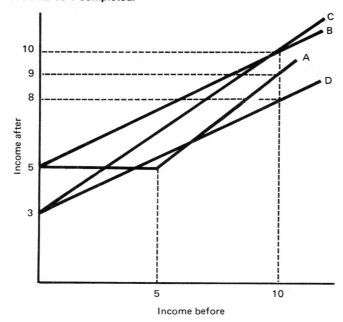

Income after

Income before

Table 36-1

20%	100%
50%	50%
30%	30%
50%	50%

Table 36-3

−5,000	−2,000	0	200	1,000	2,000	3,000	9,000
−5,000	−3,500	−2,500	−2,000	0	2,500	5,000	20,000
−3,000	−2,100	−1,500	−1,200	0	1,500	3,000	12,000
−3,000	−1,500	− 500	0	2,000	4,500	7,000	22,000

Table 36-4

10,800
0
0
36,000

CHAPTER 37
Marxism and Marxist Economics

Learning Objectives

After you have studied this chapter in the textbook and the study guide, you should be able to

Describe the labor theory of value

Explain Marx's view that workers are exploited

State two predictions of Marxism that have not been verified by history

Explain the Marxist solution for raising capital, and the problems with it

Describe the problems associated with central planning

State why and by how much the Soviet economy grew faster than the American economy in the 1960s and 70s

Explain in what respects the Soviet and American economic systems are becoming increasingly similar

List three specific effects of the Liberman reforms in the Soviet Union

State two differences between the Soviet and Yugoslavian economic systems

Describe the ways in which the government still exerts a great deal of centralized control over the Yugoslavian economy

Explain why workers' incomes tend to be more unstable and less evenly distributed in Yugoslavia than in the Soviet Union

CHAPTER HIGHLIGHTS

This chapter discusses three closely related topics: (1) the theory of Marxism, (2) the economic system of the Soviet Union, and (3) the economic system of Yugoslavia. Under these topics the chapter discusses what a socialist economic system is like, the Marxists' arguments in favor of a socialist system and against our own capitalist system, and the capitalist critique of these Marxist arguments and of their practical applications in the Soviet Union. The chapter also discusses the communist system of China.

The Theory of Marxism

Marxism is based upon (1) the labor theory of value, and (2) the subsistence theory of wages. It claims that workers ("the proletariat") are exploited under capitalism because instead of enjoying all the fruits of their labor, they receive just enough to subsist, the rest going in the form of "surplus value" to the capitalists. According to Marx the only way of resolving this class struggle is a revolution in which workers forcibly seize the ownership of physical capital from their exploiters, followed by a dictatorship of the proletariat and the eventual state of communism.

One criticism of Marxist theory is that its predictions have not been borne out by history. (1) The dictatorship of the proletariat, rather than withering away, has remained powerful in Marxist states. (2) Under capitalism workers have enjoyed rising real incomes rather than the increasing misery predicted by Marx.

Another criticism of Marxist theory is that if capitalists are eliminated some other way must be found to generate physical capital for production. The Marxist solution is to generate capital by taxation rather than by personal saving. But (1) taxes (forced saving) may be more burdensome than voluntary saving, (2) when governments invest the funds they have raised, they typically lack the inventiveness of private capitalists, and (3) some substitute must be found for the profit motive as a means of allocating capital among different industries.

The question of profit raises an important issue in the debate between capitalism and Marxism. Supporters of Marxism and capitalism alike generally agree that monopoly profits should not go unchecked. Capitalist supporters argue that this can be done through government regulation under a basically capitalist system. Marxists argue that regulation is ineffective because big business interests are so powerful that they end up controlling their own regulators. A capitalist response to this criticism is that big business does indeed have power; and so does the government. But this is better than having *all* of the power in the hands of the government—as happens in a communist state.

The Soviet System

The two important features of a socialist system are that (1) physical capital is owned by the state rather than by private individuals, and (2) the decisions on how much of each good to produce and how much to invest in each industry are made by a central government rather than through the interplay of market forces. In the Soviet Union these centralized decisions are based on 5-year plans, administered by an agency called Gosplan. These plans set yearly production targets, or quotas, for the managers of different firms. There are three major difficulties with central planning of this sort:

1. It is difficult for the government to determine a set of consistent quotas. For example, the right quota of steel to produce depends on the production level in steel-using industries such as machinery and autos. But how does one know the machinery output without knowing the output of steel (since steel is a machinery-using industry)? Since both steel and machinery are inputs in the production of the other, how can one determine the quota output of either without knowing the other? While there are mathematical ways of breaking through this impasse, it is nonetheless impossible to get quotas just right; consequently bottlenecks are common in the Soviet economy.

2. Consumers' wants tend to be ignored in the Soviet system, because the manager of each firm tends to concentrate on satisfying a quota rather than producing the type and variety of goods that consumers most want.

3. It is not clear that the Soviet degree of central planning could be made to work without a repressive Soviet-style political dictatorship. Marxists counter by saying that our freedom is enjoyed only by the rich and powerful. And they point to one apparent advantage of central planning: It produces very little measured unemployment. However, critics point out that if someone is working to produce unwanted goods this really constitutes "disguised" unemployment.

The 5-year plans of the Soviet Union have emphasized rapid growth. For example, from 1960 to 1974 the average annual rate of growth was 4.9 percent in the Soviet Union, compared to 3.8 percent in the United States (the rates have recently been lower in both countries). To accomplish this, investment in the Soviet Union is about 30 percent of GNP, compared to 15 percent in the United States. This investment is financed by taxes on consumer goods, which amount to about one-third of the price of the typical good. One reason for using this kind of tax is that it can be made progressive by taxing luxury items more heavily than necessities. (However, the Soviets have also sometimes used it to make their tax system more regressive.)

There are two reasons for believing that the Soviet and U.S. systems are converging toward each other:

1. Rapid growth in welfare programs in the United States has been reducing income inequalities while at the same time diminishing economic incentives. Meanwhile the Soviet workers are being given strong incentives (such as bonus earnings); while the objective has been to encourage efficiency, these incentives have also created income inequality.

2. In the United States the government is becoming more and more involved in production decisions, while in the Soviet Union, largely as a result of the Liberman reforms, production decisions are becoming more responsive to the market. These reforms have (a) allowed managers of firms to take orders for particular kinds of goods from their customers, (b) imposed penalties on managers unable to produce goods that will sell, and (c) allowed managers some scope in changing their prices.

The System of Yugoslavia

In Yugoslavia, as in the Soviet Union, the state owns most of the physical capital. But production decisions are much less centralized in Yugoslavia. Firms there are operated by workers, who elect a manager. This manager attempts, like the manager of a capitalist enterprise, to maximize profits, which are then distributed to the workers.

However, the government still exerts a great deal of centralized control upon the economy:

1. Although most firms are allowed to change their prices, they can do so only within fixed limits.

2. As in the Soviet Union, the government diverts one-third of annual GNP into the production of investment goods.

3. The allocation of these investment goods into different sectors of the economy is also determined by the central government.

4. The government sets out 5-year plans as in the Soviet Union (although these plans are not strictly enforced).

There have been three special problems with the Yugoslav system.

1. Some of the "worker-enterprises" have a monopoly position, which their managers have exploited by restricting output.

2. Because workers receive the firm's profits and because these profits fluctuate with market conditions, their incomes tend to be unstable and unevenly distributed.

3. There is not enough incentive to create new firms. Thus many existing firms do not face even the threat of competition.

China

Although it is difficult to get an accurate picture of what is happening in China, it appears that the recent leadership there is also moving toward a market-oriented form of communism.

IMPORTANT TERMS

Capitalism An economic system in which most physical capital is privately owned.

Socialism An economic system in which physical capital (and land) is owned by the state.

Communism In Marxist theory this is the ideal system in which all means of production and other forms of property are owned by the community as a whole and the central government has "withered away." In capitalist countries, the term communism refers to the present economic and political systems of countries like the Soviet Union. However, these countries do not refer to themselves as having achieved communism.

Labor theory of value The theory that the value of any good is determined solely by the amount of labor that goes into producing it. Notice that this labor includes not just the labor directly involved in producing the good but also the labor embodied in the capital used to produce the good.

Subsistence wage theory The theory that, in a capitalist economy, workers' wages can never rise, except temporarily, above a socially defined subsistence level.

Surplus value In Marxist theory, the difference between the total value of output (all of which "belongs" to labor) and the wages actually received by labor.

Exploitation The Marxist description of any system in which the workers themselves do not receive this surplus value.

Gosplan The central planning agency in the Soviet Union.

5-year plan A plan drawn up in a Marxist country every 5 years setting production and investment targets for each industry. In practice, these plans are revised from year to year.

Proletariat The Marxist term for the working class.

Bourgeoisie The Marxist term for the capitalist class.

Dictatorship of the proletariat According to Marxist theory this is the transitory stage after the workers' revolution, before the government withers away and the ideal state of communism is achieved.

Disguised unemployment Disguised unemployment exists if people are employed at useless tasks. This might be regarded as the Soviet equivalent of featherbedding.

Liberman reforms The Soviet reforms of the early 1960s that were inspired by the ideas of Professor Liberman and made Soviet firms more responsive to market forces.

True-False Questions

T F 1. The government of the Soviet Union does *not* regard itself as having achieved communism.
T F 2. According to Marxist theory, exploitation occurs because workers do not receive even subsistence wages.
T F 3. Marx advocated the achievement of communism through nonviolent methods rather than through revolution.
T F 4. Marx regarded as surplus value both above-normal profits and normal profits.
T F 5. Five-year plans are drawn up in Yugoslavia.
T F 6. One of the main problems of the Soviet system is that, because the capitalist class has been abolished, there is not enough investment.
T F 7. In the Soviet system consumer goods are not produced in as much variety as in a capitalist system.
T F 8. The Soviet Union has experienced a higher growth rate in the 1960s and 70s than the United States.
T F 9. One of the advantages of central planning is that it succeeds in eliminating disguised unemployment.
T F 10. In Yugoslavia the manager of a firm is elected by the workers.
T F 11. In Yugoslavia the state exerts no direct control over the amount of investment every year.

Multiple-Choice Questions

1. Investment in the Soviet Union constitutes how large a percentage of GNP?
  (a) 15 percent
  (b) 30 percent
  (c) 45 percent
  (d) Any amount, depending upon interest rates

2. The higher average growth rates in the Soviet Union as compared to the United States in the 1960s and 1970s is probably a result of their
  (a) Higher agricultural productivity
  (b) More rapid accumulation of capital
  (c) Higher rate of technological innovation
  (d) Greater political freedom

3. Marx believed that under capitalism the workers
  (a) Would and should revolt
  (b) Would revolt but shouldn't
  (c) Wouldn't revolt but should
  (d) Wouldn't and shouldn't revolt

4. Which of the following statements is *false*?
  (a) Bottlenecks are common in the Soviet economy
  (b) The variety of consumer goods is less in the Soviet Union than in the United States
  (c) The Soviet government has not been as innovative in its investment decisions as the private capitalists in western economies
  (d) Measured unemployment tends to be higher in the Soviet Union than in western countries

5. In Figure 37-1 the curve labeled *MPL* denotes the marginal productivity of labor in a perfectly competitive industry, where the wage equals *OW*. According to Marxist theory, the area of the triangle *ABW* measures
  (a) The subsistence wage
  (b) The amount of labor embodied in the output of the industry

FIGURE 37-1

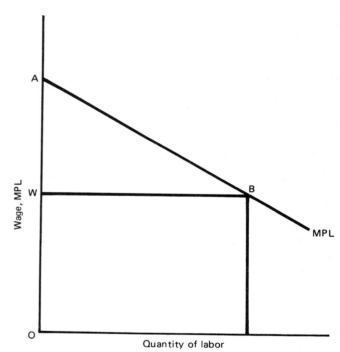

(c) Surplus value
(d) The total income of workers

6. In the Soviet Union, investment is financed mainly through
  (a) Government borrowing
  (b) Income taxes
  (c) Taxes on investment goods
  (d) Taxes on consumer goods

7. One reason why it has been argued that the economic

systems of the United States and the Soviet Union are becoming increasingly similar is that

    (a) The Soviets have been allowing greater scope for market forces in production decisions than in the past

    (b) The Soviet government is relying more heavily upon its 5-year plans

    (c) The United States government is becoming less involved in production decisions

    (d) Most farms in the Soviet Union are now privately owned

8. The purpose of the Liberman reforms was to

    (a) Increase efficiency in production

    (b) Impose stricter quotas on managers

    (c) Allow workers to own their own firms

    (d) Increase the fraction of GNP going to investment every year

9. The Liberman reforms

    (a) Made it illegal for managers to accept special orders from their customers

    (b) Compensated managers whose output did not sell well

    (c) Allow workers to elect their managers

    (d) Give some freedom to managers to change prices

10. Which of the following is *not* true about the economic system of Yugoslavia?

    (a) The manager of a firm is restricted in his or her freedom to change prices

    (b) The government allows their total value of investment each year to be determined by market forces

    (c) The government issues 5-year plans

    (d) The government allows workers to elect the managers of their firms

11. Market power in the Yugoslav system

    (a) Cannot be exercised by any firm

    (b) Can be exercised but isn't because workers operate the firms instead of capitalists

    (c) Can be exercised by firms but does not lead to inefficiency as it does in our system

    (d) Can be exercised and does lead to inefficiency

12. Worker ownership in the Yugoslav system results in

    (a) Incentives to work harder

    (b) A more even distribution of income

    (c) More incentives for production to expand in regions where firms are making losses

    (d) Lower productivity

Essay Questions

1. The textbook mentioned that while Soviet-style planning reduces measured unemployment it often replaces this with disguised unemployment. Likewise, the Soviet system does not appear to suffer from inflation as we do. In what sense do you think it might be true that the Soviets have also replaced measured inflation with a less obvious kind? Hint: Is the value of your money really constant if prices remain the same but, due to increasingly severe bottlenecks, goods are becoming harder to find?

2. Most workers in the United States save toward their retirement. Much of this saving takes the form, either directly, or through pension funds, of investment in shares of corporations. Do you think it is true, therefore, that most workers in the United States are also capitalists? Why or why not? Likewise, most people in the United States—including the very rich—do some kind of work or another. Is it therefore true that most capitalists are also workers? Why or why not? Argue the case either for or against the proposition that Marxist theory is based upon a class struggle that doesn't really exist.

3. Construct an argument in support of the following statement: "Because the Soviet system has abolished traditional capitalism, it is going overboard in support of the system of "human capitalism," thus creating a new bourgeoisie out of those who possess large quantities of human capital."

4. "The reason why economic growth has been faster in the Soviet Union than in the United States is that in the Soviet Union everyone's efforts are devoted toward the common good, whereas in the United States everyone's efforts are devoted toward their own self-interest." Do you agree or disagree? Explain.

5. Review your understanding of why land has value, from Chapter 32. How does the labor theory of value run into trouble in trying to explain the value of land?

6. Recall from Chapter 36 the difficulties of defining the poverty line. Do these difficulties also apply to defining "subsistence wage"?

7. The text pointed out two predictions of Marxism that have not been verified by history. How do you suppose the development of labor unions in the United States and other capitalist countries has helped to falsify Marxist predictions?

8. Why has economic growth been more rapid in the Soviet Union than in the United States? Do you think it would be desirable for the government of the United States to raise taxes on consumer goods and to increase subsidies of investment activities in order to bring our rate of growth up to the Soviet level? Who would gain from such a policy? Who would lose? What political problems do you think there would be with such a policy?

9. In his famous *General Theory*, Keynes said, "The ideas of economists and political philosophers, both when they are right and when they are wrong, are more powerful than is commonly understood. Indeed the world is ruled by little else. Practical men, who believe themselves to be quite exempt from any intellectual influences, are usually the slaves of some defunct economist. Madmen in authority, who hear voices in the air, are distilling their frenzy from some academic scribbler of a few years back. I am sure that the power of vested interests is vastly exaggerated compared with the gradual encroachment of ideas. . . . soon or late, it is ideas, not vested interests, which are dangerous for good or evil." In what sense does the history of Marxism and Marxist states tend to bear out this opinion? In what sense does it tend to contradict the opinion?

Answers

True-False Questions: **1** T **2** F **3** F **4** T **5** T **6** F **7** T **8** T **9** F **10** T **11** F
Multiple-Choice Questions: **1** b **2** b **3** a **4** d **5** c **6** d **7** a **8** a **9** d **10** b **11** d **12** a